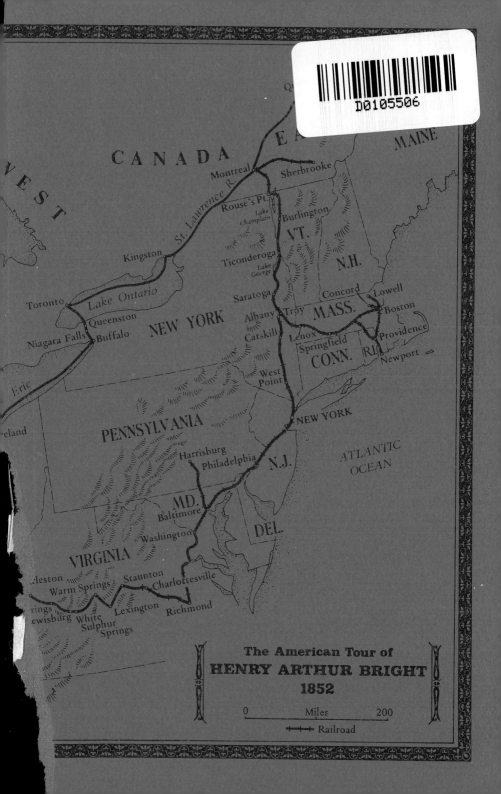

The American Tour of
HENRY ARTHUR BRIGHT
1852

0   Miles   200
†—†—† Railroad

HAPPY COUNTRY THIS AMERICA

The Travel Diary of
Henry Arthur Bright

Edited, with an Introduction

by

Anne Henry Ehrenpreis

OHIO STATE UNIVERSITY PRESS : COLUMBUS

Library of Congress Cataloguing in Publication Data

Bright, Henry Arthur, 1830–1884
  Happy Country this America.

  Includes bibliographical references and index.
    1.   United States—Description and travel—1848–1865.
  2.   Canada—Description   and   travel—1763–1867.   3.
  Bright, Henry Arthur, 1830–1884—Journeys—United
  States. 4.   Bright, Henry Arthur, 1830–1884—Journeys
  —Canada. I.   Title.
  E166.B857 1977   917.3'04'60924   77-11167
  ISBN 0-8142-0271-3

To Elizabeth Mary Lloyd
this edition
of her grandfather's diary
is dedicated
with affection and gratitude

CONTENTS

LIST OF ILLUSTRATIONS

INTRODUCTION

HENRY ARTHUR BRIGHT IN MIDDLE LIFE

INTRODUCTION

1

On May 1, 1852, the famous iron ship the *Great Britain* steamed out of Liverpool harbor, under bright skies, bound for New York. It was in effect her second maiden voyage. Designed by that quirky genius Isambard Kingdom Brunel, the *Great Britain* was the largest vessel of the period and the first steamship to use the screw propeller. After a successful run to New York in 1845, which established her reputation for speed, the *Great Britain* met sudden disaster when she mysteriously ran aground in Dundrum Bay off the coast of Ireland. A Liverpool shipping firm, Gibbs, Bright, and Company, bought the vessel, rebuilt her entirely, adding an oak keel and new screw engines, and launched her again—this time successfully. On board as she left Wellington Dock early that May morning in 1852 was Henry Arthur Bright, representing his father's shipping firm and bent on a tour of pleasure in America.

Bright's family were well-established merchants, Unitarians, and respected members of the aristocracy of commerce that flourished in nineteenth-century Liverpool. The mercantile tradition had produced there "a quiet, rich, well-bred provincial society, a little heavy, a little high-minded, much bent on good works, their interests divided between helping the poor and making money for themselves."[1] The eldest of a family of eight children, Henry Arthur Bright was born into this well-cushioned milieu on February 9, 1830. His father, Samuel Bright, came from a Bristol family of West Indian merchants; Hawthorne described him as "a gentleman with white hair, a dark expressive face, bright eyes, and a Jewish cast of features."[2] His mother's family were Liverpool bankers. When Sophia Hawthorne visited the Bright family in 1854, she wrote home all aflutter about the style in which they lived; her letter, despite its saccharine prose, is revealing:

> It is such a pretty scene: the elegant drawing-room, the recess a bow window of great size . . . looking out upon the verdant lawn . . . two superb cranes, with stately crests, walking about with proud steps. . . . Inside, innumerable gems of art and mechanism cover the tables. . . . In the evening . . . the group of airily dressed children; the tender mother in her rich brocade and lace mantle; the happy father; the agreeable governess . . . the music, talk, and aesthetic tea. . . . The grave butler brings in a tray with cups and saucers and an urn, and leaves the room. . . . There is no fuss; it is all *en famille*. . . . There is no noise at any time anywhere in the house, except the angry squall of the cockatoo. . . . It is all peace and love and happiness there, and I cannot discover where the shadow is. Health, wealth, cultivation, and

1. James Pope-Hennessy, *Monckton Milnes The Flight of Youth* (London, 1951), pp. 193-94.

2. Nathaniel Hawthorne, *The English Notebooks*, ed. Randall Stewart (New York and London, 1941), p. 188.

4

all the Christian graces and virtues—I cannot see the
trail of the serpent anywhere in that Paradise.[3]

The tone of Bright's family letters readily confirms
Sophia's impression of a close-knit, affectionate circle.

In August, 1844, when he was fourteen, Henry left
Liverpool for Rugby School. In his three years there
he came under the influence of two remarkable men:
Archibald Campbell Tait, who had only recently succeeded Dr. Arnold as headmaster, and George Cotton,
who was Bright's private tutor. As one of the School
House boys, Bright was placed under the immediate
care of Dr. Tait, whose reputation for earnest piety
led at last to his elevation as archbishop of Canterbury.
Hardworking, devout, concerned more with substantial character than with scholarship, Tait gave lectures
in divinity and modern history and kept a firm hand
on school discipline. Bright, who remained on friendly
terms with him and was later a frequent visitor to
Lambeth Palace, reminisced about Tait and his accomplished wife in these terms:

> Many old Rugby boys, now well advanced in middle
> life, will remember the time when their head master
> brought home his young wife to the school-house. He
> was young himself for the heavy duties which had
> been laid upon him. He had succeeded Dr. Arnold,
> the most renowned head master of his day. He had
> ventured on a few reforms, and the schoolboys, who
> are always the most conservative of beings, were an-
> gry and suspicious. Some time had to pass before the
> sense of his even-handed justice, of his anxious devo-
> tion to duty, of his earnest care for those who were
> placed under him, made him win first the respect and
> then the affection of masters and boys alike.

3. Rose Hawthorne Lathrop, *Memories of Hawthorne* (Boston and
New York, 1897), pp. 231-33.

Meanwhile there was, there could be, but one opinion about that beautiful and gracious lady who had come to share and lighten the head master's toil. She was, of course, known by sight to all the boys, but the school-house "fellows" had other opportunities of knowing her. Occasionally they were asked up to her drawing-room in the evening, and the evening was only too short, as she made every one at home with her kindly smile and gentle voice. Sometimes there were drawing-room games, and sometimes she would persuade one of her Irish cousins to sing for the boys some Irish songs.

But better still will be remembered her care of the boys in time of sickness. There was a sick nurse of course, but Mrs. Tait came every morning herself to see that all was right. She would talk to them all and cheer them up, and lend them books to read ("Ivo and Verena" was a favourite of hers), and make them each feel how cared for each one was.[4]

George Cotton, after fifteen years as a tutor at Rugby, went on to become master of Marlborough College and bishop of Calcutta. Remembered for his dry humor, Cotton, like Tait, established unusually close ties with his pupils. Bright's affectionate memories of him are preserved in a review of his life, written many years later:

We see him again—a Rugby master—with that calm, quiet face, which still is often lighted up with a merry twinkle of the eye or a humorous smile upon the lip. Now and then he asks some half-sarcastic question, and the boys seem puzzled as to how they are to take it, and Cotton fairly chuckles with amusement. He is always hard at work, with the threefold duties of master of the fifth form, of housemaster, and private

4. Review of Memoir of Catharine and Craufurd Tait, *Athenaeum*, Sept. 20, 1879, p. 359.

tutor. No pains are too great if only he can influence his pupils for good,—now by exciting their ambition,—now by smiling at their follies,—now by an earnest word of counsel or of warning. He discusses history with them, and reads Shakespeare with them when the work of the day is over. He prepares for them a little manual of prayers and a volume of instructions in Christianity. His favourite parting gift is Arnold's Sermons, and few boys leave without the promise of letting him hear of their future welfare.[5]

Cotton was the model for the "young master" in *Tom Brown's Schooldays*, who advises Tom to keep as his primary aim in life the desire to do some good in the world. To his pupil Henry Bright, about to enter Cambridge, he gave similar counsel, in a letter that Bright carefully preserved for twenty-five years:

> Whatever differences may exist between us in our views of the Christian Revelation [because Bright was a Unitarian], we are, I trust, agreed upon two points, —that the highest work and duty of every Christian is to do his utmost to extend Christ's kingdom among men, and that he must do this in his own heart as well as amongst others, by seeking to conform himself in all things to the pattern of Jesus Christ.[6]

With this advice in his ears, and with some of Rugby's celebrated moral earnestness stamped upon him, Henry Bright went up to Cambridge.

Following in the footsteps of his Uncle Henry and his cousin James Heywood, Bright entered Trinity College in October, 1847. As a Unitarian, he was not required to subscribe to the Thirty-Nine Articles at matricula-

5. Review of Memoir of George Edward Lynch Cotton, *Athenaeum*, Feb. 18, 1871, p. 201.

6. Ibid., p. 202.

tion (as he would have been at Oxford) and therefore could not take a degree. It was not until 1857, when the religious restrictions were lifted, that Bright received his B.A.—he and James Heywood, who had campaigned tirelessly for this reform, being the first nonconformists to do so. The atmosphere at Cambridge was thoroughly Anglican: all but two of the Fellows at Trinity College were obliged to take holy orders, and daily attendance at chapel was required of all undergraduates, whatever their religious beliefs. Bright, who took his faith seriously, was an outsider in this important aspect of college life.

His years at Cambridge were not ones of arduous application; as his friend and memorialist, Lord Houghton, put it, "the special studies of the University of Cambridge did not attract Henry Bright."[7] He read for a "Poll" or ordinary degree, rather than taking honors. This was not a demanding course: it meant, to be specific, that after passing the "Little-Go" as a trial run, he was examined in a Greek and a Latin author, the Acts of the Apostles in Greek, the history of the Reformation, and the mathematical theory of mechanics and hydrostatics. Plenty of time remained for Bright to cultivate his literary interests, which were more important to him than the laws of motion.

What really attracted him and absorbed much of his time at Cambridge was the Union Society. The Union was open to everyone, had about five hundred members, a well-stocked reading room, a library, and a writing room. It held debates every Tuesday evening, often on political subjects, and elected a board of officers each term. The kind of students who became "Unionic Cantabs" (they were rather scorned by the "reading men") were described by Bright's friend James Payn as

7. [Richard Monckton Milnes, Lord Houghton,] "Henry Bright. In Memoriam," *Philobiblon Miscellanies* 15 (1884): 5.

literary undergraduates, who write for the declamation prizes, perhaps, but are otherwise disaffected to university studies, and who, without reference to classical models, become Ciceros (or even Catilines) themselves, at the debates at the Union.[8]

To distinguish oneself as a speaker before this well-disposed audience was an ambition easily gratified.

Like Payn and other of his Cambridge friends—Reginald Cust, Julius Lloyd, and Robert Temple—Bright served a term as president of the Union. He was also active in a Trinity College oratorical society,

> which was devoted to debate, and formed a sort of nursery garden to "the Union," affording less trying opportunities over pine-apple and claret for the display of eloquence, than did the crowded Hall of Elocution in which the larger society held its sittings.[9]

The gift of easy conversational give and take, which emerges from the pages of Bright's American journal, was nurtured in these surroundings. "I like to talk with him," wrote Sophia Hawthorne in 1853; "he can really converse."[10]

The sort of life Bright led at Cambridge is reflected in the sentimental poem "Noctes Coenaeque Deum," addressed to his old Rugby friend Robert Temple (see page 447). With a talent for attaching friends and the loyalty to keep them, Bright was a welcome member of that close and privileged society. He was tall and thin, with large prominent eyes, a quick laugh, and a modest opinion of himself. Contemporary references to him agree that his surname was appropriate: he reminded Sophia Hawthorne uncannily of the merry madcap student named Eustace Bright in her hus-

8. [James Payn,] *The Foster Brothers* (New York, 1859), p. 267.
9. Ibid., p. 273.
10. Lathrop, *Memories of Hawthorne*, p. 228.

band's *Wonder Book*.[11] Julian Hawthorne remembered him as

> good-humored, laughing, voluble; with his English eyeglass, his English speech, and his English prejudices; arguing, remonstrating, asserting, contradicting,—certainly one of the most delightful, and delightfully English, Englishmen that ever lived.[12]

Lord Houghton called him "Lucidus." And George Ticknor, seeing him in Liverpool five years after Bright's American tour, described him as "full of life and cordiality, as he always is."[13] Of all personal attributes, charm is the most difficult for a biographer to convey. It clearly was an attribute of Henry Bright.

Such was the young man who, at the age of twenty-two, with Cambridge behind him, embarked on a five-month tour of America.

2

Bright's route took him from New York as far south as Richmond, and westward to Saint Louis and Saint Paul; then on to Canada for a three-week stay in Montreal and Quebec, and back through Boston to New York. Traveling in America at this time meant frequent changes of conveyance: even Bright's journey from New York to Philadelphia involved a ferry boat, railroad, steamer, and carriage. There were over six thousand miles of railroad in the United States by 1850, but the lines were still largely confined to the Northeast. In the South stagecoaches remained the

11. Ibid., p. 227. The book was published before Hawthorne met HAB.

12. Julian Hawthorne, *Nathaniel Hawthorne and His Wife*, 2d ed. (Boston, 1885), 2:21.

13. *Life, Letters, and Journals of George Ticknor*, ed. George S. Hillard, Mrs. Anna Eliot Ticknor, and Anna Eliot Ticknor (Boston and New York, 1909), 2:400.

chief form of transportation, and how miserably uncomfortable these could be may be gathered from
Bright's description of his jolting journey over the Virginia mountains. Once at the Ohio River, he changed
with relief to steamboats. These could be crowded and
mosquito-ridden with one hand-basin and a common
toothbrush for all the passengers, or comfortable and
roomy with excellent food. They were in any case
cheap: Bright notes that the six hundred miles from
Louisville by way of Cairo, Illinois, to Saint Louis
cost him only eight dollars, whereas a ninety-mile
stagecoach ride in Kentucky came to twice that
amount.

There were inevitable hazards and delays. Their
money ran out, leaving them stuck at the Virginia
springs (out of season) until additional funds arrived.
Low water held up their steamer at the rapids in Keokuk, and a calf derailed their "car" in Illinois. Bright
chronicles these events, but they do not seem to have
distressed him unduly. ("Bad food, a slow coach, jolting roads, swearing Irishmen, and an all-but-sleepless night—not much of pleasant memory to be extracted out of these," he writes, with characteristic
equanimity.) His travel companion was less fortunate.
Thomas Burder was a Cambridge friend, a serious,
frail, and disaster-prone young man, who succumbed to
all the difficulties of uncomfortable travel that never
seem to have troubled Bright. He almost lost his luggage in Washington, fell into a hole at Mammoth
Cave, and continually suffered from the asthmatic
complaint that contributed to his premature death
three years later.

But the two young men were happy in their acquaintances; they carried with them a battery of letters giving them entrée to society in almost every city.
Bright's business connections produced introductions

11

to established merchants like Charles Augustus Davis in New York and financiers like W. W. Corcoran in Washington. As Englishmen both of them were welcomed by their country's diplomatic representatives. In Canada, as the privileged guests of the governor-general, Lord Elgin, they met many of the province's political leaders. A letter to Longfellow led to the most important meeting of all—that with Hawthorne—although what was to become a firm friendship began inauspiciously enough.

> If Socrates were here [wrote Emerson in 1853], we could go and talk with him; but Longfellow, we cannot go and talk with; there is a palace, and servants, and a row of bottles of different coloured wines, and wine glasses, and fine coats.[14]

Given his choice between Socrates and Longfellow, Bright would decide differently from Emerson; and it was just this atmosphere that he found irresistible at Craigie House and in George Ticknor's comfortable mansion, with its fabled library, on Beacon Hill. A Boston wit once said that if Ticknor took it into his head to visit Olympus, he would have a letter to Jupiter in his pocket. He introduced his English visitors to such a wide group of what they would call "lions" that Bright came to regard the fortnight in Boston as the pinnacle of their American tour.

Bright was not long in America before he tried to sort out the political differences—always confusing to foreigners—between Whigs and Democrats. 1852 was the year that claimed the lives of two American giants—Clay and Webster. Millard Fillmore sat in the White House, but the presidential campaign under way

14. *Journals of Ralph Waldo Emerson*, ed. Edward Waldo Emerson and Waldo Emerson Forbes (Boston and New York, 1909–14), 8:397.

when Bright arrived came up with General Winfield Scott as the Whig candidate in his stead. The Democratic national convention, which Bright witnessed in Baltimore, selected Franklin Pierce as its surprise candidate. Slavery was the crucial issue on both platforms. The Fugitive Slave Law of 1850, which had been widely acclaimed as the "final" solution to the problem, provoked the northern states to pass stronger personal liberty laws inhibiting the return of runaways. At the Free Soil convention in August, slavery was denounced as "a sin against God and a crime against man."

The political atmosphere in America concerned Bright enough for him to write a letter to *Fraser's Magazine* on the presidential election (his first stab at journalism); but one suspects that among current publications he devoured *The Blithedale Romance* more eagerly than *Uncle Tom's Cabin*. Predisposed as he was to hero-worship, Bright felt naturally elated by his encounters with Webster and Sumner; but his conversation with the latter was about books, not politics, and he reserves his most extravagant rhapsodies for the literary society of Boston and Cambridge. Already a keen autograph collector, with the modest beginnings of what was to become a good library, he took advantage, along the way, of those American acquaintances who shared that enthusiasm. (He continued, long after he returned home, to swap autographs with Longfellow and Ticknor.) Pleasure seems to have been the purpose of the trip: the only official duty Bright records is making speeches on shipboard as the representative of the *Great Britain*'s owners. As he pursued his convivial course, from a champagne dinner at the residence of the British minister in Washington to a cookout of fresh fish in Minnesota Territory, he laid the foundation of a special fondness

13

for America that was to play a part—small, but more important than he could have anticipated—in his later life.

3

If Bright's name is remembered today, it is only because he is known as Hawthorne's closest English friend. The most unassuming of men, Bright would not have been surprised at this; in fact, he predicted it. Reading the warm references to himself in the passages from Hawthorne's English notebooks, which Sophia published after her husband's death, Bright wrote to Lord Houghton in 1872: "These few words will be the only thing by which anyone will one day come across my name."[15]

When he heard, some months after his return from the United States, that the oppressively shy man whom he had met in Concord was to be consul at Liverpool, Bright wrote to Longfellow: "I look forward to seeing him again with much interest but without much hope of 'getting on with him' at all."[16] As one of the first callers at the dismal consular office, Bright began at once to offer hospitality, introducing Hawthorne to his family (he was still a bachelor and only half Hawthorne's age), taking him to the theater, showing him the sights, bringing him recent periodicals. He immediately entranced Sophia Hawthorne with stories of the fancy dress balls, glittering dinner parties, and concerts that awaited her, if only her husband would relax his perpetual reserve. Two full years after Hawthorne's arrival, Bright wrote to Charles Eliot Norton: "Hawthorne is still with us, and all my family like him very much:—but he is very reserved and knows

15. Quoted in Pope-Hennessy, *Monckton Milnes*, p. 195.
16. Letter of May 31, 1853, in Harvard College Library.

14

few people besides."[17] Bright twitted Hawthorne about his shyness in an affectionate bit of badinage, "Song of Consul Hawthorne" (see page 457), written in 1855.

Through Bright's unceasing efforts Hawthorne was drawn a little into Liverpool society, though he never relished as Sophia did the elegant gatherings offered by Bright's family at Sandheys or by his aunt, Mrs. John Pemberton Heywood, at Norris Green. More to Hawthorne's taste were the tête-à-têtes in the consular office, where Bright dropped in about every other day.

> Almost the only real incidents, as I see them now, were the visits of a young English friend, a scholar and a literary amateur, between whom and myself there sprung up an affectionate, and, I trust, not transitory regard. He used to come and sit or stand by my fireside, talking vivaciously and eloquently with me about literature and life, his own national characteristics and mine, with such kindly endurance of the many rough republicanisms wherewith I assailed him, and such frank and amiable assertion of all sorts of English prejudices and mistakes, that I understood his countrymen infinitely the better for him, and was almost prepared to love the intensest Englishman of them all, for his sake. . . . Bright was the illumination of my dusky little apartment, as often as he made his appearance there![18]

The friendship prospered as they enjoyed excursions together, to Wales, to London, to Bright's old school and university. When Bright went up to receive his deferred Cambridge M.A. in 1860, his celebrated American friend sat in the audience. When Hawthorne embarked for Italy, it was to Bright that he entrusted

---

17. Fragmentary letter of [Aug. 14, 1855], in Harvard College Library.

18. *Our Old Home*, Centenary Edition (Columbus, Ohio, 1970), p. 39.

the manuscript of his English notebooks, with the following note:

> Here are these journals. If unreclaimed by myself, or by my heirs or assigns, I consent to your breaking the seals in the year 1900,—not a day sooner. By that time, probably, England will be a minor republic, under the protection of the United States. If my countrymen of that day partake in the least of my feelings, they will treat you generously.[19]

His consular duties and travels over, Hawthorne returned to America after a seven-year absence abroad. Three months after resuming residence in Concord, he was chided by the young friend he left behind:

> Of course not!—I *knew* you'd never write to me, though you declared you would. Probably by this time you've forgotten us all, and sent us off into mistland with Miriam and Donatello. . . . Well, at any rate I have not forgotten you or yours; and I feel that, now you have left us, a pleasure has slipped out of our grasp. Do you remember all our talks in that odious office of yours; my visits to Rock-ferry; my one visit, all in the snow, to Southport; our excursions into Wales, and through the London streets, and to Rugby and to Cambridge; and how you plucked the laurel at Addison's Bilton, and found the skeleton in Dr. Williams's library; and lost your umbrella in those dark rooms in Trinity; and dined at Richmond, and saw the old lady looking like a maid of honor of Queen Charlotte's time; and chatted at the Cosmopolitan; and heard Tom Hughes sing the "Tight Little Island;" and— But really I must stop, and can only trust that now at last you will be convinced of my existence, and remember your promise, and write me a good long letter about everything and everybody.[20]

19. *Nathaniel Hawthorne and His Wife*, 2:168-69.
20. Lathrop, *Memories of Hawthorne*, pp. 464-65.

The two men never met again. Hawthorne's death in 1864 left Bright with tangible mementoes in the form of his cherished manuscript of *The Marble Faun*, ("the gem, the Koh-i-noor, of my autographs") and letters from Hawthorne, parts of which he used to read aloud to selected friends. Six months before his own death in 1884, Bright wrote, with characteristic reticence, to Julian Hawthorne about these treasures:

> As regards your father's letters to me, after looking through them I find so much that is personal to myself or so much that I am sure your father would not have wished *published* that I shrink from giving them to the world.—Whether hereafter I may *print* selections from them to give to a few friends . . . I cannot now decide.—If I did I could, with less feeling of being egotistical, speak of my own personal relations with him, and record some of our talk:—but this I *could* not *publish*.[21]

If Hawthorne valued Bright for his amiability, his lack of pretension, his insularity and his good heart, Bright could sum up his feelings for Hawthorne in one sentence: "It is one of the best things of my life to have made a friend of you."[22]

4

The story of Bright's later life—an unhurried life of unobtrusive usefulness and quiet pleasures—can be quickly told. At one point he must have toyed with the idea of going into law, for he was admitted to the Inner Temple in June, 1850. On returning to Liverpool from his American trip, he entered his father's

21. Letter of Oct. 26, 1883, in Berg Collection, New York Public Library. This portion of Bright's letter is omitted from the transcript in *Nathaniel Hawthorne and His Wife*, 2:350.

22. Letter to Hawthorne, Oct. 20, 1863, in *Nathaniel Hawthorne and His Wife*, 2:279-80 (date from Berg MS).

shipping business, which was prominent in South American trade and responsible for the establishment of regular sea communication with Australia. After her record-breaking transatlantic run, the *Great Britain* was used to carry emigrants to Australia; and one of the ways Bright chose to entertain Hawthorne, shortly after his arrival in the summer of 1853, was to take him aboard for the commencement of such a voyage.[23] Another time he urged Hawthorne to come as his guest to the launching of the company steamer the *Royal Charter*, which stuck fast in the mud of the Dee after being nervously christened by Bright's mother—an event amusingly described in the *English Notebooks*.[24] Like his brother Heywood, who teased him for being more interested in literature than in shipping, Henry Bright became a partner in the firm.

From his family Bright acquired an acute sense of his social duty, and he soon busied himself with philanthropic sidelights of the business, establishing and administering Sailors' Homes in Liverpool. The "ship-cruelty question," involving the inhumane treatment of sailors on American merchant vessels, incensed him enough to ask his friend Milnes to bring the question before Parliament; but the outbreak of the Civil War forestalled any action. Bright also concerned himself with other humanitarian causes, such as the improvement of prison vans and the creation of homes for working girls and fallen women. His position in Liverpool led to his appointment as justice of the peace for the borough in 1865 and (on his father's death) for the county of Lancashire in 1870.

But Heywood Bright was correct to accuse his elder brother of losing his heart to literature. Bright had been home from America only six months when he

23. Hawthorne, *English Notebooks*, pp. 10-11.
24. Ibid., pp. 187-88.

suggested to John Chapman, London publisher and newly chosen editor of the *Westminster Review*, that he publish a literary journal (to be called *Chapman's Magazine*) for which Bright would provide financial backing. Negotiations continued for some weeks, but the project came to nothing, perhaps because Chapman began to drop heavy hints about wishing to find "an able young man with a small capital," whom he could use to market his publications in Liverpool.[25] In the course of the correspondence, Bright offered to write for the *Westminster Review*, and his two contributions on Thomas Moore (1853) and De Quincey (1854) launched him on a lifetime career— or rather, avocation—as a reviewer. From 1855 to 1869 he wrote for the *Examiner*, contributing reviews of a wide range of current writers that included Longfellow, Hawthorne, Swinburne, and Gladstone.

A conversation in Liverpool with Sir Charles Wentworth Dilke, proprietor of the *Athenaeum*, led to a long association with that journal, beginning in 1871 and lasting to the end of Bright's life. Under Norman Mac-Coll's editorship, the *Athenaeum* enjoyed an enviable reputation for fair-minded, authoritative criticism and scholarly dependability. Bright averaged between five and six contributions a year, devoting his special attention to the memoirs and biographies of English literary figures. He was also given for review gardening books, collections of minor English verse, and American works. When he discussed the memoirs of Catharine Sedgwick, George Ticknor, or Margaret Fuller, he could draw on his own American experiences, and his notices of Hawthorne are enlivened by personal reminiscence.[26] If Bright is partially respon-

25. Letter from John Chapman to HAB, June 21, 1853, in Trinity College, Cambridge.

26. HAB's file of his own reviews is still in the possession of his grand-

sible for the success of the *Athenaeum* as one of the chief English organs for reviewing American books, the roots of his interest must be traced back to the tour he took in 1852.

As a collector, Bright assembled what Lord Houghton calls "a charming library of readable books in fine condition," a remarkable collection of autographs (including a full gallery of Americans), and the manuscripts of a number of novels, obtained, like *The Marble Faun*, from the authors themselves. These included Trollope's *The Claverings*, Harriet Martineau's *Deerbrook* (in which he found a portrait of his American friend William Furness), and Elizabeth Gaskell's story of religious persecution, *Lois the Witch*.[27] It was Houghton, a bibliomaniac like himself, who was responsible for Bright's membership in the Roxburghe Club and the Philobiblon Society.

With a wide acquaintance of literary people, Bright came to assume the role that William Roscoe had once filled as the center of Liverpool literary life. He kept up a voluminous correspondence, for, as he wrote to Charles Eliot Norton, "I take to myself something I remember Longfellow saying to me, 'I do not like to lose a friend I have once made.'"[28] He was assiduous in offering hospitality to American acquaintances, many of whom he had met on his trip in 1852. (See "Sonnet to Longfellow in England" on page 460.) He was on intimate terms with Elizabeth Gaskell, who mothered him and gave him an introduction to Rossetti.[29] During the last ten years of his life, he was

daughter; the authorship of his *Athenaeum* reviews is confirmed by the editor's marked set in the London offices of the *New Statesman and Nation*. For Hawthorne, see *Athenaeum*, Jan. 3, 1880, pp. 14–15 and Jan. 6, 1883, pp. 9–11.

27. Milnes, "Henry Bright," p. 26.

28. Letter of Nov. 8, 1860, in Harvard College Library.

29. See Anne Henry Ehrenpreis, "Elizabeth Gaskell and Nathaniel Hawthorne," *Nathaniel Hawthorne Journal*, 1973, pp. 89–119.

20

friendly enough with Swinburne to inspire a mortuary sonnet, published in *A Midsummer Holiday* (1884).[30]

A series of contributions to *The Gardener's Chronicle,* describing the seasonal work in his garden at Ashfield, led to the one book for which Bright was (for a while) known: *A Year in a Lancashire Garden* (1879). This is an informal series of essays, a blend of flowers and literature, whose considerable popularity is now perhaps difficult to understand.[31] But Bright did not aspire to literary fame. If he could correspond with authors, entertain them at his comfortable fireside, and gather their books around him, he was content.

In 1861 he married Mary Elizabeth Thompson of Thingwall Hall, and the long, red-gabled house they built together at Ashfield, outside Liverpool, became the home for three sons and two daughters. In 1881 pulmonary disease forced Bright to seek a milder climate; but his constitution was never robust, and he did not recover. He died at the early age of fifty-four and was buried, as Lord Houghton puts it, "beneath the wreaths of his own Lancashire garden."[32]

5

Throughout his American tour, when he arrived in a new city, Bright paid one of his first calls on its Unitarian minister. This practice brought him in touch with such prominent figures as William Henry Furness in Philadelphia, Theodore Parker in Boston, and William

30. Printed on page 461. See Cecil Y. Lang, "Swinburne's Letters to Henry Arthur Bright," *Yale University Library Gazette* 25 (July, 1950): 10-22. In one of two unpublished letters to HAB, belonging to Bright's granddaughter, Swinburne agrees to read over poems written by Bright's dead brother Hugh.

31. Charles Eliot Norton, thanking HAB for a copy of this book, says that "Harry James" (in his biography of Hawthorne) should have included English flower gardens in his list of things that America lacks (letter at Trinity College, Cambridge).

32. Milnes, "Henry Bright," p. 25.

Greenleaf Eliot in Saint Louis. (How he would have enjoyed knowing that the kindly clergyman, in whose church in the "far West" he first took the sacrament, was to be the grandfather of a celebrated poet!) Since many of these men were not only distinguished in themselves, but represented various facets of a divided religion, Bright's remarks on Unitarians provide an unusual dimension to his American journal.

Bright's faith was of the utmost importance to him. His family had been Unitarian for generations, and he himself had suffered for his views at Cambridge. In the Liverpool of his boyhood, two large and flourishing Unitarian congregations, under able ministers, claimed among their members many townspeople prominent in civic and social affairs. When Bright was nine years old, the city was wracked by a celebrated Unitarian controversy that must have vitally concerned his family. Anglican clergymen, alarmed at the entrenched position of this radical faith, announced a series of lectures that would expose its dangerous errors. The three challenged ministers (James Martineau, John Hamilton Thom, and Henry Giles) duly attended the lectures; but when they delivered thirteen addresses in turn, eloquently defending their faith, the Anglicans boycotted the meetings. The series was nonetheless heavily attended, the lectures printed, and Liverpool was plunged for months into a controversy whose echoes traveled far. Few were converted, but existing convictions were sharpened and clarified. Traditional Unitarians like Bright's family must have felt that they should cling even more tenaciously to their cherished views.

These views, in brief, centered upon the belief that God is one person, not three, and that Christ, his son and messenger, is a being distinct from God. Since modern Unitarianism has moved far from its original biblical basis, it is well to remember that for those holding the faith when Bright was young, the Bible was the sole source of Christian truth. William Ellery Channing, the "father" of American Unitarianism, whose writings were widely revered in England, based his rejection of the Trinity on the grounds that it was unscriptural. In his epoch-making Baltimore sermon of 1819, which became a Unitarian manifesto, Channing stated that as "a book written for men, in the language of men," the Bible should be subjected to critical study and the exercise of reason; but it was indubitably the record of God's successive revelations to mankind. In common with other Christians, Channing believed that God's revelations found confirmation in the miracles performed by Christ. Jesus was sent from God to aid in man's redemption from sin, and his teachings were God's infallible truth.

These views came under fire from the Transcendentalists in the 1830s, when Emerson's generation began to assert that the truths of religion and morality were not dependent on the authority of the church or the revelation of the Bible, but were immediate intuitions of the divine. Consciousness itself was a reliable source of spiritual insight. Jesus was no longer viewed as the unique channel of God's will, and the miracles wrought in confirmation of his authority were dismissed. The forms and traditions of the Unitarian church were left behind, in favor of man's "inner light." The division between the orthodox Unitarians and the new Transcendental school was declared when Emerson wrote in his journal in 1837: "Once Dr. Channing filled our sky. Now we become so conscious of his limits and of the difficulty attending any effort to show him our point of view that we doubt if it be worth while. Best amputate."[33] In his Divinity School Address, which became for the Transcendentalists almost a new reli-

33. *Journals*, 4:239.

gious manifesto, Emerson declared that when Christ spoke of miracles he meant only that all of life is a miracle. He advocated "faith in man" rather than faith in Christ.

Thus when Bright met the American Unitarians, they did not represent the cohesive little sect he may have anticipated. Young radical preachers, under the influence of Emerson's writing and Parker's preaching, were speaking out for a religion natural to man and authenticated by intuition. To conservative believers, such teachings were nothing short of heretical. In 1853, the year after Bright's visit, the leaders of the Unitarian Association found it necessary to defend their faith against the charge of infidelity and rationalism. In the report issued that year they announced:

> We desire, in a denominational capacity, to assert our profound belief in the Divine origin, the Divine authority, the Divine sanctions, of the religion of Jesus Christ. This is the basis of our associated action. We desire openly to declare our belief as a denomination . . . that God, moved by his own love, did raise up Jesus to aid in our redemption from sin. . . . We receive the teachings of Christ . . . as infallible truth from God.[34]

Although the conservative majority of Unitarians prevailed for a time, the report had profound repercussions within the faith. Complicating the controversy was the issue of slavery. The radical Unitarians were nearly all abolitionists, while the orthodox—conservative alike in their social and their theological views—opposed this agitation. Consequently, the antislavery efforts of such men as Parker (who was minister-at-large for fugitive

---

34. Twenty-eighth Report of the American Unitarian Association, quoted in George Willis Cooke, *Unitarianism in America* (Boston, 1902; rpt. 1971), p. 157.

slaves in Boston) and Furness became a serious cause of discord.

The schism in the faith is graphically illustrated by the first two "Uni" ministers Bright met. In Philadelphia, William Henry Furness presided over a congregation whose complexion—it was largely made up of well-to-do merchants—was not unlike that of Bright's Renshaw Street Chapel at home. Furness was a close friend of Emerson, an admirer of the Transcendentalists, and a keen abolitionist. He had contributed to the debate on miracles by arguing that they were not performed in order to confirm the truth of Christ's teaching. On the Fourth of July in 1839 he had begun preaching against slavery to an astonished congregation that numbered Pierce Butler among its members. From that time on his pulpit was increasingly devoted to the antislavery cause, and when Bright heard him preach on Paul at Corinth, the sermon struck him as being all for abolition, though Furness never mentioned the word. In conclusion, Bright says, he asked God's blessing on "the colored man."

At the opposite extreme from Furness, George Washington Burnap of Baltimore represented the old school. A much-published author, Burnap was an aggressive defender of conservative Unitarianism and accepted the authority of the Bible without question. He made clear to Bright that he abhorred both Transcendentalists and abolitionists, insinuated that Emerson was mad (he "never thinks in *lines* but in *dots*"), and found Theodore Parker "disgusting." Bright was much charmed by Furness's forceful personality but lent a sympathetic ear to Burnap's splutterings.

Entering Massachusetts, Bright felt he was approaching the Unitarian mecca, as indeed he was. Of the two hundred and forty-two Unitarian churches recorded in the 1850 census, one hundred and sixty-three of them, with congregations totalling nearly 93,000 members, were in Massachusetts. Unitarians had long predominated among literary men, Harvard professors, judges, and the social elite. "Dear Massachusetts!" exclaims Bright in a naive paean of praise, "where Channing lived and Henry Ware, . . . and where more entirely than in any other State is it true that our people 'have kept unstained what there they sought—Freedom to worship God!' " Ezra Stiles Gannett, Channing's successor at the Federal Street Church in Boston, was only the first of a collection of "Uniparsons" he met there. On his first Sunday he heard Theodore Parker preach in the morning, Ephraim Peabody at King's Chapel in the afternoon, and spent the evening with Edmund Squire, an English Unitarian he met on shipboard. Even the Seamen's Bethel, where Charles Eliot Norton took him to hear the celebrated Father Taylor, was established with the help of Channing and Emerson and was supported almost entirely by Unitarians. Indeed, *We're all Unitarians,*" Norton assured Bright after telling a smug little story intended to illustrate American tolerance as against English bigotry. Norton did not mention the fact that his father, Professor Andrews Norton of the Harvard Divinity School, publicly branded Emerson's followers as infidels; or the fact that Theodore Parker was forced to preach his crusading sermons in the Melodeon because he had been ostracized from Boston Unitarian pulpits for his radical views.

Bright's own sympathies were with the old school. Channing was his hero, and he would hear no ill of him. He was most comfortable with sermons on orthodox topics, such as G. W. Hosmer's (in Buffalo) on retribution and forgiveness of sin. To mix politics with religion, as Furness and Parker did, Bright thought inappropriate and unwise. He did not wish to hear from the pulpit about the heroism of Kossuth or the evils of Louis Napoleon or the sufferings of the colored man. Parker's personal style he found repellent. (It was Emerson who said, "Highly refined persons might easily miss in him [Parker] the element of beauty.") Bright lacked the insight of another visiting Englishman who settled into the same close-knit Boston-Cambridge circle a few weeks after him. Arthur Hugh Clough wrote home with some indignation:

> I sometimes, when I have heard people here for example talk of Theodore Parker as if he were the scum of the earth, think that it will not do to keep silence. I have no particular love for Th[eodore] P[arke]r, but he is so manifestly more right than these people who despise him.[35]

And yet Bright sensed the smug complacency in Boston Unitarianism and disliked it. Such men as George Ticknor seemed to him to profess a faith that was fashionable and undemanding, more moral than religious.

Bright never swerved from his old-school Unitarian views. In 1856 he outlined a little book (never written) to be entitled *Free Theology by a Cambridge Man*, in which he describes Christ as "God manifest in the flesh," as well as the "ideal of humanity which God first expressed in the life of his Son." Reason he calls the groundwork and root of faith, but he also cites revelation as an evidence of God.[36] For some years (1856–60) he championed the conservative side of his religion in the pages of the weekly Unitarian newspaper, the *Inquirer*, and contributed as well to other

35. Letter of Jan. 17, 1853, *The Correspondence of Arthur Hugh Clough*, ed. Frederick L. Mulhauser (Oxford, 1957), 2:365-66.

36. Letter of Feb. 13, 1856, to a potential publisher, in the Berg Collection, New York Public Library.

Unitarian journals. He was grieved (in 1864) when he reported to Charles Eliot Norton that "our ministers are beginning to preach against the miraculous in Xtianity."[37] Among his works were hymns, religious poems, and an account of the early Arians called *The Confessor of Antioch* (1867). And in 1875 he wrote, again to Norton: "For my own part I still hold to the Conservative Unitarianism in which I was born as (at least) as probable as any thing else, and therefore not worth changing."[38]

6

Since for Bright the exercise of reason was the underpinning of faith, it is not surprising that he viewed with a skeptical eye the phenomenon of spirit-rapping that he encountered in America. The rage for spiritualism, which was in full spate in the 1850s, began on the night of March 31, 1848, in Hydesville, New York. A farmhouse belonging to John D. Fox was disturbed by mysterious noises in the middle of the night. In response to questions from the Fox sisters—thirteen-year-old Margaret and twelve-year-old Kate—the knocking spirit revealed that it was the ghost of a murdered peddler. The girls' mother summoned the neighbors, who heard answers rapped out to further questions. As testimonies to the supernatural origin of the noises were published, the fame of the Fox sisters spread, and in June, 1850, they began a series of séances at Barnum's Hotel in New York City. Horace Greeley fanned the growing mania by defending the sisters in the pages of his *Tribune*, and many substantial citizens were persuaded into believing in the new cult. Judge John Worth Edmonds of the New York

37. Letter of Dec. 28, 1864, in Harvard College Library.
38. Letter of Feb. 19, 1875, in Harvard College Library.

Supreme Court became a celebrated convert, resigned his seat on the bench, and devoted the remainder of his life to the spread of spiritualism.

The subject was thus very much in the air during Bright's visit. It became a fashionable amusement to hold séances in private houses, presided over by a medium who would ask questions of the spirits. Responses could take the form of alphabetical rapping, table-tipping, or spirit-writing. When Thackeray visited New York later in 1852, even a sober intellectual like George Bancroft did not consider an evening of table-tipping an odd entertainment for his famous guest. In Boston, Bright met Tom Appleton, Longfellow's brother-in-law and convivial Brahmin, who conducted similar gatherings in Beacon Hill drawing rooms. Bright was ready from the first to dismiss the whole subject as obvious chicanery, but found himself continually surprised that intelligent people were so credulous. Julia Ward Howe testified to Appleton's spirit-rapping abilities; Anna Ticknor, Lidian Emerson, and Catharine Sedgwick's niece all regaled their young English visitor with spiritualist stories. When Longfellow suggested that the rappings were caused by electricity, Bright took the trouble in his diary to marshall arguments disproving the notion—not so much, one suspects, for his own satifaction, as out of deference to his host.

The Fox sisters' popularity spread so rapidly westward that spiritualist circles soon proliferated in every village and town. During the 1850s an estimated one million of America's twenty-five million people professed allegiance to the new "faith."[39] William Dean Howells (born in 1837) remembered that in the Ohio of his youth spiritualism was "rife in every second

39. Howard Kerr, *Mediums, and Spirit-Rappers, and Roaring Radicals Spiritualism in American Literature, 1850–1900* (Urbana, Ill., 1972), p. 9.

house in the village, with manifestations by rappings, table-tippings, and oral and written messages from another world through psychics of either sex, but oftenest the young girls one met in the dances and sleigh-rides."[40] Bright found that Saint Louis was "a great town for Rapping"; and indeed, not only did the Fox sisters visit the city in 1852 but spiritualist lectures were regularly offered during the decade of the fifties, and a spiritualist paper was issued there. On the Mississippi steamboat bound for Dubuque, Bright and his fellow travelers were subjected to amateur experiments in table-tipping and a form of hypnotism known as "electro-biology." Such experiments served only to deepen his skepticism and inflame his indignation.

While he was delayed in Blue Sulphur Springs, Bright amused himself with reading the *Revelations* of Andrew Jackson Davis, the "Poughkeepsie Seer," whose clairvoyant prophecies preceded the Fox furor. When the "Stratford Rappings" (in Connecticut) followed the Foxes' "Rochester Rappings," A. J. Davis pronounced them spiritual in origin and later became a spokesman for the spiritualist movement. A shoemaker's apprentice with very little education, Davis, in a "magnetized" state, delivered a course of lectures in New York. Published as *The Principles of Nature, Her Divine Revelations, and A Voice to Mankind* (1847), Davis's lectures trace the evolution of the universe, describe the solar system (with details of the planets' inhabitants) and expound an almost unintelligible system of mystical philosophy. To Bright it seemed apparent that Davis's "magnetizer" must have done more than put his ignorant young subject into a trance.

Without realizing it Bright also had a quick look at one of the most celebrated exponents of the spiri-

40. Quoted ibid., pp. 7-8.

tualist movement. Thomas Lake Harris was a sometime Universalist minister who wrote volumes of "trance poetry" (dictated by the spirit of Shelley and others) and later founded communal societies based on sexual mysticism. Bright saw him and his red-bloomered wife when the stagecoach stopped near Mountain Cove, Virginia, where Harris helped establish a short-lived spiritualist community. Since outside witnesses to this community are rare (it disintegrated early in 1853), Bright's brief sketch of the village and its members provides a valuable glimpse of a curious aspect of the mid-century American scene. In fact, his accumulated observations show how intense was the national preoccupation with a phenomenon that began when two mischievous girls decided to tease their superstitious mother by cracking their toe joints against the bedstead.

7

No traveler to antebellum America could go far without running head on into the problem of slavery. The fact that Britain had abolished slavery in her colonies in 1833 underlay the condescension of some visitors; but experience of America led most Englishmen to oppose abolitionism as vehemently as they condemned slavery. Harriet Martineau, who clambered up a Boston platform to speak out in support of abolition, was a notable exception. Like most of his countrymen, Henry Bright came with an instinctive distaste for the principle of human bondage. But, unlike Dickens or Harriet Martineau, he had not made up his mind how he felt about American slavery before he left Liverpool. In his diary he notes down facts about the Negroes with the naive earnestness of one trying to comprehend an unfamiliar phenomenon. In the end his natural conservatism betrayed his judgment; but the

31

process of his education, as seen through the unex-
purgated pages of his diary, gives a better notion of
the ordinary traveler's reactions than Dickens's impas-
sioned chapter on slavery in *American Notes* or other
travelers' careful summaries of the subject.

To modern ears Bright's casual references to "blubber lips," "lubly yaller gals," and "niggers" that "don't
show dirt" are offensive; but we may be sure that such
remarks seem unusual only because they would be
edited out of published accounts. His real education
in the subject of slavery began in Philadelphia. Here,
at the house of the British consul, Bright spent an
evening talking with George Washington Smith and
Thomas Wharton, both substantial and conservative
gentlemen. Philadelphia at this time, it should be remembered, was on terms of special friendship with the
South. Its mercantile interests were much involved
with southern states; a local publisher had rejected
Uncle Tom's Cabin; and the abolition movement there
was viewed with much hostility. In answer to Bright's
innocent questions, Smith and Wharton trotted out all
the standard arguments proving the physical and intellectual inferiority of the blacks. Smith (who had
"investigated the subject from boyhood") assured him
that blacks and whites must not mix because mulattoes
all die young. Not surprisingly, in such company,
Bright could get "no certain reply" to his speculation
that Negroes might improve intellectually if they were
educated for two or three generations.

His indignation was aroused when he learned that a
black congregation had been refused admission to an
Episcopal convention in Philadelphia. He was further
enlightened when, to his amazement, he discovered
that his host in Baltimore, not himself a slaveholder,
approved of this action. (This same man would not
read *Uncle Tom's Cabin* because he claimed he knew

it was a tissue of lies.) Another Baltimore gentleman, who owned one hundred and fifty slaves, assured Bright that few masters ever ill-treated them, and that many of them refused liberty when it was offered. As he traveled farther south and heard testimonies from more slaveholders about the happy condition of their slaves, Bright came to view the action of the Episcopal convention as an example of the prejudice awaiting the free Negro who went north. "In America, south of Baltimore, you *must* sympathise with the slaveholder," he wrote on his return home; "north of it, you must still express your anti-slavery opinions with caution and reserve."[41]

Perhaps the best solution, then, was the Colonization scheme. In Liberia the free black could live secure from the white man's domination in a climate to which he was naturally suited. Bright did not realize that the paucity of blacks actually transported to Liberia demonstrated their unwillingness to go; or—as Harriet Martineau was quick to spot—that the whole Colonization scheme was not only impractical but an easy means for southerners to rid themselves of clever and discontented blacks.

Practically all English visitors tried to attend a slave auction, and Bright was no exception. The scene in the Richmond auction house provoked his bitter irony. More unusual were his two visits to black church services, in Baltimore and in Richmond, which he describes with some verve. How many travelers to this country, one wonders, ever *talked* with Negroes? Dickens conversed at length with a Choctaw Indian chief and with prisoners at the Philadelphia penitentiary, but the only black conversation he records took

41. *Free Blacks and Slaves. Would Immediate Abolition be a Blessing? A Letter to the Editor of the Anti-Slavery Advocate.* By a Cambridge Man. (London and Liverpool, 1853), p. 4.

place between a Virginia coach driver and his horses. Captain Marryat, who was given to noting down conversations with Americans at all levels, seems to observe Negroes only at a distance. Bright, affable always, had long conversations with three blacks in Virginia: a female slave in Lewisburg, a free Negress raised in South Carolina, and a mulatto waiter at the Alum Springs hotel, who had been promised his liberty if he could raise eight hundred dollars. All three struck him as intelligent, and two of them could read. They painted a picture of their masters that was by and large an agreeable one; the stories he heard of beating and branding were secondhand. Bright, sanguine by nature and lacking the moral fervor of some of his countrymen, was ready—too ready—to believe what he was told.

In the pamphlet cited above, in which he rather unwisely published his accumulated wisdom on the subject of slavery, Bright takes the line that the free Negro is so brutally treated in the North that abolition under existing circumstances would be no favor to him.

> With a political freedom which throws him upon his own resources, and deprives him of any protecting hand, the free negro of America is in a social bondage as inexorable as that which confines the slave of Virginia or the Carolinas. The latter, though in the power of one man "for better or worse," is at least safe from maltreatment by every other; the former is exposed to insult and contumely from each and all of the dominant race. (P. 7)

The arguments Bright heard from his conservative friends are all repeated, together with the comforting assertion that "the more horrible scenes of wickedness and suffering are rather the exception than the rule."

34

Uncle Tom's Cabin, warmly recommended by Furness, Bright condemns as "an appeal rather than an argument." He praises the Colonization scheme and recommends some sensible reforms, such as the observance of the marriage tie among blacks and the better regulation of auctions. Small wonder that his abolitionist friends Furness and John Jay each wrote long and detailed rebuttals of these arguments in letters to Bright, in which they deplore his logic and remind him that "slavery is a *sin!*"[42] Among his conservative friends (predictably pleased with the pamphlet), Charles Eliot Norton, reviewing it for the *North American Review,* praised its "good sense and moderation" and singled out Bright's suggested reforms for applause.[43]

When the Civil War broke out, Bright, despite his particular fondness for "dear old Massachusetts" and his Boston friends, allied himself with the southern cause. In a letter to Norton, explaining his views, he wrote, "I am so thankful that I saw America united,— and that then no dream of civil war had ever haunted any of us."[44] When Bright's liberal brother-in-law, Henry Yates Thompson, visited America in 1863 and was struck with Olmsted's *Cotton Kingdom,* he wrote home: "If anybody wants some data to judge the American question by, no better book can be found. Henry Bright ought to get it: tell him to read it and see what a charming state of society his Southern friends wish to perpetuate."[45]

42. Letter from Furness, July 1, 1853; letter from John Jay, Oct. 24, 1853, both in Trinity College, Cambridge.

43. *North American Review* 161 (October, 1853): 528-30. The review is anonymous, but its authorship is determined by a letter from HAB to Norton, Nov. 11, 1853, in Harvard College Library. Bright laments his pamphlet's poor reception in "ultra-abolition England."

44. Letter of Sept. 7, 1861, in Harvard College Library.

45. *An Englishman in the American Civil War,* ed. Sir Christopher Chancellor (London, 1971), p. 52.

8

Bright's travel diary is an informal account meant
only for his family's eyes and not intended for publication. He kept it faithfully, making entries every other
day or so, and filling in events when he missed a night's
writing. His pages contain incidental observations of
American customs, some details of sightseeing, and
mercifully brief descriptions of scenery. He was well
aware that one or two details can bring a scene to
life more readily than many pages. Of Saint Paul he
is content to say, "It reminds Loch and Burder of
Richmond on the Thames, as from a terrace walk on
the bluffs in front of the town you see the river winding
below, and fair forest land upon the other bank."
Except for Niagara, where he seems to have felt that
more was expected of him (so did Dickens), he does
not often indulge in guidebook descriptions of natural
beauty. But he was a careful observer (and collector)
of flowers—as befits an enthusiastic gardener. And he
can toss off quick sketches that capture a scene:

> There was much bustle as we left St. Louis,—much
> business and bargaining. Carts drawn by mules in
> tandem were busy bringing goods to the boat; boys
> were hawking newspapers and books, cheap reprints
> from the English, cheaper translations from the
> French; an old man begged me to buy a gun-cleaner,
> and a girl offered me a water-melon.

Or, to describe a New York dinner party:

> Madiera excellent, a white Ariadne not too warmly
> clad sat in vanille ice on a pink ice panther.

But it is his attitude to people that gives Bright's
journal its special quality. "The traveller who desires

to tell his experience of North America," wrote Anthony Trollope, who toured the country a decade after him, "must write of people rather than of things."[46] From the moment Bright writes about his companions on the voyage, his enthusiasm for meeting people becomes obvious. Dr. Pettit of Philadelphia is "my Quaker friend" after three days' shipboard acquaintance; George Riggs and Charles Sumner are "two of my friends" after as long a time in Washington; Longfellow and Ezra Stiles Gannett rapidly become "our dearest Boston friends." Less condescending than most visiting Britons, Bright did not mind talking with humble people as well as celebrities. He struck up an acquaintance with an eccentric old farmer near Blue Sulphur Springs in Virginia, who made him promise to write "just to say how you get along." With a ready appetite for experience and an ability to wring enjoyment from new adventures, however bizarre, Bright relished the fun of camping out in the Minnesota woods with two middle-aged bluestockings. (Since Mrs. Ellet's account of the adventure is preserved, we can view this encounter from both sides.) The capacity to be delighted by so many things and to take such pleasure in human interchange is very winning.

By listening to people talk and recording their conversations—sometimes in summary, better still in their very words—Bright brings to life the many characters, famous and infamous, whom he met. "I'll get quite fat here in the country," complains poor Mrs. Piggott, wife of a New York watchmaker taking up residence in the Mountain Cove community in Virginia. "You've too many wrinkles on your brow for that," retorts the gentleman medium riding in the same stagecoach. A long conversation with Charles Sumner, who was con-

46. *North America*, ed. Donald Smalley and Bradford Allen Booth (New York, 1951), p. 20.

siderably Bright's senior and by his own account "a little formidable," reveals something of that statesman's pompous erudition:

> "I told [Margaret Fuller] I had been reading Hoole's translation of Ariosto; she told me I was quite wrong —Rose's was the best. I retired full of awe at a young lady who had not only read books in the original, but knew all about every translation. Next time I read Ariosto was in the original."

Margaret Fuller's name, in fact, seems to be on everyone's lips. She had drowned two years before, but many of the people Bright met had known her and talked to him about her, and one realizes how deeply she affected those who came in touch with her.

Bright's manner of portraying people is well summed up in his review of James's life of Hawthorne:

> What we want to know is how he looked and talked; we wish to see him, to ask him questions and hear his answers. . . . Harriet Martineau relates that Mr. Carlyle once told her "he would rather read of Webster's cavernous eyes and arm under his coat-tail" than all the speculation in her "Retrospect of Western Travel," and Mr. Carlyle was perfectly right.[47]

Bright's own account of his meeting with Webster (which duly notes the "black cavernous eyes") is very appealing:

> But it wasn't his conversation, for after all we gained but little, he seemed so sadly tired and so low,—it was (as Burder said) the sitting there that was so charming.—The feeling, there I am sitting close by the greatest man in the world perhaps, close by, talking to him,

47. *Athenaeum*, Jan. 3, 1880, p. 15.

shaking hands with him, asking him questions,—so
near I could pull his nose, take his wind or anything!
it's very curious! And this is Webster, and this is
Henry Bright. . . .

One is often reminded (by his tendency, for instance,
to refer to men in their early forties as "old") that
Bright was only twenty-two.

Bright's comments on people are never searching:
he notes what he sees, often with wry humor, but he
rarely analyzes or probes. He may remark that Miss
Mary Clark, Michigan schoolmistress, bites her nails
to the quick, or that Mrs. Ellet is "impulsive, merry,
fat, vulgar"; but tolerant acceptance seems to be his
customary attitude. Being more concerned with surface
than with substance, he often leaves the reader of his
diary wishing to have further details. In the legislative assemblies of the United States and Canada, he
tells us more about the appearance of the chambers
and of the speakers than about the matter of their
discussion. We learn that Emerson went deep into the
mysteries of Christian Socialism without finding out
what he said. That very habit of uncritical tolerance
which made Bright such good company deprives his
diary of the intellectual vigor of more substantive
accounts.

Lord Elgin in Quebec receives the fullest treatment
among his gallery of celebrities, and this portion of
Bright's journal is consequently one of the most rewarding. Elgin was an unusually gifted diplomat, who
had been entrusted by Earl Grey's Colonial Office with
the task of carrying out in Canada the policy of "responsible government," recommended by Lord Durham's famous Report. As governor-general since 1847,
Elgin had altered the relation of his office to Canadian
popular government so as to surrender much of its

traditional power to majority opinion. He was one of the first statesmen to help create an empire the secret of whose strength was to be local autonomy. Although he was reviled at the time by Tory politicians for losing a valuable colony, historians now agree that he filled his role with judgment and vision. Not long after Bright's visit, Elgin wrote to a friend:

> I have been possessed . . . with the idea that it is possible to maintain on this soil of North America, and in the face of Republican America, British connection and British institutions, if you give the latter freely and trustingly. Faith, when it is sincere, is always catching; and I have imparted this faith, more or less thoroughly to all Canadian statesmen with whom I have been in official relationship since 1848, and to all intelligent Englishmen with whom I have come in contact since 1850.[48]

One of these Englishmen was Henry Bright, and the diary's record of the governor-general's conversation bears witness to Elgin's effectiveness in transmitting this faith. We are given a close-up of a seasoned diplomat in action. Like all skillful administrators, Elgin gives an impression of being indiscreet, without in fact giving anything away ("I may here tell you, what should not be repeated . . . "). In discussing current political problems—the issue of the Clergy Reserves (concerning the secularization of church lands) or the question of annexation to the United States—he makes explicit his own views, with some pride in his diplomatic successes. He takes pains to explain his reasons for signing the Rebellion Losses Bill (in 1849): a crisis in his career, demonstrating rare courage, which was misunderstood and bitterly criticized in Britain.

48. Elgin to Cumming Bruce, Sept. 18, 1852, in *Letters and Journals of James, Eighth Earl of Elgin*, ed. Theodore Walrond, 2d ed. (London, 1873), p. 126.

But at the very moment he was talking to Bright, Elgin knew that his tenure in Canada was in jeopardy; the Tory administration that had come into power some seven months earlier was uncertain if it wished to retain his services. Elgin had worked in great amity with Lord Grey, but the new colonial secretary, Pakington (whose views spelled disaster for Elgin's program), had not yet even been in touch with him. Not a whisper of this, of course, to his visitors. Grey was, Elgin assures them, the best colonial secretary Canada ever had; "of Sir J. Pakington [notes Bright] he only knew from favourable hearsay."

How infectious Elgin's enthusiasm for Canada was may be gathered from Bright's sympathetic response. "No one knows how disheartening it is,—the ignorance of the English on these subjects," he tells his listeners, "and the way in which my best efforts are neutralized by the cool manner in which they talk of giving up Canada." Taking the hint, on his return to England Bright wrote for *Fraser's Magazine* an article on Canada extolling Elgin's policy, painting a glowing picture of Canada's virtues, and deploring Englishmen's ignorance of their valuable possession. Elgin's little chat over breakfast at Spencer Wood had not been wasted.

As an account never intended to see print, Bright's diary has the advantage of uninhibited honesty over more discreet published journals. ("It seems to me that of all unsafe things," he once wrote, "the least safe is to write down every unkind and illnatured thought in a diary and leave them all to a literary executor.")[49] Bright is gossipy, but rarely unkind and never illnatured. It may be doubted, however—since it was not considered ethical for a traveler to print personal remarks about his acquaintances—if any published

49. Letter to Lord Houghton, Dec. 28, 1882, in Trinity College, Cambridge.

journal would refer to the daughter of the American president as "fat and plain" or to one of America's greatest living poets (Bryant) as "uninteresting and stiff." Certainly Bright himself would view with consternation the publication of his unguarded remarks.

It would be a mistake to claim too much for Bright as a diarist. He is addicted to schoolboy humor and dubious puns. His style, though always clear and fluent, suffers from a self-conscious literariness and a superabundance of quotations. He can make fatuous remarks. He is gullible, believing all too readily what he is told, for instance, not only by pro-slavery enthusiasts, but by the jailer at the Philadelphia penitentiary about the comfortable state of his prisoners.

But Bright's refreshing lack of condescension goes far to balance these defects. "It is the nature of an Englishman to think everything ridiculous which contrasts with what he has been used to," wrote a reviewer of Dickens's *American Notes*.[50] That is a valid judgment on most British travelers to America, but it does not fit Henry Bright. Of the two hundred and thirty British visitors between 1836 and 1860 who published their accounts, a good number were openly hostile, many more were highly critical, and even those who were well-disposed toward the country were likely to be patronizing.[51] Bright had read a good many of these accounts in preparation for his visit: he seems to be familiar with those of Dickens, Harriet Martineau, John Delaware Lewis, L. B. Mackinnon, and Sir Charles Lyell. En route he reads Captain Marryat, whose sneering tone he dislikes. In response to such negativism and prompted by his own good nature, he writes his journal in a very different spirit.

50. [James Spedding] in *Edinburgh Review* 76 (January, 1843): 499.

51. See the annotated bibliography in Max Berger, *The British Traveller in America, 1836–1860* (New York and London, 1943), pp. 189-229.

Bright is never profound, but because his comments are passing and immediate, they give the reader a direct sense of how things must have seemed to his contemporaries. And his diary has one quality that is worth a collection of other virtues: it is rarely boring. To read it is to enjoy the double pleasure of catching glimpses of American social history while becoming acquainted with an engaging young man.

9

The original manuscript of Bright's diary has disappeared, and my text is based on a typescript, made a good many years ago, which is still in the possession of his granddaughter. This has posed some editorial problems, the chief one being the need to guess at what Bright wrote when the typescript is obviously wrong. The difficulty occurs mainly with proper names, and though it is easy to amend "Fameril Hall" to "Faneuil Hall" and "Ticonduoya" to "Ticonderoga," there are other cases where I cannot be sure of the correct reading. These I have left with a [?], altering silently those I am certain of.

Since there is evidence that Bright's spelling was not always reliable, I have taken the liberty occasionally to correct it silently, or to regularize variant forms of a word. In a handful of cases I have corrected his punctuation for the sake of clarity. Gaps in the typescript are indicated by angle brackets < >, which I have sometimes filled with suggested readings. I have standardized the form of place and date in the heading to each entry, adding a date in square brackets when Bright has omitted it. The chapter divisions and titles are mine. When quoting from Bright's manuscript letters I have expanded his ampersands.

The notes are admittedly copious, but since Bright is constantly name-dropping in one way or another, their bulk seemed unavoidable. In a separate section I have printed poems by Bright that bear in some way on his American tour, and the memorial sonnet written for him by Swinburne.

10

First among my acknowledgments must be Mrs. Elizabeth Lloyd, Bright's granddaughter, who has not only allowed me to publish the diary but has heartened me with continuous, enthusiastic encouragement. At her beautiful house in Malvern, where she offered hospitality to me and my family, Mrs. Lloyd made available family letters and mementoes, as well as the thirty meticulously-kept ledgers containing her grandfather's correspondence, which are now housed in Trinity College, Cambridge. Bright's own set of his reviews has enabled me to identify his numerous anonymous contributions to various journals. The discovery of the American diary was the high point of a memorable visit.

I am indebted to the Master and Fellows of Trinity College, Cambridge, for permission to quote from the Bright correspondence; I should also like to thank the Librarian, Philip Gaskell. Lola L. Szladits, Curator of the Henry W. and Albert A. Berg Collection of the New York Public Library, has granted me permission to quote from two of Bright's letters housed there. The Norton papers and the Longfellow papers at Harvard contain a number of letters from Bright that I have found useful; I owe thanks to William H. Bond, Librarian, and to Carolyn Jakeman. I quote by permission of the Houghton Library, Harvard University.

The southern portion of the diary—chapters 5, 6, and part of 7—has been published in the *Virginia Magazine of History and Biography*, to whose editor, William M. E. Rachal, I am much indebted.

The staff of the Alderman Library at the University of Virginia, particularly Kendon L. Stubbs, has been unfailingly helpful. Other libraries must be thanked for answering my queries: Rugby School, the Cincinnati Historical Society, the Historical Society of Pennsylvania, the Library Company of Philadelphia, the Maryland Historical Society, the Virginia Historical Society, the Quaker Collection of Haverford College Library, the Boston Public Library, Duke University Library, Yale University Library, and the Mount Vernon Ladies Association of the Union.

Among friends and acquaintances who have rendered various services I must thank Fredson Bowers, Nancy Hale Bowers, Cecil Y. Lang, J. C. Levenson, Viola Hopkins Winner, David Levin, Arthur F. Stocker, Walker W. Cowen, Charles L. Perdue, Paul M. Gaston, Martin J. Havran, Walter Muir Whitehill, Esther Rhoads Houghton, Ruth Mortimer, Sarah Sedgwick, Mary W. Scott, Shelah Kane Scott, Sophie Wilkins, Joel Myerson, Carl Seaburg, and C. E. Frazer Clark, Jr. My deepest gratitude, *comme toujours*, is reserved for my husband, Irvin Ehrenpreis.

45

THE DIARY

1

THE VOYAGE OUT

Great Britain. Saturday Evening, May 1, 1852.

The steam tug had left us with all my belongings on
board, and for a good hour we stood together at the
stern, watching it as it lessened each moment, and
waving our handkerchiefs as long as we could see any
answering flutter from its deck.[1]

We then began to look around and see who were to
be our friends during the fortnight which must pass
before we could again touch terra firma:—poor Burder[2]
had too soon to disappear—his "soul" began before
mine to "sicken on the heaving wave,"—and thus made
new acquaintance of no small importance.

Foremost at least in gentlemanly bearing and courtesy was Colonel Macaulay, but true to his country's

1. The ship's log records that the *Great Britain* left Wellington Dock
at 9:10 A.M. and stopped at 10:40 to put owners, friends, and pilot on
board the steam tug.

2. Thomas Henry Carr Burder (1831–55), Bright's travel companion,
educated at Eton and St. Catharine's College, Cambridge. He was admitted to the Inner Temple; but poor health forced him to leave London,
and he was studying theology at Cambridge when he died of rheumatic
fever at age 24.

instincts he added a reserve contrasting strongly with Dr. Pettit, a Philadelphian Quaker—very Yankee—nasal twang, sallow face with marked features:—still I liked him,—the shrewdness, the loquacious good-nature, and the pressing hospitality with which he urged me to visit him in his house "tho' thou'lt find us plain folk."[3] Spite of his peculiarities he was a decided acquisition, made speeches after dinner, returned thanks for the ladies on the strength I suppose of his having a wife on board who by the way eat [i.e., ate] more determinately and systematically with knife in mouth than anyone I ever saw.

With others I made acquaintance at dinner:—Mr. Smith the inventor of the screw propeller was most civil, and gave me some information about screws, &c.,[4] and still more about one Earl and Baronets and the like ad libitum whom he knew, or wished to make us understand that he knew:—I give him credit however for having more piquant stories of his grandees than the Cambridge Don who is wont to brag of his familiarity with the Duke of Athol, "a great friend of mine. I was one day out shooting with his Grace—I tell the story merely to show what intimate terms his Grace and myself are on—and I said, 'If I were your Grace I'd promote Sandy'—Sandy you must know was under-keeper—and his Grace answered with that openness and frankness which always distinguished him, 'Sandy Mon, Sandy be damned.' "

Mr. Smith is, like a sensible engineer, going to see in what our Transatlantic brothers excel us—he will

3. Dr. William Pettit (1805–53), a self-made man who earned a fortune in the copper mines of Lake Superior. A graduate of the University of Pennsylvania medical school, he practiced medicine in his native Ohio before taking charge of the Cliff Mine in 1845. Bright visits him later in Philadelphia.

4. Francis Pettit Smith (1808–74) had labored on his invention of the screw-propeller since 1835 and so impressed I. K. Brunel that the design of the *Great Britain* was altered to accommodate the new invention.

THE GREAT BRITAIN LEAVING LIVERPOOL PIER

Illustrated London News, August 28, 1852

"For a good hour we stood together at the stern . . . waving our handkerchiefs."

travel in every "crack" steamer in the States, and come home "like a filled sponge," to use his own words.

A fast young lady, a Miss Ingall, who likes soldiers and enjoys the smell of a cigar, sat next me at dinner. She is the daughter of a Canadian officer, and knew Bob Bright[5] when in those parts.

Every one was at dinner, among them Burder—the dinner itself was good, the speeches afterwards great fun (though I rather flinched at having to return thanks for the owner of the Great Britain) and the whole day most successful.

In the evening we passed the Africa (Cunard Line) from America to Liverpool:—happy people to be so near their journey's end!—we fired salutes as our rival ships moved close past each other, and gave three hearty cheers to our brother voyagers on the broad Atlantic.

The Captain has been in full force today—most kind

5. A cousin, Robert Onesiphorus Bright (1823-96), who had an army career. HAB sees Miss Ingall again in Montreal.

and attentive, and important:—we went this evening to see his charts, and while there were startled by a sweet voice—really most sweet—singing close by us the very *un*nautical "I know a bank." Burder and myself rushed off to the music room—it was Mrs. Sedger—heroine of the "Romance of the Great Britain"—a runaway match, the lady having jilted some promised and now desponding lover, and taken her passage with the favoured one in our ship. We have been listening to her songs, and now Burder has disappeared, and I having written today's journal shall follow his example.

Monday Morning, May 3.

A splendid morning on the broad Atlantic!—the ship's motion is but little, and thanks to my friendly strap, I have as yet been perfectly well, and almost *enjoyed* myself. Everyone seems well too—on deck groups are sitting, reading and working, or pacing from stem to stern congratulating each other and the captain on the beauty of the weather, the little rocking of the ship, and the non-appearance of the "Canada" which we may perhaps still meet.[6]

Yesterday was nearly as fine though colder:—I was late at breakfast, having had an energetic fit in the night which prompted me to walk the deck with the officer on watch, and having to lie in bed with a lazy fit in the morning.

At half-past ten we had service on board—our little Captain read well, to a most crowded congregation; so crowded that many had to stand, although extra

6. The rival Cunard line's *Canada*, which held the record for the shortest run to Halifax, left Liverpool on the same day as the *Great Britain*. She reached New York 17 hours and 30 minutes before Bright's ship.

seats were brought in for us to the saloon. Service over, we sang the 100th Psalm and listened to an extempore effusion from the Revd. Mr. Balme, a worthy of the Baptist persuasion, who is author of the "Mirror of the Gospel," "Telegraph," "Telescope," "Magnet" and "Lever" of Ditto, and is now going to the New World to enlighten his brethren there with a little of his Biblical science, or rather scientific Gospel.[7] His sermon was peculiar, and his accent still more so—he hoped we should "have *peas* with God," and believe in "the mystery of Godliness." Of course he "improved the occasion," what orthodox dissenter ever fails to do so—the ship's ballast was the fear of God, the ship's sails the love of God:—we were passing grand and varied scenery, but what so grand as God's goodness, &c., &c. ad nauseam (figuratively, not literally—my strap prevented that!) He was right about the scenery—the wild bold Irish coast with its indented bays in which nestle little white cottages all with their little white chapel, and little white-sailed fishing boats moving about between us and them:—while I was gazing at the rocky headlands I was roused by a voice of singular nasal power, "Friend Bright, wilt thee answer me a question?" (Will some Quaker answer me a question as to their knowledge of English grammar, and the pronoun "thou"?)

My Quaker friend was full of getting from Halifax to Galway in six days, and saving nearly half the voyage, and to all my objections opposed such a shrewd dogged determination that it should be and must be that there was nothing more to be said but an equally dogged and very Eldon-like "I doubt."[8]

7. Joshua Rhodes Balme was ordained minister of the first Baptist church in Chicago (September, 1852) and became involved in antislavery activities.

8. A reference to John Scott, first earl of Eldon (1751–1838), lord chancellor, famous for the delays of his court.

53

Last evening was beautiful—such moonlight!—such "beautiful moonlight!"—as I told Miss Ingall this morning at breakfast just as the steward whispered at her other ear, "beautiful potted shrimps, Ma'am." But last night's moon *was* beautiful, at times shining clear and bright, at other times webbed over with a most delicate gossamer of fleecy clouds, and always leaving a lane of light across the still ocean waters which (in the touching and meaning (?) words of the Honourable Alexis) "flashed like the flowrets of yesterday." Some of the passengers saw porpoises, which I did not, but saw instead an enthusiastic young gentleman mistake the log which had just been thrown overboard for a large fish following in the ship's wake, and very small he looked when we set him right.

Colonel Macaulay pointed out a lunar rainbow last night,—I was almost too late, but just caught a glimpse of the pale prismatic colours before they passed quite away.

I had much conversation with Mr. Smith—he complains of our coals which appear detestable, and will keep us a day longer on the voyage: he gave me a good deal of information about the screw, illustrating it by a common corkscrew—for each revolution of the engine he says the screw makes three. He insists on taking me into the engine-room, and I must go I suppose, though I'm certainly *not* scientific, and shall probably commit myself egregiously among the screws and cranks, and wheels and pistons below.

Saturday Night, May [8].

In the saloon again at last, after three most miserable days![9]

9. The ship's log for May 5–8 chronicles heavy gales and high seas.

54

Illustrated London News, June 12, 1852

Pleasure and misery are ever wandering together, says the Eastern fable, through the world:—one never comes to you, but the shadow of the other dogs his steps.

Tuesday evening was really delightful. We sat late at dinner, and afterwards Burder and myself walked on deck and saw the moon making her way through a bank of clouds and lighting up the broad Atlantic. Some of the passengers were walking, others dancing to the sound of a flute or chalking lines on the deck for jumping matches.

Wednesday was "quantum mutatus ab illo,"—how sadly changed for the worse.[10]

I got up as usual, but found myself both after breakfast and dinner obliged to retire to private life, and at last resigned myself to my fate, and have been in bed ever since. It has been blowing a gale nearly all the time and I have experienced a complication of motions as disagreeable as may well be imagined. First the vibration of the screw-propeller—this I really got to like at last—the great life-pulse of the ship it seemed, and its regular steady beat was re-assuring and pleasant among the sounds of wind and wave. Then there

10. *Aeneid* II.274.

was the tossing and rolling of the vessel in the trough of the sea—alas for the children of Britain if the rocking of the cradle of the nursery is as intensely unpleasant as the rocking of the "cradle of the deep!" —and most horrible of all, the shudder of the ship, as some huge wave smote her on the side and she reeled again beneath the blow:—and such waves as some of them were!—so grandly beautiful—rising up in a black shapeless mass as high as the deck, then breaking over in a sheet of foam "soft as carded wool," and as it falls changing into a wave of a shade of green or blue between each, and more beautiful than either, while the light spray is borne away in a shower of sparkling diamonds:—but how impossible to describe what must be seen or never realized.

Wednesday was a tempestuous and to a landsman an awful night, rendered more so by the cowardice of a few in the fore saloon who gave the alarm that the ship was going down at two in the morning. Up rushed the poor ladies in a state of the most frantic alarm; it must have been the most distressing sight— women and children coming tumbling up the stairs into the cold night air, with the firm belief that they had only some few more minutes of this world left them:—thank God I did not see so sad a sight!

One accident *did* happen—a poor sailor fell off the mizzenmast on Thursday morning—some fifty feet! By some chance he escaped but slightly injured, but few escapes can have been narrower, especially with such a sea running as there then was.

Every one has been most kind to us in our misery. Captain Matthews and Captain Martin came each day to tell us the news—the Quaker Doctor also paid us a daily visit—we got quite fond of the old man, his quaint Quakerisms and Yankeeisms were as amusing, as his disposition was kindly and good. "Hath it been in thy

56

province friend to read Longfellow?" he asked me the other day—and in giving us advice about our tour he advised us to go somewhere where we should "be rowed by ingines" (Indians, i.e.) He thinks slavery in each state in America should be bought off by a sum voted by the Federal Government and left to accumulate till the bribe became tempting—the same has been done with regard to education.

But now to bed or —

Monday Morning, at Noon, May 10.

We have just come up from an expedition with Mr. Smith and Mr. Squire (a Unitarian Minister who is seeking the "Paradise of Ministers,")[11] to the engine-room and the "screw alley,"—it is a wonderful place, and we emerged feeling very dirty and scientific.

We saw, besides the engines themselves (each revolution of which, per minute, impels the ship half a knot an hour, the screw each turn making 19 feet, so that since (as I before said) three revolutions of the screw equal one of the engine,—at each revolution of the engine we progress 19 × 3 or 57 feet, making in the hour an extra half knot *nearly*). Besides the large propelling engines and the like, we saw an hydrometric, reminding us amusingly of Cambridge and the Poll;[12] it's used to ascertain the quantity of salt in the boiler. But the most beautiful little instrument is one to mark off the number of revolutions made during the voyage

11. Edmund Squire became minister of the Second Hawes Church in Boston, 1852-53—where Bright visits him—and later of the Unitarian church in Washington Village, Boston, 1857-61.

12. At this time Cambridge men who took the "Poll" examination (i.e., a pass degree) were expected to demonstrate a knowledge of hydrostatics, largely by describing such instruments as pumps and barometers.

57

—as the engine revolves, a digit is added to the whole number already marked, so that by the end of the voyage we know exactly the effect of the engine on the onward speed of the vessel.

Nothing every one assures me can have behaved better than have our engines—the bearings have never got for one moment hot, and it is believed that the Great Britain is almost a solitary instance of a first trip with no inconvenience from the over-heating of the bearings. When we came up I was graciously pleased to order down a sherry bottle for our friendly engineers, at Mr. Smith's suggestion.

We are now going over the great bank of New-foundland; the weather is hazy and the air cold, show-ing that ice is near us. This is the most dangerous part of the voyage, and the look-out is ever most strict—the Captain was himself on deck all night, not trusting the ship even to our careful and painstaking officers. The caution is really needed, as a large iceberg did come into sight yesterday at a distance of some eight or ten miles—it was some 200 feet high, and we could just see it indistinctly standing up a white pinnacle on the horizon:—some of the passengers, thanks to a good glass, saw it more clearly, and one I believe suggested two white bears upon it,—the suggestion was how-ever hardly received with the favour and gravity it doubtless deserved. I hope we shall meet with an-other *rather* nearer,—but they are dangerous acquain-tance, and it is necessary to keep them at a distance, especially since on their part they always treat one with the utmost *coolness*. An iceberg, Lyell says, is eight times as low under water, as its height above, which gives some notion of their enormous and fearful size.[13] They are most to be dreaded when nearly sub-

13. Charles Lyell, *Travels in North America* (New York, 1845), 2:84.

merged, as a ship in this dense fog and at night might so easily run against one, and be never heard of again. Another danger here is from the number of fishing-boats always at anchor for the cod and mackerel fishery—we keep up a constant steam whistle to warn them we are coming, and they in reply blow (or *should* blow, for I've not heard one yet) an omnibus-like horn in answer, to tell us where they are, that we may steer out of their way.

Among my most pleasant acquaintance is Captain Franklin, formerly of the "British Queen."[14] He is a gentlemanly and agreeable fellow, and we had a long conversation yesterday on sea disasters, and many stories he told me of the beautiful heroism exhibited in the most awful scenes by captain and crew.

Wednesday Morning, [May 12].

Last night we had a—ball!—a veritable *ball* at sea.

On Tuesday it was suggested, and we got up a little hop, but last night the Captain gave a regular soirée —not *much* like a Manchester "swarry—." All the fore-saloon passengers were asked, and all came except a few who were *serious*:—we had singing from the bride Mrs. Sedger, from our steward, from Burder, and besides others from our jolly little Captain—" 'Ere a sheer 'ulk,"[15] sung with all the pathos which the good fellow can throw into it—a sailor's hornpipe by three Jack Tars, whose steps were as varied and wonderful as an Opera Danseuse, was most successful—a recitation

14. The *British Queen* was a Great Western steamer, Edward Franklin her commander.

15. "Here, a sheer hulk, lies poor Tom Bowling," nautical song by Charles Dibdin.

by a Master Grahame was if possible more so—it was of "My name is Norval" school,[16] and the young gentleman in question was one of the best infant prodigies I ever saw. There was dancing,—Polkas, and "soft Quadrilles" "succeeded turn by turn,"—and great fun it was, and great detriment for those who respected their toes, as the vessel lurched and the dancers tumbled up against tables and chairs and one another. "Sir Roger"[17] is delightful, though as a magnificent individual from among the Fore Saloon aristocracy informed us "a very vulgar dance,"—but most assuredly from his awkwardness when he did attempt to dance it, it was hardly a contempt induced by familiarity which he felt towards so ignoble a joy.

Mrs. Squire, wife of the Unitarian Minister, Miss Ingall, and a Miss Ruch were the belles of the room. Miss Ingall is great fun—when all was over we made her come and drink hock and soda water with us, and a very merry half hour we had: afterwards Burder and myself went on deck—a glorious night it was—the stars above and the phosphorous below tried to outshine each other, and the only sounds were the ripple of the sea and the plaintive reassuring "all's well" from the man on the look-out. Just while we were sentimentalizing upon the Celestial Great Bear, up came the infernal Little Bore in the black trousers and red neck-cloth who thought "Sir Roger" low, and began to catechise Captain Martin about the screw,— "It's at the stern, I suppose—ah? Oh, indeed!—lor! and it's *really* (with a drawl which defies orthography) going round all the time?—by George!—ah!" Captain Martin had evidently hard work to restrain his laughter and Burder and myself fairly turned tail, and

16. A set piece of schoolboy oratory from John Home's *Douglas*.
17. I.e., "Sir Roger de Coverley," an English country-dance.

turned in after as pleasant an evening as I've had for a long time.

This morning is most beautiful—the bright sun, the lake-like ocean, and the light breeze are most exhilarating and delicious. The passengers are scattered about the deck, the sailors are singing as they hoist the sails.

We saw some porpoises this morning at a distance; they followed each other in an undulating line and we all agreed how easily by an unpractised eye they might be mistaken for a huge sea serpent "moving upon the face of the deep." A propos of sea-serpents, Captain Matthews told me that off the coast of Malabar—some 50 miles from land—he has seen snakes of 10 or 12 feet long lying on the water, and that *he* sees no difficulty in believing in similar creatures of larger size and more in mid-ocean.

The "Great Britain" seems a sort of marine Gretna Green: a lady and gentleman who have passed for brother and sister turn out to be wandering lovers like those in the popular and extremely silly "Off, off, said the Stranger," a song by the way, Mrs. Sedger with the sweetest of voices and strangest of tastes sang to us the other day.

But to the lovers—they want to get married before they get to New York, and I only wish the Captain had taken kindly to the idea—what fun a marriage on ship board would be! The bridesmaids were chosen, the cake preparing, the bonnet getting "done up" (or "fixed" I should say this side the Ocean), but the parson alias the Captain said "Nay"—so the marriage will be deferred for some three days yet.

I've been walking to-day with Col. Macaulay—he's a fine old gentleman and has given me a great deal of information about the natural history of America—fireflies, rattlesnakes (for which see Lake George) and bull-frogs. Mr. Squire is also a nice person, he grows upon one—he is so simple, good and earnest, and Burder likes him even better than I do. He was for some time Uni-minister or rather missionary at Idle in Yorkshire, and he tells me the common people hear gladly the doctrine of the Supreme Unity, but will not accept non-humanitarian views of the Saviour. He intends to leave us and become purely unsectarian.

A young gentleman about our age is agreeable, but has such a name—Mr. Coffin! Fancy Mr. Deadman, Dr. Rotton and Mr. Coffin all travelling together—what a funereal party!

After Breakfast, Thursday, [May] 13.

Yesterday was most delightful altogether. The morning was as fine a morning as ever rose on the Atlantic, and the evening was most amusing.

After dinner we had songs from the Captain, and the more syren-like part of the passengers, and great fun some of them were; Mr. White has the best voice —he's the man who has so long puzzled me, and whom I've always supposed to be Mr. Harrison. He must have thought my inquiries about Tom Ashton strange, and perhaps still stranger the terms of intimacy on which I addressed him.

The veritable Harrison I only discovered yesterday— very Manchesterian, but good-natured looking—hardly our "stamp" I think,—too fast, and "Je ne sais quoi."

Mr. Arkwright (Peter Crawley's friend) is the greatest puzzle to every one—a most sphinx-like man, who is unfathomable to us all. Captain Martin first called my attention to him. He believes him to be a Government spy, or something of that sort—he is always measuring and taking notes, asking questions and examining sails: he never lets out that he is in the Navy, and Captain Franklin has also been surprized at his naval knowledge and mysterious manner. I'll talk diplomatically to him in the course of the day and see if I can play the rôle of Oedipus to his Sphinx.

Mr. Manfred (J. Gregg's friend) is a nice "moyling" fellow, but I don't see much of him,—and Colonel Macaulay, Captain Franklin, Dr. Pettit (the Quaker), Mr. Squire, Miss Ingall, and Miss Innes are our great allies:—the last lady knew "Alexander Cruikshank" well, and also Ramsay—we had a long talk over my dear old friend the other night.

After this digression, during which we have been singing, and drinking healths, (suppose)—I go on with yesterday's history. Songs aforesaid were followed by a deck-walk and tea, and then we drew our tickets for the "Great Britain Sweepstakes." We had each a ticket for 5/-; every ticket being marked with some hour or half-hour of the day ranging from 12 tonight to 12 to-morrow night, and whoever draws the ticket with the hour on it at which we arrive gets the whole of the money, £8. Mine ticket was a bad one, 9 p.m., as it is supposed we shall be off the Neversink Lighthouse at noon to-morrow:—a fog has however come on, which may retard us, but this is sincerely to be prayed against malgré the Sweepstakes ticket.

Last night the Phosphorus was most splendid. I got Miss Ingall to wrap up and come with me on deck, and a pleasant enough flirtation we had looking over the ship's stern at the long wake of light behind, while every now and then we could track the passage of some large fish by the luminous water at the distance: —we had a bucket of water brought up to look at, and beautiful scintillations flashed out as we dipped our hands by turns into it. The ship was going faster

63

than it had ever gone—13 knots—and we had the comfort of knowing that in the last 24 hours we had run 300 miles.

I went up again on deck just before bed time. The sea was brighter than ever—at the bows shoals of fish were darting along in phosphorescent arrows of light, and the whole sea was alive with animal life. The wonderful ocean!—it "grows upon one," as you know it more,—so restless and huge,—never still—the slumbering bosom of the Atlantic is ever heaving, like any other life-breast—yet always stately and grand. I could have stayed all night looking at the shifting fire-waves, it was so strange and glorious.

This morning we've heard some Yankee stories, &c. from the Quaker—he amused us by the story of the man who couldn't see the city of New York for the houses! —and amused us still more by some of his own remarks. He talked politics, admires Cobden, and spoke of the time when Wilberforce was a "nice young man."[18]— Dickens' behaviour *in* America, not *out* of America, he was severe upon, and Mrs. Pettit observed as an instance of how "reprobate degraded" he was—"He was always getting drunk, and riding outside the coaches." Martin Tupper was more popular being gentlemanly, but "a vain little man."[19]

He told us much about the Indians, and recommends us to go always to the best and most aristocratic Red Men, or we shall lose caste in the back woods.

Burder was secretary of the Sweepstakes, and made rather a good one, being an awful dun!

18. Richard Cobden (1804–65), statesman; Samuel Wilberforce (1805–73), bishop of Oxford.
19. Martin Farquhar Tupper (1810–89), author of the prodigiously popular *Proverbial Philosophy*, visited America in 1851.

2

Astor House, New York. Friday night [May 14].

At last at our journey's end!—Our last day on board
was spent in toasting everybody—(I spoke on behalf
of "my owners" as the worthy Captain calls them) and
in getting up memorials to Matthews and Smith.

The entrance to New York, where we arrived at
about two was beautiful, and very—though most inde-
finably—foreign looking. The grass on the slopes of
Staten Island looked greener, the houses more ori-
entally built, and the ships in the harbour more gaily
painted than those we see in England—and yet it was
hardly these but a peculiar tout ensemble impossible
to describe, but still most striking, and doubtless owing in part to the purity of the atmosphere, and the
distinctness with which every thing stands out against
the sky.

This foreign aspect became more marked as we
came up to New York—the hundreds of absurd little
steamers, all with houses on deck, and huge paddle-

Gleason's Pictorial Drawing-Room Companion, October 11, 1851

*"The entrance to New York . . . was beautiful,
and very . . . foreign looking."*

boxes were quite unlike *anything* one had ever seen before.

There were a good many people waiting to meet us, but hardly as many as we had imagined would have been there. The truth was most people, among them Mr. Irvin,[1] fancied we should not get to New York before Saturday or Sunday. As we reached the Quay—a work of some difficulty which was only accomplished at last by dint of a shouting and bawling on the part of our little Captain, which made him as red in the face, and as hoarse in the voice as ever Captain was or could be—as we reached the Quay, Mr. Irvin, and not only Mr. Irvin, but all the < > people who

1. Richard Irvin, who served as HAB's financial agent, had emigrated from Scotland as a young man. Bright's brother-in-law described him some years later as "an oldish man of the British merchant class with fingers of right hand shrunk and stiff in a bent position" (Henry Yates Thompson, *An Englishman in the American Civil War*, p. 83).

could manage it pressed on board:—and between their kindly officious impudence and the stately grandeur of the Custom House Officers, it is a matter of no small wonder how we got on land at all.

Thanks to Captain Martin and Mr. Irvin we did, and found ourselves surrounded *by* and *in* the power of as nasty a set of slate-coloured vagabonds as it was ever my good fortune to meet.

We drove to the Irving House first—an enormous place, but with no room for us:—thence to the Astor, still bigger, where Mr. Irvin kindly introduced us, and where we did find room at the top of the house.[2] How different from an English Hotel—large, smoke-scented parlours "pro bono publico," waiters all dirty and inattentive to a degree almost ludicrous,—and the Manager at the bar (with whom Mr. Irvin really a gentleman shook hands) a brother of a general and a proportionally great man. On arriving at the Astor, not so far as the top of Bold Street from the Pier Head,[3] we found we had to pay $2.50 or rather more than 10/-, a respectable sum of money, which I own rather frightened and disgusted me; we were I believe "done" a little, but not much, people think. Railway cars must be avoided in this democratic land!

We dined at six, having asked Captains Franklin and Matthews, and Mr. Smith to dinner. We had an excellent dinner, and some good, but very dear wine, which really looked rather cheap on the card when the best Madeira was marked $12. or about £2: 10: 0 a bottle—credite posteri!![4]

Among the delicacies at dinner were a soup made of a peculiar oyster,—a white salmon, and pumpkin pie.

2. The solid granite Astor House, at Broadway and Vesey Street, was New York's leading hotel.

3. In Liverpool.

4. "Believe it, future generations!" (Horace, *Carmina* II.xix.2).

The waiting was shameful, and the waiters coolly looked over our shoulders and read the addresses of our letters of introduction we were showing to a Yankee Colonel, whom we asked to take a glass of wine with us. Equally characteristic and far ruder, were the shrieks of laughter the chambermaid and boots went into at seeing me pull out of my carpet bag a pair of hob-nailed Welsh walking shoes—they hadn't seen such things not since they'd left the old country! (They're all Irish.) This is the strangest country!—in some things so far before us—i.e.—the railways (for horses) in the streets, the electric telegraph rising all over the town, the iced water everywhere for every body, and the fountains in Broadway:—in others, as far behind us,—in their hotel comforts, attendance, the lighting of their streets, and the arrangements of their omnibusses—such things these last!—"a heavy sea's on," said Burder as we jolted away in one.

We have done two sights to-day—Barnum's Museum[5]—just opposite the Hotel, and gorgeous with paintings on the wall, and banners on the roof:—never under one roof was collected such trash—Tom Thumb's Carriage, and Queen Adelaide's Carriage,—(a model of) "The Koh-i-noor" (in glass)—n.b. of *course* the words in brackets never figure in the Bill of Fare outside—Chinese curiosities, awfully bad pictures, and stuffed birds:—the only really curious thing we saw was the "Leviathan Turtle" stuffed—an enormous and wonderful creature if—how hatefully sceptical this free-thinking land makes one!—if it ever existed.

Our other sight was a pretty little theatre—Niblo's Gardens—where we all went after dinner.[6] It was bet-

5. Barnum's Museum at Broadway and Ann Street, the most conspicuous building in New York, was opened by Phineas T. Barnum in 1841.

6. William Niblo built his theater in a summer resort at Broadway and Prince Street.

Gleason's Pictorial Drawing-Room Companion, May 15, 1852

ter lighted, better arranged, and adorned with more pretty faces and pretty bonnets than any theatre I ever saw:—Anna Thillon acted in "Robert le Diable."[7]

A jeweller's shop here is splendid—we saw there the famous Californian gold service sent to Exhibition.[8]

Saturday night, [May 15].

This morning we got up late, and went after a breakfast of "clams" and Indian corn bread to leave some of our letters, first however calling at the Great Britain (where we found every one much excited and interested in the account of our voyage in the New York Herald),[9] and at the Irving House, where we found

7. Anna Thillon (1819-1903), an English singer married to a Frenchman, made her New York debut in 1851. Meyerbeer's *Robert le Diable* was one of the greatest opera successes of all time.

8. The Great Exhibition held in London's Crystal Palace in 1851.

9. The *New York Herald* (May 15, 1852), in a detailed front-page account, congratulated the *Great Britain* for setting the transatlantic record for a screw steamer: 13 days and 4 hours.

NIBLO'S GARDEN, BROADWAY, NEW YORK

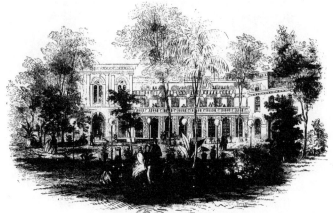

Gleason's Pictorial Drawing-Room Companion, March 6, 1852

"A pretty little theatre."

every one very slow and low at not being able to get
out owing to the rain. The Grinnells and Minturn[10]
were not at home, Duncan was, and so also were
Davis and Brooks who we find are partners[11]—Kennedy, Bunch,[12] and Jay were also out—so that our acquaintance is still but small.

I was at first awfully nervous but at last got quite
"plucky" and cared very little about my letter carrying.

We were most impressed I think by Duncan, a nice
gentlemanly young fellow, who knew Edward Gressly
and indeed seemed "au fait" at most of the English
visiting New York.

10. Moses H. Grinnell (1803–77) and Robert B. Minturn (1805–66)
owned a line of transatlantic packets and did a large shipping business.

11. Charles Augustus Davis (1795–1867), one of New York's merchant princes, author of some of the "Jack Downing" letters, friend of
the Knickerbocker authors, and a leader of society. His partner in a commission business was Sidney Brooks (d. 1878).

12. Robert Bunch, British vice-consul in New York.

Davis and Brooks also were most kind, and we've promised the former to go and see him after morning service to-morrow at his house.

This evening we went to Mr. Irvin's—a five o'clock dinner—Captain Matthews went with us. The style of house is like a foreign,—e.g. Mr. Koch's house at Frankfort[13]—handsome outside, with several good rooms opening out of one another, but all rather unfurnished looking, owing doubtless to the necessity for keeping everything as cool as may be during the intensely hot weather which is to come.

Mr. Irvin I like much—a kind honest sort of fellow, with a good-natured wife, and very ugly children (eight of them). The dinner was good—the chief peculiarities being "shad," a delicious fish and so good! —and an ice cream in the shape of a rampant white horse of vanille, prancing about on a rugged red rock of cherry water—this by the way, with one jelly, were the only "sweets"—most different from an English dinner! But the best thing there was the Madeira—such Madeira!—out and out the best I ever tasted, and, except maybe at New York, I shall never taste as good again.

We left early and called at a friend of Captain Matthews, a Mr. Paton who lives in a good house and is a great snob—thence to the "Irving" to call on the Squires and Miss Ingall,—and home.

New York reminds me more of Leamington than any English town when seen from Broadway—the trees, smart shops and "watering place" air all are similar —by the way, I'm disappointed with Broadway aforesaid; it's narrow though long, and is certainly not to be compared with Regent Street, London. New York must I fear be very disreputable:—the first words Mr.

13. Christian Koch, British consul in Frankfort, a great friend of Bright's family.

Irvin said to me on landing were "Look after your pocket—"; the first words I see at the "Astor" is a notice, "Keep your doors bolted to prevent *losses* by night,"—a most euphemistic way of expressing doubt of the honesty of the visitors at the "Astor."

A most "splendid dismal"— to use Thackeray's epithets for the Marriage of Addison and Lady Warwick[14] —a most "splendid dismal" House this Astor—so large that it's hard to find one's way in, so full you can't get a room except up four flights of stairs—so magnificent you may eat all day long if you like, and *must* pay $2.50 a day whether you eat or not,—the largest and most uncomfortable, the most popular as to visitors, the least populous as to waiters of any Hotel I ever saw, or ever hope to see. I must say, the "Irving" *seems* more comfortable, and possibly is—at least if it is not, it must be worth visiting simply to see what Yankees will stand. Mr. Jackson was right though, and the "New York" is the place to go to, and every one here tells us the same.[15]

At Mr. Irvin's we met Mr. Mitchell, rather a nice person, who gave us some valuable "wrinkles" about our future tour, and gave us much information concerning land, &c. at New York; land worth £900 some thirty years ago is now valued at £110,000—an instance of this "go-ahead" impulse.

Sunday evening, [May 16].

We've spent a fatiguing but amusing day—breakfasting in state in the "ordinary," dining in still greater

14. In the lecture "Congreve and Addison" in *The English Humourists* (delivered 1851, published 1853).

15. The New York Hotel, one of the city's largest and most fashionable establishments, was "uptown" on Broadway.

72

state with Captain Matthews and our officers, and taking supper at the Irving with our fair lady passengers Miss Ingall and Mrs. Squire.

After breakfast (we eat fried hominy for the first time and very good we found it) we went to call for the ladies aforesaid, and with Mr. Squire and them— Burder terribly afraid of being a confirmed heretic— walked along Broadway to Mr. Bellows' Church—the Church of the Divine Unity.[16] Mr. Bellows was ill, and we had a Mr. Huntington of Boston instead.[17] Saving always a black choker and a nasal twang, he seemed a nice specimen of a Uni-Minister, and gave us a really excellent sermon full of sense and eloquence on the tendency there seems to be to prefer the abstract Humanity to the concrete man,—to look after Society, and neglect the individual. There was much good in it, and even our two orthodox friends were pleased—I liked too the way he blessed us at the end, raising his hands over us, as the congregation stood.

But it was the Church itself we were most struck with. I hardly ever saw—never indeed out of Belgium— such a splendid wooden pulpit, and noble organ screen through the woodwork of which shone the rich red of a painted window. The pews were also carved wood, and the perfect taste of everything (not forgetting the slight clustered pillars supporting the roof) made the greatest impression, as we were so entirely unprepared for any architectural beauty in the States.

16. On Broadway, between Spring and Prince streets, this elaborate Gothic edifice was built by the First Unitarian Church in 1845. Henry Whitney Bellows (1814–82), a conspicuous figure in New York's social and religious life, had been pastor since 1837. Thackeray, lecturing there a few months after Bright, was also struck with the long, dark wainscoted benches, the pillared nave, and the oak pulpit.

17. Frederic Dan Huntington (1819–1904), minister of the South Congregational Church in Boston, turned Trinitarian in 1859 and became an Episcopal bishop.

From Church, B[urder] and I went to call at Mr. C. A. Davis, 1, University Place (our letter to him was from Horsly Palmer and Davis had yesterday told us to call). His house was still in winter gear—carpets down, &c. in which the contrast was strong to Mr. Irvin's house where everything was in its coolest summer dress.

Mr. Davis is quiet and stiffly kind, Mrs. Davis is chatty, merry and very like Mrs. Litchfield, the fruiterer's wife at Cambridge. Miss Davis was pretty, and French-looking, more disposed to talk than to listen. They were extremely civil, and we dine there tomorrow.

Thence to our Hotel, having dropped a card at Mrs. Gibbs en route. She seems to be the leader of fashion here, and we've been lucky to get an introduction.[18]

We dined with Matthews and the officers at three—Franklin, Perry and others were there, and a most excellent dinner we had. We two had to do most of the talking—the "middies" were shy, and it seemed hopeless work to try and "draw them out." They left however as soon as dinner was over, and Smith, Matthews, Franklin and ourselves stayed on talking for some time "de omnibus rebus" e.g. New York and Merchants' Navigation Laws, and the "Great Britain," "et quisbusdam aliis," e.g. Laura Bell[19] and the like. Burder smoked after dinner—a feat as yet unparalleled since our arrival, and worthy of all note.

The evening was spent at the Irving House (where we escorted Miss Innes) and great fun it was—how we laughed and talked, quizzed and flirted! Mrs. Squire—daughter of Rev. W. Hincks of Cork[20]—is one of the

18. Susan Annette Vanden Heuvel, daughter of a wealthy New York landowner, was married to Thomas Gibbes, of a prominent but impoverished South Carolina family.

19. Heroine of Thackeray's *Pendennis* (1848-50).

20. Possibly William Hincks (1794-1871), Unitarian minister, professor of natural history at Queen's College, Cork, 1849-53.

sweetest, prettiest, fairyest little things I ever saw, and with a good deal of fun beneath her calm and kind manner. The chief difference between the two hotels is the fact of the waiters at the Astor being an untidy dirty set of Irishmen, and those at the Irving being a neat, dapper set of niggers;—more attentive, and then they don't show dirt so soon!

By the way, how the niggers do come out on Sunday!—the *she* ones particularly; dressed in the height of nigger fashion with rainbow colours they are at least a striking addition to the strange aspect of the town!—a green bonnet with pink inside, and blue strings was a lovely head-dress for one of the sweet creatures we met.

The non-nigger part of the female population really do dress well—very French though, with tiny little bonnets perched on the back of their heads with (as Mr. Squire says) a "won't-you-kiss-me?" air about them. Now Broadway was crowded today with fair faces—not unlike a Sunday evening on King's Parade Cambridge:—Burder must be taken care of—he's susceptible to ladies, but it's the bonnets that "are the mischief" as an Irishman would say. He raves about them, and got quite solemnly in earnest on their behalf versus coal scuttles with Mrs. Squire this evening.

Tuesday, May 18.

We've just returned from a Concert given by Jenny Lind. The great Metropolitan Hall—the finest place of the sort I ever saw after our own Opera House—was crowded with people, all enthusiastic and all delighted. How could they help it? Jenny sang better and more sweetly than ever—her bird notes were more deliciously varied,—and she looked so well and happy that

75

Gleason's Pictorial Drawing-Room Companion, May 15, 1852

no one could regret her marriage for love instead of for rank or wealth. Otto Goldschmidt played her accompaniments, and was much cheered as *her* husband, probably from his looks at least his chief distinction.[21]

I never saw a lovelier collection of faces than tonight, and generally all the ladies at least were well and becomingly drest, though in bonnets, contrary to our English custom on such occasions.

The only specimen of a Yankee girl I've seen *near* yet is Miss Davis—we dined there yesterday, and had an agreeable party. She (Miss Davis) is French in manner, and Yankee in voice, but undeniably pretty, well-educated, "sharp as a needle." There was much sharp shooting during dinner, much laughing at Yan-

21. Jenny Lind (1820–87), who sang in England in 1847–48, had married Otto Goldschmidt only a few months earlier. This was her farewell appearance in America.

kee manners, and much abuse of English conceit. Mr. Davis says Lord Morpeth was popular in the States and is almost a solitary instance of an English lord who behaved himself properly "as sich."[22] Dickens was altogether "low," and Tupper got drunk, some Englishmen are overbearing, others disreputable. Davis is a nice fellow, and certainly was very kind to us, Mrs. and Miss D[avis], and a brunette cousin were also most amusing, they are all dying to see a lord, and I've promised to do my best for them if they come to England.

After dinner, Davis read us some of his own poetry on the "America Yacht,"[23] and when we at last got rid of his importunate Muse, and joined the ladies, we found Mildmay[24] had made his appearance to tea, and it was some time before we could get off, which we did just in time to hear the "Fair one with Golden Locks"[25] at the Lyceum—a most imbecile and "inadequate" piece (to use a word of Burder's) only redeemed from damnation by one clever actor, who did the part of a Crow, and danced in the style peculiar to Jim Crow, that species of feathered biped.

Such have been our evenings' amusements of these two days;—the mornings have been spent in sight-seeing and letter-carrying:—we've done our duty in this respect most properly, and have received much civility in return. To-morrow we go to a ball and dinner at Mrs. Fearing[26] and Mrs. Gibbs' (what an uninten-

22. George William Frederick Howard, viscount Morpeth and 7th earl of Carlisle (1802-64), visited the U.S. in 1841-42.

23. The yacht *America* had astonished the British in August 1851 by winning the Queen's Cup in a course around the Isle of Wight.

24. Either Henry Bingham Mildmay (1828-1905) or his brother Humphrey Francis Mildmay (1825-66), of Shoreham Place, Kent.

25. An extravaganza by J. R. Planché (1796-1880).

26. Probably the wife of Daniel Butler Fearing, one of New York's elite.

tional hysteron proteron—or Anglicé "cart-before-the horse" sentence I've made of this!) Next day we dine at Mr. Kennedy's at six—a noticeable hour as we have heretofore been asked at five.

Mr. Irvin took us yesterday to see the Custom House, Exchange and the like, all doubtless described in Appleton's Guide in greater detail, and altogether better than anything I could attempt.[27] One word to say that I was a *leetle* disappointed is all I've room for, though the white marble pillars in the Exchange are certainly worthy of all commendation. The Post Office however is a truly characteristic and interesting place —it was an old Dutch Church when New York was New Amsterdam, and the Knickerbockers and the Vandermeulyns had not been supplanted by the Gibbs and the Browns.[28] A curious metamorphose has taken place in the old building, and the sorting of letters (most of them by the way in a dirty yellow envelope) has taken the place of the singing of psalms. Among the more foreign peculiarities are the Irish women with great strings of Bananas for sale in this part of the town—beware of bananas!—they are the very nastiest fruit I ever tasted—something like a pulp of nicely compounded rhubarb and sugar. The "oyster plant" which we tasted to-day at our "Ordinary" (for the first time honoured by our presence) is also a matter of caution—like an elongated oyster in look, like a detestably bad one in taste, it's perhaps the least inviting vegetable extant.

But "revenons à nos moutons"—to have food and get back to sights—we saw yesterday Trinity and Grace

27. The Custom House (1841), a massive imitation of the Parthenon, was at Wall and Nassau streets. The Merchants' Exchange, an even larger Grecian pile on Wall Street, boasted gigantic Ionic columns, each of which weighed 45 tons and cost $3,000.

28. The Middle Dutch Church at Cedar and Nassau streets (dedicated 1729) was used as the U.S. Post Office, 1845-75.

The Merchants' Exchange, Wall Street

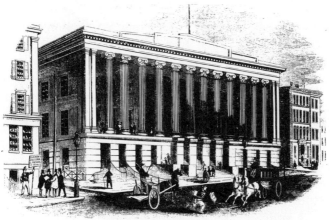

Gleason's Pictorial Drawing-Room Companion, December 11, 1852

*"The white marble pillars in the Exchange
are certainly worthy of all commendation."*

Church, the two most beautiful Episcopal Churches in
the town, or perhaps in America.[29] They are of a most
splendid Gothic, and full of painted glass—inferior I'm
free to confess to ours in England, being too Arabesque
and meaningless in design, too fresh and gaudy in
colouring, yet the effect is very beautiful and peculiar,
as every window in both Churches is painted, which
I never saw in any Church of the same size in England.
In beauty of wood-carving our Unitarian Church here
excels both the Episcopal.

Today Smith, Franklin, Matthews and ourselves
went over to see the Navy Yard at Long Island. Some
of the first engineers in America were with us, and
we were received with the utmost "impressement,"
especially Smith who was introduced by one Yankee to

29. Trinity Church at the head of Wall Street (designed by Richard
Upjohn) and Grace Church at Broadway and Tenth Street (designed by
James Renwick) were both completed in 1846.

79

another as "Mr. Smith of England—the Great Screw man."

One of our friendly guides amused us much by his calm Yankeeisms. He told us several strange stories which are I suppose true of the way American houses are lifted and moved from place to place, "so that," he added with the utmost gravity, "a man sometimes wakes in the morning and finds himself in another part of the town." He then told us of a diver who had got up some heavy pieces of machinery from the sea at a depth of 90 feet, "they were all recovered but one, and that had apparently gone down head foremost and we believe they got it out at the other side." After this sort of calm lying one sees but little absurdity in the stories so constantly told of Yankee romancing, e.g. how the weak and dying horse required another horse to draw his last breath for him. While speaking of Yankee stories, I heard two new riddles yesterday— When does a steamboat Captain assert himself not a Captain? When he says "Ease her, back her, stop her," (he's a bacca-stopper).[30]

"Spell a blind pig in two letters?" "Can't do it." "Well then, P.G." "But P.G. doesn't spell pig?" "Don't it? P.G. does spell pig without an eye (i)—therefore P.G. spells blind pig."

Why is a free black like the "sweet south on a bed of violets?" It's stealing and giving odour.

The dockyard was in beautiful order, and the "North Carolina" which we were taken over is a splendid frigate. The old Port Captain (Peck) who had served *once* under Collingwood[31] received us most hospitably, showed us everything, and made us take a glass of wine

30. A "bacca-stopper" is a device for tamping down tobacco in a pipe.
31. Cuthbert Collingwood, Lord Collingwood (1750–1810), vice-admiral.

with him. The decks of the "North Carolina" (80 guns) are most spacious and lofty.

We will try to see more of Long Island, the towns of which have increased enormously of late. In 1820 the population of Brooklyn was 30,000, it is now more than 100,000. Williamsburg has also increased wonderfully—in ten years from 5 to 35,000 inhabitants.

We found our way to the "Battery" this afternoon. It reminds me somewhat of "Mainlust" at Frankfort.[32]

Wednesday, [May 19].

This morning after breakfast Mr. J. Jay called.[33] He is a barrister, an agreeable man and a strong abolitionist. He asked me to dine with him to-morrow to meet Jenny Lind. Alas! we are already engaged to Mr. Kennedy, and we have been regretting it ever since. Mr. Jay pleased us much by his unaffectedly kind manner, his anxiety to serve us, and his enthusiasm about slave-abolition. We are to drive out with him tomorrow to the country place where he is staying. He told us a curious story about a slave he had assisted to escape. The slave *had* escaped once, but being on a steamer bound for Maryland feared to be retaken, and made the best of his way in a little boat (taken from the ship) to land. He was indicted for larceny, and put in prison, but fortunately Mr. Jay procured a pardon for him the very day before his punishment of imprisonment was over; he was let secretly out of the prison, while his *master was in asking for him,* and is now in

32. The Battery was then New York's most delightful promenade, with shaded gravel walks and a glorious view.

33. John Jay (1817-94), leader of the New York bar, was deeply involved in antislavery activities; later he was minister to Austria.

Canada. The Herald is very indignant with Mr. Jay, and I insert the paragraph in which the case is noticed in a letter to that paper—which is, however, I hear considered an inferior journal—the Courier is the best, at least for family reading.

HERALD. May 28.

SINGULAR FUGITIVE SLAVE CASE— MANOEUVRES OF THE ABOLITIONISTS.

To James Gordon Bennett, Esq.,
Editor of the New York Herald:—

Will you give to the public the following statement?

On or about the first Sunday after Easter, A.D. 1849, a negro slave, named Nicholas Dudley, the propperty of Dr. Allen Thomas, of Ellicott's Mills, Anne Arundel county, Maryland, escaped from his owner, and came to the city of New York.

In April, 1850, this slave Dudley was arrested in the city of New York, charged with the robbery of a Captain Rowland. He assumed the name of James Snowden. He communicated with his master, informing him of his situation. A son of Dr. Thomas thereupon came to this city, and found Dudley in the Tombs.

Mr. John Jay, a lawyer of this city, somewhat known as an abolitionist, became the counsel of the negro, and advised him not to return to his master, but to plead guilty to the offence of which he was charged, and temporarily remain in the State prison. The negro took his advice, plead guilty, and was sentenced, on the 13th day of May, 1850, to the State prison at Sing Sing, for the term of two years, by the name of James Snowden. About the first of April last, Dr. Thomas, the owner of this negro, wrote a letter to his Excellency, Washington Hunt, Governor of this State, stating the above facts, asking whether the negro had been pardoned, and expressing his intention to reclaim him at the expiration of his sentence, viz: May 13th instant.

To this letter, Dr. Thomas received the following reply in the hand of Gov. Hunt, in person:—

STATE OF NEW YORK, EXECUTIVE DEPARTMENT, ALBANY, April 20, 1852.
Sir:—On examining my records, I find that no pardon has been granted to James Snowden, nor is there any application before me in behalf of such a person.

Very respectfully, Yours,
WASHINGTON HUNT.

Dr. Allen Thomas, Ellicott's Mills, Md.

Upon receiving this letter, Dr. Thomas made all necessary preparations to reclaim his slave at the expiration of his sentence. The second proof under the tenth section of the Fugitive Slave Act, was perfected, and Allen Thomas, Jr., with a witness as to identity, came to this city on the 8th of May, inst. He found the United States Marshal and his deputies courteous and desirous to fulfil their duty in the premises. Charles S. Spencer, Esq. was employed as attorney. The necessary papers were prepared; the proper warrant promptly issued by George W. Morton, Esq., U.S. Commissioner, and on the eleventh of May instant, two days before the expiration of the sentence, Deputies Marshals Talmadge and L. D'Angelis, with the warrant, accompanied Mr. Thomas to Sing Sing. They arrived there about 2 o'clock P.M., and immediately proceeded to the prison. On going through the same, and examining the works, the boy was found to be missing, and information was given to Gen. Lockwood, the agent, of the object of the visit. The keeper, Mr. Robinson, was represented to be unwell, and lying down. Gen. Lockwood expressed himself willing to render all assistance in his power, and said that the negro was still, as far as he had knowledge, in the prison. Robinson soon made his appearance, took Gen. Lockwood aside, and made to him some communication. Soon after Gen. L. stated to Deputy Marshals Talmadge, and L. D'Angelis, and Mr. Thomas, Jr. that he had been informed that the negro had been pardoned and released that morning, and at the same time produced the pardon of Governor Hunt. Upon examination, the pardon was found to have been given on the 11th, the same day of the discharge by his Excellency, Washington Hunt; without any publication or notice in either the State paper, or any paper in this city, and without notice to the District Attorney of the city and county of New York, where the conviction was had—with of necessity, a full knowledge of all the facts, and with, beyond doubt, the express purpose of defeating the reclamation of the slave. The marshals and Mr. Thomas returned to the city on Friday the 14th of May. In the proceedings of the American and Foreign Anti-Slavery Society, convened in the Tabernacle, in the city of New York, the following—as appears by the report in The New York Herald—was said by—

REV. MR. RAY (a colored brother)—Do not go away; I have something very interesting to tell you. Two years ago, a poor panting colored man came to this city, from Maryland. He became a cook in a vessel between this port and Providence. He was discovered, and a man went to him and said he should go to Maryland with him. He refused to do so, and then a charge of stealing was got up against him. He was put in prison, and his master came to his cell and demanded the boy as his property. John McKeon would not consent. He said the boy must be tried on the charge of stealing. His lawyer and friends advised him to plead guilty. He did so, and was sent to prison. Steps were taken to get him out; but the idea was abandoned, as it was feared it would be known by his master. However, as the time drew nigh that his period of imprisonment had expired, the brethren felt very uneasy, and Dr. Pennington went to Albany and succeeded in getting Governor Hunt to release him. His time is not out until to-morrow; but he is flying today beyond the reach of his enemies. (Applause)

A BROTHER here stated that the owner wrote to a

84

keeper of one of the prisons, asking him where the slave was, that he might take him when his period of imprisonment expired; but his letter was never answered.

MR. RAY.—Oh! yes. I forgot to mention that.

The *modus operandi* of the defeat of the reclamation is, by the above extract, quite satisfactorily explained. These facts without comment, are submitted to the public. By the act of the Governor of New York, committed with a full knowledge of the position of matters and its results, the owner of the slave Dudley, alias Snowden, has been deprived of his property, and a convicted felon once more loosened, to prey upon the property of the citizens of the North. Whatever remedies in the premises the claimant has, civil or otherwise, against any of the parties to this wrong, will be promptly and fearlessly enforced.

ALLEN THOMAS, Jr.

New York, May 17, 1852.

A propos of papers the advertisements in the American Papers are so delicious I shall have ample space here to insert some of them.

E. Lyon, No. 424 Broadway.

OH! IS IT POSSIBLE!—CAN IT BE TRUE
That sensible people will harbor so long
Rats, roaches, and all the nasty crew,
When the Exterminator is sold for a song!
We refer you to the following list;
They declare the nuisance shall not exist:—
Mr. Hodges, Carlton House.
L. Delmonico, Delmonico's Hotel.
Clarke & Baily, Howard House.
Capt. Flowers, Pacific Hotel.
Mercer House.
Empire City House.
Johnson's (late Shelly's) Restaurant.

J. Taylor, Confectioner, Broadway.
Upson's Restaurant, Broadway and Leonard Street.
John Genin, the Hatter.
L. B. Buisse, No. 43 John Street.
P. V. King, No. 41 South Street.
Benjamin Wood, No. 10 Macdougal Street.
Wm. H. Underhill, No. 430 Broome Street.
Washington Market Clerks, Watchmen, Butchers,
Fishermen and all the others.
Centre Market the same.
Thousands of others could be named—
So you see the Exterminator is famed.
Believe not certificates from the press.
 Which others publish, but please inquire
Of the persons above if what we profess
 Is true. Gold is refined by the fire.

COSTAR'S Vermin and Insect Exterminator—Depot, No. 444, Broadway, New York—wholesale and retail. To be had of all the principal druggists in the United States, Canada, &c.

A LADY IN LIMBO—IN A CASE BEFORE A JURY the other day, in the Municipal Court of a neighbouring town, the witnesses were unable to recognise the prisoner, on account of the color of her hair and eyebrows, which had been converted from a sandy-colored red to a most beautiful glossy black, by the use of BOGLE'S incomparable Electric Hair Dye, which may be had, with other articles, at the store of A. B. & D. Sands, 100 Fulton street; Rushton, Clark & Co., 273, and Rice & Smith, 727 Broadway; Wm. H. Cary & Co., 245 Pearl street, and by the druggists and and perfumers throughout the world.

EXCURSIONS—INTERESTING TOUR THROUGH EUROPE—A foreign gentleman of a learned profession and of courteous manners, who has travelled for more than five years all over Europe, and is a perfect connoisseur of the paintings and statues, etc., of all the European galleries of art, wishes to engage as amanuensis or companion with a gentleman or lady who proposes to go to Europe. City references exchanged. Apply by letter, prepaid, under the address of "Europe," to the Herald office.

EMPLOYMENT FOR EVERYBODY GUARANTEED.—Messrs. Bradley & Jones continue to send to all parts of the United States, their fifteen easy and ready methods of realizing from $6 to $25 per week. Numerous thankful letters prove that they have been a blessing to many. Depend, it is no falsity, it is a certainty, and without risk. Direct, prepaid, inclosing $1, box 282 Post Office, Baltimore, Md., and they will be sent by return mail. All, of either sex, in town or country, having a few idle hours, may be benefitted by these valuable instructions. Patent right secured.

"A LIGHT HEART AND A THIN PAIR OF BREECHES go merrily through the world."—Thin Breeches as well as thick Breeches, thin Coats and thick Coats, Vests, grave and gay; Pantaloons, white and black, brown, green, &c., can be had, at all prices, at SMITH & RICE'S, 102 Fulton Street. Call and buy.

BEWARE!
Have a care;
Don't buy poisonous trash,
When a quarter, hard cash,
At Lyons' laid out,
All the bed bugs will route,
And make roach, ant, and flea,
Commit felo de se.
LYONS' Powder and Pill,
All insects and vermin will certainly kill.
124, Broadway.

A WIFE WANTED.—A young lady of not more than 35 years of age, intelligent, amiable, affectionate, and respectable looking, American, English, French, German or Italian. The subscriber is a man of 27 years, intelligent, enterprising, ambitious, good looking, amiable, genteel, affectionate, temperate, virtuous and proud. Was never married. He has been in the jewelry business eight years. Lost most of his money by a fire. He is very desirous to become a husband and father; and would marry a Lady if there was mutual attachment, and be everything a kind husband could be—provided the lady could loan him $5,000 or $10,000 to start in business again. He has the best of references: is from a good family, and an American. Notes addressed to T. S. FRANKLIN, New-York Post-Office, stating where an interview can be had, will be strictly confidential.

TRIBUNE. May 19.

DR. C. BARNES, a medium of Spiritual Communications, has taken lodgings at Earle's Hotel, Park-row, where he may be seen during the day and evening. Dr. B. will also make arrangements to visit circles in private families, for the purpose of giving physical and mental demonstrations of spiritual agency. He is supplied with abundant testimonials of the satisfactory nature of these exhibitions.

WANTED TO ADOPT—A LITTLE ORPHAN Girl, from 1 to 4 years of age; must be of English or American parentage. Any one knowing of such a child, and can give satisfactory information concerning the worthiness of its parents, may find a good home and kind friends for it, by addressing, any day this week, R. C., Tribune Office.

TRIBUNE. May 19.

BALTIMORE SUN. June 4th.

MATRIMONIAL.—A GENTLEMAN, WORTH $20,000, wants a wife worth $10,000. Communications received until the 1st of July next, at which time answers will be returned. References exchanged. Address Wm. Adderley, Post Office.

BALTIMORE SUN. June 4th.

TEN DOLLARS REWARD.—Ran away on or about the 21st of May, CHARLES HAMILTON BRENT, colored, quite dark, aged about 13 years, had on when he left, light cap, dark pants and large sleeve apron, with patent leather belt. The above reward will be given when delivered to or information left of his whereabouts at NICHOLAS BRENT'S, Raborg street, between Pine and Pearl streets. I caution all persons not to employ or harbor him.

BALTIMORE SUN. June 4th.

NOTICE.—I forewarn all persons not to trust my Wife, SUSAN HOWE, on my account, as I will pay no debts of her contracting after this date.

HENRY HOWE.

June 3d, 1852.

SLAVES WANTED.—We are at all times purchasing SLAVES, paying the highest CASH prices. Persons wishing to sell will please call at 242 PRATT ST. (Slatter's old stand). Communications attended.

BALTIMORE SUN. June 10th.

A WIFE WANTED.—A PROFESSIONAL GENTLEMAN, 33 years of age, wants to form an alliance with a young and beautiful WIDOW, or YOUNG LADY of respectability and high standing in society. Parents, guardians or others having the confidence of qualified ladies, should address "L. L. LEANDER," Philadelphia, Penn'a., as delicacy and secrecy make it desirable that the first step should be taken by others than the lady herself. A shorter or longer correspondence by letter is expected to precede a personal acquaintance. Exertions in his behalf by third persons shall be liberally rewarded.

NEW YORK TRIBUNE. June 9th.

MATRIMONIAL.—A GENTLEMAN, an American, 30 years of age, having an income of over $3,000 a year from his real estate, whose time is much occupied in its management, desires a Wife, a Lady by birth and education, not over 25 years old, and attractive in person, with not less than $10,000 in her own right, which will be secured to her. To prevent imposition, a reference of the first character will be given and required prior to an introduction. Address A. G. S. CRANE, N. Y. Post-Office.

N. Y. TRIBUNE. June 9th.

MEN WANTED.—Twenty men, to sell an article wanted in every family. Agents are making $20 per week. Agents for Boston, Philadelphia, New-England, the Western and Southern States, are wanted. They can make $1,000 per annum with a small capital. Call or address, postpaid, No. 317 Bowery.

N. Y. TRIBUNE. June 9th.

PROTESTANT SERVANTS WANTED—Cooks for $8 to $12, Laundresses, Waitresses, Nurses, and Ladies' Maids, for situations in first-class families— now ready at No. 148 Grand-st.

N. Y. TRIBUNE. June 9th.

THREE FEEDERS WANTED.—Apply at the Press Room of this office. None but sober hands need apply.

NEW YORK HERALD or *TRIBUNE. June.*

Birthdays of Great Men—SHAKSPEARE was born in April, Burns in January, Milton in December, Napoleon in August, Washington in February—so their greatness is not confined to any season; Tailor M'Kimm himself was born in July, which probably accounts for his many warm friends, who purchase clothing at 17 Carmine Street.

NEW YORK HERALD or *TRIBUNE. June.*

A MERCHANT TAILOR, in whom there is no guile, can be found at 116 William street, named Clarke, who will make to order a most beautiful dress or frock Coat for $16; the very finest $20; a "recherche" single breasted frock Coat, from $10 to $12; other garments in proportion. Summer goods made up and in the piece.

NEW YORK HERALD or *TRIBUNE. June.*

NEWPORT, ho!—Rum or no Rum, Holmes will re-open his Daguerreotype Rooms in Newport 1st July —all in first rate order—to take pictures of the citizens and strangers, whether they are drunk or sober, in a style unsurpassed, and seldom equalled. Rooms in New York, No. 289 Broadway.

NEW YORK HERALD or *TRIBUNE. June.*
THE MOTHER'S HOPE.

The mother gazed on her beautiful boy,
Blooming in health and end full of joy,
And she thought that disease might wither his bloom,
And her dear one haste to the mouldering tomb.
So to Root's she sped with eager pace,
And procured her darling's "sun-drawn face;"
And now she knows, that chance what will,
Her eye can gaze on her darling still!

ROOT'S Gallery. No. 363 Broadway.

We spent to-day in going over the "Art Union" picture gallery—a truly wretched exhibition—hardly a fine painting there:—a landscape of Kensett was the best and "bad's the best" here—truly Brother Jonathan is behind us in one particular.[34]

The Dusseldorf Gallery *was* pleasing, having nice pictures by good German artists.[35] An hour in the Franklin Museum, where a man balanced a heavy cart wheel on his nose, and several ladies gave us several very bad "Poses Plastiques."[36] This, and a look at the Church Dr. Dewey had—the Church of the Messiah—very ugly and painted in villainous taste as a Gothic Stage Scene is painted—filled up our morning.[37]

We dined at Mr. Gibbs, 5th Avenue. Mrs. Gibbs is a nice chatty woman, and not so formidable as we imagined the leader of the New York fashion would be. Mr. Gibbs is a pompously good-natured man, very proud of his family who spell their names "Gibbes" with an "e" (which I see I haven't always done), and very anxious to let us know that the millionaire Mr. Astor who owns the Astor House is "my son-in-law."[38] "My son-in-law" was asked to meet us—a red-haired,

34. The American Art-Union bought paintings from contemporary American artists and distributed them by lot to its members. The landscape by John Frederick Kensett (1816–72), who had settled in New York after many years of studying abroad, was an English-looking scene entitled *A Holiday in the Woods.* Bright meets Kensett later at Niagara Falls.

35. The Dusseldorf Gallery was in a large hall over the entrance to the Church of the Divine Unity.

36. This rather dubious establishment in Chatham Street, under George Lea's management, featured models portraying such scenes as the Rape of the Sabines, Adam and Eve, and the Greek Slave.

37. Orville Dewey (1794–1882), Unitarian minister, was pastor of this church on Broadway, near Washington Square (built 1839). It was of rough granite, with a square front.

38. The marriage of John Jacob Astor (1822–90) to Charlotte Augusta Gibbes was one of the glittering social events of 1846.

big moustached man, rather like Major Warr, but plainer, and altogether hardly attractive. His wife, whom I took in to dinner, is a sweet, ladylike unaffected woman who hardly speaks through her nose at all. Mirabile dictu! The dinner was good, and there was some of the finest gold plate on the table I ever saw.

After dinner we walked across the street to Mr. Fearing's where there was an evening party. I asked Mrs. Gibbes why she did not get a bath chair for that sort of thing—she said she *daren't*—she would be hissed and hooted all down the street if she attempted such a thing. Oh! free and enlightened country!

At Mrs. Fearing's were some forty people, among them Mr. and Mrs. Bancroft who treated us very kindly and hoped to see us on our return.[39] Bancroft I find is not popular—his talent is acknowledged, but he is thought a "slimy" politician, and not quite straightforward:—he is not supposed either to be very aristocratic or gentlemanly;—to us he was most civil and talked for some time with each of us,—of Jenny Lind he said "She came to America, Mr. Bright, a lonely Una—she is canonized, and is now a Saint Cecilia."

The Jones, Sidney Brooks, and other N.Y. fashionables were there:—there was a little dancing, a little supper, a great many tender adieux, a wet walk home, a sherry-cobbler, and an end to a very agreeable evening.

Everybody is kinder and more hospitable than the last, and it's well we don't stay or our heads would be turned by the civility we receive.

39. George Bancroft (1800-1891), Massachusetts statesman, historian, and former minister to Great Britain.

Thursday Night, [May 20].

A "couleur de rose" day!—one of the pleasantest and most noticeable I ever spent! Directly after breakfast (we were shamefully late by the way at this necessary meal!) Mr. Jay came and took us with him and Mrs. Jay to hear a rehearsal of Jenny Lind at the Metropolitan Hall—we were almost the only people there, and as soon as we entered, Jenny came up and sat by us. Mrs. Jay introduced us, and Jenny (who was in excellent spirits) turned and said in sweet low broken English and with the merriest smile—"From the old country—when did you come? Dear old England!—I shall be so glad to see it again. How is the Queen and all of you there now?" Mrs. Jay asked if she wasn't sorry to leave America. "No," she said, "not altogether, —your climate doesn't suit me—such terrible winters as they have here would kill me—you are lucky to have come at this time of year," (she added to me)—"and then, you know," she said to Mrs. Jay who asked if she had not had great happiness in America from her marriage, &c. "if I have had great happiness I've had my greatest sorrow." She has never got over her Mother's death, and she is still in deep mourning for her. I spoke of Liverpool and the Yates'[40]—she desired to be remembered to them, and said how greatly she admired the Philharmonic Hall—"it is so good for the voice, so beautifully arranged and lighted:—oh, it is really enchanting!"

She sang very sweetly as ever, and so naturally and enthusiastically—no affectation, and with a perfect "abandon;"—her ear is splendid, and whenever any unlucky musician got the least out of time, she threaded

40. A prominent and philanthropic Liverpool family.

94

her way among the orchestra, and launched out indignantly at his devoted head.

She is very plain and old-looking, but with a quiet humourous good-natured look which is very pleasant: —she is, however, Mrs. Jay says, awkward in Society and is constantly giving offence by not speaking except in monosyllables, &c. She seems "*uncertain*," but today she was (Mrs. Jay says) "in her best way."

Otto Goldschmidt is a nice little gentlemanly man when you see him near, but we were not introduced to him.

From the Rehearsal we drove out to a house of Mrs. Jay's father in the country.[41] It is beautifully situated on the banks of the Hudson, and I never saw such a splendid suite of rooms: it not only eclipses anything I've seen at New York, but anything I've seen in England in a place so unpretending and hospitable:— a beautiful drawing-room, library, dining-room and some 2 or 3 rooms besides, all opening out of each other and all furnished with a luxury and magnificence, fit for any nobleman's house.

Mrs. Jay's little girl is a beautiful little thing and quite won our hearts.

After the prettiest lunch, oysters and lobster, hock and champagne, shaddock and banana, we left, though with some delay as the "carriage wanted fixing" the servant told me.

We dressed and went to Mr. Kennedy's—fancy our horror!—they were at dinner, and it was a dinner party —a beautiful one too—gold plate, oak-panelled room, flowers and dessert frenchwise on the table—it was perfect! Mr. Kennedy was civil, Mrs. Kennedy (a Lenox

41. Mrs. Jay (Eleanor Kingsland Field) was the daughter of Hickson W. Field, prosperous New York merchant, who built the New York Hotel.

by birth)[42] as gracious as could be expected under the circumstances, and the company most "select" (as Elliott would say).

Mr. Astor the elder—the richest man in America—was there:[43]—Mr. Aspingwall, a "rising man"[44]—Mr. Cogswell (librarian of the Astor Library), a man far more eminent in literature even than Bancroft, they say,[45]—and our old friend Mr. Davis,—(with others,—about 18.) We had much pleasant conversation, and I gleaned information on several points.

Culinary:—

Grouse much prized,—pheasant and hare not much thought of,—cheese hardly ever eaten:—all these are English luxuries, and good for presents.

Antiquarian, &c:—

The date of Sir P[hilip] Sidney's death very doubtful. The Bostonians are raving about genealogies, and a "Genealogical Magazine" is published there.[46]

Horace Mann is not thought much of (i.e. by New York fashionable) and was well shown up by Bristed[47] (N.B.—Mr. Kennedy is the only man who speaks well of this last gent).

Botanical:—

The Ailanthus Japonica (the tatoo or "tattow" tree)

42. David Sproat Kennedy's wife was one of the five daughters of the millionaire Robert Lenox.

43. William Backhouse Astor (1792–1875).

44. William Henry Aspinwall (1807–75), merchant, chief promoter of the Panama Railroad.

45. Joseph Green Cogswell (1786–1871), teacher and librarian (since 1848) of the Astor Library.

46. *The New England Historical & Genealogical Register* began publication in 1847.

47. Horace Mann (1796–1859), educator; at this time in the House of Representatives. Charles Astor Bristed (1820-74), in *A Letter to the Hon. Horace Mann* (1850), defended the enlightened philanthropy of his grandfather, John Jacob Astor, against Mann's attacks. Bristed would be of particular interest to HAB as an American who had spent five years at Trinity College, Cambridge.

is much cultivated in New York because it does not habour caterpillars:—the tulip tree is likewise popular.

Etymology:—

The muffin men in New York call out "tou cow," French "tout chaud." Is language "a gift of God" or "a creation of man?" Cogswell thinks the latter.

We ended the day by seeing a good farce "Popping the Question" at Burton's Theatre.

New York Mems:—

N.B.—The only letter *I* have not given is one to Mr. Bellows who I believe is very ill.

Dr. Moore, Mr. Minturn I have not seen.

Mrs. Davis, Mr. Jay (Hon. J) are nice people to send letters to. The Jays have travelled in England in the best circles, have been to a Queen's Ball, have lunched with Duchess of Sutherland, &c. and are quite unaffected, and entirely *un*snobbish.

Mrs. Davis wants autographs.

Bryant and Horace Greeley[48] are still to be seen by us at New York.

So among places, the City Hall, water works, and Greenhill [i.e., Greenwood] Cemetery.

Mr. Jay wishes to be remembered to Mr. R. Rathbone,[49] and desires me to tell J. Kenyon[50] to send letters to him.

48. Bright did call on poet William Cullen Bryant (1794–1878) just before leaving America, but he did not see Horace Greeley (1811–72), editor of the *New-York Daily Tribune*.

49. Richard Rathbone (1788–1860) of Liverpool.

50. John Kenyon (1784–1856), poet and philanthropist, friend of the Brownings and other literary figures.

3

PHILADELPHIA

United States Hotel, Philadelphia.[1]
Saturday Night, [May 22].

Yesterday before leaving New York, we called on Mr.
Grinnell (who was most civil) and left cards on the
Davis', Fearings and Gibbes. From Mr. Irvin we got
money $250 each, and from Mr. Tomes we bought pis-
tols and then—for Philadelphia.

"Variety is charming" as we all know from our
schoolboy copy slips—therefore the journey from New
York to Philadelphia is charming, changing as we did
from ferry boat to railroad, from railroad to steamer,
from steamer to carriage. The railway carriages have
often been described—they resemble the Belgian second
class, and here there is but one class.

The country is like English country, and there is little
to remind you that you are not at home, except that
snake (or worm) fences take the place of our hawthorn hedges, and give a strange look to English-like

1. Dickens also stayed at this hotel, on Chestnut Street, between Fourth
and Fifth.

fields with their irregular cheveaux de frise. Flowers too are scarce, maybe a solitary dandelion or a hermit buttercup, and that is all—generally the fields are grass "simple."

Our steamer on the Delaware was large and comfortable, and the river looked strangely picturesque as we saw it by the pale light of stars and the "red light" of—*not* the "planet Mars,"[2] but the signals on the steamer funnel. We found our dear friends the Captains waiting for us, and hailed with delight an hotel not too large to be comfortable, nor too magnificent to be looked after while there.

Philadelphia. Sunday, May 23.[3]

Yesterday poor Burder was ill, and could not go out, so Franklin, Smith and myself found our way to the Fair Mount waterworks—they are very pretty and must be a great resource for idle Philadelphians. I amused myself by thinking how puzzled an Englishman would be were I to attempt to describe our ramble there as of course a "genu *ii*ne" Philadelphian would describe it. "We walked along the banks of the Schuylkill (pronounce *School*kill) on a day when not a breath of wind stirred the leaves of the locust tree, and gazed now at the wire bridge below the School, now on the statute of the immortal Graff.[4] As we returned

2. Cf. Longfellow, "The Light of Stars."

3. This was Burder's twenty-first birthday, which he evidently celebrated on his sickbed. Exactly a year later he wrote to HAB: "This is my birth-day; a year ago I came of age in a very unobtrusive manner in New-York [*sic*]!" (letter of May 23, 1853, at Trinity College, Cambridge).

4. Frederick Graff (1774-1847), chief engineer of the Philadelphia waterworks. A ride to Fairmount, and a walk across the wire bridge, was a usual Philadelphia recreation.

Gleason's Pictorial Drawing-Room Companion, September 20, 1851

*"We walked along the banks . . . and gazed
now at the wire bridge."*

many a rapid spider web rolled past us, and the bo-
hoys looked at our distanced car in triumph."[5]

On our return we looked in on the Mint. Most of
the eng*iii*nes were idle, but we saw enough to interest
us for a good half hour—the smoothing the coins' edge,
the stamping them were going on, but most interesting
of all was the engine which set the whole in motion—
"the very poetry of machinery," as Burder said of an
engine we saw at New York—so smooth, so noiseless,

5. That is, "boys in speedy carriages ('spiders') outdistanced us." Pok-
ing fun at inflated American rhetoric was a standard recreation of foreign observers beginning with de Tocqueville.

so steady—moved every crank and iron rod in the en- . gine's frame.

Captain Matthews introduced me to Mr. Peter the Consul;[6] a fine old man who knew Uncle Henry in his M.P. days,[7] when Peter was Member for Bodmin. His wife is in Jerusalem and he stays at home, having been very ill lately. He is full of information and has been helping some young Cornish man in writing a book on American Institutions, &c. He condemns the use of Ballot, and says that the "godless" system of education in New England makes the most knavish "tricky" set of fellows though without many gross vices. But he is most indignant, and very properly so, at the Episcopal Convention just held here, at which the majority decreed that a certain black congregation should not be allowed to send deputies to the convention on account of their colour!—a godly set of men this Episcopal Convention, but after all perhaps as good as their neighbours, who are too many rank slave holders and pro-slavery men.[8] On the subject of immediate abolition—in other words, throwing upon the country a set of uneducated, idle fellows—there may be two opinions, and I own I do not take the extreme line,—but that when men of colour are free men and Christians—

6. William Peter (1788–1853), politician and poet, member for Bodmin, 1832–34, consul at Philadelphia, 1840–53. "He is an English gentleman of good family . . . an agreeable, well-bred, cultivated person. He has received great attention here & enjoys society, eating & drinking more than any man I ever knew" (*A Philadelphia Perspective The Diary of Sidney George Fisher*, ed. Nicholas B. Wainwright [Philadelphia, 1967], p. 108).

7. Henry Bright (1784–1869), M.P. for Bristol, 1820–30.

8. HAB discusses this event, as an instance of American bigotry, in his pamphlet *Free Blacks and Slaves* (1853). He quotes the opposition argument that "like the Indians" the Negroes "should be regarded as in a state of pupilage, still fostered and kept under the wing of the Church." This pamphlet provoked a letter from John Jay, who told Bright triumphantly (October 24, 1853) that the Episcopal Convention of New York had just admitted a colored church (letter at Trinity College, Cambridge).

and many of the free men are most intelligent fellows—
they should be excluded from a religious right by their
brother freemen and fellow Christians is perfectly
monstrous and disgusting.

The leading abolitionist here is Dr. Furness our
minister.[9] He has alienated many of his congregation,
which spite of his talents and high character has been
constantly growing "fine by degrees and beautifully
less,"[10] from the Doctor's harping too exclusively on
this one thing. I hardly think a Unitarian minister should
sacrifice the interests of truth in religion to the interests of truth in politics. An abolitionist would
doubtless though put it otherwise and say it was sacri-
ficing sectarian prejudice to the rights of Man.—
"Utrum horum mavis accipe."[11]

Dr. Furness is I fear injudicious, and through his
agency, at least in some measure, was brought about
the separation of Mr. and Mrs. Butler.[12] They went to
his Church, but Mr. Butler left it, because Dr. Furness
was always preaching *at* him as being a slave-holder.
Mrs. Butler still held to the Doctor, swore by abolition, and thanks to her temper which is awful, and this
difference of opinion, the separation took place which
Dr. Furness—too late—did all in his power to prevent.

Still, he is a splendid man, so earnest and eloquent,
so simple (in black coat and neckcloth) and urgent. We
were both delighted with him:—his sermon was on
Paul at Corinth and how God may raise up the weak
to confound the strong—and how *we* must labour to do

9. William Henry Furness (1802-96), distinguished Unitarian clergyman, a native Bostonian, and lifelong friend of Emerson; pastor of the
Philadelphia church, 1825-75.

10. Matthew Prior, "Henry and Emma."

11. "Take whichever of these you prefer."

12. The marriage of Pierce Butler (1807-67) and the actress Fanny
Kemble (1809-93) ended (1849) in a divorce in which Furness acted as
intermediary.

102

WILLIAM HENRY FURNESS, CA. 1850

*"So earnest and eloquent, so simple
(in black coat and neckcloth) and urgent."*

good, the first step to which is to "see with our own eyes" what is evil and not to let our impressions be swayed by mere fashion or prejudice. His sermon was all I think for abolition, though he never mentioned the *word*, but in his prayer he asked God's blessing on "the coloured man." The service concluded with the singing of "Charity" by *one* good female voice and a blessing from the Minister, to whom I gave a letter, and he promised to call on us tomorrow. The Church is a neat Grecian building,[13] the congregation pretty good—the *fans* very numerous; by the way, ladies here have regular *Sunday* fans which they leave with their hymn books in Church:—at the Church of the Messiah at New York I counted seven fans in one pew!

But speaking of abolition and Dr. Furness, has taken me away from my account of yesterday. Our Quaker friend of the "Great Britain" took us to see the Franklin Square, where squirrels in dozens were playing about as tame as possible and coming for bread which little children threw them. We dined at the Girard House, a splendid Hotel,[14] with Captain Matthews and a Mr. Snyder, and afterwards Burder, myself and the Dr. and Mrs. Pettit drove to Laurel Hill Cemetery—a beautiful spot, a spot which "makes you fall in love with death" to use Shelley's well-known phrase on Keats' burial place,[15]—on the wooded banks of the Schuylkill among flowering magnolias, dark pines, and green willows are many of the prettiest monuments I ever saw,—one with a dove on a marble pillar and "our Kate" inscribed—another with only "Isabelle"—one, a lamb lying upon a cross with "My father" for all epi-

13. The Unitarian church at Tenth and Locust streets was designed by William Strickland (1828).

14. On the north side of Chestnut Street, this large hotel (1,000 guests) had opened only this year.

15. Or rather, to misquote Keats's words (in "Ode to a Nightingale").

104

taph,—and some with rarest flowers clustering round
them or woven into wreaths upon them. Among the
most splendid monuments is one without a name—
simply because the man to whose memory it was
erected is still *alive*.[16]

In the evening I went to a cousin of Dr. Pettit's,
who has written a discourse which the Dr. gave me.[17]
There was a small party, quiet people, with a small
house, a small supper, some good nigger melodies and
some execrable American champagne—"Catawba"
they're pleased to call it. Franklin and Smith were
there, Burder was too unwell, Matthews was too much
engaged to come.

The other events of yesterday were the taking a bath,
and the sending the paper-case to Mr. Bonnell, whom
I have not seen, he is busy for Allibone is from home.[18]
To-day we went to Dr. Furness; drove to Fair Mount,
passing a curious covered bridge, dined at the Hotel,
saw the Captain and Smith off, and spent the evening
at Dr. Pettit's:—he is really quite a nice person, well-
informed and far-travelled, and most kind to us. His
house is beautiful, every convenience—even the
servants—strange to say he keeps only *two men*, no
women at all—have marble chimney-pieces in their
rooms and a splendid Bath Room for themselves. The
house is marble-fronted—the steps are "small bits of

16. "The salutary effects of ornate and well-preserved cemeteries on
the moral taste and general sentiments of all classes, is a most valuable
result, and seems to have been appreciated in all ages, by all civilized
nations" (*A Guide to Laurel Hill Cemetery* [Philadelphia, 1851], p. 20).

17. William V. Pettit delivered an address in the Pennsylvania House
of Representatives on April 6, 1852, that advocated the Colonization
scheme for Negroes. It was published by the Pennsylvania Colonization
Society (1852).

18. Samuel Austin Allibone (1816–89), literary lexicographer, had not
yet begun his *Critical Dictionary of English Literature and British and
American Authors* (1858–71). He was at this time with the Insurance
Company of North America. Mr. Bonnell was perhaps his assistant there.

unpolished marble—that's all," as the worthy Quaker modestly remarked. The basins in each room are supplied with taps for warm and cold water, the garden has its little fountain, the drawing-room its scagliola pillars, &c. &c. Such is a house of a Republican and a Friend!

Philadelphia is a noble town—trees everywhere in the streets and courts, so green and pretty. The houses faced with white marble, which if only polished would be dazzlingly beautiful—as a city it is a more striking one by far than New York, me judice, and certainly more clean.

Tuesday Afternoon, May 25.

Yesterday early Mr. Bonnell and Dr. Furness called upon us. Most pleasant is Dr. Furness though "he's done an immense deal of harm" as a Mr. Wharton[19] with a slavery tendency told us last night at Mr. Peter's where we dined. We heard much about slavery there from our host, Mr. Wharton, and Mr. Washington Smith,[20] all talented and superior men.

Mr. W. Smith gave me much information on this subject of slavery. The colonization plan seems the most popular, gradually drafting off the blacks to Liberia, &c.[21]—but then again arises the question, who will till the rice-swamps, and cultivate the cotton plantations of the South? Will the plan of introducing Chinese answer?

19. Thomas Isaac Wharton (1791-1856), lawyer, author of *Digest of the Decisions of the Supreme Court of Pennsylvania* and Wharton's *Reports* (1835-40).

20. George Washington Smith (1800-1876), wealthy, well-traveled, and a bachelor, was a founder of the Franklin Institute and the Pennsylvania Historical Society.

21. The American Colonization Society (est. 1817) had purchased a tract of land in Liberia for American Negroes; but by 1860 only 15,000 had settled there.

106

What would be the effect of amalgamating the black and white races? I asked. To this it appears there are various difficulties. Nature hardly seems to countenance such a union of race. The conformation of the negro differs from that of the white in several respects—the colour is obvious,—the glands emitting a most offensive odour under the arm pit, the projecting heel, the side shin—all show a natural distinction between the two families of the human race, which does not exist between us, and the Indian, the Mongolian and the Malay. The result of such a union as I proposed would be simply the extinction of the blacks—the Mulattoes *all die young*, and the nearer white the Mulatto descendants are, the more susceptible are they of disease, the more certain of an early death. Mr. Smith has never (and he has investigated the subject from boyhood) seen more than three Mulattoes in his life above 60 years of age.

The intellectual qualities of the black man are inferior—an instance like F. Douglass is "the exception that proves the rule."[22] A man by no means of first rate talent is heroified *because* he is black—can there be any better proof of the intellectual inferiority of the race—an inferiority by the way, most strikingly shown in the features, if physiognomy be the least worthy of trust. The negro is imitative, often cleverly so, like a well trained monkey or the "learned pig" (to which highly respected animal Wharton was pleased to compare Douglass) and that is all. Negro children are as sharp when children as any white "brats," but when the childlike imitation rises to manly invention, the negro is not merely distanced but altogether left behind. He is hardly ever educated, hardly ever can be educated beyond a certain point—for hundreds of years

22. Frederick Douglass (1817-95), abolitionist, published the *Narrative* of his life in 1845.

the negro race has existed (some by the way, and I shocked Mr. Wharton by saying so, believe Adam to have been a "coloured gentleman," which certainly upsets Mr. Smith's hypothesis of the impossibility of raising the negro race, that is, *if* all mankind were born from *one* pair)—and no one great man has the negro race produced.

To a question of mine as to whether if educated and cultivated for some two or three generations the negroes might not be able to cope in intellect with the whites, I could get no certain reply—no such experiment has ever been tried, but it would, I think, have at least a probability of success, as we so generally see properties (physical and mental) of an ancestor descend to his posterity, whereas at present the negro ancestor has nothing to transmit but ignorance and debasement.

Our dinner conversation of slavery has already drawn me so far from the sights of the morning, that I had better push them away for another page or two more, and describe more accurately still our dinner and conversation.

Mr. Peter is a delightful old man,—an enthusiastic Whig, an enthusiastic Cornishman. He was intimate with the Duke of Sussex, and played whist with the Duchess of Inverness as his partner,[23] "I've always liked her—she kept her temper so nobly, when I lost her the game by a revoke." "Mistress of herself, though China fall,"[24] muttered the clever and sarcastic Mr. Wharton—an eminent lawyer, who has written many volumes of digests and reports, who is a zealous Yankee and anti-abolitionist, and who was rather angry at some of our English and No-Slavery impertinences. He

23. The duke of Sussex was Augustus Frederick (1773–1843), sixth son of George III; the duchess of Inverness was his wife.

24. Pope, *Moral Essays*, Epistle II.

laughed much at our laments about the heat of the weather, and when we told him of the jellified state in which we were, he asked, "if you do such things in the green tree, what will be done in the dry?"

Mr. Peter says Uncle Henry used always to have a different reason for what he did from everybody else, and his Whig friends could never manage him. Kenyon he says is a delightful fellow, and from him Dickens received a letter of introduction to the worthy Consul.[25]

Mr. Peter is an author—he showed me a letter on American schools he had sent to the Economist, and *gave* me a translation of his of Schiller's "William Tell." To Burder he gave a translation of the Agamemnon.

Among other mutual friends he talked of the < > and told me that Lady < > had been given to drinking in former years—est-il possible?

After dinner Mr. Smith took us to the Athenaeum Club, where are to be found all the American and English papers and magazines—a great lounge while at Philadelphia, which is so pleasant—I don't know when we can leave it.

Mr. Allibone on whom I called yesterday, has persuaded us to go and spend to-morrow evening at his country house to see his farm, &c., and Mr. Josiah Randall (the old democrat drops the "Mr." on his cards)[26] had over-persuaded us to stay and dine with him on Thursday to meet Mr. Peter. Randall is a friend of James Heywood[27] from whom I got my letter,

25. A few months later Kenyon also gave Arthur Hugh Clough a letter of introduction: "Wm Peter was a Christchurch man, then a barrister— . . . He is a fair Scholar, loves poetry and is a high gentleman to the backbone" (letter of October 26, 1852, *The Correspondence of Arthur Hugh Clough*, 2:324–25).

26. Josiah Randall (1789–1866), leading Philadelphia lawyer and later political adviser to President Buchanan.

27. James Heywood (1810–97), HAB's cousin and M.P. for North Lancs., 1847–57.

and also of John Heywood,[28] with whom we had business:—he will give us a letter to Fillmore,[29] he says.

We finished yesterday evening in seeing Celeste act in the "Willow Copse," and an infernal (literally *uncelestial*) farce afterwards.[30]

But now for our morning doings of yesterday. With Mr. Bonnell (whom Burder hates, for he said Burder had an American face, and an American voice!) we went to see the Girard College[31]—a splendid Parthenon-like building, all white marble,—floors, and roof, pillars and steps all the same material. I never saw anything more magnificent or more useful. Orphans of Philadelphia are educated here, and boarded in white marble houses close by! From the roof there is a fine smokeless view of the city. Thence to the Penitentiary—the first place where solitary imprisonment was tried:—it answers admirably, and Dickens' stories about its evils are, Mr. Peter (who investigated each instance) assured me, *pure invention!*[32] The man who showed us round was a most intelligent fellow, and he says that except in cases where there is a predisposition to insanity, the effect is perfect; in cases where insanity is likely to ensue, the patient is sent

28. Probably John Pemberton Heywood, banker, of Liverpool; another relative of Bright's.

29. Millard Fillmore (1800–1874), president of the U.S., 1850–53.

30. HAB saw Celeste (1814–82), celebrated French actress, in the opening night of Dion Boucicault's melodrama at the Walnut Street Theatre; the farce was W. E. Burton's "Deeds of Dreadful Note."

31. Stephen Girard (1750–1831), French-born banker and philanthropist, founded this college for poor white orphan boys (opened 1848).

32. Dickens's chapter on Philadelphia in *American Notes* is largely devoted to this penitentiary and the evils of solitary confinement; he creates a nightmare vision of what such a life would be. Peter, requested by the Philadelphia Prison Society to investigate the later history of each prisoner Dickens described, found that with one exception they were "doing well" after discharge.

110

GIRARD COLLEGE, PHILADELPHIA

Gleason's Pictorial Drawing-Room Companion, September 4, 1852

"A splendid Parthenon-like building, all white marble."

to work in a beautiful garden with the gardener, and a cure often takes place.[33]

Each cell has a little court attached, where the prisoner may walk for an hour every day. When in his cell he is supplied with books, and paper, and instructed in shoe-making, tailoring, weaving, or any other trade for which he has a "turn." One cell was painted all over by a German prisoner,[34] another occupied by a female was hung with worsted work!

The confinement is really solitary, no walking about in company with others as in England, no meeting

33. Bitter controversy divided the champions of this solitary confinement system in Philadelphia and partisans of the rival "congregate system" used at Auburn, N.Y., where the prisoners were allowed some contact with each other during the day.

34. Cf. Dickens: "In another cell, there was a German, sentenced to five years' imprisonment for larceny, two of which had just expired. With colors procured in the same manner, he had painted every inch of the walls and ceiling quite beautifully" (chap. 7). Since this cell is also mentioned by Frederika Bremer, perhaps it was a showpiece for visitors.

111

others in chapel on Sunday. The gaolor and chaplain are admitted to them, and that is all. On Sunday any Minister of any persuasion may stand on an elevated platform and preach to the prisoners, whose cell doors are partially open, so that the preacher's voice, echoing down the galleries may reach them all, if they choose to listen.

The last good feeling or instinct which leaves a prisoner the gaolor told us, is the love of beauty. When they no longer care to have things nice about them, their case is desperate! The books in their library are too serious, he tells me,—"our life here is too sad and real," one prisoner said to him, "we can't always be reading religious, melancholy books—we want stories to make us forget." The only prisoner we saw was the librarian, an old reprobate with whom Burder had some talk—"speculations in trade" first got him into difficulty, he said—and in difficulty, said the gaolor with a grin, he's been 37 years.

Our tame gaolor was so civil and gentlemanly, I didn't quite like to offer him anything—on going away, I said, "We're much obliged to you,—were I in England I should offer you something, but—" my delicacy was soon checked by a "well, I guess I shouldn't refuse it if you did," and the half dollar was pocketed.

To-day we have seen the Academy of the Natural Sciences, where is a collection of stuffed birds, most like other collections of stuffed birds, and certainly not so many as at Leyden. The Philadelphian Library[35] where Mr. Bonnell took us, and where we found lying open on the table a book of Heraldry and Pictures of George IV's Coronation.

Mr. Wharton took us to the Academy of Arts, where was many really fine pictures, and several celebrated

35. I.e., the Library Company of Philadelphia, then on Fifth Street, founded by Benjamin Franklin.

112

Gleason's Pictorial Drawing-Room Companion, October 16, 1852

ones, such as West's "Death on the Pale Horse"[36]—
a very different collection to the New York one!

We dined at 3½ at the Lady's Ordinary (after spending an hour at the Athenaeum). We had several strange
dishes, and one of stewed frogs—"Grenouilles sautées
à la Provansal" as the bill stated—and very good they
were,—little sauced legs of white meat rather chicken-
like.

Wednesday, Noon, May 26.

Yesterday at 6½ we went to Mr. Bonnell's for tea.
Affection was all he had to bestow, he said. Alas! it
was very true, except indeed a fit of indigestion which
had succeeded the eating of some very hot heavy cake
in a very hot close room with a smell of very hot ran-
cid butter!

Still I must not be ungrateful—they were really very

36. The oldest art academy in America (1805) was then on Chestnut
Street between Tenth and Eleventh streets. The canvas by Benjamin West
(1728–1820) was painted in 1817.

kind to us, and old Mr. Bonnell is quite a nice person. Young Bonnell told me that a question of some political moment in Pennsylvania is whether there should be a duty on foreign i.e. English iron, as the extensive importation of it is destroying entirely the mines of the State, which from the scarcity of labour are most expensive to work.

At 8½ we went to Dr. Furness. Here we found a party of some twenty people, most agreeable and nice, many of them. Miss Furness is rather *my style*—a pretty Jenny-Lind-like girl, with small hands, a merry laugh and a good voice.[37] I had much conversation with her and have promised to send her from England the "Rainy Day" and "Burk." She is very clever and well-informed—"blue" if you like, but a decidedly pretty tint:—she talked of Fanny Kemble, who was their constant guest—she was perfect, thinks Miss Furness, and when I ventured with some trepidation to hint at her tolerably well-known deficiency of temper, all I got was "she's impulsive, that's all."

Of Margaret Fuller[38] neither Dr. or Miss Furness or Miss Ware (daughter of Henry Ware)[39] thought much. The Doctor's chief feeling was one of pity for her extreme plainness, but as Miss Furness says, her admirers never seem to notice it, "Margaret was *sumptuous*" on such and such a night, they say,—"such a word to use too, sumptuous," (Miss F. added) "it re-

37. Annis Lee Furness (1830–1908), later Mrs. Caspar Wister, captivated another English visitor some months later: "Have you heard Miss Furness of Philadelphia sing? She is the very best ballad singer I ever heard" (Thackeray to William B. Reed, February 14, 1853, *The Letters and Private Papers of William Makepeace Thackeray*, ed. Gordon N. Ray [Cambridge, Mass., 1945–46], 3:203).

38. Margaret Fuller (1810–50), Transcendentalist, friend of Emerson, drowned with her husband and child in a shipwreck off Fire Island.

39. Henry Ware, Jr. (1794–1843), leading Unitarian clergyman and professor at the Harvard Divinity School.

minds one of O'Connell's toast, that sumptuous and elegant woman Mrs. Burdett Coutts."[40]

Dr. Furness regrets that the book was ever published and thinks it calculated to do much harm.[41] Miss Ware always disliked Margaret, who she says, repulsed her,—and another gentleman talked of her (not at Dr. F's though) as a sort of spiritual Bloomer and denied that she was ever *married*.

On slavery I had but little conversation with Dr. Furness—he recommended "Uncle Tom's Cabin"[42] as a splendidly written and very true book on it, and told us of a slave holder who read it till tears came. It was in a railway carriage, and an inquisitive Yankee asked, "I guess you're ill now." "No!" "Then perhaps you've lost a friend." "No, *but that damnèd book!*"

Burder and I have both bought a copy and expect to gain much useful knowledge from it. "Thorpe by Mountford"[43] we've also bought.

Unitarianism as a sect perhaps, the Doctor told me; does not increase in America, but more orthodox Churches are daily becoming liberal and approaching nearer to our views. Bancroft was a Uni-Minister, Fillmore (the President) is also a Uni, and has just appointed Dr. Dewey as *Chaplain to the Navy*, an office which Dr. Furness, who is touched on the peace question, thinks he should never have accepted.[44] "Dr. Dewey has completely lost himself," he said.

40. Daniel O'Connell (1775-1847), the Irish politician; Angela Georgina Burdett-Coutts (1814-1906), philanthropist, who included Ireland in her catalogue of good works.

41. I.e., the *Memoirs* of Margaret Fuller (1852), written by Emerson, William Henry Channing, and J. F. Clarke.

42. Published in book form in March, 1852, and immediately a sensational best seller.

43. *Thorpe, a Quiet English Town, and Human Life Therein* (1852), by William Mountford, Unitarian minister.

44. Dewey resigned this post after a few months.

We were both much pleased with our evening—the company were most intellectual, the ices undeniably good, and Miss Furness sang well and rather like Miss Blundell.

Wednesday Evening, [May 26].

To-day we went to see the lunatic asylum near the town. I had never seen one before, nor did I much care about so painful a sight—Burder was however curious to see it, and we went. The Doctor to whom we shewed a card of Mr. Wharton's was most civil. The building is very fine, and all the arrangements are perfect. The rooms are lofty and well ventilated, and the gardens are extensive and pretty. They (the poor inmates) have reading rooms and museums and everything is done to reconcile them to their sad fate.

One thing the keeper told us which was curious—the negroes are hardly ever insane when *slaves*, as *freemen* they often become melancholy-mad and the like, feeling there is no one to take care of them and take an interest in them.[45]

On returning to the town we bathed, wrote journal and dined—after which Mr. Bonnell and Mr. Allibone came to take us into the country. We went in Mr. A's carriage, which took us along some very bad roads to an old farm of his which he used once to live in. The country round is very pretty—rich fields of rye and

---

45. This notion gained much currency after the census of 1840 published figures showing that insanity was much more common among free Negroes than among slaves. When Bright repeated this theory in his pamphlet *Free Blacks and Slaves*, it brought the following retort from Furness: "It is a terrible misfortune to lose one's intellect, but it is a worse evil to have no intellect to lose. The slaves are as a man so imbruted that they are not up to being crazy" (letter of July 1, 1853 at Trinity College, Cambridge).

clover, none divided by hedges, but many by rows of the American cedar (a cypress?)—the woodlands and copses, white with the flowers of the Dogwood, and beautiful with a pink azalea-looking flower which grows some foot and a half above the ground and called by him "the wild honeysuckle," though obviously a different species of plant altogether to our common honeysuckle. Another flower I also found which was unknown to me—a white privet-like blossom growing with the "azalea" plants.

In the garden round Mr. Allibone's we saw many beautiful and to us rare trees and flowers. The "all-spice" or "shrub" (as the Americans call it, never using "shrub" as we do) with its dark brown fragrant blossoms reminding me so of old Ham Green[46]—the prickly acacia with its formidable spikes,—the white magnolia still in bud,—the Sassafras, the Locust and the Tulip tree—all clustering round the pretty farm looked strangely un-English and curious.

With Mr. Allibone's dwelling house we were also pleased, though we preferred the farm ourselves.

He has a large family—some 9 or 10 children, and we found a party of friends and relations there to meet us—we were introduced to everybody and got on I think very well. I like Mr. and Mrs. Allibone very much indeed, kinder hearted and *better* people I have rarely met, but he *will* chew, and *she* can't help speaking through her nose. Some of their daughters are sweet-looking girls, and my impression of the whole family is very pleasant indeed. Mr. A. gave me an autograph of Clay's[47] and promised to send us over some apples from his orchard, which are very famous.

After tea we had a great deal of singing from some

46. The estate outside Bristol belonging to HAB's grandfather Richard Bright.

47. Henry Clay (1777-1852), statesman.

nice girls, many "nigger" songs among them,—and then great platesful of ice, more singing and then we went away.

Burder got into conversation with a singular young woman who is secretary of an "Anti-Matrimonial Society" which numbers some 30 members from 16 to 22 —lovely girls some of them, he heard! They say "man is deceitful" and so forth, and are themselves evidently believers in the doctrines laid down by the old aunt in Bernard Mandeville's book on this point.[48]

I learned several curious things in the course of the evening. Mr. Allibone's house and the other houses in Hamilton Village though some two miles from the town are marked on maps, &c. as being in the town, and the lane in which Mr. A. lives is called a "street." The distances between two parallel streets at right angles to another is called a "square" here; a "block" in New York. And this "square" phraseology is used quite out in the country as the word street (I before said).

By the way, I forgot to mention that part of our drive to-day passed through a pretty cemetery near Mr. A's. Cemeteries here are all the "rage"; people lounge in them, and use them (as their tastes are inclined) for walking, making love, weeping, sentimentalizing, and everything in short: very different from Harvey's "Meditations among the Tombs" would be those of some of the fair Philadelphians![49]

Thursday Evening, [May 27].

To-day we spent a quiet morning, buying books and carpet bags, and walking about the town. Our greatest

48. In *The Virgin Unmask'd: or, Female dialogues betwixt an elderly maiden lady and her niece* (1709).

49. James Hervey's popular "Meditations among the Tombs" (1746–47) were evangelical and high-minded in tone.

exertion was in making farewell calls on Dr. Pettit and Dr. Furness—at the former place only Miss P. was at home, and our conversation chiefly turned on the vivacity of a Quaker "Meeting." At Dr. Furness' we sat an immense time talking to him, his wife and daughter. They are really delightful people and Burder is equally charmed with them; the Dr. has given us several letters and added for me an autograph of Dewey's. I asked how I should like Dr. Burnap, our Minister at Philadelphia[50]—Miss Furness laughed, Mrs. Furness said nothing, and the Dr. expressed a curiosity to know what their answer would be. Mrs. F. at last told us that probably the first thing he'd do would be to take down all the books he'd written from their shelf and say "Here is the produce of my brain!" a conceit only surpassed by that of Martin Tupper, who, going up to be introduced to a lady at New York, said "How do you do, Madame—I suppose you've read my books? No! Oh then, of course you're going to!!"

We are seriously thinking of writing "English travellers in America and what the Americans think of them." How it would sell, and how libellous it would be!

We hear that Lady Emmeline Stuart Wortley was *horridly dirty*, and that poor "Victoria's teeth were perfectly *black*!"[51]

Dickens is said never to have seen the best set in America—he was called upon, and made at once a "lion" and a "victim" by all the hunters for notoriety in New York, while the better set, like the Jays, kept aloof altogether.

---

50. A slip for Baltimore. George Washington Burnap (1802-59), a prolific writer, was Unitarian minister at Baltimore, 1828-59. He belonged to the conservative wing of his church, at the opposite extreme from Furness.

51. Lady Emmeline Stuart-Wortley (1806-55) visited the U.S. in 1849-50 and published her *Travels* in 1851. Victoria was her daughter.

Frederick Peel[52] was so reserved that he was put down a "fool" by J. Randall much to Mr. Peter's indignation, who didn't at all like poor Sir R's son to be "writ down an ass."

These stories however I got from various quarters, and they must not be put down to the Furness'.

In the evening we dined with Mr. Randall. We met Governor Coles, an excellent man, who, born a slaveholder released his "niggers," and gave them each a tract of land in Illinois for them to cultivate, and they have one and all turned out excellently.[53]

Dr. Jackson was there,—the most eminent medical man in America, who is now attending Henry Clay;— he is quite an agreeable old fellow, and we had some pleasant talk.[54]

A Mr. Sykes was there, who has lived much in Paris, and who is a singularly handsome man, and quite pleasant. Mr. Ingersoll,[55] most repulsive to look at but intelligent, talked to me about the Penitentiary and capital punishment.

Two sons of Mr. Randall are good specimens of young America, and from the eldest I got a good deal of political information.[56] I find it hard to understand the difference between Whigs and Democrats, but from my conversation with young Randall and from other sources I make out that the principal distinctions are as set out next page. The Presidential Election is exciting everybody—the Whig candidates are, Fillmore,

52. Frederick Peel (1823–1906), second son of Sir Robert Peel.

53. Edward Coles (1786–1868), born in Virginia, became governor of Illinois, 1822–26, and a prominent abolitionist.

54. Dr. Samuel Jackson (1787–1872) was indeed eminent, but Clay was in his last illness and died a month later.

55. Probably Joseph Reed Ingersoll (1786–1868) or his brother Charles Jared Ingersoll (1782–1862), both distinguished lawyers.

56. Samuel Jackson Randall (1828–90) went into politics and served later as a congressman from Pennsylvania.

120

Webster and Scott, and the Whig National Convention decide which shall be their man. The Democrats in their Convention then select between Cass and Buchanan, and the fight is between the chosen Whig and the pet Locofoco.[57]

Whigs.	Democrats.
I.　Have an aristocratic turn—their stronghold is the Eastern cities.	I.　Carry favour with Irish Emigrants, &c. and are always trying to send to Congress men of the people. The West back woods &c. is their strong point.
II.　Are generally Protectionists.	II.　Are freetraders.
III.　Are anxious to consolidate the federal Government.	III.　Wish each separate State to be as independent of Washington as possible.
IV.　Wish the Government to retain the lands.	IV.　Desire to give up to the people some government lands.

The National Bank question is now among the things that *have been*.

The Georges,[58] Randalls, and indeed almost everyone we've met are *Whigs!*

57.　The Democratic National Convention met the following week (June 1-6) in Baltimore and nominated the dark horse Franklin Pierce instead of Lewis Cass or James Buchanan. The Whig National Convention (June 16-21) chose Winfield Scott over Daniel Webster or the incumbent Fillmore.

58.　HAB's Baltimore host.

The dinner at Mr. Randall's was good—*French* like Mr. Kennedy's in having the dessert on the table all the time. I took Miss R[andall] in to dinner, which seemed curious considering the number of old grey-headed "fogies" who had to toddle in by themselves. Mr. Sykes offered to take us if we would stay till Saturday, to his cousin's, Mrs. Rush's, who has the most beautiful house perhaps in the United States—12 receiving rooms! it is the great lion of Philadelphia, but can only be seen on Saturday mornings when the lady gives a "reception."[59]

After dinner we talked about the "Ballot." I insinuated a doubt of its efficacy—all the Americans screamed at me. I quoted Mr. Peter—he was voted prejudiced and the like—bribery was unknown they said:—there was "betting" on the vote, and even fraudulent votes which could not be helped,—prisoners have been let out of prison by the Governors to vote for their friends—but—there was no bribery! Happy country this America, and impossible-to-be-improved institutions!

I asked if there would ever have been repudiation if it had not been that the ballot concealed the vote, the unmasked man would have been ashamed of. Mr. Randall said "yes"—Mississippi avowed and gloried in repudiation, acting as if a private individual, and acknowledging herself the only State liable as an individual to be sued, *if repudiation be winning!*[60] (Mr. Peter to whom I have spoken since denied that

59. Mrs. James Rush, formerly Phoebe Anne Ridgway, daughter of a wealthy Philadelphia merchant, built the magnificent "Rush Palace" on Chestnut Street in 1843.

60. Mississippi's Union Bank was established in 1838 with bonds sold to the United States Bank of Pennsylvania; when the Mississippi bank failed, the bonds were repudiated. The issue was still simmering, and in 1853 Mississippi disregarded the court's decision that she must meet the obligation.

there was *at the time* any *expressed* wish to repudiate, but quis sciat? muttered each man as he dropped in his ballot ticket. On ballot Mr. Peter declares that the inspectors shuffle away one card for another to suit their views.)

Philadelphia Mems:—

Send letters to Mr. Peter, Dr. Furness, Dr. Pettit, and Mr. Allibone.
Did not call on Col. Randall.
I must send Miss Furness some plants and songs.[61]
Mr. Allibone—grouse?

61. Bright, not one to forget a promise, had his sister copy out some songs for Miss Furness and sent some plants as well. Ten years later Furness wrote him that "our two laburnums and the hawthorn are perpetual memorials of our two young English friends" (letter of December 17, 1862, at Trinity College, Cambridge).

4

BALTIMORE

Baltimore, Mr. George's. Saturday Morning,
[May 29].

Yesterday morning we packed, called on Mr. Peter, who was as agreeable as ever, and bathed. Here Burder contrived to splash all his clothes so horridly that within half an hour of the train's starting he was found sitting by the side of his bath in a patience-on-a-monument attitude, trying to drain the water out of his stockings, and to empty the water out of his boots. I rushed to the Hotel, and taking a friendly nigger into my confidence, sent a suit of dry clothes to the dripping animal, who by dint of a great effort got ready in time for the train to Baltimore.

The country is rather pretty, between the "Vilige" and the "Monumental" Cities,—thick woods with a "clearing" or "shanty" the greater part of the way.

We pass the Susquehanna by a steamer, and the two Gunpowder falls by bridges. The scenery is everywhere quite pretty, with wooded banks sloping down to the water.

The railway comes quite into the town, and at the Depôt we met Mr. George—*as ever.*[1] Their house is beautiful, everything in good taste, and some capital pictures. It's most pleasant to have so kind a "Home amongst Strangers."

Their eldest son is to be Surgeon and is full of his chosen profession,—both he and his brother are good *artists*, and have painted several pretty things. Mrs. George reminds me so of home,—she asks so affectionately after everyone, and seems so glad to see us, and to me it's no small pleasure to meet one familiar face again!

This morning Mr. G. took us over his new house, which he will get into in October. It is magnificent, or rather *will be*, and worthy of its possessors. Everything is so light and airy, and cheerful,—the rooms are so spacious, and every convenience is to be found there.[2]

Our good friends are *not* slave holders, which is a relief, nor are they Abolitionists—Colonization men is the word I believe which expresses the party to which Mr. G. belongs, and as far as I can see, and read (from Mr. Pettit's Pamphlet) their principles seem the only sensible and practicable view of this most difficult question.

Monday Night, May 31.

These two days have passed quietly enough away. We have had several kind visitors, among them Dr. Burnap and Dr. Stewart,[3] our host and hostess are the

1. Samuel K. George (1810-71) had met Bright's family in Liverpool in 1847 and married an English girl.
2. The Georges' new house was at 71 Mount Vernon Place, in the choicest residential section of Baltimore.
3. Perhaps David Stewart (1813-99), a founder of the Maryland Col-

most hospitable of hosts and hostesses, and we have gained much information about slavery. We breakfast at 9, and dine at 4, and with the exception of a glass of iced water or a cup of tea we get no more food in the day.

We have neither soup nor pastry of any sort at dinner, but among the Baltimore delicacies we have soft crabs, and fresh strawberries, besides delicious ice-cream.

The weather is hot, and we sit quiet in the early morning—after twelve pay calls—and go out in the evening—such beautiful evenings! I took a drive with Mr. George to-night. The country is finely wooded, and all along the roadside were white-blossomed acacias, with an occasional Tulip tree, or a flowering magnolia: —otherwise, save the absence of hedges the country was like England,—pretty country houses among tall trees, pretty country villages with their whitewashed < > and hardy rustics:—all this was like the old Country.

This morning we went to pay calls with Mrs. George. She is a good chaperone and initiated us into some of their "simple ways" as she called them. A young lady may walk anywhere with a young gentleman through the town, but if he dare to offer her an arm, and she is venturesome enough to accept it, you are put down by the gossips as *engaged*.[4] Their perfect readiness however for an *armless* tête à tête walk was curiously exemplified to-day on our calling on a young lady whose uncle has a fine collection of pictures. After

lege of Pharmacy (1840) and a founder (1847) and lecturer of the Maryland Medical Institute.

4. "I remarked that it was not very unusual at Washington for a lady to take the arm of a gentleman, who was neither her husband, her father, nor her brother. This remarkable relaxation of American decorum has been probably introduced by the foreign legations" (Frances Trollope, *Domestic Manners of the Americans*, chap. 20).

talking to us for five minutes—she had never seen us before—she asked if we would call to-morrow and she'd take us to see aforesaid uncle's collection. We accepted of course—of course imagining that Mrs. G[eorge] would go with us as chaperone. What was our surprize to find that this had never entered the young lady's head, and Mrs. G. had herself to ask for an invitation.

The Uni. Church is a handsome Grecian building with a fine dome.[5] Dr. Burnap is much what Dr. Furness said he was, with good-nature and bad delivery:—many of his remarks are shrewd. His great horror is of the Transcendentalists, with an almost equal abhorrence at the doings of the abolitionists.

Of Emerson he seems to have no very exalted opinion, and more than insinuates he is mad. He says Emerson never thinks in *lines* but in *dots*, he is without logical reasoning power,—and his sect is *not* increasing. Margaret Fuller was quite without religion, he said, —and as for Theodore Parker he is *"disgusting."*[6]

Burnap told a good story of how T. P[arker] called on Carlyle in London with a letter from Emerson, and found Carlyle blacking his boots. He talked on all subjects, but on all subjects did the cynic Prophet "snub" him. One card remained—emancipation!—here Carlyle *must* agree with him, must sympathize with him!— "Sweep the niggers into the sea!—into the sea with them!" was the sympathy he found![7]

5. The Unitarian Church at Charles and Franklin streets was designed by Maximilian Godefroy (1818).

6. Theodore Parker (1810-60), celebrated preacher and minister of the 28th Congregational Society in Boston, excluded from orthodox Unitarian pulpits because of his Transcendental views.

7. Thomas Carlyle (1795-1881), on the contrary, wrote to Emerson (October 31, 1843) after this meeting: "Parker is a most hardy, compact, clever little fellow, full of decisive utterance, with humour and good-humour, whom I like much" (*The Correspondence of Emerson and Carlyle*, ed. Joseph Slater [New York and London, 1964], p. 350).

127

When Miss Martineau was in America, she stayed with Dr. Burnap—her conceit was intolerable—arguing with him on philosophical necessity (in which she firmly believed) she ended by asserting that everyone would agree with her "*who had brains in his head.*"[8]

As long as you admired her, she was most amiable, you were discriminating and excellent—woe to you should she suspect that you did imagine that the world might contain a genius equally profound—you were ignorant and unworthy.

Her jealousy was disgusting—with Mrs. Burnap (and others) she constantly abused Miss Edgeworth[9] whom she accused of being a "tuft hunter," and was always aiming some poisoned shaft at <her?>.

Mrs. Burnap assured her that her books were great favourites of hers and in America generally, but in one case (at the end of Belinda) she did feel angry with Miss E. for making a black man marry a white woman, and said she nearly threw the book across the room in disgust.

This incident Miss Martineau relates, saying that Miss E. is unpopular all through the States, and generously throwing the Aegis of her protection before her.[10]

Oh! Harriet Martineau!

8. Harriet Martineau (1802–76), Unitarian writer and a keen abolitionist, visited America 1834–36. Burnap was not her intellectual match.

9. Maria Edgeworth (1767–1849), novelist, whose *Belinda* appeared in 1801.

10. "It was in Baltimore that I heard Miss Edgeworth denounced as a woman of no intelligence or delicacy, whose works could never be cared for again, because, in Belinda, poor Juba was married, at length, to an English farmer's daughter! The incident is so subordinate that I had entirely forgotten it; but a clergyman's lady threw the volume to the opposite corner of the floor when she came to the page. As I have said elsewhere, Miss Edgeworth is worshipped throughout the United States; but it is in spite of this terrible passage, this clause of a sentence in Belinda, which nobody in America can tolerate, while no one elsewhere ever, I should think, dreamed of finding fault with it" (H. Martineau, *Retrospect of Western Travel* [London, 1838], 1:141).

Tuesday (before Dinner), [June 1].

We have now been some four days in a slave country, and we haven't been shocked once. The "niggers" look comfortable and happy—they are spoken to kindly, are treated well, and may be seen walking merrily along with "lubly yaller gals," Lucy Longs and Mary Blanes, or driving them about in carriages with sometimes a white driver.

The slaves in Baltimore are on the decline, and we hear that in 20 years probably (Dr. Stewart) there will be no slaves in Maryland. Here slavery is certainly mild enough. Many of the blacks are well educated, and we went on Sunday to a black Methodist Church, where we found a large congregation, rows of blubber lips and a superior coloured gentleman to hold forth to and edify congregation of blubber lips aforesaid.

He really preached well on the "Lord's House," though some of his expressions were droll, and his pronunciation more so. "How do you feel to-night, Sinner?" was one of his oddest remarks. His illustrations were curious—a story amused us about a gentleman and an Indian who were talking of getting to Heaven, when the Indian said he had the best chance. The gentleman must throw off his houses, and horses, give up his pomps and vanities, the world and the flesh —while "I", said the Indian, "need only throw away my old blanket, and here it goes."

After the sermon there was a collection for defraying the expenses of the Church. $51.22 had been collected in the morning, and they now got several more dollars from charitable and pious darkies, egged on by the eloquence of a speaker who assured them that "to give to the Lord was to lend to the poor," and that for every dollar they gave they would be at once repaid, as he once was by picking one up from the ground or otherwise. The whole Service was good, and a fair specimen

129

of the more intelligent negroes—in the South, alas! they are anything but intelligent, for they may not be educated,—such an education as would but show them in its true colours their degradation and misery, without giving them freedom would but take away their light-heartedness and make them unhappy;—it would be indeed cruel, the kindly Dr. Stewart, who himself owns 150 slaves, assured me; and where slaves *are unhappy from their slavery*, every good man, he says, should and would release them. Otherwise in "blissful ignorance"—never working till 10, or after 50 years of age, with one-third of each day at his own disposal, the negro slave often leads so pleasant a life as to refuse liberty were it offered to him. Few masters ever ill-treat their slaves,—they would lose caste if they did, and many instances are told of slaves who refused to leave their masters and become free.

But even were they free they would hardly gain much advantage from their position:—It may be impossible to abolish slavery at present, it is certainly not impossible to treat the free black with some consideration, and respect if his mental attainments render him worthy of it.

What was my surprize on expressing disgust to Mr. George on the result of the Philadelphian Episcopal Convention to find he approved of it, and justified such approval by asking how I should like servants, for instance, placed on an equal footing with oneself. To my objection that they were *not* servants, he opposed the home thrust—the stock one of the South set—How would you like a black man to be intimate with your family and marry your sister? To this I answered that physical causes were an objection to cousins marrying, but that I should certainly not exclude my male cousin from the house lest my sister should marry him:—moreover, one can hardly imagine English ladies

130

having so peculiar a taste; if they had they'd better be off to Liberia at once. At Boston the free black is allowed to vote by law, and *one* was elected to the State Legislature, but custom, and Society would not allow him to sit, and he resigned.[11] Spite of the pseudo-liberality of the American citizens, the black is insulted there in a way unknown in the South.

Wednesday Afternoon, [June 2].

I will at once finish the remainder of the digested slavery "cram" I have acquired, and for the present get rid of the subject.

A coloured freeman may own an estate, and has been known to possess slaves—but this is rare—indeed except in two instances which Dr. Stewart mentioned where a white father had left his personal property to his illegitimate Mulatto children—I never heard, or could hear of a case;—always excepting the most common one in which a free man *buys* his own wife and children, and even then he generally sets them free, otherwise strange anomalies would occur—the son would of course inherit his father's property, and have his own mother as slave, being himself a slave all the time!

In but few of the States are the Free Blacks allowed to vote, and among the many advantages which would ensue from the abolition of slavery in Maryland would be that by a substitution of white labour the political importance of that State would be greatly increased, for as the representatives are chosen by universal (white) suffrage, the State would then return

11. Not until 1866 did Massachusetts become the first state to have blacks sit in its legislature.

131

13 or 14 members instead of 6. Another advantage would be the social one of raising up an intermediate class between owners and tillers of land, which cannot exist when there are only the Great Slave owner and the poor slave. Such an intermediate class of tenant farmers would facilitate the transfer of property and be productive of much benefit.

The only difficulty is in the doubt whether the white man can become sufficiently acclimatised to stand the heat. Dr. Stewart thinks he may, at least in the cotton and tobacco plantations:—in the rice swamps even the white man (though this is doubtful) might be induced to bear the weather, and he is at least not so subject to pleurisy and the like as the negro.

Thursday Morning, [*June* 3].

The days pass along so pleasantly and quietly—we pay calls, and shop (at "Stores"). To be sure the weather is hot, about 92 in the shade, and we are all lazy together,—still we enjoy ourselves extremely and I endorse Sarah's[12] opinion of my host and hostess with all my heart. Some of the houses are beautiful—such pictures as many possess I have rarely seen in England, certainly never in America.

One morning we see the Catholic Cathedral which has also fine paintings,[13] another time we go up to the top of the Washington Monument whence is a glorious view of the city, and to-day we have been with Mrs. George to see the Athenaeum and Mercantile Library,

12. HAB's oldest sister, Sarah Elizabeth Mesnard Bright (1832-1909).

13. The first Roman Catholic cathedral in the U.S., designed by Benjamin Latrobe (1821), contained two paintings: a Descent from the Cross by Pierre Guerin, and Baron Charles de Steuben's picture of Louis IX burying his soldiers at Tunis.

where we found English Reviews and American papers.

Baltimore is famous for beauty—an adorable Miss Draper—an angelic (a French angel) "Ella Chapman" (N.B. Don't know whether she's Miss or Mrs.), and a much to be commended Miss Briène, under whose sweet patronage, after one day's intimacy, we went to call on the aforesaid "Ella." (Strange are the customs of Baltimore.) You may call on young ladies, walk with young ladies, drive with young ladies, and no one dreams of chaperons, but—offer a young lady your arm and all the old maids in Baltimore say you're engaged, and the poor young lady, if not engaged, is a flirt and shocks the morality of the strict and proper in the simple unsophisticated town.

Monday Morning, [June 7].

To-day we leave Baltimore. We have done a good deal since I last wrote, but when I'm in the house, I've so much talking to do, that my poor journal has to go to the wall.[14] The Green Mount Cemetery is

14. One event HAB omitted from his diary (but described elsewhere) was a Democratic mass meeting that he witnessed in Monument Square: "A platform was covered with branches of green hickory—an emblem of the party—and here stood many of the leading delegates and politicians of the Democrats. The square was filled with people, who were listening attentively, and cheering slightly the sentiments of the various speakers. 'That is good,—good, sir,' was an expression, Indian like in its laconic approbation, that one heard most frequently from the satisfied 'sovereigns.' Among the speakers was a young fellow from the West, not unlike the pictures of Shelley. On stepping to the front of the platform, he pulled off his neckhandkerchief and threw back his coat—'We from the far West must have clear throats before we speak,'—and then he began, and I must own I never heard such grand declamatory eloquence before; were the affectation of Democratic vulgarity which prompted him throughout once cast away, the beauty of his language, the sweetness of his accent, the variety of his modulated tones would make this young politician of. Indiana an orator of no mean pretensions" ("The Presidential Elec-

Gleason's Pictorial Drawing-Room Companion, May 8, 1852

very pretty though inferior in beauty to that at Laurel Hill, Philadelphia. We saw there the monument mentioned in "Across the Atlantic" on a living man—a Mr. Watchman; the lines were:—

> What need the pen rehearse
> A life well spent;
> A man's good deeds are
> His best monument.[15]

Under Mr. Watchman's own epitaph is one to his wife who *is* dead. In the height of his distress the poor widower forgets to be grammatical. What has

tion for America," letter written from St. Louis and signed "A Cambridge Man in the West," *Fraser's Magazine* [September, 1852], p. 349).

15. John Delaware Lewis, a contemporary of Bright's at Trinity College, Cambridge, describes this monument in *Across the Atlantic* (London, 1851) and regrets that he had no pencil to copy down the inscription. Mr. Watchman was still "hale and hearty, living and carrying on business," but at his death, Lewis says, "there will be nothing to do but to pop him in" (pp. 156–57).

Lindley Murray[16] to do with the wailings of the bereaved?

> *Like* a bud nipped from the tree,
> So death has parted you and me.

Query: was Death ever called bud-like before?

Among our constant visitors at the Georges has been a Colonel Bliss who has, mixed up with a good deal of rubbish, given us some curious information. The best cure for a snake bite, he says, is Spirits of Hartshorn, while a grass called "Dragon's tongue" is a remedy against the fang of the rattlesnake. It always grows where the snake is found—the bane and the antidote.

Among the women of N. Carolina and Virginia (*not* the Georges say, of the highest rank) the chewing of snuff is as common as it is deleterious. [This was confirmed by Mr. Peyton at Lewisburg—the landlady of the chief hotel at Winchester—one of the greatest people in the town—he saw do it, and in an advertisement of a young lady's school at Lewisburg "No snuff-taking allowed" appeared, or words to the same effect.][17] Some too eat a peculiar clay.

Dr. Plummer of the Presbyterian Church has also called on us.[18] He told me he has seen more suffering among the free blacks of Philadelphia in two hours than among the Southern slaves in 20 years. He kindly gave us some letters to Virginia. He is highly esteemed and is an eloquent preacher (as we heard yesterday) of the M'Neil school.[19] I cannot say I

16. Lindley Murray (1745–1826), "father of English grammar."

17. This sentence must have been added later (cf. p. 194).

18. William Swan Plumer (1802–80), pastor (since 1847) of the Franklin Street Presbyterian Church.

19. Hugh McNeile (1795–1879), an eloquent evangelical preacher at Liverpool, and canon of Chester Cathedral.

quite liked his pulpit manner, and Burder thought he looked drunk, especially when he turned in the middle of his sermon and spat on the floor!

An English fellow, about our age, Anderdon, quite a nice fellow he turned out, has been here.[20] We are to meet him at Washington and we must go together to the Springs, &c., and on to Cincinnati, where he will leave us for Lake Erie.

On Friday Burder and myself went off to Harrisburg on the Susquehanna, and returned on Saturday. It is 5 or 6 hours from Baltimore, and the drive is really beautiful. Harrisburg is the capital of Pennsylvania, and has about 8000 inhabitants. The Inn, I believe the best one, we went to is Harris Hotel. The Susquehanna reminds me of the scenery round Windermere, very pretty and highly wooded. The Black Locust or False Acacia, the wild Cherry and other trees border the river, and cluster on the little islands.[21] A strange red-winged black bird (or *Starling* as Anderdon says it's *improperly* named) flew past us as we drove along. Two drives we took, one along the river and back by the canal,—the other into the woods and hills on the bank that faces the House. Here I found the yellow oxalis and other uncommon flowers. We got a boat too on the river, but it leaked, and the current was strong and we were sulky, so that it was rather a failure our rowing. The boat belonged to a gardener-looking man who pocketed the half dollar we offered for the use of the boat and gave us a note to his brother at St. Louis, "a young gentleman like you"; brother was to take us into prairies, &c. our hospitable boatman-gardener friend with the sweet name of "Symeon Oyster" told us.

20. John Edmund Anderdon (b. 1830), educated at Balliol College, Oxford.

21. See Bright's poem "The Susquehanna River" (p. 451).

136

We enjoyed our little "outing" amazingly, and on our return found Baltimore calming down from its democratic excitement, having elected an unknown man Pierce, after 49 ballots, as its presidential Candidate.[22] The Whigs have their turn now.

In the Railway Car with us were several of the Pennsylvanian Country people—Germans—who talked all the time in that language to each other. There are many of them in this State.

Before I close my Baltimorean journal, I'll note down sundry things which have struck me or I've heard since I've been here:—

A child's funeral occurred next door yesterday; the day was odd—Sunday—the hour was odd—5 o'clock in the afternoon, and the arrangements seemed to me oddest of all. People were asked to attend who were no relation or had any claim to be there. The Georges went and some 30 others we saw going into the house, just as they were without any additional black crape or bombazine. At last every one had arrived;—a white hearse with white horses and a black driver came to the door, and a considerable number of carriages. Little children stood at the door and watched. We drew our chairs closer to the window and watched too! At last the Minister, Dr. Burnap, appeared and stepped into a carriage and drove off; then came the little coffin borne by some 4 or 5 men, who placed it in the hearse and then got themselves into a second carriage and drove off, followed by the hearse. Then came some 3 or 4 carriages for the mourners, and then another and another for the general company, till at last the procession started with 2 carriages in front and *12* behind, besides a number of gentlemen who walked by their side to the cemetery.

22. The surprise nomination of Franklin Pierce (1804-69), later fourteenth president, resulted from a split Democratic party.

Dr. Burnap, Mrs. George told us, delivered an address at the house and another at the grave, spoiling the last by quoting poetry. They were very fond of funereal poetry here—as fond as Mrs. Canning I met at the Custs[23] was of "Dirges." I insert here some notices of Deaths from newspapers curious for this and other peculiarities. There were no plumes or other adornments on the carriages we saw.

DIED.

On the 2d instant, JOHANAH COUGHLAN, aged 60 years, a native of the Parish of Doneraile, County Cork, Ireland.

Her friends are requested to attend her funeral on this (Thursday) afternoon, at three o'clock, from her late residence, Canal street, near Wilk street.

On the 2d instant, of consumption, MARTHA McELROY, in the 23d year of her age.

> Why should our tears in sorrow flow
>   When God recalls his own,
> And bids them leave a world of woe
>   For an immortal crown?
>
> Her toils are past, her work is done,
>   And she is fully blest;
> She has fought the fight, the victory won,
>   And entered into rest.
>
> Farewell, dear Martha, thou hast left us,
>   We thy loss most deeply feel;
> But 'tis God that hath bereft us,
>   He can all our sorrows heal.

Her friends and acquaintance are requested to attend her funeral, on to-morrow (Friday) afternoon, at three o'clock, from No. 145 Pierce street.

23. Reginald John Cust was a Cambridge friend of Bright's.

On the 1st inst., THOMAS, aged 3 years, 2 months and 24 days, second child of Thomas and Caroline Conner. (Frederick papers please copy.)

The servants in America are very odd—chiefly blacks, they hate and fear each other, and one reason the free Blacks won't go to Liberia as willingly as one might expect is that they are afraid of their own colour, and have a constant dread of being *poisoned* in some fit of vindictive rage. They are generally, to all appearance at least, most civil to each other, calling each other "lady" and "gentleman." Fancy two coloured women coming to Mrs. George who wanted a cook, and on her turning to one and asking her something about it, the woman coolly saying, "It's this *lady*, Madam, who wishes to be cook."

A Concert at Harrisburg.

I had very nearly forgotten to mention:—A Madame Krollman,[24] who sang nicely and was really pretty except a gap where some truant tooth had lost its place; a Mr. or Herr Krollman who was decidedly plain, but fiddled cleverly, and a M. Wolowski who did the piano part of the business were the performers. It went off very fairly—about 100 people at half-a-dollar sat and listened to the "Grand Musical Feat Festival," and Judge Francis Wolowski the Manager no doubt turned an honest penny by the concert. The last scene was enthusiastic:—a salute to France, when the lady holds a Tricolour Banner, a Madame La Borde gave her.

Yesterday we took a long walk together to a lovely spot where the tulip trees are magnificent. To-day

24. Mme Krollman (otherwise Mary Shaw) began her stage career as a child in New York City.

Burder stayed in, and our hostess and myself went shopping and paying calls. Dr. Stewart was the only person we saw; he was most civil. The shops were all good, the people only tolerably civil.

I feel quite sad at cutting adrift from such a pleasant house as we have found here. The Georges have been kindness itself, and we both look forward to meeting them at Newport in the Autumn!

5

WASHINGTON

Nat[ional] Hotel, Washington.[1] *Tuesday Night,*
[June 8].

We arrived here last night after a journey of 1½
hours from Baltimore—a journey only marked by our
seeing fireflies for the first time flitting over the rail
side fields, or darting in and out of the hedges, bright
as sparks from blacksmith's anvil, and numerous as
gnats in the woods of our England. Then Burder (just
like him!) nearly lost his carpet-bag, but finally were
glad to find ourselves in very fair rooms (which we
had telegraphed for at the cost of 10 cents), in a very
dirty and astor-like hue.

We found Anderdon here, and after agreeing to meet
at breakfast, did the four preliminary flights of stairs
and went to bed.

1. Built in 1827, on the corner of Pennsylvania Avenue and Sixth
Street. Frederika Bremer described it in 1850 as "a kind of hot oven
full of senators and representatives, of traveling gentlemen and ladies"
(*The Homes of the New World*, trans. Mary Howitt [New York, 1854],
1:447).

To-day we called and left various cards—the Riggs[2] and Corcoran,[3] on Sumner,[4] on Pierce (Senator for Maryland),[5] on Curtis[6] (a friend of Webster's and Mr. George's, as was Pierce also) and on Synge at the British Legation.[7] Horace Mann and Matheson were not in town, and Pennell[8] had been in England nearly a year!

The only persons we found in were Messrs. Corcoran and G. Riggs; they were both civil and we dine with Corcoran on Thursday:—our deepest obligation to him is however, for his having introduced us to the President. It was a day when Fillmore receives strangers from 12 to 2, and about the latter hour we drove up with Mr. Corcoran to the "White House,"—a handsome Grecian house with nice shrubberies, &c. round it is the "White House." There was no sentinel at the gate, no porter at the door, no footman in the hall. We walked in just as we were through a fine hall and a good room into a plain and scantily-furnished, though handsome, drawing-room, where stood the President talking to several gentlemen, while on chairs all together sat the President's wife, and the President's daughter, and the President's sister, with other august members of the President's family. Mr. Corcoran introduced us. Fillmore shook us each by the hand, was

2. George Washington Riggs (1813–81), Corcoran's banking partner.

3. William Wilson Corcoran (1798–1888), wealthy banker and philanthropist, founder of the Corcoran Art Gallery.

4. Charles Sumner (1811–74), U.S. senator from Massachusetts and noted abolitionist.

5. James Alfred Pearce (1805–62), lawyer and U.S. senator from Maryland.

6. George Ticknor Curtis (1812–94), distinguished lawyer and United States commissioner.

7. William Webb Follett Synge (1826–91), diplomat and author, attached to the British legation in Washington, 1851–53; a friend of many literary men.

8. John Croker Pennell (1825–65), British diplomat attached to the Washington legation, 1849–51.

142

graciously pleased to say he was glad to see us, and graciously pleased to ask how long we had been in the country, and then desired Corcoran to introduce us to the ladies. We were then trotted off in front of the Woman circle. The President's ladies bowed and we bowed—no one spoke, and we were glad to find ourselves at an end of the ceremony, and close to a Mr. Campbell, an American gentleman, who is to marry Miss Fillmore, on dit.[9] She, Miss F., is fat and plain. Mrs. Fillmore is ordinary, and the President himself, with a large dignified appearance and a good-natured look, is the best of the family as far as externals go.[10] Our observation however was short, for after a little conversation with Campbell, Corcoran thought it time for us to be off, so we bowed round the circle again, and vanished, taking a peep as we passed of a magnificent reception <room> used on State occasions. The unfurnished look is partly owing to the weather, and partly to the fact that the "White House," though a splendid *dwelling* can be but little more of a *home* than the Mansion House to our own Lord Mayors!

The President can be approached by any one on "reception" days, and had we liked we might have introduced each other without breach of etiquette. No one however, is expected to stay more than some 5 minutes, which is all the time that can be allowed one person. The whole appearance of the reception reminded me a little of one of Whewell's "Teas and stand ups."[11] When we were there only some 10 people besides the family were in the room!

9.   Fillmore's only daughter, Mary Abigail (1832–54), died unmarried.

10.   In his letter to *Fraser's Magazine* about the American election, Bright describes Fillmore: "A good natured presentable (no small praise in this country!) dignified personage, is President Fillmore; a 'model president,' his friends call him, and his enemies concede that he treats everybody with suavity and courtesy, and 'is proud to make your acquantance,' with an air of as much sincerity as a president need have."

11.   William Whewell (1794–1866), master of Trinity College, Cam-

We went afterwards to the Capitol. It's a very hand-some Grecian building, for description of which see Guide Book.

The Senate was sitting with closed doors, so we went to the House of Representatives. Each representative has his desk, with pens, ink, paper, books and news-papers upon it, and by the side of each desk stands the representative's "spittoon." A private desk and a private spittoon with some $8 a day and a prefix "Hon."—happy man is a member of the American Con-gress! The House of Representatives I own disappoint-ed me, there was but little spitting and no whist-ling![12] Many of the Representatives are gentlemanly and one at least—the Member for California—a dis-tinguished-looking man.[13] We heard nothing of interest, and soon adjourned to the National and thence to see Lola Montez act *herself* at the theatre.[14]

The house was very empty for so interesting a piece —the Parquette pretty full, the boxes only about a third occupied. Lola is still beautiful, her eyes are black as ever, and she is still animated and piquante. Au contraire her voice is shrill, except when in the low notes she reminds one of the affectations of Celeste by her faint foreign tone. What a temper she has is ob-

bridge, and professor of moral philosophy. Cf. Leslie Stephen's remark in the DNB: "Though he [Whewell] was anxious to be hospitable, his sense of the dignity of his position led to a formality which made the drawing-room of the lodge anything but a place of easy sociability."

12. Nearly all English visitors commented on the prevalent Ameri-can habit of spitting; Dickens in *American Notes* remarks on the appalling condition of the Senate floor and on the number of "honourable mem-bers with swelled faces."

13. Both the representatives from California—Joseph W. McCorkle and Edward C. Marshall—spoke at some length during this session, on Cali-fornia affairs.

14. Lola Montez (1818–61), adventuress and dancer, made a great hit in a sketch of her own life, *Lola Montez in Bavaria*. As the official mistress of Ludwig I, she virtually ruled the country until his abdication in 1848.

Gleason's Pictorial Drawing-Room Companion, March 13, 1852

"We got on the 'floor of the house' and
saw everything and everbody admirably."

vious from her acting, the gusto with which she tears
to pieces a bouquet in the first Act and the way she
tossed away a piece of paper she held when just behind the scenes, and *not* acting, made her viciousness
very apparent. Her acting however *was* hardly acting
—it was nature itself, and no doubt she really did be-
have pretty much as the acts she did. Of course allow-
ance for the rosy tint in which all her actions appear
must be made, still the whole thing is interesting and
as honest as can be expected. I forgot to mention
that Crampton[15] asked us to dinner, which we had to
decline.

15. John Fiennes Twisleton Crampton (1805–86), minister with the
British legation. He was recalled in 1856 when he offended the American government by recruiting soldiers for the Crimean War. At this time
he was a bachelor with a large house in Georgetown.

145

Before Dinner, Wednesday, [June 9].

To-day at eleven we called on Webster.[16] I sent up my card with Burder's name on it, and Kenyon's letter and waited outside. A negro woman with a turban-like cap desired us to come in. We were shown into a prettily-furnished room, with a fine picture of its owner over the mantlepiece, some old carved wood chairs and books upon the tables—among them were one by Tupper and a "Day at Tivoli," by J. Kenyon himself.

At last in came Webster; he was glad to see a friend of "that agreeable gentleman John Kenyon Esqre. so full of information," and sitting down opened and read the letter, snorting hard over it all the time. We sat and looked at the mighty "Great Westerner!" he is now old and shaky, a mere "wreck," still I can never believe that his personal appearance could have been at first sight as striking as I had been led to imagine; he is hardly tall enough for that,—but yet as you look upon him more closely and see that heavy ponderous brow, and those black cavernous eyes, you believe at once in his Majesty—"A king among men." But the letter and the snorting were over. He told me he had written to Kenyon himself last week a letter of introduction. He inquired our route and asked us to come to his house this evening at eight, and see Mrs. Webster, hinting also his wish we should dine on Friday with him.

From his house we went to the Legation. We were pleased with Synge and Loch[17] (an Englishman who

16. Daniel Webster (1782–1852), at this time secretary of state. Catharine Maria Sedgwick later wrote to HAB: "You were indeed fortunate in catching some of the last gleams of Webster's life" (quoted in HAB's review of Miss Sedgwick's *Life and Letters* in the *Athenaeum*, July 20, 1872, p. 74).

17. John Charles Loch (1825–1902), educated at Eton and Trinity College, Cambridge, later settled in America and worked for Cunard.

was there, and who knows the Denmans, &c.). Crampton (Envoy Extraordinary and Minister Plenipotentiary are his titles) was there also and again pressed us to dine this evening at six.

Synge and Loch then took us (Anderdon joined us at the National) to the Senate. Through our attaché friend's good offices we got on the "floor of the house" and saw everything and everybody admirably. King (the new Democratic Vice-President Candidate) was in the Chair.[18] Cass was there with spectacles and a brown wig;[19] Stockton, Navy Secretary, spoke on National Defences, but only a few words.[20] Charles Sumner was there and made us a great many speeches about being a bachelor and having nothing to offer us, but being anxious for "further conversation" he spoke much of Kenyon, nothing of Russell Carpenter.[21]

We again explored the House of Representatives, and then adjourned to a luncheon of devilled crab and sherry-cobbler.—Thence to the Patent Office, a sort of Museum Place where are to be seen Franklin's walking stick, Washington's coat, Atahualpa's hat, a shred of Pizarro's flag, the "effects of Mr. Smithson," founder of Smithsonian Institute,[22]—the shawls &c., given to various Presidents which the Constitution won't let

He joins Bright and Burder in Cincinnati and travels with them as far as Buffalo.

18. William Rufus Devane King (1786-1853), senator from Alabama and formerly minister to France.

19. Lewis Cass (1782-1866), senator from Michigan, formerly secretary of war and minister to France.

20. Robert Field Stockton (1795-1866), senator from New Jersey, was not navy secretary but had a distinguished naval career. He spoke in favor of completing the building of a war steamer.

21. Russell Lant Carpenter (b. 1816), a Unitarian clergyman like his more famous father, Lant Carpenter.

22. James Smithson (1765-1829), English scientist, left his entire fortune to the United States government "for the increase and diffusion of knowledge." The Smithsonian Institution was inaugurated in 1846.

them keep, and other equally interesting and valuable relics. We then left our kind cicerones and returned home to write and dress for dinner.

Synge is quite a nice fellow, and Loch a good specimen of a Cambridge man. How different in style from the Oxonian Anderdon! Every man sees through spectacles of his own colouring.

Synge told me that when he was at Boston a lady asked him whether in Poetry he preferred "the aesthetical or the esoteric." With great presence of mind he replied "he was not prepared to give a categorical answer. He thought it depended on the apophthematical postulates!" The transcendental lady said no more!

To Washington itself I'll devote one page. If asked for a description of it in short I should say:—"it's a huge suburb."[23] You never feel you're in the "town," a long wide street lined with Ailanthus[24] and tulip trees and with houses of every shape, size and colour on each side. Now a fine residence, then a cottage, now an open space, then a shop and so on. Such is the general character of Washington. The Pennsylvanian Avenue is the finest, the houses are more continual, and the Capitol seen at the end of the Ailanthus Avenue has a noble and imposing effect! Many of the public buildings are certainly magnificent.

23. Washington, then a rather scruffy southern town, was to Harriet Martineau "a grand mistake"; to Dickens "the City of Magnificent Intentions"; to Emmeline Stuart-Wortley "a vast plantation with the houses kept far apart."

24. In a paper I saw at the Blue Sulphur there was a petition mentioned as having been presented to the Senate for the "putting down" the Ailanthus as a *nuisance* in the city of Washington. It has I believe an offensive smell. I'll back the Jamestown weed to beat it in this particular. [H.A.B.] (This note must have been added later.)

Wednesday Night, [June 9].

A memorable evening has this been—one to be thought upon hereafter. We dined at Crampton's— Anderdon, Loch, Synge, a Martin (son of *the* painter)[25] and ourselves. It was a pleasant party—champagne *at* dinner and cognac *after*,—the Minister affable and good-natured, and everything very agreeable. Synge told us how he had been cloroformed at Dublin and found himself with only a wide open[26] and pair of socks in a cellar when he woke. Crampton told me that the wires between Whig and Democrat were quite worn out, and he wondered they had no new divisions.

The dinner over, Synge with Anderdon as protégée, Burder and myself went to Webster's.

When we entered *he* was not in the room, but came in afterwards. We talked much to Madame, and Synge bewailed in a most diplomatic way the manner in which *one* with a European reputation was unable to be chosen President at once, or perhaps at all.[27] Mrs. Webster responded in a heart-felt tone. She talked to me of Mr. Kenyon, and his kindness, and her gratitude,[28]—she told me how she enjoyed England, and in short gossipped "very prettily," and much like any one else.

At last on the departure of some unknown gentle-

25. John Martin (1789-1854), English historical and landscape painter. His eldest son, Charles (1820-1906), who was in America at this time, became a well-known portrait painter.

26. I.e., a "wide awake"?, a low-crowned, soft felt hat.

27. Webster's perennial presidential aspirations were shortly to be crushed again, when the Whigs nominated Winfield Scott (1786–1866) in his stead.

28. One of the Websters' first social engagements, on arriving in London in 1839, was a breakfast at Kenyon's where they met Wordsworth, Samuel Rogers, Hartley Coleridge, and Monckton Milnes.

man Webster came and took her place—stiff and cold, "lymphatic" (Synge's word) and tired, the old man shewed great good-nature in talking at all to two young Britishers, nameless, rankless, like ourselves. He looked sadly worn and talked slowly and seemingly with difficulty and fatigue. He spoke of the stranger-races crowding to America, and how "the world was averaging itself, the over-peopled Europe flocking to under-peopled America." He spoke of the Senate and how it has deteriorated thanks to the increased number of delegates from new States. He told us how 12 years ago he predicted the superiority of the Americans in agricultural implements over the English, and how the Exhibition had proved it;—he talked of Pennsylvania and New York as emphatically the Agricultural States and believed we should enjoy Boston.

But it wasn't his conversation, for after all we gained but little, he seemed so sadly tired and so low,—it was (as Burder said) the sitting there that was so charming.—The feeling, there I am sitting close by the greatest man in the world perhaps, close by, talking to him, shaking hands with him, asking him questions, —so near I could pull his nose, take his wind or anything! It's very curious! And this is Webster, and this is Henry Bright, and, till you'd noticed the superb forehead of the former, you'd never guess what a long, long distance there was between them as they sit there talking together, till Webster gets quite sleepy and we rise to go.

A Miss Page[29] is staying with them; she flirts with Anderdon chiefly!

After this we strolled and heard a bit of Democratic Speechifying at the "Mass Meeting." The great men

29. Probably Hariette W. Paige, Webster's niece (by his first wife).

150

had finished, but a Colonel Wight of Pennsylvania was haranguing effectively and well.

We did not stay very long, soon feeling tired of the noise of the tongues and smoke of a Democratic bonfire,—a restorative Cobbler, a parting with Synge, and then to journal and bed, having first ascertained that a report of Henry Clay's death at the National is unfounded, if true it were indeed, as Crampton said "a sad memento more" for Webster (now 73).[30]

Thursday, June 10.

At half-past eight we three left for Mount Vernon. The steamer started at nine, and we lounged about the wooden quay and gazed on the Potomac's muddy green waters, till all being at last ready we started. But pride may have a fall; steamers may receive a check, and with hardly 20 yards between us and the land we struck! Never tell me again the story of the Kentucky steamer that could sail on *dewy grass*. I don't believe a word of it—the Thomas Collyer struck in water where you could hardly see the bottom, thanks partly to consistency of the water, but anyhow it struck.[31]

Off again at last she steamed us along down a river

30. Clay died on June 29; Webster's death followed on October 24. HAB wrote to Longfellow in November, 1852: "I need hardly say how shocked I was to hear of the death of Mr. Webster,—it seems such a short time since we were at Washington, and he was kindness itself to us,—*then* too full of hope of being—(just about this time too,)—chosen President of your great Nation" (undated letter in the Harvard College Library).

31. The *Thomas Collyer* was purchased in 1860 by the Mount Vernon Ladies' Association of the Union, to carry visitors from Washington to Mount Vernon.

a mile broad to *Alexandria*—Not the associations of Alexandria the Great hang round this place, yet it is sometimes visited, for here Washington went to Church![32] On again now to Fort Washington—high walls, cannon balls in piles, reminding one of schoolboy problems,—and sentinels are common to all such places. The view is Fort Washington's own, and very beautiful it is, wooded knolls, winding river, &c.

Then to Mount Vernon—at last! We all disembark—people, *things* in straw hats, and red neckties, pick flowers, or rush up to the tombs to explore.

We were fortunate; Synge had given us a letter to Mr. Washington (J. A. W.) whom he slightly knew, and we were summoned into the presence of his Great Great Uncle's Great Great Nephew.[33] The Great Great Nephew is very hospitable, but badly off. As Synge remarked, he reminds one of the "Last Heir of Ravenswood."[34] A black woman servant, rooms with the paint cracking off, and gardens untrimmed look poverty stricken, as also the way he asked us to take *spirits* with him:—a glass of whiskey (ripe whiskey) and water we did not refuse, and then he shewed us the curiosities of the place, many of which are not generally shewn. Mr. Washington is evidently very proud of everything which was the General's. He shewed us the General's "Self-interpreting Bible,"[35] and "Adam's Astronomy,"[36] with the great man's autograph in

32. Washington owned a pew in Christ Church, Alexandria (built 1773), which he occupied regularly from 1785 until his death.

33. John Augustine Washington (1821-61) lived here until 1860, when the building was taken over by the Mount Vernon Ladies' Association.

34. In Scott's novel *The Bride of Lammermoor.*

35. *The Self-interpreting Bible . . . To which are annexed marginal references,* ed. Reverend John Brown (1792). This Bible remained in the family when the bulk of Washington's library was acquired by the Boston Athenaeum.

36. George Adams, *Essays on the Globes* (1789), bought by Washington on February 10, 1790; probably sold in 1876.

them. A book on "the Late War," by Lord Erskine[37] with an autograph letter on the title page in which he, Erskine, says he has associated with "Many exalted men, but for Washington alone he felt an *awful reverence*," and hopes "the evening of his life" may be serene. Then there is in the hall the key of the Bastille, and a picture of its capture, sent by La Fayette, a portrait of Louis XVI. sent by himself; an original bust of Washington's[38] and other family relics. A fine room with a magnificent marble chimney-piece we also saw, though it is not generally shewn, as a man had broken off one of the Cupid's arms with which it was adorned.[39]

In the garden we saw a magnolia the General had ordered to be planted—a splendid tree with no branch low enough to pluck a leaf from; however I found one on the ground!

Washington's tomb we also saw. It rests in a sort of Mausoleum, and is very plain with only his name and shield upon it—stars and stripes, though not arranged as in the national banner.

Then there is a curious little picture of the General elaborately framed. It is broken off some old clay mug, and is the best likeness extant. Behind it is a clever and beautiful anonymous inscription to the great man, which Mr. Washington read to us with "une larme dans sa voix."[40]

37. Thomas Erskine, *A View of the Causes and Consequences of the Present War with France* (1797), now at the Boston Athenaeum.

38. Modeled in clay from life by Jean Antoine Houdon, celebrated French sculptor, in 1785. This bust, the key to the Bastille, and the portrait of Louis XVI are still at Mount Vernon. The picture of the Bastille was sold at auction in 1891.

39. This Italian marble chimney-piece, with three sculptured panels showing agricultural scenes, was presented to Washington in 1785 by Samuel Vaughan of London.

40. The so-called Pitcher Portrait, the eulogy on the back written by an unknown Englishman, was sent to Judge Bushrod Washington by John R. Smith of Philadelphia. It was sold at auction in 1891.

The House is white and wooden with odd verandah. It commands a fine view. Most of the rooms are small and old-looking; the ceilings are covered with cornice like composition ornaments, and the staircase is rather handsome.

Mr. Washington gave us each a hickory stick, and then we returned to our boat and reached the town at three, delighted with our host. He is not unlike Captain Martin, and though a *leetle* rough a nice person.

Richmond, Virginia. Sunday Morning, June 13.

The evening of the day on which I last wrote we dined at Mr. Corcoran's, the great banker.[41] It is a beautiful house, with a noble picture gallery with the "Greek Slave" as its chief ornament.[42]

Corcoran is a widower, and there were only gentlemen, among them the Mexican Minister[43] and two of my friends, Riggs and Sumner. Sumner sat next me at dinner (there were about 20 there!), and the wines and plate, &c. were not more striking than the "feast of reason, &c." with which Charles Sumner delighted me all through dinner,—and that is saying much, for it was certainly the most sumptuous dinner I ever saw. Three huge pieces of gold plate in the centre of the table, and gold knives &c. with the dessert. The wines, ices, and so forth were delicious,—of the rest of the dinner I remember nothing I was so busy talking. Sumner spoke of Emerson. I never look at him with-

41. Corcoran lived at 1611 H Street in the Swann mansion (built 1822), which he bought from Daniel Webster and much enlarged.

42. The *Greek Slave* by Hiram Powers (1805-73), American sculptor, exhibited in 1851 at the Crystal Palace. took Europe by storm. Its nudity shocked contemporary taste.

43. Don José de la Vega.

154

out the reflection, future ages will wish to know how Emerson looked, what he said, how he lived. Emerson forms an angle between me and posterity. Longfellow too is a delightful person,—his "Golden Legend" *may not have been* written had not "Faust" been written, but it is no imitation.[44] The passages charged with blasphemy are necessary to give a true picture of the Middle Ages; the poem is in fact a series of tableaux; an omission of the Miracle play would destroy the honesty, would do away with the entirety of the pictures. Yet Longfellow should have explained this in notes;— weaker brethren and critics would then be unable to find any fault, and I entreated him to let me write some explanatory commentaries on it. He would not, but *now* he writes saying "he repents in sackcloth and ashes."[45]

Hawthorne lives near Emerson—very shy and quite unused to Society. Margaret Fuller I remember well. I had when at College to call there one day, having been to a party there. I was much frightened for everybody talked of her as a genius, &c. and a tête-à-tête (for I found Mrs. F[uller] out) was a formidable prospect. I nearly sank through the floor, as I found myself sitting by her trying some small talk. My fear increased when she began to catechise me on my reading. I told her I had been reading Hoole's translation of Ariosto; she told me I was quite wrong—Rose's was the best.[46] I retired full of awe at a young lady who

44. Longfellow's dramatic poem (1851), dealing with a prince, his beloved, and Lucifer, was based on *Der Arme Heinrich* by Hartmann von der Aue. Critics accused him of plagiarism (he had disguised his source), and some found the miracle play obscene.

45. Longfellow actually wrote Sumner (January 16, 1852) that he wore an unfavorable English notice of the poem "as a kind of hair shirt." He did provide notes for David Bogue's illustrated edition of 1854, and they appeared in all subsequent editions.

46. John Hoole's translation of *Orlando Furioso* was published in 1783; William Stewart Rose's in 1823-31.

155

had not only read books in the original, but knew all about every translation. Next time I read Ariosto was in the original.

Sumner himself is a little formidable—will quote Latin. "Mihi multa cogitanti,[47] how does Cicero go on with it? Senator is a pretty name. There were however more Senators at Rome than there are here. How many were there; let's see."

When in London I breakfasted with Sydney Smith;[48] many notorieties were there, and I was young. I chanced to say that the Americans ventured to re-judge the decisions of the English Critics, and award favour to the unfavoured in their own country. This to *Sydney Smith!* "An instance," he called out. "Carlyle," I said. "Spite of his mistake in style, his extravagant opinions and so forth, he often irradiates a dark subject as if with a lightning flash." "We know nothing of him here," said Sydney Smith statelily. I felt put down—an awkward pause ensued, and I was most uncomfortable. Presently a gentleman came round from the side of the table, pulled a chair near me and whispering, "I thank you for what you've said. I am perhaps the only person here who appreciates its truth; let me see you when in London often." He threw down his card,—it was Monckton Milnes![49]

47. "To me pondering many things."

48. Sydney Smith (1771–1845), one of the founders of the *Edinburgh Review*, noted for his remark, "Who reads an American book?"

49. Richard Monckton Milnes (1809–85), politician and litterateur (later one of HAB's closest friends). The breakfast was in 1838, when Sumner was 27; his enthusiasm for Carlyle was derived from Emerson. Cf. a letter from Sumner to George S. Hillard (December 4, 1838): "Young Milnes (whose poems you have doubtless read) told me that nobody knew of his [Carlyle's] existence; though he, Milnes, entertained for him personally the greatest regard" (Edward L. Pierce, *Memoir and Letters of Charles Sumner* [Boston, 1893], 2:22). After Carlyle's death in 1881 Bright recalled this story in a letter to Milnes, and added, "What a pleasure to you to know that you were almost the first Englishman to appreciate him" (letter of December 28, 1882, at Trinity College, Cambridge).

Of Miss Barrett I have the highest opinion, but she is no artist.[50] You must be genius and artist before you can succeed, and somehow woman never is the second except perhaps in letter-writing. Mrs. Norton's small poems are sometimes artistic,[51]—Mrs. Hemans' are sweet but "chambermaid-like."[52] Maria Del Occidente, an American lady whom Southey calls by this name is excellent though little known,[53]—but Miss Barrett constantly disappoints one; some poor line (H.A.B. I quoted an illustration "Dips deep in velvet roses *and such things;*"[54] Sumner agreed with me.), some weak expression spoils a passage.

Sumner is much abused by the Southerners, for he's a strong Abolitionist; he's hated by the Whigs because he's turned Free Soiler, and he's detested at Boston because he turned out Winthrop.[55] Still he's agreeable, a gentleman and a scholar, and was made very much of in England. Mrs. Webster spoke highly of him *privately* the other day to me, though she said his political opinions prevent them from seeing him now.

We left Corcoran's—every one did—at nine, and refusing an invitation to smoke with Riggs, went to see Lola dance—(as in play bill). She looks larger and finer dancing than acting, and is certainly a striking woman. We came in too for the latter part of the play in which

50. Elizabeth Barrett Browning (1806-61), whose *Poems* appeared in 1844 and *Sonnets from the Portuguese* in 1850.

51. Caroline Elizabeth Sarah Sheridan Norton (1808-77), English poet and novelist.

52. Felicia Dorothea Hemans (1793-1835), English poet whose lyrics were very popular in America.

53. Robert Southey gave the nickname "Maria of the West" (Maria del Occidente) to Maria Gowen Brooks (ca. 1794-1845), Massachusetts poet, whose first volume, *Judith, Esther, and Other Poems*, he praised.

54. From "Casa Guidi Windows," part 2 (1851).

55. Robert Charles Winthrop (1809-94), former senator from Massachusetts, defeated by Sumner in 1851.

she made a terrible "lapsus linguae" in the most patriotic part, saying with tears in her eyes (!) to some benevolent Countess, "I hope that your *safety* to me will not endanger your own *kindness!*" Worthy of Livingston in the Union![56]

Next morning we went out with Synge and Loch to call on Madame Calderon, but unluckily she wasn't well enough. She is English by birth and with her sisters kept a school in Washington.[57] Her husband is, I hear, a fine specimen of a Spanish gentleman, and dotes on her. We saw the Smithsonian Institute—a beautiful building in Norman architecture; the style is approved in a book by Mr. Owen lately published.[58] There are interesting pictures of Indian Chiefs, and one of a Mexican View. Large cactuses of the <*sketch*> shape. It must be an extraordinary country. On our way back we called at a book store and learnt from the man that Dr. Dewey was in Washington.

We dined at Webster's. Mrs. Webster had asked several people to meet us—some 16—chiefly young people as she said, for us. Webster was there, silent and gloomy, but very civil. He desired me to take Miss Page, his wife's niece into dinner, and talked to us about the "Smithsonian Institute," and the Indian pictures there.[59] Every distinguished chief who came

---

56. Probably Richard John Livingstone (1828-1907), who had been with Bright at Trinity College. HAB was president of the Union in 1851.

57. Frances Erskine Inglis Calderon de la Barca (1804-82), born in Scotland, author of *Life in Mexico* (1843), wife of the Spanish minister in Washington. The school she kept, with her mother and her eldest sister, was at different times in Boston, on Staten Island, and in Baltimore.

58. *Hints on Public Architecture* (1849), by Robert Dale Owen, the social reformer. As congressman from Indiana he introduced the bill under which the Smithsonian Institution was founded and served as chairman of the building committee.

59. At this time the Indian portraits at the Smithsonian were those by John Mix Stanley (1814-72), which were almost all destroyed by fire in 1865. The story that follows may possibly concern George Catlin, whose famous Indian Gallery Webster (among others) unsuccessfully tried to

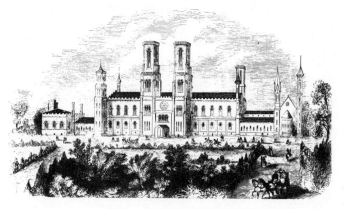

Gleason's Pictorial Drawing-Room Companion, April 24, 1852

"A beautiful building in Norman architecture."

to Washington was painted formerly. A painter was ordered to sketch one of them and he desired the man to sit down,—intending to reduce the expense by only doing a half-length of the man—for the purpose. He drew himself straight stiffly up—the "limner" again bade him sit—again he drew straight up, at last ejaculating "Legs and all," to the amused and astonished artist.

At Webster's was the Brazilian Minister's daughter[60] and others, to most of whom we were introduced. The dinner was good. I sat next to Miss Page and Anderdon—my right place, for a slip of paper with a name was laid on each plate. In the centre of the table was a vase of mixed artificial and real flowers. Miss Page was quite a nice girl and made me promise to call on her at Boston. On Anderdon's right sat a "blue" who told him of her tour to London, and how she had

persuade Congress to secure for the nation. Catlin's portraits, however, were painted not in Washington but in Indian territory.

60. The Brazilian minister was Pereira de Sodré.

159

rushed up and shaken hands with *the* Duke[61] as he came out of St. James' Chapel, and how some weak English friends were shocked in consequence. Anderdon hardly sympathised, I fear.

After dinner came in some Spaniards to whom Webster lamented "I have no Spanish on my tongue," and we shortly took our leave,—Burder and myself,—for Dr. Dewey's, to whom we had sent a note mentioning our intended invasion. He was very glad to hear of Liverpool people and gave us letters to Miss Sedgwick[62] and Bryant. Washington's duty is light, requiring a sermon a week for nine months, and that's all, but it doesn't agree with him, and he seems to pine for his New England home.

That night before I went to bed I had the felicity of losing my pretty watch. One of the house servants had helped me to pack. When he left the room the watch left it too. Of course *he* knew nothing about it, and the chances are *I* shall know nothing about it either.

61. I.e., the duke of Wellington.

62. Catharine Maria Sedgwick (1789-1867), novelist, living in Lenox, Mass., where HAB later visits her.

160

6

RICHMOND TO ALUM SPRINGS

[June 13 Continued]

Early on Saturday we started for Richmond—half our journey by boat down the Potomac, the other half by rail ("cars" they say here) through Virginia. The Potomac is certainly a pretty river, and the steamer a good one. The inland country is really beautiful— thick woods with flowering tulip trees, catalpas, locusts and others—among them I recognized for the first time a kalmia shrub, fields blue with some salvia- like flowers.

We were delighted with the drive, though I confess we were dusty, hot, and thankful when we got to the end of it. The American Hotel is the only comfort- able "house" we've as yet seen, very civil people who are really anxious to make one comfortable.[1]

1. The American Hotel, at the corner of Eleventh and Main streets, was praised in a contemporary account for its "excellent table, attentive servants, pleasant, richly furnished rooms, and obliging assistants" (*Gleason's Pictorial Drawing-Room Companion* [April 23, 1853]).

After dinner we left letters on Mr. Hobson,[2] with whom we had a long conversation, and also on Mr. Scott[3] who took a drive with us to a cemetery (the usual *park* of an American town) where there is a beautiful view of the river with its numberless little islands, and where we found a wild yellow cactus (?a prickly pear) growing.[4] Poor Burder grasped at it energetically, but too late found that "if every rose has a thorn," every cactus has one no less. His hands were covered with subtle and venomous little darts. I escaped better, but not altogether, and the rest of the drive was spent in sucking our fingers!

Monday at Noon, [June 14].

Yesterday I wrote home and in my journal in the morning, while the others patronized the Presbyterian Church. After dinner Mr. Scott and Mr. Hobson went with me to the *African* place of worship—a Baptist Church capable of holding 2000 people—the largest Church in the town.[5] My kind friends sat one on each side of me, each with a "quid" in his mouth, and a spittoon at his feet. Didn't they chew jollily, and spit accurately, and smell pleasantly during this operation, and didn't I feel comfortable when I reflected how only the evening before I had told Mr. Scott (son of the old

2. John Cannon Hobson (d. 1873), tobacconist and president of the Exchange bank. His imposing Greek Revival mansion at 409 East Main Street was built in 1847.

3. James Scott (1773–1861), another tobacconist, who emigrated from Scotland in 1798, lived half a block away from Hobson on South Fifth Street.

4. Hollywood Cemetery, opened in 1849 as a "rural, decorated cemetery," so called because of its holly trees.

5. The First Baptist Church (the African Church) at the corner of Broad and College streets.

man who drove with us) that we—that all Englishmen
—hated spitting and thought it a most nasty habit?[6]

At last the Church filled, and the service commenced with a series of hymns given out by anybody
who had pluck enough to begin, and taken up by anybody who had enthusiasm enough to follow. They all
sing well, this tabooed race, and in capital time. A
negro prayer, fervid and in a wailing voice followed
from a distinguished member of the congregation, who
lamented "our many bewanderings." Then a very bad
sermon from a pert young white parson who dwelt
much on the virtue of "patience."[7] Poor souls, they've
need of it! Then a prayer from another of the congregation in whom we recognized the cabman who drove
us the night before, and then a blessing from the
white parson—hymns between each of the prose parts.

We now prepared to go, but what was my surprise
to find that the *interest* was but beginning. A hymn
was struck up in the middle of the Church, every one
rose and joined in; a solemn dark gent begged there
would be no *stamping*,—he was very partially obeyed—
the hymn grew louder and assumed a jig tune with a
"Hallelujah" sort of chorus. The chief performer
raised his hat on an umbrella and gently waved it;
the "ladies" at one end of the Church, the "gentlemen"
at the other sang each verse chorus with greater gusto;
they moved their heads in time to the singing, and
gradually increasing (the "ladies" chiefly) bobbed up
and down in a solemn manner at first, getting faster
and more energetic, and laughing in the most delighted
way. It was the drollest sight I ever saw. C[oun]t
Hamilton's Moussellina couldn't have kept her counte-

6. Mr. Hobson only chews on Sunday, he told us. [H.A.B.] Smoking
was not permitted in church, but chewing was.

7. It was illegal for Negroes to assemble except under the guidance
of a white preacher.

nance,[8] and the young lady whom the "Golden Goose" moved to a smile,[9] would have giggled still more heartily had she seen the nigger ladies, in smart bonnets, and shawls, with waving fans, and tossing heads bending and rising, and singing, and shuffling as I saw them yesterday in the Baptist Church at Richmond.[10]

The slaves *seem* happy. Hobson tells me his father has offered to free his and send them to Liberia with money to start there with, but—*none of them will go*! —a fact for the writer of "Uncle Tom's Cabin" and the like. It tells well at least for some of the "Mas'rs."

Mr. Randolph set his blacks free, with money to buy land in Ohio—a Free State.[11] The free Ohioans however wouldn't have them, and it was many long months before the poor fellows found a home in the more secluded parts of the State, during which time many entreated to be again made slaves in old Virginey. Another gentleman wished to free his slaves, but did not know how or where to settle them, till at last a suggestion was made that he should take them down the Ohio as if bound South,—and the keen-scented Abolitionists would do all they could to get them to escape, and would *probably succeed* and save him all further trouble. In Indiana, State Government hopes to do away with slavery, allowing no slaves to be brought into the State, no traffic to go on in the

8. A beautiful princess who never laughs in Anthony Hamilton's tale "Les Quatre Facardins" (1730).

9. In this fairy tale another solemn princess laughs for the first time when she sees a procession of people stuck to a golden goose.

10. "The African Church on a Sunday I am told is a perfect blaze of pea-green, crimson, ear-rings, lace collars, satin and velvet which the poor darkies wear" (Thackeray to Albany Fonblanque, March 4, 1853, *Letters*, 3:229).

11. Nearly four hundred slaves belonging to John Randolph of Roanoke (1773–1833), freed under the terms of his will, tried in 1846 to establish themselves in Mercer and Shelby counties in Ohio.

State, and offering after some years itself to buy and maintain the slaves that still remain! State Governments should do more than they do do on this subject; they should not allow separation of wife and husband, they should regulate auction sales, and appoint Commissioners to enquire into the state of a man's negroes, especially on the Plantations!

Monday night, [June 14].

We were taken this morning by Scott Junr.[12] and Hobson Junr. to see a slave auction.[13]

In a common barnlike open room was a platform on which a black middle-aged woman was standing. She was well-dressed, but looked stupid and vacant, except when a young Mulatto man who had to show her off chucked her under the chin or shook her rapturously by the hand, or stroked down her white apron for her. Twenty or thirty men round were bidding listlessly and slowly, while the auctioneer screamed out the various bids. At $600 they took her down, but soon put her up again and a Mr. Townsend secured her for $615 when she was finally knocked down. Another girl now appeared, also very black and "warranted sound and healthy," the auctioneer said, "only," he added in a lower voice, "the woman says she's sore eyes every spring, but then they don't know nothing about that sort of thing." Ignorant niggers! "Let the young lady pass," he said. A space was

12. Scott's son, James A. Scott, followed him into the tobacco business.

13. Thackeray's friend Eyre Crowe, visiting the same auction rooms on Wall (or Fifteenth) Street some months later, described them as "low rooms, roughly white-washed, with worn and dirty flooring, open, as to doors and windows, to the street" (Eyre Crowe, *With Thackeray in America* [New York, 1893], p. 131).

Harper's Weekly, January 24, 1863

"Twenty or thirty men round were bidding listlessly and slowly, while the auctioneer screamed out the various bids."

cleared and the "young lady" was trotted down the room to show her paces. The interest increases. One man pulls open her mouth, another examines her foot and leg, the sore eyes seem a myth, the rest of the body is so healthy. The bids increase and $610 is offered by Mr. Nixon and accepted!

Mr. Scott had a drunken coachman he wished to part with, but a delicacy—an absurd qualm—prevented the sale while he was there to witness it, and the man was taken down again. Charming sight this human

166

auction!—flesh and blood and the auctioneer's hammer disposing of it! The desire of possession—one of the 5 desires according to Whewell[14]—must be so pleasantly satisfied, and the feeling of having a fellow being yours, and yours only, to beat or pat on the back, on whom to vent all the passions, good or bad, which want an escape valve, on whom to wreck vengeance if you're sulky, or to be benevolent with very little trouble if you're amiable. And then the way in which one's vanity must be tickled by being "Mas'r" supreme, paramount, undeniably lord and sovereign. Truly Mr. Nixon and Mr. Townsend you must be happy men, and every good Christian must "wish ye joy of yer proize mons."

Now for a few facts about the negroes. They are superstitious and Hobson told us that his Uncle could always find a negro thief by calling his men, reading Bible to them and putting rice in their mouths. The thief is so certain of some necromancy that his "tongue cleaves to the roof of his mouth," the saliva is secreted and when the rice is spit out, that from the thief's mouth is perfectly *dry*! They believe also in Witchcraft, &c. The S. Carolinians talk African dialect mixed with their English. The children of a family get much attached to an old nurse and call her "Mammy." The black nurse sometimes *gives suck* to a white child.

We were this evening at Mr. Scott's, and we heard two black slaves (one of Hobson's) play the banjo and sing negro songs. They were several of them very good, and sang really well—the banjo and the tunes are *really*

14. Whewell in his lectures on moral philosophy at Cambridge enumerated four leading desires of man: personal safety, possessions, family, and civil society. The desire of knowledge he considered of a secondary nature.

nigger, the words are *white*, and were originated by a man called Sweeny from New Orleans.[15] "Lucy Neal" our friend sang comically, "Uncle Ned" was tragical, and "Old Virginey" rather so too. They seemed to enjoy the fun very much—one of their heroes "shaved his corns with a railroad wheel."[16]

This morning we also saw tobacco warehouses and tobacco factories; curious and rather intoxicating we found them. All employed are negroes except the overseers. We heard some of them singing hymns.[17] There is a fine Statue to Washington in the Capitol.[18]

The river is very pretty and in the afternoon we three went in a sailing boat on it with a Mr. Scholefield who keeps a Julep saloon and would not let us pay him, only *treat him*—and a Mr. Taylor who *was* an "Aristocrat," educated at Cambridge U.S., spent everything, and looking at 36 more like 63 is now head waiter or superintendent of a second-rate Hotel in the town.[19] He was full of information and told us how Edgar Poe had swam down where we were sailing— 5 miles against the tide—and how Edgar Poe might

15. Probably HAB was told about Joe Sweeny (1813–60), a famous black-face banjoist who traveled throughout the south in the late 1830s and 1840s.

16. Probably "Old Dan Tucker," who in another version "combed his hair with a wagon wheel."

17. Cf. a contemporary account of a Richmond tobacco factory: "Here I heard the slaves, about a hundred in number, singing at their work in large rooms; they sung quartettes, choruses, and anthems, and that so purely, and in such perfect harmony, and with such exquisite feeling, that it was difficult to believe them self-taught" (Frederika Bremer, *The Homes of the New World*, 2:509–10).

18. Houdon's statue was executed in 1788 and placed in the Richmond Capitol in 1796.

19. W. Jacqueline Taylor, assistant superintendent of the City Hotel, at the corner of Main and Fifteenth streets, may have been pulling Bright's leg. If he was "educated" at Harvard, he did not receive a degree there.

have been a very wealthy man but drink ruined him, as we've reason to believe it did our informant.[20]

In the evening we went (I said already) to the Scotts —drank coffee, talked small talk, eat ices and listened to negro melodies and then—Good-night!

Charlottesville. Wednesday at Noon, [June 16].

We arrived about 1½ yesterday, having started at 6½ —not a hundred miles to go and such a time about it. The day was hot, and the cars were dusty, but the country was rather pretty, and the Hotel here (close to the station where those who went on to Staunton got out and dined) new and cool-looking with civil people and three large swing fans set in motion above the tables by a little "nigger."[21] After dinner we went to call on Mr. Jefferson Randolph to whom we had letters. The road was bad—worse than any road I ever saw. The most awful rocks to get over, hills to climb up, a considerable river to ford through, and after all the finding Mr. Randolph from home, and Mrs. R. not disposed to ask us in. We had heard so much of Virginian Hospitality that we expected a bed and a razor volunteered at once. Our disgust may be imagined when a cold "Where are you staying" was all we got from the Virginian planter's family.

The house looked like an English farmhouse,—a light Mulatto girl came to the door and the *look* of the

20. Edgar Allan Poe (1809–49) spent much of his boyhood in Richmond. The swimming feat, which became a Richmond legend, occurred some twenty-eight years before, when he was only fifteen.

21. The hotel was Smith's Central Hotel, located east of the Virginia Central Railroad Station.

thing was, I think, a disappointment.[22] Jefferson's own house Monticello is near here, but that we cannot see.[23] In the evening Burder and I took a stroll and then we all sat in the porch looking at summer lightning and fire-flies.

This morning we went to the University, about a mile from the village. It is a nice-looking place built all for coolness,—the students' rooms opening out on a porch verandah shaded with trees at the end of this avenue. Rather like the arrangement of Downing is the Lecture Room, Library, &c.[24] Library a round room with a dome is rather handsome.

The Students are about 600, professors 15. Session from June to October,[25] and no more vacation even at Xmas. The College Church is taken year and year about by some persuasion; just now a Methodist has it, and he's so much liked he probably will keep it one other year.[26]

A man may take his degree as soon as he is fit for it, and some go down after one session. It's a comparatively new place, founded by Jefferson, and as the cicerone had to own to Burder has produced no great man yet; Harvard still rules supreme.

We leave by the train (by which yesterday we got here) for Staunton. The country round here is pretty,

22. Thomas Jefferson Randolph (1792–1875), Thomas Jefferson's favorite grandson, built a white brick cottage at "Edgehill" about 1830.

23. At this time Monticello was owned by Commodore Uriah P. Levy of New York City, who used it only as a part-time residence.

24. The buildings of Downing College, Cambridge, are also built in Greek revival style around a large open quadrangle. The University of Virginia library was then in the Rotunda.

25. Or rather, October to June.

26. The Reverend Ballard E. Gibson did retain the chaplaincy for 1852–53 and was succeeded by an Episcopalian. It was part of Jefferson's plan that the university be thoroughly undenominational.

THE UNIVERSITY OF VIRGINIA, CHARLOTTESVILLE, 1856

"It is a nice-looking place built all for coolness."

but the Hotel is badly situated for *view*, though admirably placed for profit, and every one is most obliging.

Lexington. Friday Night, [June 18].

After some few miles of rail we had to "Stage"—5 miles an hour—to Staunton.[27] Several University Students were in the "Stage," and amused us much by some of their College stories, &c. I asked if they had a Debating Society there and found they had four, of which the "Jefferson" is the most distinguished.[28]

They may be out all night, and the poor professors get shot at if they attempt interference.[29] After a "Mint julep" at a half-way house, and a friendly parting at Staunton, they went their way and I saw them "no more," as says J. Bunyan's Pilgrim.

The Inn at Staunton is comfortable (Virginia House), but we left early next morning by a private "trap" for Lexington.

Fine mountain scenery here as in the crossing the Blue Ridge to Staunton. We dined "en route" at Fairfield. We reached this town at seven, took tea in company with some performing War dancing Indians, and called on Col. Reid, quite a nice hospitable person.[30]

This morning Burder was asthmatic, Anderdon was

27. The railroad across the Blue Ridge mountains to Staunton was not completed until 1854.

28. The other three were the Washington Society (founded 1835), the Philomathian Society (1849), and the Parthenon Society (1852). The last two were short-lived; the Jefferson Society (founded 1825) still flourishes.

29. A reference to the notorious shooting of Professor John A. G. Davis by a student on the Lawn in 1840.

30. Samuel McDowell Reid (1790–1869), who succeeded his father as clerk of Rockbridge County and was a trustee of Washington College.

bilious—poor Burder regularly gave in, Anderdon "made an effort" and came with me to the Natural Bridge. The road was pretty good, but the 17 mile journey took a good three hours *odd*. When we got there we lunched and then hurried to the top of the bridge. The view was fine, but the view from below is finer still. High escarped rocks covered with vegetation rise from the banks of a little rivulet; at the height of 200 feet they are joined by an arch so simple and massive, so unspoiled by "man's device," and so unlike anything one ever saw before, that the first view of the Natural Bridge is one of those rare scenes never to be forgotten.

The guide tells you of people in the rock, of Washington's name written on it, and fifty other equally important personalities.[31] One doesn't care for them, or think of them while staring upwards in a stupid amazement at so grand a work of the Great Architect.

Round the glen are wooded mountains, one of which the rattlesnake haunts; another where the "painter"[32] may be seen. What a finish they give to the picture as you see their green heights filling up the entrance of the dell.

It's a beautiful spot, but my pen is as powerless, as my pencil, and I will only add that after a comfortable dinner and a long talk with an old man who remembers when Washington had no houses, and when the first stone was hewn for the Capitol.

We returned home, collecting rare flowers on our

31. "To this arch it has ever been the attempt of visiters to throw a stone, and we recollect it to have been stated, years gone by, that the only successful competitor, in this feat of physical power was General Washington, who, it was also said, cut his name higher than any other person, upon the perpendicular rock" (Joseph Martin, *A New and Comprehensive Gazetteer of Virginia* [Charlottesville, 1835], p. 431).

32. I.e., the cougar or puma.

way, and happy in finding our interesting invalid on the high road to recovery.

Alum Springs, Rock Bridge Co., Virginia.
Sunday, June 20.

Yesterday Anderdon and myself rode with Colonel Reid over his *farm—plantation* I find is only used of tobacco, cotton, and other Southern productions, not of wheat and (Indian) "corn" which the Colonel chiefly grows. Burder was still too unwell to go with us, but we had quite a pleasant ride over fields and through woods to a spring where the water was delicious. A glorious place our kind old guide told us for a "barbe-cue," a sort of picnic where the meat is cooked on the spot. We saw no negroes at work, but we heard the old Colonel inquiring affectionately after a sore hand one of his blacksmiths had contrived to get. A détour to see the Military Institute of Virginia followed, where Colonel Reid introduced us to a Colonel Smith[33] (to whom we afterwards found Hobson had given us a letter we had forgotten), who shewed us over the place, made us explore the washing-houses and dining rooms, and told us the regulations imposed upon the Cadets. They are never allowed wine or spirits; they have to be in by ten, and are subject to many (we should say) most vexatious rules.

Anderdon and myself dined at the Reids at two; they are solemn stupid people, (the ladies at least) who regretted we could not spend a "peaceful Sabbath" at Lexington, disliked large towns because no one

33. Francis Henney Smith (1812-90), professor of mathematics and first superintendent of the Virginia Military Institute, which he served for fifty years.

174

knew them, and talked enthusiastically of the felicity of being a slave.

We started for this place at 5 and arrived at 9½, the distance being 18 miles, so that we just went at the rate of four miles an hour. The wood scenery was beautiful, but night closed in long before we got to our journey's end. The fire-fly was darting among the bushes, and the tree frog was making his dismal cry as we drove along.

The Alum Springs are situated in a nook surrounded by wooded hills; the Hotel is large and round it are some twenty little houses, each with four double-bedded rooms for the accommodation of visitors. The water is said to be admirable in scrofulous cases, and a Dr. we met at Lexington was ambitious to send a barrel to the Queen! The lovely scenery and fine mountain breeze doubtless is often as effectual a remedy as the slimy water.[34]

We've just come in from a ramble in the woods—the highest trees, I think, I ever saw, with an underwood of flowering kalmia, among which are glancing the most splendid butterflies of enormous size, vivid colour, and beautifully serrated wings.

I never saw anything more luxuriant than the kalmia bushes here,—white and pink and other wild flowers quite unknown to me growing every here and there among them. Among the other attractions of the place is the constant supply of venison which the neighbourhood of wild deer affords to the water-drinking patients.

I have been much amused and interested by a Mulatto waiter in the Hotel, who looks on us with much interest and coolly tells us he never saw "such delicate

34. John and William Frazier built up the Rockbridge Alum Springs in the early 1850s as a rival to White Sulphur Springs.

175

ROCKBRIDGE ALUM SPRING, VIRGINIA

From *Album of Virginia*, illustrated by Ed. Beyer, 1858

"The Hotel is large and round it are some twenty little houses."

things as we are—just like girls, but prettier girls than ever come to these Springs." Our appearance fascinated a dark lady in Lewisburg equally. I have had a long conversation with him [i.e., the waiter] since, and spite of his impudence he is a very intelligent fellow. Born of a Mulatto slave and a white father, twenty-five years of age, he learned to read from a child of his master's who passed his cottage on his way to school. He is a shoemaker by trade but is anxious for liberty. This master who is a very good man has told him that he may go as waiter to the Inn here, and when he has saved $800 he will give him his liberty for that sum; the sum is high, but the poor fellow would fetch a far higher price if his health were better —lucky for his hopes of freedom that it is *not*.[35] He has a wife and child who belong to another master, who has promised to free them when the man has freed himself. He intends to go to Liberia he thinks, as in the State the slave is better off than the free black, and either Liberia or Jamaica (I dissuaded him from the latter) is where he wishes to go. Many blacks, he says, dislike Liberia, having an impression that it is unhealthy and that they will die early if they go there. Canada too is not so favourite a place as formerly; "the pure blacks are the most *ignoramus* set," he tells me, and their principles are so low a *white negro* often does not like associating with them.

CHARACTERISTIC OF AMERICA.

Everything in America has a tendency to "run to a level." I don't mean by this a "levelling tendency," for that generally implies a *mere* "pulling down."

35. Many of the Negro servants at this hotel were themselves suffering from scrofula; they were slaves farmed out for the summer by their masters to work and take the cure simultaneously.

Now in America there's a pulling down and a raising up at the same time—if every mountain and hill is brought low every valley is at the same time exalted. I never saw a more *mediocre* country—no extreme of luxury, no extreme of poverty—not so many fine scholars or fine gentlemen as in England, but fewer uneducated men and fewer (except perhaps in the far West) miserable wretches. You see this running-to-a-level peculiarity in the most insignificant instance, —in every instance. The carriages are the shabbiest, the "hacks" the best I ever saw,—the gentlemen are least refined, the people the most intelligent of any nation I have come across. The Unitarian is the most orthodox of Unitarian, the Trinitarian the most liberal of Trinitarians perhaps any where to be met with.

The newspapers illustrate this fact.—Their number and (we should say) inferiority, their cheapness and their large circulation shew how they too accommodate themselves to this Republican tendency, while the high-prized Magazines fit for the aristocracy of the country, are hardly read even by them, and the English ones are usually preferred.

7

TOURING THE VIRGINIA SPRINGS

Warm Springs, Virginia. Monday Noon, [June 21].

After dinner yesterday we left for the Bath Alum Springs—the distance was about 20 miles, the time rather more than four hours:—it's a doubtful pleasure touring through Virginia,—until one has travelled in these regions one never understands the discomforts of a coach ("Stage")—such heat and dust, and such jolting, now across a watercourse, now against a branch of some felled tree. You try to sleep and wake up suddenly by an excruciating shake which first pitches you against your next companion, and then heels you over against the coach side with a thump, probably against some trap knot which makes your side and arm ache for the rest of the journey; then if the coach is full, 8 others are crowded into it besides oneself—three in each seat, and a third seat with face to the horses which accommodates three more:—a crowd anywhere is a nuisance, but a crowded coach is positively infernal! Yesterday however we were fortunate, only one inside besides ourselves, and spite of the other inconve-

From John B. Bachelder, *Popular Resorts and How to Reach Them*, 1875

"Such heat and dust, and such jolting."

niences of such travel, the scenery was splendid enough
to condole us not a little. Such views as we slowly
gained the crest of some mountain spur of the Alleghanies and looked down over hill after hill wooded
with all the varied forest trees of these regions—nothing
but trees to be seen except where some white little
cottage peeped through them in the valley below, and
some few fields with the tree-stumps still standing
showed that some attempt was making to reclaim this
wild district. Three times have I seen fine forest scenery.
Once in Belgium when, passing through the forest of
Saint Hubert at nightfall, I saw the fires of the char-
coal burners lighting up the scene, and glancing like
beacons from the tops of woody hills. A second time
when from the tower of < > I saw the Autumn
forests of Germany on the hills of the Odenwald, with
round gray castles peeping from among them, and
quaint little German villages nestling at their feet.
But *for wood* these Virginian forests excel both of them

180

immeasurably,—a sea of woods, as Bancroft said to Burder—ridge after ridge of hill-land rising one after the other like sea-waves, and all covered with the greenest foliage.

The Bath Alum Springs are not unlike the Alum (Rock Bridge) springs, but we stayed there only a short time, as we were anxious to sleep at the Warm Springs, especially since we found the host of the Bath Alum sulky and indisposed to furnish us with a carriage, while we were disposed to get on. The only thing then was to walk, and off we started, sending on a man on horseback (we came across) for a cart from the W[arm] S[prings] for our luggage. It was a glorious evening walk—five miles—from seven to half-past eight, the kalmias in the woods were more beautiful than ever, and the wild cry of the "whip poor will" as he darted across our path reminded us that we were walking by night in an American forest.[1] Burder first recognised his dismal note, repeated like the cuckoo's over and over again.

We told ghost stories, and had we been in the Hartz or Black Forest, might have conjured up some wild Huntsman or Dunro.[2] Even in the Northern Catskills the fate of Rip van Winkle might have taught us reverence for the Spirit World—as it was we were as sceptical as superstitious, and quite prepared for a supper and bed in one of the "cabins" which surround the great hotels in each of these springs.

This morning we rose before six and went to disport ourselves in the famous warm baths, whence this place derives its name and its celebrity. In a large

1. The scene inspired Bright to poetry: see "Two Views of One Object; or, the Kalmia Brake" (p. 452).

2. The wild huntsman is a spectral hunter who frequents the Black Forest in medieval legend and in such ballads as Burger's "Der wilde Jäger." "Dunro" (a misreading of "Demon"?) eludes me.

Rotunda Building is the bath, the warm medicated water changing each minute, running out and bubbling up from its mysterious source, the temperature is about 96 and it is said to be the most delicious bath in the world. This I don't believe,—first because a warm bath is never, I think, so truly pleasant as a cold one, and secondly because there's a slightly unpleasant Aix water-like smell and taste about it which, though not strong, is quite apparent, and thirdly because you feel unrefreshed and relaxed after it.

After dressing and breakfast we went out pistol shooting in the woods, and then returned, read, slept, and wrote, and are momentarily expecting a call to a two o'clock dinner. The price of these places per day varies from $1.50 to $2, a reduction being made for those who stay some time.

The feeding *now* is decidedly bad, but the season hardly begins till July so that we are no fair judges:— One thing we find disagreeable—it is most difficult to get wine here—at Lexington the chief hotel is a temperance one, at the next best they couldn't give a sherry-cobbler; at the Alum Springs there was nothing, and at the Bath Alum it was perfectly detestable. Luckily we brought a small supply of brandy with us, and thus we are tolerably independent. We breakfast at 6 or 6½, dine at 2, and supper about 7. The Hotels are generally badly kept, and in several indescribable ways uncomfortable.

White Sulphur Spring. Wednesday Morning, June 23.

The evening (Monday) after writing, dinner and a siesta, we strolled up the Mountain which we came over the night before. The view I have already endeavoured to describe—the beauty of the wood Lea was increased by the sunset running on and flushing the tops of pine knolls, and lighting up the peaks of distant hills. I never saw a scene which struck me so much, and over which I should have lingered longer.

Yesterday we left the Warm Springs at 6½ and arrived here at 6 in the evening, the distance being 42 miles. The near woods through which we passed were wilder than ever, the hills were covered with them, and the Alleghanies which we crossed were themselves covered with vegetation; the kalmia, the wild rose and other plants formed a thick underwood, and the purple phlox was growing luxuriantly in places beneath them. A Black Snake, some 5 feet long (which unfortunately I missed) darted across our path, and disappeared in the thickets.

(N.B. The black Snake is said to be harmless, and will destroy any Copper head or Rattle-snake it comes across.)

We dined at Callaghan's house,—a most comfortable little Country place, and got a good dinner and a good Sherry Cobbler which was a novelty worth recording.[3] The people were civil, took in newspapers, and were I to travel this way again I should certainly stop there in preference to the second-rate Springs, where we stayed lately. The scenery too is most beautiful, and one only regretted that we must hurry on and not linger to explore the wild surrounding country.

The "White Sulphur" has pretensions about it, which no other Spring in the State can aspire to—it's *the* Spring of Virginia, and in the season 900 people dine here. The season however does not begin till July,

3. According to Jerome Bonaparte a few years earlier, Callaghan's was "the best tavern in the mountains," celebrated for its milk and fried chickens (William D. Hoyt, Jr., "Journey to the Springs, 1846," *Virginia Magazine of History and Biography* 54 [1946]: 126).

so that we were now only about 50 in number,—the baths aren't "fixed," the billiard-room is shut, there is no band playing and no balls going on. Still it looks rather a nice place, with a might-be-gay-some-day air about it, as Burder said. The Hotel proper consists of a Coach-office, an enormous dining-room and a post office. A barber's shop is close by on one side, a ball-room on the other, and near it the Temple-covered Spring where the water comes bubbling up with a "healthful and horrid" smell of egg like sulphur, hardly so noxious however as the Aix water, and, I *believe*, resembling the Harrogate. Round the Hotel in every direction up the hill slopes are rows of little cottages ("cabins") with a verandah in front of each where the guests sleep. There are 2 double-bedded rooms in each, each room with two doors, one opening on the hill, the other on the lawn leading down to the Hotel.

We have been drinking the water last night and this morning, but do not think we shall repeat the experiment:—I wanted some medicine myself, and my two glasses have been most efficacious.[4]

To-day it's raining, which is a bore, but it gives us a good opportunity for getting on with our journals:—how long we stay here depends entirely on whether we have money enough to get on with. I wrote to Mr. George asking him to send $100 for me here, but it has not yet come, and unless the landlord will lend us the "necessary" we are fixed till it arrives.

Speaking of money I will take this opportunity—thanks to the rain I could hardly find a better one—of

4. "The White sulphur acts, when taken in doses of two or three glasses at a time, as an alterative, exercising on the system much of the salutary influence, without the evil effects of mercury,—used in larger quantities it becomes actively diaretic [*sic*] and purgative" (Joseph Martin, *A New and Comprehensive Gazetteer*, p. 24).

scribbling down sundry observations which this money of America calls for.

The division into dollars and cents, the money itself is admirable, and the decimal coinage is in all respects to be commended and imitated—each dollar is worth 100 cents, or rather more than 4/- sterling, the rate of exchange being about 4.87.

But if the *money* is good, the *coinage* itself is villainous—"the worst in the world," a good Whig told me the other day, "and all owing to the Democrats."

To their coinage there are many objections:—

1. The inconvenience of carrying about large silver dollars is obviated in two ways, each worse than the other:—the gold dollar coin is so small as to be liable to be lost constantly. Smaller than an English fourpenny bit, it is the most absurd and disagreeable little coin I know, though better than the other plan they have of a paper currency of dollars:—small notes in Germany or anywhere are not always very pleasant, but I never got hold of such pestilential little bits of paper in my life as you get in the United States. Then too the Bills of dozens of different banks are current, but it often happens are current only in one particular State, and the annoyance to a stranger is often very great. If however a tradesman refuse to take a note they will generally change it for you at the Hotel.

In my pocket now I find two notes, one of "The Bank of the Union" with a picture of two ladies supporting the shield of America with the legend "Prosperity and Liberty," also a head of Washington, a cotton-loom and an eagle. The other is from the "Farmers' and Merchants' Bank,"—its devices are a head of someone unknown, a sentimental "Square" looking at a river, and a figure of "America" with a cap of freedom on a pole.

I must I think have had more than twenty notes from *different* banks since I came to America.

2. Another objection in the coinage is the use of Spanish money which has become very common, and as in the case of the quarter dollar (25 cents) almost entirely supersedes the American piece. It—the Spanish—is a larger coin and puzzles a stranger a good deal.

3. There are several coins which are of no good that I can see except to *confuse* and *annoy*.

The natural division of American money would, I think, be:—dollar, half-dollar, quarter dollar (which they have), ⅛ dollar (12½ cents or 6d), $\frac{1}{16}$ dollar (6¼ cents or 3d nearly), which they also have, *but in Spanish money*.[5]

This division of American money is, I think, in every respect the best, and the other American coins, the Dime (10 cents), half Dime (5 cents) and 3-cent piece are, it appears to me, perfectly useless, and very liable to get mistaken for the ⅛ and $\frac{1}{16}$ dollar coins.

4. In each State the coins have different names:— The ⅛ dollar (about our 6d) is called in

New York	"a shilling"
Boston	"Nine pence"
Philadelphia	
Washington	"eleven pence"
Richmond	or "Levy"
&c. &c.	
New Orleans & West	"a bit."

The $\frac{1}{16}$ dollar (about 3d) is generally called

In the South	a "fip" = "5 pence"
	a "Piccayune"
In New York	a "sixpence."

5. Mexican and Spanish coins were legal tender until 1857, when a new monetary law caused the adoption of decimal coins.

Gold Coins of America.

20 dollar piece
10   "   "
5   "   "
2½   "   "
1   "   "

Silver Coins.

Dollar
Half Dollar
Quarter Dollar
⅛ Dollar or 12½ cents
¹⁄₁₆ Dollar or 6¼ cents
Dime or 10 cents
Half Dime or 5 cents
3-cent piece

Copper Coins.
Cent

Thursday Morning, [June 24].

Yesterday it poured the whole day; the trees were dripping round our "Cabin," the walks on the slopes were deserted—the Sulphur Spring looked miserable and dank, and forsaken. We did stroll out for a little walk when the showers ceased, and that was all we could do, except wait for the mail in hopes that it might bring a letter from George and some money. Fortunately for us it did, especially since the landlord here refused to lend us "tin," for our journey. Virginian hospitality! I don't believe in it! When in the North everybody told us we had no idea of the kindness and hospitality we should receive in the "Cavalier" State. Cavaliers and hospitality have, I fear, died out

187

together. In Richmond they were kind, our good friends, but we were there two days and were never asked to dinner, only once to tea. At Lexington Col. Reid did as much for us as a good-natured sort of farmer could who was a teetotaller and gave no wine on his table. But at Charlottesville when we called on Randolph, and sending in our letters to the lady (when we heard the Master was from home) asked leave to walk through the grounds, all the answer we got was an enquiry of "where are you staying?" and we had to find the best of our way back again.

Coming from Charlottesville we travelled and fraternized with a lot of University men, but except a Mint-julep they never offered to do anything whatever for us,—never volunteered to show us the lions of Staunton, or invited us to their houses!

Now all this to an Englishman would show no want of hospitality—indeed it would appear odd in England if these good people had done anything more for us— in America however it is different, and I verily believe that in the North we would have received more kindness than we have done travelling through the much-vaunted Virginia.

Last night Anderdon and myself played Picquet; this morning we sit writing and reading.

Lewisburg, Saturday Evening, [June 26].

"Such is life" as one always says when anything disagreeable happens! Here we are "cribbed, cabined and confined" in a second-rate Inn in a second-rate Virginian town. Last night we arrived here from the "White Sulphur,"—last night Burder got a violent attack of asthma from walking up a steep hill to "ease the stage," and

188

this morning I found myself alone, with Burder wheezing in bed and Anderdon gone to Cincinnati. Luckily they are extremely nice people here, anxious to do everything to make us comfortable, so that we might easily be worse off than we are. We have found too a decent Doctor,[6] who has been cupping and physicking the poor fellow this morning, and he is now better. The cupping was much original looking but I believe efficacious;—two tumblers each with a piece of lighted paper in it were inverted and clapped upon his back— the air being thus exhausted, each tumbler became fixed like the receiver of an air pump and raised the skin up into it. This counter-irritation had the effect of drawing away the tendency to chest-inflammation and is certainly a clever plan. The Dr's. pet medicine appears to be "Lobelia." He is clever at wild flowers, gave me the names of several of mine which I showed him, and in exchange for a specimen of an odorous white shrub flower (a species of anemone, I believe,) made me a present of one of the yellow violets immortalized by Bryant.[7] He is collecting a hortus siccus for the Smithsonian Institute at Washington. I've been spending the day in a search after amusement. One half hour was passed at the Book Store, the owner of which I was startled at hearing called "Judge." He was a civil, respectable fellow though his choice of books was small and dreary, being chiefly scholastic and religious, Methodists' Hymn Books and M'Guffey's First Readers. Thence I strolled into a newspaper office for a copy of the Lewisburg Chronicle. I entered the shop or office ("Printing Office" over the door) and was startled to find myself in a bedroom of

6. Probably John A. Hunter of Lewisburg, who took his medical degree at the University of Pennsylvania in 1841 and later served as a surgeon with the Virginia forces during the Civil War (see p. 197).

7. In his poem "The Yellow Violet."

far from uncomfortably large proportions, with a little table at which were sitting the Editorial "We,"—two gentlemen from whom I had the satisfaction of buying a copy of their influential Journal, price 5 cents.

Eating and sleeping, with a stroll up a hill, several sits with Burder and a little letter of introduction writing for Anderdon in the shape of one epistle to Collingwood,[8] and three to Philadelphia to Mr. Peter, Dr. Furness and Dr. Pettit—this has filled up the remainder of my day.

The last day at the Sulphur was spent very quietly with nothing more interesting than a stroll or two in one of which Anderdon and I saw the ball-rolling beetles mentioned by Lyell (Vol. II.)[9] In the middle of the road we saw six pair of beetles, each pair busy in rolling along a ball rather larger than this. <sketch> One fellow got on the top and weighed it over while the other pushed at the same time. The one on the top of the ball was very clever and reminded me of the man at Franconi's[10] who used to perform a somewhat similar feat. We were much puzzled to guess what their object was in such labour. They appeared very "shiftless" as Ophelia Vermont would say (Uncle Tom's Cabin). But poor little darkies they were, Lyell says, in search of a soft place in which to imbed their precious freight and were most unsuccessful while we were watching them.

There is an English Mr. Peyton here. I sat next him at dinner, and he lent me an "Illustrated." He has come here to buy land for the Irish emigrants, and has chosen some lying between here and the White Sulphur.

8.   A friend in Montreal (see p. 326).

9.   It was in Virginia that Sir Charles Lyell observed these beetles (*Ateuchus volvens*) (*A Second Visit to the United States* [New York, 1850], 2:245–46).

10.   A traveling circus.

He is much interested in mountain deer shooting, but has as yet been unsuccessful.

We have heard of Scott's nomination. "Oh, blind and slow of heart" Americans not to choose the greatest man in the country!

One reason why Webster is not more supported is that in 1812 he opposed war with England violently, belonging to what was called the "Hartford Convention." Also the Whigs feel their only chance of a President is a *General.* Harrison and Taylor[11] they managed, Clay they never could. The red-coated frenzy of the Americans seems childish to a degree and more worthy of a drawing-room flirt than a great and powerful and very intelligent nation.

Sunday Night, [June 27].

Burder is, thank God, much better—has come down and been out—and seems pretty well again. One great annoyance is that we must wait till Anderdon can send letters from Cincinnati for us—it delays us a week here pottering about at the Springs when we should be in the far West.

Among the greatest discomforts of country life here is the food—breakfast at 6½—hot everything, no cold bread to be had and hot rolls, hot biscuits, hot wheat bread and hot corn bread all ready to give you any species of indigestion you may prefer:—then how the people eat—while I'm asking the b'hoy for a second cup of coffee, and chewing away at a tough beefsteak, each mouthful of which requires a considerable time for mastication—I suddenly find myself alone—

11. William Henry Harrison (1773–1841), ninth president, and Zachary Taylor (1784–1850), twelfth president, were both major generals.

somehow or other everyone else has finished, their cups of coffee get down "slicker" and their beefsteaks are ground by some mysterious internal process with which English stomachs are unacquainted.

To-day I've been twice to church—once in the morning with a Dr. Rice the *State* Senator,[12] to the Presbyterian—this evening with a Mr. Somebody staying at the Hotel, to the Methodist.

The Churches were alike, the services alike, and the congregations were about the same. Here the <resemblance> ceases. The Presbyterian tone of Minister and congregation was cold, stately, practical, and quiet—the Methodist was fervid, energetic, canting (in its better sense) and undignified. In the one the choir sang, in the other the people,—in the one the people listened to the prayers, in the other they were constantly ejaculating "Amen," "God bless us," "Oh, dear," "That is true," etc., etc.—in the one the old minister took for his text "Do to others as others should do to you," in the other, one of the two parsons (the other did the prayers) harangued us on a passage in Hebrews. The Presbyterian's sermon was against "Ardent Spirits"; the Methodist's on "faith" and *Moses' trust in Christ* and "manifestations of the Spirit," and so forth. Certainly the former gave us the best, but a very crotchety sermon, implying rather strongly that if you sold a Mint-julep you'd go to a "worserer place" for your pains—that's all!

12. Possibly John T. Rice, member of the Virginia House of Delegates from Richmond and Westmoreland counties.

Blue Sulphur Springs. Tuesday Morning, June 29.

Yesterday was Court opening day at Lewisburg.[13]
There was much spitting, smoking, haranguing,
brandy-smashing and the like going on at our Hotel.
Judge ——— held Judge Somebody else by the button-
hole, or threw his arm round his neck, and stood in the
entrance hall and confidentially, quid in mouth, talked
to his illustrious colleague—and as everyone did the
same, and the Hotel got more crowded and more dirty
every moment, we congratulated ourselves that we
had secured our "hack" and were going on. The Court
itself we looked at—a "Magistrates' Court" they call
it:—Magistrates or Judges or—whatever be their proper
name—sitting on a raised bench, afforded a striking
coup d'oeil of dirty shirts, rather twisted neckties,
non-pareil coats, and greasy faces, and likewise furnished divers studies of spitting which, however, I
will not attempt to describe—I could hardly do justice
to so grave a subject.

Great too were the Judges at dinner time! The
first, ten-minute-before-dinner, bell had rung, and
thick and pressing as the crowd which this time were
gathered round the Koh-i-noor cage, and by faith believed it a diamond, thronged the legal magnificoes
of Lewisburg round the stairs leading to the dining-
room. Now the dining-room certainly couldn't hold
more than half of them,—moreover if we didn't get
near the window, the dining-room was so dark that
we should have to dine under difficulties of no small
magnitude. Burder, myself and Peyton, an Englishman who is staying here held a council of war,—what

13. The western branch of the Court of Appeals and the District Court
of Chancery brought many prominent jurists to Lewisburg.

could we do? We couldn't push away these long Westerners (strapping men many of them), and yet dinner was an object for we were very hungry. "A window is there?" I suggested in an interrogatory tone. "Yes," said Peyton, and hurrying into the garden we got through the window and had just seated ourselves in the best places when the dinner-bell sounded, the door was thrown open, and the rush took place—such a rush!—and only about half found places at last. However it mattered little except to the weaker brethren who had an affection for a clean cloth. Ten minutes is ample time for an American to dine, so that the excluded had no long time to wait.

This Peyton is quite a nice Irishman—in the Army, "I guess," for he asked me to call on him at the "Army & Navy Club" when I come to London. He's been buying Mountain land at 2/- an acre—8000 acres—for some Irish Emigrants. His land lies near the White Sulphur. He is an amateur author and threatens to put in print our dinner adventure of yesterday. He tells me he has been much among the woods on shooting expeditions and a "native" told Burder the other day that he was the best shot at anything "on the wing," he (the "native") even said "from a cat downwards."

Peyton quite agrees with us about the no-hospitality of the Virginians. He had a letter to a General Harman some time ago, in some remote district, and next morning as he was going to leave it struck him he ought perhaps to offer something to his military host. "What, General, am I indebted to you?" he asked. "Two dollars, I reckon," was the hospitable reply. I don't doubt the story the least.

Yesterday on our road to this place, one of our horses "was took worse," and we had to wait for some three hours or more while our dark driver first went to look for animals in the field near a farm, and

194

then rode back to Lewisburg for a fresh pair. We asked leave to rest in the porch of the farmhouse; we got a nod in reply. We asked for some water, and the spring was pointed out, but no one volunteered to get us any—no one offered us bread or anything whatever, although we were there between 4 and 7 in the evening when the farmer's own supper was doubtless going on. It was a great relief when we found our nigger-driver coming back, and ourselves driving on over the (Blue Sulphur—Muddy Creek) mountain, remarkable for the most splendid ferns I ever saw. We arrived here about nine. We could hardly be in nicer quarters —civil landlord, clean rooms, good attendance and capital eating. The scenery round is like all the Watering Places here—low woody hills slope down to the valley near the head of which is the large Hotel, with the "cabins" connected, and the Sulphur Spring a short way off under a fine Grecian Temple (which wants a little whitewash, by the way), and approached through an avenue of trees. We intend to do some riding during our forced sojourn here, and write "to the letter" as Lewis Arundel says.[14]

When at Lewisburg we "heard tell" of a Mr. Montgomery from England, who is travelling through Virginia and wishes to join us in our Western travels. I suppose he'll be here in a day or two. We feel curious about him!

The woman servant at Lewisburg is a slave and had a conversation with me about it. She asked whether we had slaves in England, and having told her of our freedom from any such "peculiar institution" I asked if she would not like to go there. "Yes, if you'll buy me, and take me there,—but you must own me, you

14. In the novel *Lewis Arundel; or the Railroad of Life* by Frank E. Smedley (1852).

know, when you get there." That, I told her I couldn't do, but asked if she wouldn't rather be free there than slave here. "Yes, *if I were sure of getting on*, but I'm dearly fond of old Virginey, and I'm very well off, and unless I was certain of being comfortable in England I'd rather stay where I am." And this, I imagine, is the feeling of most of the slaves in these parts:—this woman was educated, she could read, and picking up an old newspaper in my room, asked leave to tear away the "Poet's Corner." "I'm a great hand for poetry whenever I can get it." She is very religious, and asked both Burder and myself what Church we belonged to. A *Unitarian* she had never heard of before. She was interested about flowers, and brought me several for me to tell their names.

The man at the farm I mentioned a page or two ago told me that slavery was indeed a curse, but that abolition would be a greater. He can, he told me, never trust a black man to tell him the truth about anything, and one white man does, he thinks, three times the work.

Wednesday Afternoon, [June 30].

Yesterday in the afternoon we walked to a Mr. Hamilton's farm[15] to see if riding horses could be got to take us to some waterfalls some 20 miles off. We were received by two young ladies of the family and asked to stay till "father returned." This we declined doing, and on our way home we met a man on horseback whom we suspected might be the gentleman himself.

15. Probably Jacob C. Hamilton (b. 1796), who inherited a fine farm near Blue Sulphur from his father and built a large brick house on it in 1840.

"Are you Mr. Hamilton?" "Good afternoon, gentlemen." "We've been calling, Mr. Hamilton, to ask—"
"My name's not Hamilton—strangers, I guess;—you're
from England, ah? Now neither of you'll be more than
one-and-twenty—You're in best health, I guess (to
Burder), and you're the oldest (to me). From England!!
Well now, and do you ever expect to get safe back
again? You've fathers and mothers at home I know—
rich old fathers—ah? and you've come here through
Lexington. I've a son at Lexington; I wish you could
have seen him when you were there, that I do!" We
found the old man hard to shake off—he told us of his
own complaints, his diseased liver and other matters
of equal interest, and seemed most unwilling to part
with us. We saw an American hare (an uncanny little
fellow) in our walk.

In the evening we took another stroll up the lovely
glen at the back of the house, and after sitting together we went to bed in good time:—no sleep for poor
Burder again though! We had to get a Doctor to him
in the middle of the night, and the cupping that he
had to go through was tremendous—and after all to
find, as we did this morning, that it had all been in
vain, and after the Dr. had gone he still sat with his
head between his hands gasping each moment for
breath. It was very disheartening! however further
cupping, a good deal of emetic-taking, and two large
mustard plasters have done their work this morning,
and he's now sitting under the shade of the verandah
outside our cabin.

The Dr. (Hunter) is, I find, a good botanist,—his
hortus siccus of the American flowers is beautiful—
accurate—and every specimen capitally dried. He has
given me much information about the few flowers I
have collected, and makes me regret extremely that I
was not in time to see the Rhododendron in flower,

197

and the *acres of azaleas* of different colours which cover parts of the surrounding Mountains. He has no apprehension, he says, about rattlesnakes in his botanical excursions. To make yourself drunk with brandy as soon after as possible is supposed to be the best remedy, and in the only case that has come under his notice it was most efficacious. A black girl had gone to an old barn for some hen eggs; she put her hand into the nest and felt what she believed to be the hen pecking it, but the hand at once began to swell, the barn was searched and a rattlesnake was discovered. The girl however recovered as soon as ever the drunken fit went off.

We got as much into the Dr. line here as at Glyn[16] we became parsonic in our acquaintance. I went for a shower bath to a large bathing place near the Hotel and connected with the Sulphur Spring. A Dr. Martin[17] received me, and informing me that Dr. Morpeth[18] had used the medicated baths some time, was pleased to order a shower bath to be got ready for me. He was exceedingly civil, assured me that the water had good tonic qualities, offered me a "servant" (i.e. a "slave") to rub me down, and gave me a book with an account of his own medical prowess in it.

We've just done dinner—venison, etc., strawberry pie and ice cream,—not despicable, by any means, is the feeding here—the corn bread too is the best I've tasted, and the port wine juleps—a new thing to us—are very commendable indeed. Fashions vary much

16. Perhaps Glynn in County Wexford, Ireland—or in County Antrim, Northern Ireland—where Bright went on holiday?

17. Dr. Alexis Martin, a Frenchman who had been a surgeon in Napoleon's army, served for many years as resident physician at Blue Sulphur Springs.

18. I.e., Lord Morpeth, who visited the Virginia springs in 1841 and wrote a poem about them.

198

in America! the landlord hadn't made a *sherry cobbler* for four years.

Look Here!   Look Here!

Once more, in the town of Lewisburg, a new and fashionable Tailor shop. Clear the track and let me go down to A. J. Brads, *new* and *fashionable tailor*, and get my measure taken for a new suit of black. Here is the place if you want fashionable clothes made in the height of the fashion and to save money. He is the man for me. He is determined not to be under-worked by any other tailor in this section of the country. He warrants everything entrusted in his care to be done with neatness and durability. Come on, and he will show you that there is nothing in this advertisement but what is true. Come, and he will prove it to all who will honor him with a call at the fashionable tailor shop of A. J. B. He works very low for cash or good country produce, of all kinds except cabbage. A reasonable time allowed. Come on, gentlemen, to the saving institution of

ANDREW J. BRADS.

Feb. 5, 1852.

8

WAITING AT BLUE SULPHUR SPRINGS

Blue Sulphur. Monday, July 5.

Here we are still and here we must wait,—ennuyée to
a degree! We eat and sleep (poor Burder still asthmatic can't always do that), bathe, talk to Doctors,
read and write. The weather's been wet and we have
made no long expeditions. Indeed I should have had
to make them alone, as Burder can't walk far at present. When will letters come? Wednesday at latest, I
hope.

The only information I've gained here has been on
the subject of the Rappers.[1] "Most knaves or fools?"
I asked the worthy Dr. Hunter, with some little flip-
pancy it repents me. "Very intelligent persons," was
the answer I received. One must be cautious here,—
I approached the question with greater delicacy and
increased respect and soon learnt how matters stood.

These Rappers, who've settled near the Hawk's Nest,

---

1. The phenomenon of rapping spirits was at its height in the 1850s
(see Introduction).

which we pass en route to Charleston, *wrap* themselves in a certain mystery, which has its due effect
on the people—of this district. No doubt some easy
legerdemain suffices for some, for others the "Mediums" (*media* isn't Rappist lingo, only Latin) are not
in the right spirit and cannot communicate with the
other world. These *mediums*, be it said, are beautiful
young ladies, and perhaps their attractions have some
influence with the departed Franklins, Washingtons
and St. Pauls who attend their levees, for their "spirit"
like Barkis "is willing."[2] However that may be, and
however the juggling is performed, we know not, but
as yet the Rappists have not been caught at a disadvantage. One of the mediums, I hear, is reported to
have said "if Mr. Scott (Rapper-in-chief) is deceiving
me, he is doing very wrong."[3] Curious that the Mediums
don't know themselves whether they see Franklin and
the rest! Otherwise people here don't seem superstitious,—"the faded fancies of an elder world" have but
few believers, as Bryant would gladly own—and I can't
hear a good ghost story for Temple[4] "No how." Mrs.
Astor told me the nearest approach to one in New
York—how a house was said to be haunted—how an
adventurous maid of hers hunted in a garret and
fainted, and how it turned out that she had seen what
she believed a coffin with *one leg* in it, booted and
spurred,—a cork leg only it seems when examined—
which had belonged to some military and one-legless
former possessor of the house.

2. In *David Copperfield*.

3. James L. Scott, a Baptist minister turned spiritualist, learned in a
vision that he should leave Auburn, New York, and establish a new
spiritualist community in Mountain Cove, Fayette County, Virginia (now
West Virginia). Taking about one hundred believers with him in 1851,
Scott ruled with divinely inspired power for two years until dissensions
and pecuniary difficulties destroyed the community.

4. Robert Temple (1829-1902), HAB's close friend both at Rugby and
Trinity College.

Ghosts however are not the only horrors in *or* out of the world. Many stories of another nature are horrible too which one hears here,—in perilous duelling stories. I never came across such a bloodthirsty, butcherous (a coined word, I fear, but expressive) set of ———never mind a substantive. I should have a good chance of being called out myself if anyone saw this journal of mine.

To-day, e.g. talking with our good Dr. here, and some other men on duelling and University squabbles, he told us a story of a row occasioned by a duel at his College. "It would never have been known," he said, "to the Professors, but I *cut up that Francisco so with my knife*, he had to take to his bed for a pretty considerable time;" and no one looked disgusted, only smiled pleasantly, and went on with the conversation.

Instances of duels in this State and the neighbouring ones were mentioned:—one personage who honours Mississippi with his residence has killed *eleven* men in duels, and still lives free and openly; he doesn't sleep much at nights I'm told!

The terms of one duel of some celebrity about here were that each should have three pistols and "finish off" with Bowie knives.

In another the challenged (challenged by a notorious dueller and "crack" pistol shot) proposed a grappling on the top of the capitol. This was voted barbarous and vetoed:—Secondly (for, of course, they might as well die together if *he* was to die), he suggested that they should both sit on a barrel of gunpowder and so make their "exits":—also barbarous—that wouldn't do. At last as a civilized and very humane plan they were to fight with muskets so near that *the muskets lapped*:—this was done, and by some chance the ball of the bully but grazed the other's arm, while he fell dead.

202

Henry Clay's duel with Randolph I heard of from another quarter:—Henry Clay—heroically enough—fired before time, and missing, had to receive his opponent's fire in return. Up started the man, naturally indignant with the (shall we say) impatient, impetuous Statesman, and after holding the pistol close to Clay's face to see if he could frighten him,—a proceeding which Clay seems to have borne with a composure worthy of a German student at the Initiatory rite of the Illuminati—raised it, and with true magnanimity fired it over the Kentucky hero's head.[5]

I've mentioned else-where that a Charlottesville Professor was shot. He ventured out one night, when all good Professors should be in their beds, in search of some *masked* students, who were pleased to enact the gentleman-bandit in the neighbourhood. They were discovered,—up walked the professor to unmask the nearest, click went cock of the pistol,—a minute more the professor was dead, and the man soon after in custody. He was *bailed* for some few thousand dollars, forfeited his bail and escaped by the contrivance of his friend.[6]

Such is the value of life in Virginia! Our English refinements in duelling provoked a smile not altogether without contempt in it from *my friend!*

Yesterday was memorable as being the *first time* I've seen "whittling" in America, where I've now been some 7 weeks. English travellers exaggerate awfully on this practice, especially Marryat whose work I've just been reading.[7] I don't like it at all—in a bad spirit

5. This celebrated duel, precipitated by Randolph's insulting Clay in Congress, took place on April 8, 1826.

6. See p. 172 and n. Professor Davis, lingering for a few days after being shot, refused to identify his assailant; but Joseph Semmes was discovered on the evidence of a flawed bullet and finally brought to trial a year later. Freed on $25,000 bail, he skipped town and disappeared.

7. Captain Frederick Marryat, commenting on this habit in 1839, says

with the chief object and aim—the cutting up of Miss Martineau, with whose book this is no more to be compared than "Moonlight unto Sunlight."[8] The diary part, I think really *poor*, and the only value of the book is contained in some supplemental chapters in the end, among which there's one on "Language" which I'm bound to say is delicious. Imagine a member of Congress saying he considered a certain assertion "*catamount* to a denial," and (on being corrected) declaring "that I am not so ignorant of our language as not to know that catamount and tantamount are anonymous." This of course might just as well have happened in England, still it's a good story.

America is certainly odd. Yesterday Dr. H[unter], talking of some disease said, "The effects of doing so and so, depends on a man's temperament. I should give Quĭnīne ad Īnfĭnĭtum."

Revenons à notre Marryat. He attacks Miss Martineau with an inconsistency of statement only surpassed by the spitefulness of the attack itself. After speaking of Jefferson's ill-treatment of his slaves he says, "this is Miss Martineau's good and great Jefferson." Elsewhere he affirms, "I can give the reader a key to Miss Martineau's praise or condemnation of every person mentioned in her two works. You have but to ask the question, 'Is he or is he not an Abolitionist?' " "Reconcile these statements," as they used to say on a Cambridge examination paper. The first charge (on the fourth page—no time is lost in commencing the battery) is that Miss Martineau has been

that "a yankee shewn into a room to await the arrival of another, has been known to whittle away nearly the whole of the mantle-piece" (*Diary in America, with Remarks on its Institutions*, ed. Jules Zanger [Bloomington, Ind., 1960], p. 147).

8. Marryat's account is certainly tactless and unflattering, with frequent gibes at Harriet Martineau's *Society in America* (1837) and *Retrospect of Western Travel* (1838).

hoaxed, and a "gentleman" in Boston showed him two pages of fallacies which he had told her with a grave face:—either the gentleman was gratifying the captain by hoaxing *him*, or if he *did* tell a string of falsehoods to a stranger—lady—the disgrace rests on him not on the lady. Anyhow Miss Martineau is not to blame.

But poor Miss Martineau can say nothing right. She asserts "America has solved the great problem, that a republic can exist for 50 years," but, adds Marryat, "such is not the case. America has proved that under peculiar advantages a people can govern themselves for 50 years, but, &c.," and then follows an assertion that America is not as it was in Washington's time.

Allowed,—but what's that to do with it? Is America a republic? Was America a republic 50 years ago? Yes. Then America "has solved the problem" &c., and Miss Martineau is right.

And what, en passant, is the exact difference, according to Marryat, between a Republic and a "people who govern themselves?"

However Miss Martineau is big enough and—(oh! no! ladies are never *old enough*) to take care of herself, so I shall not undertake her defence farther.

On one point Marryat is undoubtedly a good witness—perfectly impartial and altogether unprejudiced; —on religious controversial questions, on religious questions of any kind, he, like Gibbon, is probably altogether to be relied on, rising very superior to all such.

His testimony then is that "Massachusetts and the smaller Eastern States are the stronghold of religion and morality. As you proceed from them farther South or West, so does the influence of the clergy decrease" —this is at least some consolation to us heretics, as Massachusetts is probably the only district in the world, except a section of Transylvania and the city of Geneva, where Unitarianism is dominant;—the effects are that Massachusetts is the most religious, moral, and the best educated (see Marryat's chapter on Education: "the State of M[assachusetts] is a school—it may be said that all there are educated") State in America. And this too *without cant*. Massachusetts gave every vote she had at the last Whig Convention for Webster. The Southern States objected to do it because he had led a wild life and occasionally took brandy! These are some small specks on the Southerners themselves which 'twere well they removed first, thinking on a proverb about Glass Houses and the throwing of stones!

Tuesday Evening, [July 6].

A Richmond paper tells us of the death of Clay—long expected, and much lamented. It also shows how Webster bears the nomination of Scott—or rather how he tries to bear it. A serenading crowd comes to him at night, which he addresses out of window in his nightgown,—"the Convention have doubtless used their *best discretion*" he says; he himself will sleep well after it. "This is a serene and beautiful night, gentlemen,—thousands of stars in the heaven—they *rule the night*; a few hours and they *disappear*—the *sun* has risen." He then bids the people good-night, and the Whigs say he approves of the nomination—"credat Judaeus apella,"[9]—I don't. "Poor proud" Webster (to use the epithets Miss Barrett applied to Byron),[10] he must indeed flinch at so heavy a blow—to be defeated by Gen. Winfield Scott!

9. "Let the Jew Apella believe it" (Horace, *Satires* I.v.100).
10. In "A Vision of Poets."

206

To-day Burder and myself took a drive in a small carriage, but we did not get, as we had hoped, to the top of the Blue Sulphur Mountain, as it was rather late. This evening I've had a long conversation with Dr. Hunter on the animal world of Virginia. He's a well-informed man on such subjects, and has received a charge from the Smithsonian Institute people to report on the "Flora" and "Animated Nature" (as Dr. Goldsmith calls it)[11] of this section of the State. One story he told me, which he will vouch for:—it looks improbable,—so do some of Gordon Cumming's stories[12]—but they are both probably equally true. A friend of Dr. Hunter's wounded a deer, and followed it by the blood-track through some woods in the county of Fayette. After a time he came across a rattlesnake which he killed,—a little farther on was another—then another—he kills them in turn, and goes on; but the more he advances the thicker grow the snakes. "These grow like Hydra's heads." A second Hercules, he kills some forty or fifty, but they are getting too many for him, and as he puts an end to one, another rattles close by. He turns tail now and brings some more friends to the fray. On they go on the old track—the rattlesnakes more in number than ever. However their opponents are a match for them, and still they advance. At last they come within sight of a large rock lying open to the sun, and several feet in length. A stifling pest-like smell rises up round it, while upon it some thousands of rattle-snakes are disporting themselves, some basking, others wreathing in quaint windings, and others "giving tongue" with their rattle tails. The Virginian battalion went no farther on their expedition.

11. Oliver Goldsmith's *History of the Earth and Animated Nature* was among his last published works.

12. Roualeyn George Gordon Cumming (1820-66), known as "the Lion-hunter," author of South African hunting tales.

Smaller companies of snakes are in like manner often found. They meet in the spring, and leaving their "den" as summer comes on, get back to their rendez-vous in the "fall." As I'm writing Dr. Martin comes in and makes me a present of a *"rattle,"* which has still a power to "please" *when the snake's dead.*

In our conversation to-night Dr. Hunter told me that we were waxing theological about them. The most eminent Unitarian in America,—the "king" of them is Mr. Campbell of Mississippi, and next to him Mr. Clapp of New Orleans![13] Most fickle fame has never sounded their praise our side the water, but has brayed out the names of Channing[14] and Dewey instead! General Scott is, I hear, a Catholic.[15]

The dominant religion here seems to be the Presbyterian—further west the Catholic:—the Baptists and Methodists are poor people and blacks, the literary patronize Unitarianism or Episcopacy. By the way in Marryat's book is a copy of some of the old Puritan laws of Massachusetts, such as:—

"No one shall *run* of a Sabbath day or walk in his garden or elsewhere except reverently to and from Church.

"No one shall travel, cook victuals, make beds, sweep houses, cut hair or shave on Sabbath day.

"No husband shall kiss his wife, and no mother shall kiss her child upon the Sabbath day.

---

13. Theodore Clapp (1792–1866), a New Englander who spent 35 stormy years in New Orleans, was expelled in 1833 from the Presbyterian church in a heresy trial that achieved nationwide notoriety. He thereafter became a Unitarian. I cannot discover a Unitarian Mr. Campbell.

14. William Ellery Channing (1780–1842), considered the father of American Unitarianism.

15. Scott was a lifelong Episcopalian, but was represented by the Democrats as pro-Catholic because one of his daughters had been a nun and others were educated at Catholic schools.

"No one shall read Common Prayer, keep Xmas or
Saint's day, make mince pies, dance or play on any
instrument of music, except the drum, the trumpet
and the Jew's Harp."

Thursday Morning, [*July* 8].

Still no letter—hope deferred of a surety! Well I
suppose "the time is at hand" for us as for the fair
Lily in Goethe's Tale,[16] and to-morrow we have every
right to expect our letters and our money,—which is
more precious I can scarcely say.

I have been looking over a curious book—a thing
John Chapman raved about a short time since, "Revelations of A. J. Davis Poughkeepsie Seer and Clairvoyant."[17] A son of a common country shoemaker, he
is put into a mesmeric state and delivers a series of
lectures on Astronomy, Anatomy, Theology, and
Heaven knows what all blended into one system and
published as delivered.

It's a strange story—the evidence is very strong to
prove that he had no education which could account
for his wonderful knowledge, and even if he had somehow acquired it, the mystery is as great, for no instance perhaps is on record of a boy of 19 discussing
some subjects with apparent originality and depth.

16. The tale is the celebrated "Märchen" that concludes *The Recrea-
tions of the German Emigrants.* In the course of its magical events, the
beautiful Lily is told three times that "the time is at hand."

17. The full title is *The Principles of Nature, Her Divine Revelations,
and A Voice to Mankind.* By and through Andrew Jackson Davis. Published in 1847 by his "magnetizer," Dr. S. S. Lyon, and his "scribe,"
the Rev. William Fishbough, this volume consists of 157 lectures delivered in Manhattan while Davis was in a state of trance. John Chapman
(1822-94), publisher, and editor of the *Westminster Review* since 1851,
had published Davis's work in England, testifying himself to its moral
value and scientific insight.

He "employs technical terms and even foreign words and phrases with the greatest facility, yet sometimes *mispronounces*." An extraordinary case—how can it be accounted for; either there is some juggling somewhere, or this is a *Revelation* which announces to the world the condition of the planets, &c., tells us that the inhabitants of Jupiter assume an inclined position, "inhabit well-constructed edifices, whose form corresponds to that of a *tent* rather than a house on Earth," &c., and "do not die, but rather sink into repose by an expansion of their interiors;"—either all this, and much to the same purpose is infallibly true, or (as I said before) there is some chicanery at work. Now being a *little* sceptical, I'm not going to swallow all this, even when gilded by an assertion—a revelation—of the truth of Unitarianism.[18] But where can we find a flaw? The lectures were given before people of all kinds,—the boy could not have had the instruction beforehand, or indeed the necessary time to get them up. How was it managed?

I thought over it for some time, and had resolved to place it among the unfathomable deceptions of "Mysterious Ladies," "Electro Biologists," and so forth, until I noticed that during these lectures "The faint vital forces still remaining in his system are only sustained sympathetically *by the presence of the magnetizer whose system is* by an ethereal medium *blended* and *united with his own*."[19]

The thought at once occurs:—if the magnetizer's *life* is thus present to the magnetizee, why not his *mind*? If mesmerism is true the mind of the manipulator has indeed a very potent effect on the patient

18. In that Davis declared that Jesus was a perfect man, but not divine.

19. Bright quotes from the introduction to the book, written by the "scribe," William Fishbough.

(or victim). Now this Dr. Lyon is a Doctor of Medicine, by no means infallible, for but four asteroids (with alas, errors countless) are mentioned as existing—but probably very capable of writing this book. He seems already to have made use of Davis in investigating diseases, and now will turn an honest penny through the publication of this.[20] If this theory is improbable, I can only say I see no means of denying the inspiration of this book, and believing in the tent-houses in Jupiter, the orang-outang like "humans" which possess Mercury, and the two belligerent races which distrust Venus. Allowing however that the mind of this Dr. Lyon so impregnates Davis that he merely becomes his mouthpiece, and that they are Dr. Lyon's revelations which the gaping scribe and editor delivers to the world, the difficulty is got over, and the full value of the book determined.

And this is come out by two or three "trifles light as air," but still worthy of notice. First this will account for the errors in the book, as overthrowing its supernaturalness. Secondly the character of Davis, who really seems a quiet, truthful fellow enough, is freed from all suspicion;—in these mesmeric sleeps he speaks, he knows not what, and when awake of course he knows nothing about it. Thirdly this hypothesis explains his use of technical terms and foreign words and yet *mispronunciation*. The words, &c. are so many inaudible dictations from Lyon which he (Davis) naturally enough can't pronounce at times. Then lastly, in the "Address to the World," Davis is made to go through the mental and other qualities of his witnesses, and places this Dr. Lyon *last on the list*:—an unlikely thing when one remembers the position of supreme

---

20. Lyon was a successful doctor in Bridgeport, Connecticut; Davis, in a clairvoyant state, diagnosed the diseases of his patients.

importance in which Lyon stands to him,—a most likely and natural thing, if Lyon arranged it all himself.[21] We are also assured in the same place that this Lyon is "opposed to all dissimulation and will present those things which form a part of his mind not in *speech*, but in general deportment and *action*"—Why so anxious to tell us that this Dr. doesn't *dissemble*—qui s'excuse s'accuse—it looks as if the Dr. did dissemble and wrote it himself;—and what does the last part of the sentence mean,—perhaps some Sphinx-like allusion to the true state of things.

Still it's unsatisfactory, and I can hardly hope this theory of mine, though the best I can get at, is true.

Since writing this I see a paragraph in the Introduction to the book which before escaped me, in which the Editor says:—"we know that such a thing (as sympathetic influx from others) could not be," *he himself*, he says, is incapable of giving it (no one suspected him!); *but Dr. Lyon is never mentioned* (whom we might suspect), except indeed "the other who could have little difficulty in proving that his mind has not been overburdened with knowledge on these subjects" —is the worthy manipulator. Few men's minds are *overburdened* with knowledge on any subject.

But it strikes me the editor is hardly so confident on this point as he would give us to believe. Of course he mustn't show his misgivings at the last moment with some seven hundred and eighty something pages of revelation before him, ready for an eager public; yet does this ring a little hollow and doubtful. "If this law of sympathetic influx however is *admitted* (italics are 'his'n', as a nigger says), it should be duly *explained* and *defined* before the conclusion is formed

21. "The MANIPULATOR, Dr. Silas Smith Lyon, is physically constituted so as to be able to impart a congenial influence to the system of the speaker, whereby the transition of the natural faculties to the spiritual sphere has been accomplished" (pp. 3–4).

that it may not, under certain circumstances,[22] be a medium through which *spirits* of the higher world may transmit their knowledge to mankind on earth. Certainly the sympathetic transmission of a thought from one person to another is quite as inexplicable as would be the transmission of the thought of a disembodied spirit to a person duly susceptible to sympathetic influx." By no manner of means!

"As touching this subject, however, see the author's remarks on Animal Magnetism, Clairvoyance and the source of his impressions in the forepart of this volume, in which the nature and ground of his claims are duly set forth." A notable plan for proving the genuineness of a book by an appeal to the assertion of it contained in the book, i.e. proving a thing to be true by assuming it doesn't lie!

(Davis derives the Trinity from Zoroaster and his predecessor, and says, "Let *us* make man" is derived from the early myth, in which the "us" means Brahma, Vishnu and Siva.

"Jesus was a good man, a noble and paralleled Moral Reformer, considering him as disconnected from all those unjust things that are in the New Testament recorded of him. He did not profess to be the Son of God in any other sense than that of a Branch, as all are, of the Great Tree of Universal and eternal Causation. He was a Type of a Perfect Man.")

Sunday Morning, [*July 11*].

Still here. To-day if our letters do not come, we must throw ourselves on Mr. Burster's[23] generosity and get him to let us go without paying our fortnight's

22. The text reads "under favorable circumstances."
23. George W. Buster (1803–68), owner of Blue Sulphur Springs.

bill. We are sick of the place. The Ohio is getting low, and our time short. Our days have some monotony about them:—breakfast between six and seven,—read and write, sit by the Spring and drink—dinner between twelve and one, read and write, etc., tea about six, a stroll, and that's about all.[24] Waiting for the Stage is one excitement, talking to Dr. Hunter another,—listening to "Would I were with thee," on a cracked piano by the wife of a Salt-work man on the Kanawha a third, —and there I think one's amusements end. Dr. Hunter took me out "snake-hunting" the other day. All in vain. We walked along "Snakes' Run," and other haunts of the reptile, but divil a snake could we see. A terrapin tortoise squatting upon a baby "buoy" in the little creek here was some compensation. Well, I should like to see a snake before we leave this country.

We have also made acquaintance with the red bird and the blue bird since we have been in this place, and with the croak-bellow of the Bully-frog.

During our snake hunt we came across a fine fat old farmer, a glorious dog, who is well-natured and well-informed, a Universalist, though without a parson to drive him, a hater of the French, of Rappers and Methodists, a lover of the English, Anti-humbug and Reason;—knows Grecian history moreover and quotes you how Aristides (a uni-syllable Aristides) said to Peri*cals* (Pericles):—"Strike me, but hear me."[25] I think I shall call on him again to-day. Mr. Clapp, Universalist Minister of New Orleans is here. Burder

24. Writing poetry was one way to while away the time. See "Soul's Memories" and "A Debt of Gratitude to Shelley" (pp. 454, 455), both written at Blue Sulphur Springs.

25. Bright's farmer muddles the heroes of two celebrated anecdotes. The phrase comes from Plutarch's life of Themistocles and was Themistocles' response to a threat by Eurybiades. The story about Aristides concerns the illiterate citizen who voted for Aristides' ostracism because he was tired of hearing him called the Just.

has talked to him, finds him a nice person, Europe-travelled and liberal—a Unitarian except in name. I must try to get acquainted with him.

Yesterday I heard an American legend for the first time. A little boy who at times frequents the Spring here, and who may be seen at times indulging himself with the fascinating amusement of spitting and catching the sweet saliva upon his naked feet as it falls. This "in-dividdle" being asked a question by some burly sulphur-water-drinking farmer answered (as Americans often do to save articulation), "Um-um." "Why do you say *"Um-um?"* demanded the burly man. "Those are the devil's words:—the Devil was asked a question, when he had one (I fear me the Devil only makes bundles of one sort,—my friend gave no substantive) under one arm, another under the other, a third in his mouth. The Devil didn't wish to drop the mouthmorsel, and to the question only answered 'Um-um.' So they are the Devil's words. I wouldn't use the Devil's words again if I were you."

Monday Morning, [July 12].

Yesterday afternoon the letters came from Ander-don—English ones for Burder, none for me—nor, says Anderdon, is there any money waiting for us at Cincinnati. This must at once be looked into. A good-natured <   > lends a cheque of his own for $100, so now we owe him $75. The only thing I got were two letters from George, one of which about the Whig Convention I insert for obvious reasons.[26]

26. George described the strife and bitterness of the convention, but ended on this note: "The return of all to a unit, the submission of each to the slender majority for Scott, is a picture which can only be seen in

George evidently believes in principles not men.

In the evening, and again this morning, I paid the jolly old farmer a visit—Mr. Standige. Last night he showed us some of his "Corn" growing near ten feet high, and really a beautiful crop. He told us of an Irishman who on first seeing Indian corn believed it to be tobacco, and as he saw the curled ear sheath, assurance became doubly sure and he pointed it out exultingly as the "tobacco *twist* mon, don't ye see it?"

He also—the Virginian, not the Irishman—took us to see a dead black snake he had killed, black above, grey below, some 3½ ft. long. This morning he showed me a tobacco field—the plants are young and look like cabbage rows exactly. My friend is an East Virginian by "raising," but has now been some time in this district. He remembers when the Indians still frequented these parts, and was at Richmond when the first representative of Kentucky passed through it and pitched his tent—a literal tent—on Capitol Hill.[27] He is of Scotch origin himself, his grandfather came over from that country. He is very curious about the "Rappers," and has made me promise to write and tell him if they are "Humbugs"; "in any case," he added, "just send us a line—never mind how short—just to say how you get along, even if it only like Caesar's from Spain to the Senate, 'Veni, Vidi, Vici,' came, saw, conquered sir." He's certainly a glorious old fellow. I found him at 8½ this morning with two white labourers—he doesn't like slaves—in his wheat (bearded wheat) field with "scythes and cradles," which may be used in our

the *United* States—*and we are united.* Now we all go into the fight with Scott as the standard bearer of our party, and we shall sweep the land with all the resistless force of the avalanche, but with none of its destructive fury."

27. As a boy, Clay lived in Richmond (1791 to 1797), first working as a clerk in a retail store, and then studying law. But this may refer to a later tour.

England (Burder tells me they are), but I never happen to have seen them.

Dr. Hunter has given me some fossils and a bottle of snakes. People are very good-natured. A lady here, Mrs. Brooks, quite bores us to take letters to the Kanawha bank and the Saline. She gave me a receipt for Indian Corn Cakes (Green).

9

WESTWARD TO THE OHIO RIVER

Charleston, Kanawha, Vir[ginia].
Wednesday Night, July 14.

We left the Blue Sulphur in a small carriage after
dinner on Monday, and after a pleasant drive during
which we had from Sewell's Mountain a view very
little, if at all, inferior to that near the Warm Springs,
we found ourselves at last safely lodged at Frazer's,
a little Inn in the mountains, where we had gone to
avoid the long stage journey of the next day to Lewis.
A quaint little Inn is Frazer's—so dark the rooms you
can hardly see in some of them, and in Burder's bedroom without a candle not at all. The table in the
sitting-room is covered with law books, and on inquiry
we find that Mr. Frazer, our worthy landlord's father,
is *High Sheriff of the County*.

Next morning, as the stage would not come before
two, we went out with Mr. Frazer, his dog "Jim,"
and his trusty gun, squirrel-shooting. On our way we
passed a little stream (Creek—rather "Crik" they call
them here), fringed with Rhododendron out of flower,

and a superb sweet-scented white Azalea in full bloom. Farther on in a "glade" (we call 'em our landlord said) we saw the yellow evening primrose (Austurea) and found the underwood consist of species of St. John's Wort, growing some six feet high, and just breaking into golden star blossom. In this wood we came across the finest trees we have yet seen in America—a sycamore required eleven paces to span it, and I found six paces only just enough to get round a large cherry whose height was proportionate.

Our squirreling was unsuccessful; we had started too late, and the little fellows had "retired into private life." To be sure "Jim" did see one, and barked at the bottom of a very high tree for some ten minutes in a most praiseworthy manner; but "Jim" had the advantage of us, and after peeping up into the branches for some time we gave it up as a bad job and walked off. We were unlucky however, and did not come across another.

In the middle of the wood runs a very wild picturesque river—Meadow River—some 50 yards across. The trees hang over it, among them the pine, not a common tree about here. By the side we found a part of a raft which had been used for crossing; the lashings were of the wild camphor, "which," said our guide, "is a mistake; the wild vine is better for that."

The rest of the morning we spent in reading, listening to a thunder-storm, and eating dinner, and about three found ourselves inside the Stage with a curious party enough. An M.D. with a young wife giving suck to a baby, and a little boy without shoes or stockings, "to harden his feet" his father said. Also a New York watch-maker, Piggott by name, who with his wife were going to settle at Mountain Cove, the "Rapper" village near Lewis (where we are to spend the night).

Of course we availed ourselves of the opportunity

and got considerably more Rapper news than I've room for in this journal. "Rappers" by the way the good folks don't like to be called—"Spirit Believers"—the wife told me was the name they went by among themselves. A spirit had revealed this "Mountain Cove" to them and they were going to settle, put up a printing press and—of course convert the world—the scoffing world—into a full and entire belief in ghosts.

The origin of this "pernicious superstition" I was going to write, but it strikes me Christianity was so called at its commencement, and I won't dignify "Rappism" by the term. The origin of this ridiculous nonsense seems as follows:—In a house in Western New York reputed to be haunted, the children of the family grew so familiar with some Rapping Spirits, that in joke they proposed to try who could *rap quickest*.[1] The Spirits accepted *the challenge*, and by degrees, rapped in answer to anything the young 'uns asked. The story got wind, and the Rappers got founded. Their theory is this. We are surrounded by a Spirit World, which we cannot see, for our Spiritual eyes are shut. These, the denizens of the Spirit World, can however announce their presence by sounds, but even these are inaudible or unintelligible save to some few gifted ones, who are the Mediums between the Shades and the Substances—Spirit and Flesh.

Sometimes these Mediums write a *spirit-letter*, as well as interpret Rappings. They sit down and their hand, apparently without volition on their part, writes that which appears to you written by some departed friend. Sometimes a spirit-letter comes without a Medium,—as when one gentleman sitting in his room and playing with a piece of writing paper, turned it

1. Margaret Fox, who with her sister Kate started the movement, confessed to the chicanery forty years later.

over and discovered a letter from some deceased friend. Sometimes the Medium will speak in a voice of some friend of yours whom he has never seen—so Piggott professes to have heard his Mother's voice.

Such was the information which we obtained from our Rappist friends, who moreover assured us a "Medium" was sitting on the box of the Stage—a fine handsome man the Medium looked when he descended in the course of our journey, and honoured us by placing himself on the seat with us—not altogether courteous though was this Spirit Medium. Perhaps Franklin and St. Paul and so forth like plain spoken people. "I'll get quite fat here in the country," said poor frosty, and much-diseased-in-the-liver Mrs. Piggott. "You've too many wrinkles on your brow for that," jeered the Medium to the poor old soul; and she bore it very meekly. I suppose we ought all to bear anything with resignation which comes from one who talks with Spirits! We had once rather a notion of trying our luck with the Medium, but the chances were considerably against our getting much information. In the first place, perhaps the Spirit World won't come at all,—they don't like scoffers and unbelievers, nor will they rap in answer to a question of idle curiosity. Suppose however an answer is vouchsafed, it is as likely as not to be a lie—bad spirits abound as well as good, and bad spirits sometimes give answers, and bad spirits always lie,—therefore if you *do* get a Spirit answer, which is *improbable*, it may turn out a lie, and the Rappists are no jot the less confident and tell you a bad spirit answered—that's all. There is another peculiarity about the Spirits which "light of nature" would lead one to imagine: they dislike towns, and answer most freely in the country, where the air is less gross, say the Believers,—where the people are more simple, says the sceptic. The Spirits appear contemptuous on religious sects—they believe in the Trinity, my companion, the ci-devant watchmaker, rather doubtfully said;—"they deny eternal punishment," he asserted very positively.

That the Non-medium believers are generally sincere I do not doubt for a moment,—that there is juggling in it I think equally certain,—but that there is much good-feeling and enthusiasm in the best I must believe, for the affection with which these good people were greeted in the pretty Mountain Cove village by their old friends was quite touching, when they left us this morning, and among the Rappists who came to meet them I saw much apparent fanaticism of expression, no hypocrisy. They are farmers chiefly and their corn (Indian) and wheat fields look most flourishing. They are now building a printing office whence will issue their converting all-powerful paper.[2] The leader of them—one Scott—I did not see. The man on the Stage was Shannon, and a wild-looking brother who welcomed them was a Dr. Harris[3] with a Bloomer wife or daughter (Bloomer being used for the first time in America) all in suit of red ditto.[4]

But now back to yesterday's journey. We did 19 miles in eight hours, and got to Lewis about eleven, the only incident on the journey being the loss of my wide-awake out of window while I was dozing. Luckily there was a store at Lewis, so that the inconvenience was of no very long duration. On the road I saw for the first time the red blossoms of the Shumach tree—

2. The first issue of *The Mountain Cove Journal and Spiritual Harbinger*, edited by James L. Scott and T. L. Harris, appeared just two weeks later, on August 1, 1852.

3. Thomas Lake Harris (1823-1906), a Universalist minister converted to spiritualism by Andrew Jackson Davis, became famous as the author of mystic poetry and later founded his own communal societies.

4. Amelia Jenks Bloomer (1818-94) popularized her famous costume in the 1850s.

a beautiful tree with leaf like the Ailanthus—and noticed the woods of flowering Spanish chestnut which were really superb.

A good supper awaited us at Lewis, and a lie down for some 3 hours, as we started again soon after three in the morning, and have been jolting along ever since.

It will give an idea of the Stage travelling here when I say that yesterday from Lewisburg to Lewis—some 47 miles—the Stage took 16 hours—rather less than three miles an hour. To-day the road was not so bad and we did 57 miles in that time; but imagine the agonies of 16 hours' travel, with less than an hour's rest for a ten o'clock breakfast-lunch, after which we fasted till we got here for a seven o'clock dinner-tea.

Some ten miles from Lewis is Mount[ain] Cove, where we dropped the Rappists (as I have already described),—a little farther and the coach stops to give you a view from the Hawk's Nest—a precipitous rock rising some 1000 feet from the New River, and from which you see the River winding along below you through a gorge of wooded hills. Very close the river looks, but he is a good flinger who can throw a stone into its stream from the beetling rock he stands on. A most glorious view it was. The "Morning Mist" which Festus Bailey quotes as so proverbially slow going "off the hills"[5] still lay in wreaths on the mountain tops, but did not obscure the view. The woods were as thick and varied as any woods I ever saw, and the river itself now lay in still pools, now chafed itself white against opposing rocks. Our stay was necessarily short, and we jolted on again to breakfast at the Falls of Kanawha, which I had intended to explore, but breakfast had "charms to soothe" the hungry stomach which the Falls had not, and Romance was sacrificed

5. In Philip James Bailey's colossal cosmic poem, *Festus*.

to Digestion. The drive was beautiful certainly along the banks of the Kanawha, now alas, infested by Cholera.

But we were certainly glad to find ourselves about seven o'clock at Charleston, passing however on our way the Salt Work, and the Burning Spring of Natural Gas, which I was sorry we could not stay to explore. Charleston is a beautiful little town on the river side, and several pretty country, or rather suburban, houses round it. As we entered we heard for the first time the loud chirping of a locust-like insect called the "Katy-did," which makes a great commotion among the trees. I never saw such splendid *corn* crops as those on the river banks here—certainly the valley of Kanawha is more rich than anything we've seen, except perhaps part of Pennsylvania.

"The Financier" stern—which boat on the Ohio.
Thursday Night, [July 15].

At last we find ourselves sailing down the river "of the Ohio" in as nasty a little steamer as I ever hope to see—still it *is* the Ohio, and we've done with *Staging* "it may be for ever," and I sincerely trust it will. Anything so miserable as has been our condition for the last two days I never felt. To-day we started from Charleston about 4½ and went on to a wretched little wayside Inn where we breakfasted. The Inn was ten miles from Charleston, and we had still 38 to go, which we accomplished by 3½, rather good travelling on the whole, and not far from 5 miles an hour, whereas the Stage which took us from Frazer's to Lewis two days ago, had got through 47 miles in 16 hours—rather less than 3 miles an hour.

We had only two companions on our journey to-day—one, a poor old negro woman, and the other a Captain M'Lomas from Barboursville. The negress was a free woman, and though uneducated, very intelligent. She told us her whole history;—how attached she had been to her Mas'r and his family in South Carolina where she was "raised," but how her Mas'r's love for drink had deprived him, first of his own fortune, and then of her "old Missi," and he had to sell his negroes. She was bought by a Western Virginian (whose house she pointed out), who freed her at his death, and his son had given her a house to live in. She was well-off, she said, and had "200 chickens." Her masters had always been good to her, and her only grief had been about her children, some of whom had been sold far away, and one daughter who did live near her had just died. She was very unhappy just then about this and longed to go to Guyandotte where her old Missi is staying to get some comfort from her. "Whenever I go there," she says, "we always have a good cry together, and I always go back with little things they've all given me." She says she would not be a slave again for anything, but believes that for many who *can't get on themselves*, slavery is a very good thing, and there is now less cruelty than formerly, though cases still occur. One she mentioned as having occurred near where we were passing—a Dutch Dr. Sershen (or some such a name) had beaten his slaves so awfully that one ran away, and being re-taken has been *in chains* ever since:—a female he sent to prison, and her back was a mass of lacerations, when she was stripped to put on the prison dress.

A pious old lady was our friend. She talked much on religious topics and told us how she was converted from Methodism to Baptism (is the word used in this sense?), and how she thought the good of any sect might be saved. "I goes in for no sect in particular; I goes in for the Methodist and the Baptist, and the < > too I hope. I goes in for all." Witchcraft, she said, many coloured people believe in,—"but I don't —for a good Spirit wouldn't want to come back to earth, and a bad spirit wouldn't be let to." She also disapproves of the contortions in which Camp-meetings throw excitable ladies. She was pleased to call us "true gentlemen," and promised not to hurt any of our "contraptions" as she entered the Stage.

Our other friend talked about the Superiority of the South, and how Boston was full of "Unitarians, Millerites and Mormons." He was however an intelligent fellow, fine, tall and handsome, though rather gaunt, a little like Harcourt, I thought.

Guyandotte is a small place on the Ohio here, as broad perhaps as the Rhine in Cologne. We dined, and waited three hours, during which I searched the sandy, pebbly beach for shells, which I hear are very beautiful, and found for my pains something suspiciously like our English domestic limpet.

At last to our joy we saw this thing coming along, hailed it, and here we are:—a horrid little boat, but paradisaical after the staging of the last three days, and besides we do go some eight miles an hour!

Friday Morning, [July 16].

The accommodation is disgusting; one wash-hand basin for all the passengers,—the common toothbrush I have *not* seen. The food is as bad—they haven't even milk and the coffee is taken pure and undefiled. The river is pretty—low hills covered with wood, on one or both sides of the river, just leave room for some farm-

226

ing in the valley-land between them and the Ohio. Small villages, and occasionally a good-sized town like Maysville (where the cholera has been bad this year) dot the banks here and there, while boats of various sorts ply up and down between them. We stop at Maysville for 10 minutes and little boys come on board, one with a basket of very green apples, another with a miscellaneous store which he brings to me with "have a toothpick, sir?" The water of the Ohio is much muddier than I expected, but this may be owing to the season at which we see it.

American Words and Pronunciations.

hack	carriage (hired)	Nátional
hackney	horse	advertísement
boy	waiter	genuíne
store	shop	engíne
lightning bug	firefly	geenyus (genius)

One gentleman wishing to assure me of the luxury of the Southern Steamers told me that after dinner there were figs, almonds and "a world of děsěrt" on the table.

10

CINCINNATI AND LOUISVILLE

Burnet House, Cincinnati.
Saturday Night, July 17.

When we arrived here about seven last night we found
Loch was here, and a large parcel of letters from England, containing the most astonishing news—good and
bad—six letters full. Sarah's engagement,[1] poor little
Theo's death—to read of both in the same half hour,
and to write congratulation and condolence, each
most sincere and heartfelt, and both together—it was
sadly strange. However, I must not mix up home affairs in a journal, so shall go back at once to the
Burnet, and Cincinnati, and what we've seen and done.

First then, this *is* a wonderful town—an Aladdin-
Palace town,—streets and stores, hotels and Banks and
Churches all built in 50 years, and a river which half
a century ago used to wind round Indian Forts and
log-huts, now washes the homes of 130,000 people.

---

1. HAB's oldest sister had become engaged to George Melly of Liverpool. Melly was a Unitarian and a Rugbean, but not (as Bright confessed
to his mother he would have preferred) one of his Cambridge friends.

It is a beautiful town moreover, with several good public buildings, with trees in the streets, and a busy gay look about it—the "Queen City of the West." In one thing it resembles an English City—there is *smoke to be seen*, for west of the Alleghanies lie the bituminous coalfields, and Cincinnati having certain factories about it, is really not so new and American-looking as the Eastern cities. Numbers of steamers line the town, reminding one of New York. Several of their names struck me as curious for different reasons,—"Duchess," "Lady Pike," "Childe Harold," "Guzman[?]," "Sparhawk," "Swampfox," "Wm. Noble," &c. &c.

The Burnet House is, I think, the best Hotel I ever saw—certainly the best I've seen in America.[2] It is enormously large and makes up 380 beds or more, and is also very clean,—the rooms are beautiful, the bath rooms good, the food very fair, and the bar people civil. We are both delighted with it, Loch too has found it very comfortable since he has been here. Here we see mosquito curtains for the first time. Our modest beds each wear a white net veil thrown all over them from top to toe.

Last night and this morning I have mostly spent in writing—to Synge, Irvin, George, Sarah, Bessie, Aunt Min, George Melly—so now I have nearly done my duty. I have also got the money from the bank for which Mr. Irvin gave me a letter,—have left the parcel on young Hart, who was from home—have called on Livermore[3] who was out,—have bought books, paper and flower presses,—have had rather a "fine thing" in moustaches shaved off—have sat for a considerable time in a news-room reading English papers,—and have

2. The Burnet House, Cincinnati's principal hotel, was at Third and Vine streets.

3. Abiel Abbot Livermore (1811-92), minister of the Cincinnati Unitarian Church, 1850-56; later president of Meadville Theological School.

BURNET HOUSE, CINCINNATI

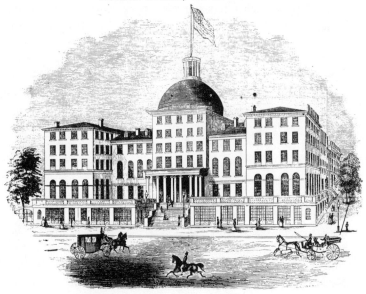

Gleason's Pictorial Drawing-Room Companion, July 26, 1851

"The best Hotel I ever saw."

passed part of the evening with the Kings[4] to whom
Mr. Peter gave us a letter. Loch has been with us all
day, and we hope to get him on with us to St. Louis,
&c. He's a nice fellow and we get much information
on many points from him. We have also seen to-day
some machine-carved woodwork which is extremely
pretty, and with which we have rather fallen in love.
It is the invention of a Mr. Wood of England who

4. Rufus King (1817–91), grandson of the famous Rufus King of New
York, was prominent in Cincinnati educational and civic work. His wife,
Margaret Rives King, daughter of Dr. Landon Rives, was one of the city's
most brilliant hostesses.

"came to grief" from railway shares and is now doing his best in Cincinnati to get on, and I don't doubt will. One instance of how an active fellow may push his way in this country I came across in the steamer here. Some seven years ago, an Irish boy came over from Donegal,—quite poor, and without friends here. He came to New York, and after getting his name, &c. put down, went to Canada, where he told me he *spent*—and I rather think *wasted*—four years. Back to America, he goes into a Store at Pittsburgh, and makes £40 the first year in wages. He and a friend then set up for themselves a store at Cincinnati,—they are doing well, *having*, more than once, made £35 *in a day*, and probably when next I come to America I shall find my friend—a shrewd, intelligent fellow full of information—Senator of Ohio, or otherwise a great personage,—Webster was a farmer's son, Clay a miller-boy!

This Irish fellow says he's travelled in Louisiana and most of the slave States, and has seen more misery in a month in Ireland than in all the time he's been in America. I got into conversation with him by asking him what language he was talking to a brother passenger—it was Irish!

The Kings on whom we called, are very pleasant people, but I don't think we gained any particular information from them. The letter to Mr. Scarborough which Irvin gave us we have had no opportunity to deliver.

Among my feats to-day I find involuntary theft is one. I went with Burder to look at some eye-glasses, and find I put one into my own pocket!—a shop-lifter with a vengeance—and such a hideous glass too!

Now to mosquito curtains and bed!

Mammoth Cave Hotel, Kentucky.
Wednesday, July 21.

On Sunday we separated. Burder and Loch went to
hear the Bishop of Ohio, I to Livermore's. The congregation was tolerably good, and I was amused by the
way the good pastor who was going to have an "out"
told his flock that the next Service in the chapel
would take place on the 1st. September. Livermore's
sermon was particularly good on "Who doeth great
wonders, for His mercy endureth for ever,"—showing
how the Supreme's goodness is manifest in ordinary
as well as extraordinary marvels, and how the strong
intuitive persuasion of his goodness makes the people
turn away from the gloomy orthodoxy of the Churches
to the more benign and comforting fancy-dreams of
Andrew Jackson Davis and the like.

After *Chapel—Church* by the way in America—I
made friends with Livermore—a kind, quiet, middle-
aged man, in look something like Mr. Maskery with a
dash of Harison in him. He asked me to go to the
Catholic Church with him in the afternoon, but unfortunately we were engaged to Mr. King for a drive
—and a very pleasant drive it was!

The suburbs of Cincinnati are extremely pretty
(really very pretty) with good houses and good gardens. We went to see some of them—a young Mr.
Longworth's place[5] and a Mr. Wheeler's.[6] At the
former we saw the lady of the house, sister to King's
wife, and wife to the heir of the Astor of Cincinnati.[7]

---

5. Belmont, the Longworth mansion, with its vineyards, conserva-
tories, and art treasures, at the foot of Mount Adams, was for generations
the pride of Cincinnati.

6. Possibly the banker A. J. Wheeler, who lived in Clifton.

7. "Young Mr. Longworth" was Joseph Longworth, who married Annie
Rives, sister to Margaret Rives King. In 1850 his millionaire father,

She is an agreeable person and gave us some very fair Catawba[8] and a button-hole bouquet. Wheeler we did not see, but from his grounds we have a beautiful view of the city and the river. A nursery garden we also walked through. The petunias were particularly fine, and several of the trees were well worth seeing.

Next morning we started for Louisville in a really fine river steamer with an enormous saloon, < > feet long. Mr. Livermore called before we started and kindly made me a present of a Cincinnati Guide. We started at 11 and got to Louisville in about 12 hours. Our chief amusements were eating, and finding the cool places in a hot boat and on a hot day. At Louisville we went to the L[ouisville] Hotel and got but little sleep, as the stage left at 4. My sleep was only an hour, as fortunately I had to finish a letter, and it was lucky I *did* sit up, as our luggage did not come from the steamer, and we could not have started at all next morning if a black b'hoy had not come down with me in search of it.

Yesterday was undoubtedly I think the hardest day I remember. We could not get inside places, and had to bake and broil outside the stage in a boiling and baking sun:—it was nearly twelve when we reached the Inn—Bell's—seven miles from hence—which we were to sleep at. It was a comfortable little place, and the landlord rather a character with a celebrated drink of peach brandy and honey.[9] "Capital peach brandy!" said a Scotchman who had come on the stage with us, "and when I was here some time ago with Mr. Wilson

Nicholas Longworth, paid—second to William B. Astor—the highest taxes on realty in the United States.

8. Nicholas Longworth developed the Catawba grape of Cincinnati into a flourishing wine-making enterprise.

9. "The proprietor of [Bell's Inn,] with his snow-white locks, and rough, but kind manners, is a curiosity in himself" (Elizabeth Ellet, *Summer Rambles in the West* [New York, 1853], p. 256).

—the celebrated Mr. Wilson, the Scotch melodist, you know, Sir—you've read his travels of course?[10]—well, Sir, Mr. Wilson was delighted with this peach brandy, and took so much it quite got into his head!—now really I recommend you to try it!"

This morning we got here about eleven and spent a quiet, comfortable morning, and after dinner equipped ourselves for the Cave. Burder and myself appeared in "pink," Loch in yellow, and a lady in a happy compound of each colour. There was a black guide, the lady's husband, and three men whom I will not venture to characterise except by saying that I had not been ten minutes in their company without thanking Heaven that I was an Englishman. The best of the three was a man whom the others bullied and called "Missouri" as a patronymic Scotch-wise.

A striking thing is the contrast between the warm air of the sunshine and the cold draught from the cavern entrance; it reminded me of the contrast we are told exists between the upper and lower houses on an Andes village;—a step and you are in a hot blast, another and you are in the coldest wind. We each had candles, or rather lamps, and in Indian file marched into the coldness and the dark. The first thing that struck me was the extreme dryness of the cavern, in this differing very much from the Trou de Hans;[11] the roads too were somewhat better. Some of the names of the places we saw amused us extremely and some of the remarks of the tourists still more,—"This is the Bottomless Pit," said our Guide, "175 feet deep." "This, gentlemen, is the Wild Dome—look how *wild* it is!" "This is the Devil's *Pulpit*!" But the poor pulpit will

10. John Wilson (1800–1849), Scottish tenor, visited America in 1838 and again in 1849. He wrote a pamphlet entitled *A Visit to the Mammoth Cave of Kentucky* (Edinburgh, 1849).

11. The Han Grotto in the Lesse Valley, near Dinant, Belgium.

soon go to "tarnal smash" for every one carries away a piece as a relic. One man came up to Loch and said solemnly "It is easier to imagine the sensations which one feels in the cave than to experience them. I can wonder, I can admire, but I am not overcome!" Another remarked that he could not "realize light."

We shall see more of the cave to-morrow,—at present I'm rather disappointed in it. Farther on in the cave it becomes damper and the stalactites are fine, but as yet I've seen finer in Belgium, and the only thing which struck me as really very peculiar and grand is an effect of the roof in one gallery, when as you look up, you see what appears the sky with stars dotted over it— the illusion is perfect, and I own I could hardly persuade myself that it was one. There are some pretty little springs of water, but as they are said to be diarrhoeic we let the eye only drink of them;—a Gothic Chapel—no more Gothic than I am, but adorned with some fine stalagmite pillars, is another lion worth seeing.

We travelled seven and a half miles and to-morrow we go much farther. One thing however I have discovered since I've been in America—that *size* itself except when seen at a glance is hardly ever (perhaps never) altogether a satisfactory thing—it can never come up to your ideas, you can't realize it, and there is no one single coup d'oeil, no one view—and it is from the coup d'oeil that the impression is left upon the mind and which is really grand. The grandeur of the great rivers is best seen on the map—the glory of the great cave is best appreciated by guide-books' dimensions—so with the lakes undoubtedly.

But disappointment is not the only feeling I have about the Cave, to which I am indebted for the most terrible fright I ever had. There was a vast chasm which one had to jump over:—one of the men offered me his arm, and I cleared it with a spring—Burder was already over and moved a little on a side as I reached the rock on which he stood. Imagine my horror, on hearing a crash, and seeing that the poor fellow had stepped backward into a hole and was falling down—God knows where!—Loch and myself felt—imagine what we felt!—the hole was luckily narrow, so that the fall was gradual and slow, as he could support himself by his elbows against rock-projections; still we saw him going lower and lower and crashing against the sides as he fell, nor was it for some minutes after he was hauled up, and we found him but little hurt that we could get over the shock:—a few inches wider, and the fall down that black abyss would have been indeed terrible.[12] Our horror however was soon turned and kindled into indignation by the screams of laughter by which "Missouri's" friends greeted the accident. They *must* laugh, had it been their own brother, "who'd have bowie-knifed them for their pains" suggested Loch afterwards. Such callous brutal disregard to life, such want of sympathy with suffering, or pain, or fear, can I think and hope exist nowhere but in the Western States of this great nation!

How can I better show "what like" are Kentuckians than by this scrap from an Albany paper of July 24th describing Clay's funeral.

Several disgraceful affrays occurred in Lexington on the day of the funeral and the evening preceding, arising out of those family quarrels which are cherished with such rancor in some parts of Kentucky. Mr. Frank Telford met Major Thos. Redd in a bar-room, and immediately shot at him with a revolver. Redd

12. Cf. the first sentence of a contemporary guidebook: "Accidents of no kind have ever occurred in the Mammoth Cave" (*Rambles in the Mammoth Cave, during the year 1844,* By a visiter [Louisville, 1845], p. viii).

was not dangerously wounded. Two other parties, belonging to belligerent families, whose members never meet without attempting each other's lives, were brought together on this occasion, for the first time in ten years. They met on the crowded streets of Lexington, and immediately exchanged shots; not, however, with serious result. These occurrences are so common in this State that little excitement was produced, and no attempt was made to arrest the parties.

Louisville Hotel, Louisville.
Saturday Night, [July 24].

The next day Loch and myself again explored the Mammoth Cave. Poor Burder could not come, and as we did not wish to be bored by the queer folk who went with us before, we and our guide wandered our own way. We passed along a curious narrow passage in the rock called aptly enough "Fat Man's Misery,"[13] and crossing a natural bridge over the river Styx, we at last reach Lake Lethe over which a boat took us safely, and then Lake Echo on which we rowed for some time. High rocks frowned down upon us from either side, and the lantern light placed on the prow, gleaming on the black water and the rugged crags lit up a most wildly picturesque scene. The boatman sang, and the echo chimed in with and lengthened out the words of "Carry me back to old Virginny," till the last notes were lost (as it seemed) among the labyrinth river windings. We then returned, as we had to get back in time for the stage, and so missed the gypsum

13. "The Winding Way is one hundred and five feet long, eighteen inches wide, and from three to seven feet deep, widening out above, sufficiently to admit the free use of one's arms. It is throughout tortuous, a perfect *zig-zag*, the terror of the Falstaffs and the ladies of 'fat, fair and forty' " (*Rambles in the Mammoth Cave*, p. 71).

237

formations which are said to be very beautiful, but to see which we must have stumbled along through three dull miles of cave with nothing whatever to see. We did some 6 miles and were only three hours. The only incident on our road to Bell's (where we had to sleep as the stage was quite full) was the sight of the first live snake I've as yet seen. It was a "spreading adder" with a frog in its mouth—it was a beautiful creature about two feet long with a striped (longways) yellow and black skin. It soon came to grief, poor thing, as an energetic passenger jumped out and smashed it with a stone, to the relief doubtless of the half-eaten frog. This is I believe a very poisonous snake, though too *slow* to be very dangerous.

Yesterday we left in a carriage for which we paid $20 for Elizabeth-town, half way to Louisville. It was a hot but not unpleasant drive, and I saw some of the most splendid wild flowers imaginable. The mullen and the ironweed, each eight or ten feet high were among the most frequent:—the latter bears a purple flower like a cineraria. In the woods too I found the lilac and white hollyhock and a yellow flower with black eye which grows in our garden,[14] and which assuredly I never expected to see all along a road-side growing in the greatest luxuriance. The asclepias were also beautiful, and several other plants of whose names I am quite ignorant.[15] Unfortunately I had left my drying press at Louisville, and was unable to preserve any.

After a good night's rest at Elizabeth-town, we started this morning for L[ouisville]. We wished to get a private carriage, but the hackman was exorbitant,

14. No doubt the black-eyed susan.

15. "The whole route from Elizabethtown to the Cave, passes through what was until recently a Prairie, or, in the language of the country, 'Barrens,' and renders it highly interesting, especially to the botanist, from the multitude and variety of flowers with which it abounds during the Spring and Autumn months" (*Rambles in the Mammoth Cave*, p. vi).

and we had a vulgar prejudice against being "done," so that we again took to the stage—patronized "the sock and buskin" (as Anderdon says). Burder was choleratic and went inside, I sat by the driver on a fraction of a seat between him, and a fine-looking Kentuckian, and Loch was perched on an < > of carpet bags at the top of the stage.

It was a wretched journey—so hot to begin with, such a thunderstorm, and sheet-like rain to go on with! —we were perfectly drenched and had to extemporize a little dressing when we stopped to dine.

At last "weary and way-worn" we arrived here between six and seven, supped, read papers and so forth.

My Kentucky friend was a nice fellow, and very intelligent;—a firm admirer of slavery, and the first I have met who does *not* wish it done away with. The latter part of the journey I sat by Loch who was agreeable as ever.

When at Bell's, I spent half an hour in gleaning eccentricities from a Louisville paper. Among the advertisements were close together, "Mules Wanted," —"Slaves for Sale," and on another column a perfumer's notice of the queerest named scents I ever came across,—"Extract of Flowers of Ashland," (Clay's place) "Extract of *Chry*stal Palace," and "Extract of New Mown Hay." How tame an English perfume looks set side by side by these. But most amusing of all was a blank verse poem on the Death of Henry Clay, "which," (says the Editor) "is a noble tribute from one of our country's 'finest poets.'" I wish I could have taken it all down just to show how an elegy ought to be written, and in "how fine a frenzy" the fine poets of America can display their patriotism and their grief.

Achilles was not the only hero immortalized in verse,—Clay also has his Homer!

239

How eloquently the Statesman's eloquence is described, and how we long to have heard *him*, whose "lightest tone was as a lightning peal." And how ready we are to mourn his loss, and call on thee "old ocean dark with viewless waves, And all ye little streams" to do so too, for alas!

> Who now shall guard
> The helmet and the destiny of State
> When storms and darkness wildly hover round,
> With such a gallant hand?

This is a poet indeed! Longfellow must soon sink into the obscurity whence he sprang,—Bryant and Whittier be all forgotten, for in Webster's words "the sun has risen!"

In this same paper was a Dr's advertisement:—"My method is strictly *eclectic*, and on this system the greatest confidence may be reposed."

Some of the Kentucky language is curious. A man being asked the other day how he was, replied, "Like about common" to his interrogator and to my amusement. One fellow whom we were talking to about the trees of the neighbourhood, replied to our question of "Is there much poplar about here?" "Pretty smart I reckon—upon the knobs!" N. B. "Reckon" is the word here, as "guess" is in the North. The phrase "to Yankee" is in these Western States equivalent with "To do," "to cheat." "They'd Yankee you finely," I heard a man say one day. Sundry hampers of wooden nutmegs, wooden hams covered with canvass, &c. have occasioned this calumny on New England States. (N.B. At St. Louis' Concert a man portraited Yankee manners, &c.)[16]

16. This sentence must have been added later (cf. p. 256).

Louisville. Sunday, [July 25].

I went this morning to the Unitarian Church here. The congregation was thin, and Mr. Heywood[17] like Mr. Livermore, was going to shut up and "flit" next week. The sermon was on the death of a Mr. Lowe, "a good man and a just," as the text said, and I own the whole sermon was too like a long churchyard epitaph to please me; he seemed to have had every virtue under heaven, this Mr. Lowe, and very touchingly were we told that once he sent Mr. H[eywood] $20 for charity, at another time $100 for the Meadville College.[18] After the service I introduced myself to the parson. He was very civil, and believed himself related to the Heywoods "of ours."[19] He knows R[ussell] Carpenter and hopes to come himself to England before long. The Meadville College is, he says, prospering, and the Theological Department at Cambridge[20] is fast improving.

In the evening we left a letter at Dr. Gross'[21] from Mr. King of Cincinnati, but he was out, and afterwards amused ourselves by going to the Episcopal Church—I say amused ourselves, as we really went for something to do, and were more fortunate than we deserved in hearing an extremely good sermon in many respects, though the clergyman did *not* draw the obvious analogy I expected would follow from his opening description of the enslaved Israelites. I suppose enslaved negroes are too delicate a subject for pulpit

17. John Healey Heywood, minister to the Church of the Messiah in Louisville, 1840–80.

18. Unitarian theological school in Meadville, Pennsylvania, est. 1844.

19. Through his paternal grandmother, Bright was related to various Liverpool Heywoods.

20. I.e., the Harvard Divinity School.

21. Dr. Samuel D. Gross, surgeon.

oratory. One remark of his, if not strictly true, was at least ingenious—that Commerce and Religion go together, as in Egypt, Palestine, and Italy it *was*, as in England it *is*, as in America it *will* be![22]

22. In a letter to his mother from Louisville, dated July 25, Bright writes: "We have just finished dinner—lamb chops, and tomatoes, hoe-cake, egg-plants fried in batter, chocolate pudding, curacao-jelly, punch à la Romaine, such has been my dinner, so that you see we do not feed badly in this Western Country. You may always know an American or an Englishman by the way he eats, as *we* pay a respect to the digestive organs that our cousins this side the Atlantic never dream of, and we are always the last to rise from the table."

11

LOUISVILLE TO SAINT LOUIS

On The Ohio. Tuesday, [July] 27.

The Fashion Steamer started with us at about one o'clock yesterday;—she has 100 passengers on board, draws about 3½ feet water, and is by no means a bad boat.

The river banks are much prettier than above Louisville, and occasionally some little bit of rock is seen peeping out among the woods which slope down to the Ohio; the river is cleaner too I think, and broader. We have passed this morning at least two nice-looking country houses, and a green island or two, also several rafts with droll little houses upon them, which are making their way to New Orleans to be sold for wood, and several Kentucky flat boats with the genuine Ohioan boatman in them;—the greatest scamps in America I believe are these men, reckless dare-devil fellows, who besides dancing, singing, and marrying pretty wives—(the chief accomplishments, as I think, for which the song immortalizes them)[1] have few scruples about the more energetic pursuits of thieving, bowie-knifing, and the like. I am a little disappointed in these far-famed river boats. The large saloon is very large, and furnished with tables and chairs,—no sofas, or bookcases, or further comforts of any sort. The sleeping places—rather smaller than those of the Great Britain—have each two doors, one opening into the saloon, the other into the passage which runs between the House on deck and the ship's sides. These sleeping places have two berths, and a looking-glass, and that's all! There are no washing utensils of any sort, so that the absurd few who are given to that exploded custom, adjourn to the barber's shop where some four basins are ready to supply their wants. Of course the barber's shop is public, so that face and hands are all you can possibly clean:—no one, as far as I saw, cleaned their teeth except ourselves, nor did I see here the common tooth-brush, which was ostentatiously displayed in the boat from Cincinnati to Louisville.

We breakfast at 7, lunch (if you can) at 11, dine at 1, sup at 7; between times we talk, read, write, sleep, look at scenery, and try to be cool.

There are too, I fear, mosquitoes about these boats, but as yet I've escaped. I saw one for the first time the night before last at Louisville. How it sang round me, and settling for a moment, eluded my avenging hand, and calmly hovered round me singing again in calmest contempt. Luckily I had one resource, and by dint of noise and shaking of bed-clothes kept

1. Boatman dance, boatman sing,
   Boatman do most anything,
   Dance, boatman, dance.
      Dance all night till the broad daylight,
      Go home with the girls in the morning.
   Hey, ho, boatman row,
      Sailing down the river on the Ohio.

(American folksong)

him for one short minute at a distance from me,—then down with the mosquito curtains,—my enemy was shut out, and I was safe, and triumphant as ever besieged chieftain when spite of the foe he had raised the protecting drawbridge. I could hear my mosquito still, but it was my turn to be contemptuous, and little cared I for him now, as he sang, and hovered, and dashed round the curtains he could not pass.

On board here yesterday I bought a book explaining Freemasonry—it's not worth keeping though *true*. One page about the signs I stick in here, as they are doubtless curious and may be interesting to some.

I also insert an advertisement of a newspaper and two advertisements *from* a newspaper, both characteristic of America.[2]

The Mississippi. Wednesday Morning, [*July 28*].

The Mississippi!—Father of Waters! River of De Soto! At last we find ourselves upon its waters! Just before breakfast we reached Cairo,—a wretched little place in Illinois, swampy, choleratic, ague-ridden, mosquito-bitten, but which—for Man has declared it as certainly as the witches declared Macbeth's elevation —"will be great hereafter."[3] The Rothschilds' money has done something, the projected Illinois railway will do more, and Cairo washed on one side by the Ohio, on the other by the Mississippi, with a line of rail running past it from North to South, must malgré ague, cholera, and mosquitoes, be one of the greatest and most central spots in the Union.

2. These are missing.
3. Dismal Cairo, described by Dickens as "a place without one single quality, in earth or air or water, to commend it" became the "Eden" of *Martin Chuzzlewit.*

At present however, the Levée, or raised mound of earth, a Hotel, and some half dozen cottages are all the signs of a city which Cairo can as yet show;—as it is considered a *deadly* place to live in, so was New Orleans, and yet it is now as bills of mortality (crede Lyell) declare, the healthiest town in the country, except for some two months in middle summer.[4]

We drop a passenger or so at Cairo, and then leave it and the Ohio together. The dirty green water of La Belle Rivière looks pure and limpid by the side of the liquid mud we are now cutting through. I never saw such abominable looking water—the foam as it breaks away from our bows is more brown than white, and looks half solid with dirt. And yet there is a prejudice —a superstition—that the water is delicious to drink—at least most travellers say so—Lord Wharncliffe however, told Loch *he* for one thought it bad, and as far as *eye* can tell, his lordship certainly has the chances in his favour.[5]

As yet, the scenery here is like that of the Ohio,— a broad stream, wooded banks, not much in themselves, but rendered beautiful by the bright sunshine which shifts from side to side as the river winds in graceful curves along its course. Last night, too, the Ohio was very fine,—the woods came low hanging over the river, which broadened out into a lake-like surface—the sun set magnificently in front of us, and a full moon rose up behind our boat. A solitary heron crossed the stream before us, and "darkly painted on the crimson sky,"[6] in another moment was lost among

4. Lyell was astounded when a doctor showed him a statistical table proving that in 1845 New Orleans had a lower mortality rate than Boston (*A Second Visit to the U. S.*, 2:97).

5. John Stuart-Wortley, 2d baron Wharncliffe (1801-55), may have accompanied his sister-in-law, Lady Emmeline Stuart-Wortley, on her American travels in 1849-50.

6. Bryant, "To a Waterfowl."

the forests of Illinois. There were no houses on the bank, no boats upon the water, and were it not that the heavy pulsing of our engine reminded us that we were, after all, in civilized land, and on a much frequented track, we should have half expected to see some Indian canoe shoot along from under the bushes that fringed the river.

This is in many respects very wonderful travelling: —400 miles from Louisville to Cairo, down the Ohio, and 200 miles from Cairo to St. Louis, up the Mississippi—taking some three days and nights to do in all, and the expense for this,—the passage, sleeping accommodation, very fair food,—only $8, or about £1: 15: 0, while by stage from Louisville to the Mammoth Cave (only 90 miles) we had to pay $16.

There are some very queer people on board the boat, and very cool people moreover. Twice when I've laid down a volume of De Quincey[7] for some few minutes have strange, coatless, black-handed men whom I never saw before, asked me to lend them the book, and read it, and I hope understood it, and I'm sure dirtied it, and hardly thanked me when they gave it back to me.

They swear too, abominably, do many of these men —"In the Name of the Great L—" is no uncommon oath, and "My G—" is as frequent as "Mon Dieu" in Paris.

Among the passengers we've made friends with a rough-looking farmer yclept Primrose. His grandfather was a third son of Lord Rosebery's in Scotland, who took refuge in this country during the '45.[8] He talks of revisiting his relatives in England—how horrified they'd be with the poor fellow!

---

7. Thomas De Quincey (1785-1859), essayist.
8. The 1st earl of Rosebery was Archibald Primrose (1661-1723), who had six sons.

We pass places with strangely assorted names—Commerce, Thebes, Cape Girardeau,—the latter reminding us that we are in the old French territories, and that the Catholics are still dominant—at Girardeau, a Catholic Seminary is the most striking building.[9]

The scenery is getting bolder—rocky bluffs 100 feet high rise up on the Missouri bank, and the sand bars covered with a low growth of cotton wood are less frequent as we get further up the river. The Mississippi has in places much the appearance of a lake of no inconsiderable size, and girt with a wood belt on every side. A large snag which here and there we pass, and a rotting half sunk steamer which we saw just now remind us that this is one of the dreaded Western Waters—bugbear of English mothers with itinerant sons!

It's past ten—I've just finished a claret "Sangaree," and we've just past the little town of St. Geneviève. It has been a splendid evening again, the sun setting red and cloudless in the west, and the reflection in the thick waters of the Mississippi reminding one of the effect of sunset over an ice-field, the colour vivid, though softened and subdued, while the trees in their reflections grow indistinct in form and shape.

Loch thinks the river not unlike the Mersey at Runcorn,[10]—and this I can well imagine.

Planters' House, St. Louis.
Thursday Night, [July 29].

We arrived here this morning, and found ourselves about eight o'clock comfortably breakfasting at a capital Hotel, next best I think to that at Cincinnati.[11]

9. St. Vincent's College (founded 1843).
10. Near Liverpool.
11. Planters' House was opened in 1841 on Fourth Street, between

The day has been so hot that before dinner our excursions were confined to a book store opposite, and a bath and shave at a barber's. Really, a barber's shop in America is a splendid institution, and well worthy of all praise and imitation; and in no city yet have I seen any Figaro's establishment equal to the one here. Over the door he is called thus—"Importer of Human Hair"—horrible expression in this West, painfully suggestive of Indians and scalps!

Our dinner was excellent—green turtle soup, baked pike with claret sauce, fried frogs, &c. &c.—a noble dinner, and winding up with the first melons we have as yet seen. After dinner, we drove about to leave our letters, to Mr. Eliot from Dr. Furness, Dr. Pope from Dr. Rives of Cincinnati, and Mr. Kenneth Mackenzie from Mr. Irvin's friend. Mr. Mackenzie[12] was the only one we found in, and he received us very kindly, though I fear we were more struck by the beauty of his house than his own attractions. Indeed St. Louis, so far from having the appearance of a semi-barbarous-newly-inhabited-by-Christians town is a most magnificent city, hardly inferior to Cincinnati. The stores are splendid, especially those appropriated to the twin professions of barber and druggist. The Churches are extremely handsome, and the streets filled with good houses and fine trees.

We prolonged our drive to what is by courtesy called a Prairie at the back of the town,—I thought an English common the more striking of the two, and Burder murmured some remark of Dickens' about "a brickfield without the bricks" which it also resem-

Chestnut and Vine. Dickens described it as "built like an English hospital, with long passages and bare walls, and skylights above the room-doors for the free circulation of air" (*American Notes*, chap. 12).

12. K neth Mackenzie (1797–1861), a Scottish emigrant, made a fortune the fur trade and was known among the Indian tribes as "King of the Missouri."

bled.[13] *The* Prairies however, are farther west than this, and I almost fear we shall not see one.

We employed the evening in drinking and prowling about. The heat was so excessive that ices, iced water, milk-mush, coffee, soda water and syrup were all in turn imbibed to return to this outer world in clouds of perspiration. It was terribly hot, 95 in the shade, and I heard people sighing for New Orleans where at least they would get a sea breeze.

We looked into a Bowling Saloon for a minute or two—falsely so named—"Skittle Ground" or "Nine Pin Alley" would be the true name for it.

We also looked into a Lecture Room—a man was holding forth on—or rather against—Spiritual Rappers, and exposing them as far as he could. This is a great town for Rapping, and the worthy lecturer told us how at some exhibition or other there were 150 people and 1500 spirits present:—10 spirits to each!—a somewhat large proportion. He also said that at another manifestation held in a medical hall here, he (Rev. W. White—spirit-unbeliever) proposed that 12 raps should be given on the head of a skeleton which was there and so placed that no trickery could be employed, while of course the sound would be peculiar, and inimitable on the spur of the moment.

Alas! no spirit would come. Dr. Franklin *had been* peculiarly brisk, but Dr. Franklin would not come when most wanted.[14] It was beneath Dr. Franklin's dignity, at last suggested a believer, to knock on a skull. Really, if Dr. Franklin forfeits the "otium" in which it may be presumed he lives in another "better land" to rap in medical Halls at the request of illit-

13. Dickens did travel thirty miles east of Saint Louis to see a prairie, but he made this remark about Washington.

14. The spirit of Benjamin Franklin was the one most frequently invoked at such séances.

250

erate "mediums,"—he might, I should think pocket his "dignity"[15] too for one night, especially when the conversion of the Rev. W. White depended on his so doing.

Alas! "poor Richard!"—vanity has still its votaries in the spirit land, and a love of truth, and of enlightening unspiritual Man gives in to a fear of losing dignity. The cherubs of *"bottomless"* sagacity might laugh to see thy ghostly hand tapping on that poor empty head,—ridicule has ever a potent influence,—still, Dr. Franklin, for once thou shouldst have braved it! —we should have believed in thee. As it is, indeed, poor Richard, we can't,—few do, fewer soon will, "O Richard, l'univers t'abandonne!"[16]

By the way, why can spirits be heard and not seen? "To be seen and not heard" was during at least one portion of their earthly career a maxim they were to act on: "the tables are now turned," and they go on the other tack. But how can they if they are spirit? To be *heard* is a peculiarity of matter as much as to be *seen*—it is only matter acting on one sense instead of another, and we must remember that it is not even by voice,—that is, by sounds independent of visible material substance—that they communicate with man, according to these mad theorists, but by *rapping* or by sound caused by something acting on matter. Now here is the chief absurdity of these Rappists. *Spirit* acting on *matter* cannot create sound. Spirit is *imponderable*, while a rap upon a table or wall is the noise occasioned by a force or weight acting upon the table.

Now force is, to use the mechanists' definition,

15. *Otium cum dignitate* ("leisure with dignity") was Cicero's motto on entering public life.

16. Blondel's song, sung at the dinner given to the French soldiers at Versailles, October 1, 1789.

"that which tends to change the state of a body's rest or motion"—weight "is the force a body exerts through the power of gravity." "Utrum horum mavis accipe"[17] as the Latin Grammar says, and it is clear that whether the rap is occasioned by a force or a weight, there is in each case a *pressure*, which it is absurd to suppose could be produced by spirit.

It is curious the excitement these Rappers cause,—the way they are spoken of—the half-belief they obtain. Superstition does in truth seem inherent in Man —the American who would look "foul scorn" on a haunted house, a ghost story or a fairy tale, is at once caught when a thin veil of Science is thrown over what is quite as absurd and quite as childish;—there must be "glamorie" in it, else no man of sense could fail to see beneath the Coan robe[18] the old jugglery and deceit and Cagliostro-charlatanism.

No! Superstition seems fated to rule the "night side" of the world,—the weak and foolish. As one form of it is exploded, another springs into being—as one dies, another is born—"Le Roi est mort—vive le Roi!"

Friday, July 30.

Dr. Pope[19] called this morning, and we found him an agreeable nice person. He took us a longish walk, in the course of which we saw

I. The fire-company's depot, chiefly remarkable for a baby bear of the grizzly variety, which was

17. "Take whichever of these you prefer."

18. *Coae vestes* were light transparent garments for which the island of Cos was famous in the days of the Roman Empire.

19. Charles Alexander Pope (1818–70), surgeon and professor of anatomy at Saint Louis Medical College. Civilized and urbane, he had pursued his medical studies in Paris before settling in Saint Louis in 1842.

chained in the yard,—and for a large quantity of nasty-smelling peas which by no means tempted us.

II. A large New Orleans steamer was the *second* "lion"—if the *bear* be counted the first. The "James Robb" has a Gothic saloon of 300 feet, is all furnished in exquisite taste in white and gold, contains baths and every other luxury, and is really well worth seeing. This steamer cost $83,000, and will last probably about four to five years: it draws 7 feet of water and gets to New Orleans in less than 5 days. We afterwards saw another, the "J. Symonds," larger still and as splendidly fitted up. Judge its splendour when the door handles to some 20 or 30 berths were each one of those glass things used in England for paperweights.

III. The Medical College built at the expense of Dr. Pope's father-in-law, Col. O'Fallon.[20] It is a fine building and admirably arranged, and sumptuously fitted up with horrible pictures of eccentric diseases, —horrible pictures *because* they are so good and lifelike, and terrible.

In the far West to come across an institution of this sort, with a full staff of professors, and with accommodation in it unrivalled in the U. S. is indeed curious, and shows, as Dr. Pope said, "the American acts for the future."

They *are* a wonderful people after all:—15 years ago there were only 17,000 inhabitants, now there are upwards of 100,000 and it is still increasing enormously and *will be* the "Metropolis of the West" as the Guide Books fondly call it.

Our kind friend would treat us to a julep and soda

20. Pope married Caroline O'Fallon, only daughter of Saint Louis's first citizen, Col. John O'Fallon. Immensely proud of his son-in-law, O'Fallon built for him the fine medical college at Seventh and Spruce streets.

253

water, providing for our creature comforts as for our intellectual improvements.

About 4½ Dr. Pope called again for us, and took us out to his father-in-law's, Col. O'Fallon.[21] This gentleman is a great man here, as we learned at once by seeing O'Fallon St., and O'Fallon Avenue marked upon the map. He lives some 4 miles out of town, and has really a beautiful place of 1500 acres, with pretty gardens, a nice little park and a capital house. In the garden were some little mounds of up-turned earth made by a rat or rabbit-like animal called a gopher; while some larger swelling hillocks in the orchard were remnants of Indian encampments. I told the old gentleman that I had not seen so nice a place in America, and he said that Lord Morpeth had told him the same; he seemed very proud of his estate and gave me all manner of information about it. He has a good many slaves, but in his will he told me he had made a provision that all born after a certain date should be set free and sent to Liberia; "by this means," he said, "the slaves being *educated for freedom* will be of use in the colony, and by degrees slavery will be banished from Missouri." Henry Clay has made a similar provision in his will, so that if other Kentuckians follow his lead, "ol Kintuck" will also be free one day.

Col. O'Fallon has made his enormous fortune by a judicious purchase of land round St. Louis and in other places. At present he has a plan for building a manufacturing town opposite to St. Louis in Illinois, and has been getting all the land there into his possession. Certain railways he has also large shares in,[22] but his old

---

21. Col. John O'Fallon (1791–1865) was in turn a soldier, Indian trader, army contractor, merchant, and philanthropist, deriving his huge fortune largely from shrewd real estate investments.

22. HAB wrote to his father, after this conversation with O'Fallon: "Another good way of making money is by taking shares in some of these

purchases round St. Louis of land at $100 an acre, which is now worth $1200 an acre, must have been his best investment.

Mrs. Pope is a charming little woman, shy but very sweet. She was in the terrible Great Western storm she told me,[23] and she described with much feeling and pathos the Communion taken together at midnight when they thought all was over, and how a hymn said to her mother when a child, "Jesus Lover of my Soul" came to her mind, and how even then it comforted her to say it over, and how it consoled her to think that she and her husband were at least dying together. She told me too, of a poor young girl who was with her then, whose story sounds like a page torn from some romance. She met her at Paris where her husband, a Dr. Drew, was dying, and Mr. Pope as a countryman was asked to attend the poor man. His young wife had married him for his wealth at the entreaties of her father, who must have sold the old homestead if she had not sacrificed herself to a man she did not love, on condition of his clearing off the family encumbrances. Her husband died of consumption at Paris, and she was thrown upon the kindness of the Popes with whom she returned to America. She refused to put on mourning for her husband, declaring it would be hypocritical to do so, and refused likewise to touch a farthing of his money. She has since married a Mr. Hunt, and lives at Baltimore:—her beauty is very great, and (Mrs. Pope said) Frederick Peel was quite smitten by a picture Mrs. Pope had showed him of her. My fair friend travelled in England some 5 years ago and was

Western Railways. The line from St. Louis to Cincinnati for example *must* pay 12 per cent at the lowest estimate, the more sanguine say 20."

23. The *Great Western*, designed by I. K. Brunel and launched in 1838, was the first steamship employed in regular service between England and America.

delighted with it; she promised to send me autographs of Clay and Madame Calderon, whom she knew, having been at school kept by her sister Miss Inglis.[24]

Mrs. O'Fallon I did not talk much to, except to ask for more coffee at tea-time and so forth—she seems a nice sort of person enough. We had a capital tea, and a good supper of "buffalo tongue" when we got back to the Inn.

By the way, Col. O'Fallon talks of coming over to England before long.

St. Louis. Monday Evening, August 2.

The boat by which we intended to go to-day was so bad that we have determined to wait for the "Brunette" of to-morrow. Saturday passed quietly, except that in the evening we found our way to a concert; to-day has also passed quietly, except that we have graced a stupid little theatre with our distinguished presence.

Sunday was a day which I must always remember as the day on which I first took the Sacrament. I had intended to go to Church in the morning, but missed my way, and heard instead a wretched "raw head and bloody bones" sermon from a man into whose Chapel I got by accident.

In the afternoon I determined to try again, and at last found myself in a beautiful Church, Gothic, with fine organ and painted windows. Service was going on, and I remained while Burder and Loch strolled on to Mr. Mackenzie's. I found the Service was Sacrament, and my first impulse was to turn away. But then I thought how I had intended to stay before I left home, and that although I could not now kneel by my mother's

24. Cf. p. 158.

side and take it for the first time, I could at least think that perhaps she too, so many thousand miles off had received the Sacrament this very day, and it seemed a sort of bond to her and home. And here too was the farthest point I should be from home, and here was the remotest congregation of Unitarians in the world, and it was a pleasant feeling to think that I could pray with my fellow-Christians in this far West as I had learnt to pray in my own family, and be united with them as fellow-believer and fellow-worshipper in the same Communion of the Lord! God grant the good resolutions I have formed pass not away!

Mr. Eliot the Minister, whom I made friends with afterwards, and who apologized for not having called, is a very kind old man; he made me come and take tea with him.[25]

St. Louis, he says, has increased wonderfully. In the last 15 years, have sprung up 19 out of 20 of the houses in the town. The Unitarian congregation was formed by himself, and now numbers 250 families. Their Church, which is strikingly beautiful (of brick faced with white stone), cost nearly £18,000, and *will* hold 1200 people, and *does* hold above 1000 every Sunday.[26] Mr. Eliot looks upon the prospects of Unitarianism in the West as most encouraging, and believes that in the East it is not declining. Fillmore and Webster, Bryant and Longfellow, are Unitarians, and General Pierce is supposed to be one too.[27]

25. William Greenleaf Eliot (1811–87), grandfather of T. S. Eliot, came from the Harvard Divinity School to Saint Louis in 1834, organized the Unitarian church there, and remained its minister until 1872. Active in educational and philanthropic affairs, he founded in 1853 Eliot Seminary, which became Washington University.

26. The Church of the Messiah, at the corner of Olive and Ninth streets, was completed only a few months before.

27. Franklin Pierce, technically an orthodox Congregationalist, became an Episcopalian a few years before his death in 1869.

Margaret Fuller he met at Boston, when however she was less talked of than our own Miss Martineau; he also saw her at Rome. As a daughter and sister she was unexceptional, and it was only when "on the plane of intellect" that her oddities commenced. Out of her own circle she would be considered "a queer stick of a girl." She was treated very injudiciously by her admirers, and had too often a sharp disagreeable way of speaking and of saying rude things.

Mr. Eliot came over to the Exhibition. He tells me he likes in England the reverence and respect the lower classes pay the higher in our country. "We can't get anything like such deference in this country —not even from a coloured man!" He dislikes slavery, and believes Missouri will soon be freed from this social curse.[28]

I may here mention that Mr. Eliot's Prayer Book is excellent!

To-day we called on Mr. Mackenzie to bid him goodbye. He gave us letters to the Upper Mississippi, and kindly took us to the Insurance News Room. Dr. Pope we also called on, and he gave us a cholera prescription, and a pamphlet of his own.

Another gentleman I met at Mr. Eliot's, went with us to the Mercantile Library. They have 40,000 volumes already, with a fund of £1000 a year for fresh purchases, and are now erecting a magnificent building for some £20,000, as the present rooms are too small for the Society's use.

Such a taste for literature speaks well for St. Louis, and I must acknowledge that I have been more pleased with this town than any since I left Philadelphia. We have met many agreeable people, have eaten the best

28. Eliot was in favor of emancipation as early as 1834 and was later a potent force in keeping Saint Louis and the northern portions of Missouri loyal to the Union.

258

WILLIAM GREENLEAF ELIOT, CA. 1854

Courtesy of the Unitarian Universalist Association

hotel dinners we've yet seen, and have found the stores good, the servants, &c. obliging, and the whole place very pleasant, and with an air of gaiety about it. An election for State Governor is going on now—but we've kept well out of the way.[29]

N.B. One of the theatres is built in an ellipse and is extremely pretty—the nicest I've seen in America.

29. General Sterling Price was running on the Democratic ticket against the Whig James Winston.

12

UP THE MISSISSIPPI

J. M'Kree Steamer, just left Nauvoo.
Thursday Afternoon, [August 5].

On Tuesday, after a last dinner at the best of dinner-giving Hotels, we found ourselves again on steamer board, bound for Galena. It was a pretty little steamer yclept the "Brunette," but unfortunately so full that our accommodation was hardly of the best, being all three, and a stranger as well, in the smallest of cabins without shelf, drawer, cupboard or any convenience of any sort.

There was much bustle as we left St. Louis,—much business and bargaining. Carts drawn by mules in tandem were busy bringing goods to the boat; boys were hawking newspapers and books, cheap reprints from the English, cheaper translations from the French; an old man begged me to buy a gun-cleaner, and a girl offered me a water-melon. At last we started, and just as the evening closed in, we saw where the Missouri pours its waters into the clear current of the Mississippi—clear thenceforth no longer, losing so, much beauty, gaining apparently no health. The red sun was setting over the western waters of the mighty tributary, and we were discussing the comparative merits of water and tide, French cooking and the junction of two large rivers; few will doubt which subject of contemplation is most generally interesting and exciting!

A wretched night, followed by a not very comfortable day, during which however, for the first time on the Missouri bank we saw a Prairie—a small one of a mile or two long, and perhaps a mile or two broad judging from a belt of wood which girt it at some distance.

It was a large level field with grass like mowing grass, full of flowers, chiefly of the yellow sunflower look.

About 12 at night we arrived at Keokuk where the rapids begin (or rather end) and where the water was so low (having fallen three inches in one night) that the Captain decided on waiting till morning and then returning us half of the passage money (to wit $3). This he did, and we were landed at a miserable little town, and had to find "a hack and team," (in English, "coach with two horses") to take us to Montrose, twelve miles off, at the other end of the Rapids. This we fortunately accomplished after a hasty cup of coffee (no parody meant on Scott's "hasty plate of soup!")[1] and passing a richly cultivated country, where every corner of untilled land was gorgeous with golden and purple prairie flowers, we arrived at Montrose, and took our luggage on board on J. M'Kree, and tried to take berths for ourselves, which however we could not manage to get; so where we sleep to-night, and whether we shall sleep at all to-night, the Fates only

1. This was an unfortunate phrase of Winfield Scott's in a letter to the secretary of war, May 25, 1846 ("Your letter . . . received . . . as I sat down to take a hasty plate of soup"). It was seized upon by the press as proof of Scott's ineptitude.

262

know, and the Furies perchance, in the shape of some of these horrid-looking black stewardesses.

We now got two little boys to pull us across from Montrose in Iowa (Ioway pronounced) to Nauvoo in Illinois (Illinoy pronounced) as we wished to see the ruins;—ruins in America are a veritable lion—of the Mormon temple,—the illustration to one of the strangest and saddest chapters in the history of this great country.[2]

Nauvoo is finely situated, as the river makes a horse-shoe bend round the promontory on which it stands. The hills rise up behind in gentle slopes, and conspicuous upon one of them stands the marble front of what was perhaps the most splendid building west of the Alleghanies.[3] Now only the front wall remains, and the town itself which once had a population of 14 or 15,000 now rejoices in one of 800 or less! Notable and praiseworthy effect of religious persecution! It is now partially settled by some 400 Frenchmen under M. Cabet,—a socialist community,—"quiet, peaceable people," said the worthy landlord of the little Inn where we dined, "but they don't get on like the Mormons."[4] We did not learn much about them, and we regret that we were stupid enough not to make friends with one of them, a blue-bloused Frenchman of whom we asked the way. At present we hear they all dine together—sufficiently inconvenient one would think, if the sect makes converts while at Nauvoo. I

2. Nauvoo was founded by the Mormon leader Joseph Smith in 1840, and in 1845 was the largest city in Illinois. Religious persecution drove the Mormons from Nauvoo in 1846.

3. The fabulous Mormon temple was 128 feet long, with thirty pilasters, an octagonal tower and dome; it could accommodate 3,000 people.

4. Etienne Cabet (1788–1856), founder of the Utopian sect called the Icarians, brought 280 of his followers to Nauvoo in 1849, after malaria had decimated his earlier settlement in Texas. The Nauvoo community prospered and expanded until Cabet's expulsion and death in 1856.

*"What was perhaps the most splendid
building west of the Alleghanies."*

wonder why they came to settle *here*,—the Mississippi banks are here flat except just above the town, and uninteresting, and the country from absence of all trees and presence of any amount of sand and dust is by no means unlike New Brighton.

We staid some time loitering by the Temple. The front is quite perfect—three doors with circular windows over them, and figures of the Sun with hands holding trumpets:—the Mormons are no prophets! and inside an inscription:—

<blockquote>
The House of the Lord
Built by
The Church of Jesus Christ
of Latter Day Saints
Commenced April 6th, 1841.
Holiness to the Lord.
</blockquote>

"Commenced 1841"—and in 1846 all destroyed except this one wall, and this one inscription![5]

We walked away and waited for our steamer to call on its way up. Loch picked up on the shore a beautiful shell which he gave me, he also saw a turtle or two pushing up their noses from the water.

At the beginning of this day's diary, I say "left Nauvoo,"—true enough;—but some miscreant—ship's clerk, I think—has been left at Montrose, so we go back in search of him, and here we are waiting till the ship's clerk turns up! and at Nauvoo we shall probably have to wait again, as some ladies have rushed meantime to see the Temple, and ladies always keep everybody waiting!

5. Actually the temple was complete in 1846 when the Mormons left Nauvoo; it was gutted by fire in 1848. The Icarians purchased the ruins in 1849 with the intention—never fulfilled—of rebuilding the structure.

Nominee Steamer, above Galena.
Saturday Night, [August 7].

We have just been having a curious amusement in shape of a "manifestation" of Spiritual Rapping—that absurd and wicked chicanery—which has, they tell me, destroyed the intellect of one of the New York judges[6] and has, during the past year added 50 lunatics to the asylums of Ohio. The cabin was crowded with eager faces, and at a deal table was placed a brace of "mediums,"—silence was enjoined,—four dirty hands were laid flat out upon the table in question, and the performance began. The table moved—that is, the side opposite the performers (marked A.) tipped up. <sketch> A child was placed on A. to keep it down, but again the table moved. Unfortunately, we were skeptical—Western people are, it's only in the East that Rochester and the Miss Foxes are believed in.

"If moved by spirits," we suggested, "let the end *next you* be tipped up." Our suggestion came to naught. "Let a big man sit at A. and you put your hands in the *middle* of the table—and let us see then." They complied, and the table did *not* move again, but one of the mediums complained of stomach-ache in consequence of the man's weight. Our "Presto Quando" was far better done. Two amateurs then tried the experiment,—everything was most satisfactory, and the big man was raised, and we heard of no stomach-ache. Another man whose wild eye and strange rough manner were suggestive of a somewhat shaken mind, then performed well enough some of the marvels of electro-biology,[7] and his success was the more conspicuous from the failure of the other gentlemen.

6. This was Judge John Worth Edmonds of the New York Supreme Court, who became a convert to spiritualism in 1851 through the Fox sisters' séances.
7. A process of inducing hypnotism by gazing at metallic discs.

This man had amused himself in the morning by counting votes[8]—51 for Pierce, 27 for Scott, was the result of the election—hurrah for the Democrats!

The "Rapping" I have since heard is a "cracking of the toes,"[9] and a gentleman in New York can *rap* as well as any of the professionals. Burder can do it a little. How shameless in their chicanery the Misses Fox and others must be to make a trade of such imposture—a religious imposture moreover.

> By the crackling of their toes
> Something wicked this way goes.[10]

Yesterday evening about 12 we arrived at Galena, which is some 7 miles up the Fevre or Febre River, now always called by the pleasing name of Fever River. It was very dark, and Fever River is very narrow, so that it was a work of some difficulty, the navigation up to the town, which we reached at last, very tired and hungry. For the last evil there was no remedy at that time of night—for the former there was—so we turned in at once, and slept soundly till about six, when we had to dress, &c. as the "Nominee" started at eight.[11]

To-day the scenery of the Mississippi improves. Rocks stand out boldly from now one side, now the other, the finest perhaps on *Iowa*.[12] They are a good

8. I.e., on shipboard.

9. A confession to this effect, repeated by a relation of the Fox sisters on April 17, 1851, was published in the *New York Herald*; but it had little effect on the spread of the movement.

10. Cf. *Macbeth* IV.i.44.

11. The *Nominee*, for many years commanded by Capt. Orrin Smith, had a reputation as the finest boat on the Upper Mississippi.

12. "There's nothing that strikes me more than the thought that in my 'old not all-forgotten' geography lessons at Miss Hunt's and Mr. Hope's these States of Iowa and Wisconsin were never mentioned, indeed they weren't States then to mention, and one looked with a sort of awe about lands supposed to be shared only by the Red-man, and the shaggy buf-

From *Picturesque America*, ed. W. C. Bryant, Vol. II, 1874

*"We see many rafts with families on them,
and a little hut in the middle."*

height, but the middle of the river is so enormous they hardly show to advantage. The islands are innumerable, some mere sand banks from which a grey waterfowl lazily rises as we approach, and flies away to some more sheltered nook; others green with trees and herbage, hardly so luxuriant we fancy as in lower parts of the river.

We see many rafts with families on them, and a little hut in the middle; by night the fires and lights from these floating floors look strange and weird, and have

falo, and yet here one is travelling in steamers, drinking iced water and eating melons, the buffalo gone and the Red-man going after him, villages springing up everywhere, and new prairie land everywhere getting into cultivation" (letter from HAB to his father written between Nauvoo and Davenport).

268

a sort of stationary jack o'lantern appearance in the water.

The towns on the bank of this Mississippi are a disappointment. Dirty-looking, built of wood without regularity and without taste, I never saw less inviting places. In the midst of a region of wood, they stand without a tree near them—bleak, bare, shadeless log houses. They are with respect to shade of trees what the Ancient Mariner was with regard to water:—

> Water, water, everywhere
> But not a drop to drink,

and the difference which might have been made in these settlements is very great. The two best I've seen are Davenport and Dubuque—the former is most "puffed" in Guide Books, but I think without sufficient justice; it is certainly a large town, with another (Rockport) on the opposite (the Illinois) bank, and an island picturesque from an old fort between the two;[13] but the town hardly looks so clean, the hills certainly do not look so varied as the town of Dubuque, and the slopes which hang above it.

Sunday, [August 8].

This morning we realised we were indeed on Free soil again in no pleasant way, viz, by the rudeness, and impertinence of one of the Free Blacks who wait on board. Loch asked him a question, and got no answer,—another, and the negro had still "lost his tongue" as completely as any village girl in England

---

13. Fort Armstrong on Rock Island, built 1816.

when you ask a question. Loch grew impatient, and pulling some things out of his hand, said, "Boy—what do you mean,—answer, sir." The secret was out—he had addressed the fellow as "Boy" at first, and with a malignant look, and a voice as spiteful as sulky, "I'll show you if I'm a Boy—I'm a man as much as any one else. I'll show you I'm a man," &c. &c. Loch of course complained to the steward, and he being also a "darkie" does not seem to have given much redress. The fact is, the term "boy" is only used in slave States, and *implies* a slave, a fact I never knew, believing it to be only another word for "waiter," and the same use of "boy" as of "garçon" in French. Loch had forgotten this too, or rather, as I think, he had forgotten that we were no longer in (or between) slave States.

At Prairie La Crosse we for the first time and to our great amusement and delight saw real wild Indians. I had just finished breakfast when Loch called me to look at some five figures in red and white blankets which were descending the slopes on the Wisconsin side. They entered the steamer, and were at once "the observed of all observers,"[14] as may be well imagined.

Of the tribe of the Winnebagoes, they had been cranberry-gathering in the "Badger State" and were now returning to their tribe beyond St. Paul. The chief was a rather fine-looking man who smoked much, wore a head-dress of feathers, and fondled a little dog he brought with him.

Another's dress was as nearly of Nature's giving as decency could allow of, consisting of long grass with a band round the loins and a red blanket which would constantly slip off, and display his red proportions. In his back hair, among the greasy plaits was twisted a

14. *Hamlet* III.i.162.

tobacco pipe. These aboriginal aristocrats of America, like some of the anything but aboriginal aristocrats of England, adorn their faces with paint—two of them had painted one cheek with yellow ochre, the other one with red, and not the cheek only, but the whole side of the face, as if to let you see how he, the Weneagle of the Crag Maylee[?], looked when in good health, and how his complexion would appear in bilious fever or when jaundiced. Another had painted his *whole* face yellow,—a sort of greenish yellow—which gave it a slightly *moss-grown* appearance. They brought a horse with them, which was, as someone said, *not* an Astbyan[15] idea of "a stud of the Prairies,"—a poor, ricketty animal, and tended by an inferior Indian, a peculiarity in the clothing of whom led you to suppose that he had spent a *wearing* sedentary life of late.

These poor Indians talk but little English—one asked me for a sixpence, but beyond that his attempts at conversation were unsuccessful, though by the way, I did learn that some nasty green apples on board were the objects of his longing, and I did my best to get him to understand that he would get 20 for the half-dollar Loch kindly gave him.

After we had gone some way we stopped, and the Captain put two of them on shore, because they would not pay their passage. We saw them disembark, and sit with their picturesque red blankets on the hill slope, but unfortunately did not understand the reason of their deserting us, or we could easily have got up a purse for them. However, we have been told they probably had money after all, and are not to be pitied. These Winnebagoes are indeed very rich people, their tribe consists of 1400, and the Government pays them a large sum of money—so large that it is computed

15. A misreading, perhaps for "Assiniboin," an Indian tribe?

that the father of a family may get £100 a year—yet
these poor fellows are always dirty and miserable,
they drink, and gamble, and lie, and cheat more than
any other tribe, and are perhaps the worst specimens
one could see.[16] As I write, two of them are squatting
on the cabin floor playing some game of cards of the
Beggar-my-neighbour species. The Red man must
have learnt this game—often to his cost—from *his*
neighbour of the lighter skin.

The Stockbridge Indians in Wisconsin are almost,
perhaps entirely civilized. They till the ground, dress
like Christians, and *are* Christians, attending also the
Congregational Church.[17]

On the Minnesota side we saw an Indian wigwam,
a small tent-looking, brown-coloured affair. Many of
the Indians about here live and roam about like our
English gypsies. At the foot of Lake Pepin we took
in another Winnebago; there were several more upon
the bank wishing to come on board and bring two
horses, but they were moneyless and our Captain was
inexorable.

Lake Pepin itself—alas! the evening—the twilightless
American evening—closed in just as we entered it. It
must be very beautiful, with its bold shores, and its
three-mile expanse of water. It extends 20 miles, and
the upper end is, I believe, really very grand; indeed
for the last 60 or 70 miles has the scenery of the Mississippi been magnificent. Soft green hills rising from
the water, each crowned with a Cybele turret of
rock,[18] reach a height of 500 to 800 feet, *we guess*.

16. Among Indian tribes the Winnebagoes had a reputation for their
wealth and their filth ("people of the stinking water").

17. The Stockbridge Indians—peaceful, well-educated farmers—mi-
grated to Wisconsin from New York between 1822 and 1833.

18. Cybele, wife of Cronos and mother of the gods, was worshipped
under the guise of a block of stone.

272

MAIDEN'S ROCK, LAKE PEPIN

From *Picturesque America*, ed. W. C. Bryant, Vol. II, 1874

"Lake Pepin itself—alas! the evening—the twilightless American evening—closed in just as we entered it."

It is extraordinary the castellated appearance of these "bluffs," they are really very striking, and Loch agrees with me in thinking finer than any natural objects on the Rhine.

This steamer is very full, and last night we had to sleep on mattresses spread on the floor among a row of some thirty in the middle of the cabin—a plan more sociable than pleasant! This morning, Burder and myself found ourselves getting into political controversies —Burder with the Magnetizer, myself with an Irishman, a true Celt, who hates the English and would march with sword in hand under Meagher's lead to attack—and of course take—the Canadas.[19] He wished to get some more oppressed Irishmen to America to *teach them*, and then they would all sail each to

19. Thomas Francis Meagher (1823-67), Irish nationalist, had been transported for his revolutionary activities to Van Diemen's land; but he escaped and landed in New York in May 1852.

England, and in a few days London, Liverpool and Manchester would be a heap of ashes!

He was impossible to argue with. Poor people were poor in England because of the Government—that terrible Government, which he asserted (Loch says he got it from the Democratic Review)[20] wishes to play off Orangemen and Catholics against each other for *political purposes.* He has a perfect "craze" on this point (to use a word of Dr. Linney's) and really believes these monstrous absurdities: in vain to urge the Queen's Colleges,[21] stopping of Processions,[22] &c.— all and each of these most sensible conciliatory acts was but an incentive to sectarian hatred:—what strange "judicial blindness!"

Another fellow we've been talking to, tells me that Campo Bello, New Brunswick is a wretched island 6 miles long, and Admiral Owen a "d----d old skywind," or some equally intelligible thing.[23] Poor Admiral Owen! what has he done to offend my worthy friend, a respectable ci-devant ship-carpenter. An Englishman like "ithy" Hope,[24] as regards the beauty and choice elegance of his language, we found amusing; he keeps a store at St. Paul's. A travelled American, a St. Louis iron-founder and others we have also fraternized with; among them, by the way, a nephew

20. Loch probably referred to a long article on the Irish question—highly critical of British policy—in the *Democratic Review* of February, 1852 (pp. 97–128).

21. Peel's policy of establishing Queen's Colleges in Belfast, Cork, and Galway (1845) as secular institutions was meant to be conciliatory but proved dangerously controversial.

22. Processions of the vehemently anti-Catholic Orange Society had been forbidden by law.

23. Probably William Fitzwilliam Owen (1774–1857), who surveyed the coast of the North America in 1847.

24. Thomas Hope (1770–1831) published anonymously a risqué oriental romance called *Anastasius* (1819). My guess is that the sobriquet derives from "ithyphallic" (obscene).

of General Cass'. Mr. Cass, so nearly nephew to the American President, has hardly acquired that refinement of manner so useless in a new Democratic Republic.

13

IN MINNESOTA TERRITORY

St. Anthony's. Tuesday Night,
August 8 [or rather 10].

"Eureka! I have seen it—Lake Pepin and the 'Laughing Water—Mina-haha' "[1]—so say I in the words of a fair writer to the Tribune newspaper, whose sweet acquaintance I imagine I have made; at least, there is a lady here who writes for the Tribune and is very learned and quite capable of using Greek words "for the sake of emphasis or expression," as the Latin Grammar says of the use of "tu."[2]

She travels with a friend—like Wordsworth's Louisa, "fleet and strong"[3]—full of information, botany, geol-

---

1. The name was not yet eulogized by Longfellow ("The Song of Hiawatha" was published in 1855).

2. Elizabeth Fries Lummis Ellet (?1818–77) was a prolific writer and contributor to magazines. A vocal champion of women, she was married to a chemist and lived in New York City. Her travelogue, which appeared in the *New-York Daily Tribune* in August and September, 1852, was published in an expanded version in 1853 as *Summer Rambles in the West.*

3. In "Louisa. After accompanying her on a mountain excursion."

ogy and what not. She has just been a walk with us, and has kindly enough been naming the plants I've collected to-day "from the hyssop that grew"[4] upon the bluffs upwards.

We arrived at St. Anthony[5] about 3 o'clock to-day, from St. Paul's, which we reached yesterday evening. The only incidents of travel since I last wrote up to St. Paul's were, sticking for some hours on a sand bar, and seeing an Indian village. The latter was curious enough—it belongs to the Sioux, who came running out of their wigwams to gaze upon us—a rabble rout of squaws and boys chiefly, the boys with bows and arrows in their hands, the squaws with children at their backs; they are not considered so fine-looking as the Winnebagoes, though a larger and more powerful tribe. How they hate the Chippeways, and how the Chippeways hate them! It is curious when one looks at this civilized part of the country, at St. Paul's or St. Anthony, where the book stores are excellent, and where one gets *ice-cream* at dinner, to reflect that we are still among Indians, and that only last year a Chippeway crossed the Mississippi at St. Paul's into the Sioux country, and killing some old foe of his, recrossed, bearing back his scalp in triumph.

Among all the Western towns, few can beat St. Paul's in rapidity of growth.[6] Four years ago the Sioux Indians were boiling their maple sugar where the

4. Cf. 1 Kings IV.33.

5. Now part of Minneapolis.

6. "Indeed it is surprising how much has been accomplished within three years, at the beginning of which there were about a dozen log houses. . . . Now the number of inhabitants is twenty-five hundred or more, and there is an air of brisk progress and life about the place. . . . Some very handsome buildings are in progress; the new State-House, the Catholic church, and other public edifices" (Ellet, *Summer Rambles*, pp. 77–78).

"Rice House"[7] now stands, and now frame and brick houses are springing up in every direction, and you will find many *luxuries* of life in this far-away town.

Perhaps the beauty of the situation acts as an inducement—it certainly would to me—and Mr. Rice[8] (who called on us this morning) says that Miss Bremer declared it the most beautiful site she ever saw.[9] It reminds Loch and Burder of Richmond on the Thames, as from a terrace walk on the bluffs in front of the town you see the river winding below, and fair forest land upon the other bank.

With St. Anthony I will not say I am disappointed, but it is certainly very inferior to St. Paul's. It is situated like the latter town but without the fine "bluffs" hanging over the river. An island here divides the Mississippi into two streams: the left hand stream is literally *covered* with timber which is floating in readiness for the saw-mills; the other is clearer, though here too huge logs of wood show that if the beautiful and the useful can't be united, the former must go to the wall, or rather to the yet unspoiled West. Near the foot of the island though still broken by it, the Mississippi flings itself over a smooth ledge of rock perhaps twenty feet high, and chafes away among the opposing blocks below. It is a striking scene enough from its breadth even when cut in two, and it is a striking thought—these are the falls of the Mississippi! Talk of the falls of the Rhine, a paltry river! Here is flow-

7. A large hotel, with new and elegant furniture (according to Mrs. Ellet), built by H. M. Rice.

8. Henry Mower Rice (1816-94), Minnesota pioneer, Indian commissioner and later U.S. senator. Shrewd in business and engaging in manner, he settled in Saint Paul in 1849 and became one of the territory's most influential men.

9. Frederika Bremer (1801-65), the Swedish author, visited Saint Paul in October 1850; she thought Minnesota might become "a glorious new Scandanavia" (*The Homes of the New World*, 2:56).

ing a stream which has already come a thousand miles, and has yet another two thousand to accomplish before it finds its rest in the bosom of the Gulf of Mexico.

On the banks we found some little shell fossils and several rare flowers, and we hear that Tufa (a petrified moss) is seen along its shores. We will try to find some before we leave, but to-morrow we have promised to make an expedition in a waggon with the authoress and her friend to see a wild lake, which, though known of old to trappers and the like, has only been explored by the civilized world during the last two or three months. We shall probably have to bivouac in the woods with our fair friends![10] Mr. Rice told us of it, and also recommended us to see a lake called after himself, where is some admirable fishing. He is well up in all this country, having travelled for six months without sleeping in a house: he is an energetic fellow and is now very rich, possessing much land at St. Paul's, the value of which will soon be immense. At present it would be a good investment, as between these two rising towns (only an hour's distance from each other) land may be bought—excellent farming land too, for $15 an acre; but in Illinois, quite as good land and nearer larger towns is sold as cheap.

We were reminded to-day that we were no longer in "the States" by an old ferryman of whom we asked

10. "When one or two resolute spirits are determined upon an undertaking, it is easy to find co-operators. . . . I found M[ary Clark] arranging some flowers to dry, with an agreeable English party, who had brought letters to her friend Mr. Rice, and through him been introduced to her acquaintance. 'They had,' as she said, 'been on the Alps, been on the Apennines—admired the banks of the beautiful Rhine, and looked on the cliffs of the Upper Danube—were familiar with all objects of interest in nature or art in the British Isles, and on the continent, as well as the various phases of social and political economy abroad, and favorably disposed to acquaintance with our own society and government' " (*Summer Rambles*, pp. 118-19).

the way to a spring of water; he told us, adding, "and you won't find better water in the *Territory*." There are at present, I *think*, three Territories belonging to the American Government,—Minnesota, Utah, and Oregon—(possibly New Mexico is one also).[11] These Territories may return only one member to Congress, who however, may not vote, only speak, but as soon as the Territory has acquired a population of 75,000 then it becomes a State and is admitted to a full share of the privileges of the Union.

Were I to settle anywhere in Western America, it would, I think, be in Minnesota, and at St. Paul's. The summer weather is not too hot, as there is always a pleasant breeze on the top of the "bluffs," while in the depth of winter, even while the thermometer is 30 or 40 below zero, no one suffers much from cold, as there is not the biting wind which the Southern winters bring with them. Mr. Rice assured us that he has walked without overcoat and slept in the woods without inconvenience when the cold was at one of these marvellously low points.

Minnesota is called the "Western New England," and was the first to follow Maine in passing the law called "The Maine Liquor Law," which prohibits the sale of spirituous drinks in that particular State or Territory. Of course the law is evaded, and no doubt brandy acquires a double charm from being "tabooed" by the wisdom of the lawgivers. Such a law in free America! The Queen vetoed a similar one passed in New Brunswick, as interfering with the *liberty of the subject*.

11. It was.

Thursday Night, [*August 12*].

We have to-day returned from a delightful expedition to the all-but-unknown lake, with Mrs. Ellet and Miss Clark. Our ladies are both of a certain age,[12] plain and strong-minded, so that no scandal could arise—Honi soit qui mal y pense,—why mayn't three gentlemen and two of the fairer sex excursionize together and bivouac together, and not be thought singular for it?[13]

Mrs. Ellet is of the genus Author, species Bookmaker, she writes "for a consideration" for the Tribune, has written either for the same *or* for fame, "Women of the Revolution," "Families of the Bible," and has now in the Press "Pioneer Women of the West." (By the way, the "Eureka" Tribune letter was not by her.)[14]

She is something like my notion of Fanny Butler,—impulsive, merry, fat, vulgar,—with a good deal of information and good deal of good humour. Miss Clark is "Preceptress of a school" in Michigan, so the argus-eyed newspapers assert.[15] She is pedantic and plain, admires Mrs. Ellet and bites her own nails to the quick or below it.

Mrs. Ellet told me several things worth noting,—

12. Mrs. Ellet's birthdate is usually given as 1818, in which case she would at this point be 34 (Bright was 22); but *Notable American Women* (1971) gives evidence that she may have been born in 1812.

13. ". . . Though a few adventurous young men may [camp out] for a frolic, any women who should venture upon such an innovation could hardly fail to find themselves styled 'come-outers' and 'independents'. . . . The idea of women going [to see the lake] was hooted at as quite out of the question. . . . This masculine selfishness in appropriating the first sights of fine scenery . . . determined us on a visit to the far-famed lake" (*Summer Rambles*, pp. 99, 116–17).

14. Cf. p. 276.

15. Miss Mary H. Clark established with her sister a female seminary in Ann Arbor in 1839. Its principles included attention to health as a sacred duty, outdoor exercise, and cheerfulness of temper.

MRS. ELIZABETH F. ELLET, CA. 1847

Godey's Magazine and Lady's Book, February 1847

"Impulsive, merry, fat, vulgar."

anecdotes of great people with whom she has been thrown at various times. Margaret Fuller was extremely agreeable but terribly ugly; you were first repelled from, but then drawn to her with singular force; she and Mrs. Ellet were much together at one time, they used "to stand treat" in turn at pastrycooks, for ices, and Margaret used to catechise her friend as to the feeling of Love, &c. of which she had then at least not the slightest idea. Margaret Fuller and Mr. Emerson (my fair informant told me) once went together to see Fanny Elssler in some ballet—("The Sylphide" I heard elsewhere); after a silence of some time, she turned to her friend, "Ralph, this is Poetry!"—"Margaret," was the reply, "this is Religion."[16]

Mrs. Dana, Mrs. E. knew well;—a small, scraggy little body with sweet voice and red corkscrews each side her face. When a widow of forty she conducted a flirtation with a young fellow of 25, and all but proposed to him—"he saw the snare and he retired" as Mrs. Ellet learnt from himself when at Mrs. Dana's request she endeavoured to "make up between them." Afterwards she again got a young gent in tow,—flaming red was his hair, ditto his face. She has now married him, and having become a good Episcopalian is doubtless an admirable wife to her Parsonic husband with whom she has since gone West.[17]

Henry Clay my fair acquaintance also knew; at a party he offered her his arm,—it was the left one—

16. This celebrated anecdote was already legendary; Charles Fenno Hoffman repeats it as "a good story afloat" in a letter to Rufus Griswold of February 19, 1845. Emerson and Margaret Fuller went together to see Fanny Elssler (1810–84) in *Nathalie* in October 1841.

17. I do not know which Mrs. Dana is meant; it cannot be the wife (or mother) of Richard Henry Dana, Sr. or Jr., or Charles A. Dana, the best-known members of the family. But the story illustrates Mrs. Ellet's taste for gossip and marital meddling—gifts that she had already exercised in New York circles against E. A. Poe and that were later turned with vehemence against Rufus Griswold.

someone noticed this to him, when he replied that a gentleman should always give the lady his left arm, his *right* was then free to defend her.

Mrs. Ellet has kindly promised to send me some autographs of the more noted of living Americans.

But now for our excursion. After breakfast we started in an open char-a-banc with three seats, each holding two, each facing the same way. The first part of our road lay over Prairie land, where there was some slight track: before long we had left this, and skirting the Cornelian-pebbled shore of Lake Calhoun, and several smaller lakes, one of which still unnamed we christened Lake Ellet,[18] we entered the woods. Here all path ceased, and we pushed our way through a brushwood of cornus (dogwood), oak and shumach generally as high as our wheels, sometimes higher than our heads; for long miles on either side nothing to be seen except this "oak opening" or "scrub prairie" as they call it, gay in places with the yellow flowers of the golden rod, the helianthus or sun-flower, and the black-eyed Rudbeckia with its reflexed petals. Of this district it may be truly said, what of the Alleghanies was falsely said by Campbell, "Lake after Lake interminably gleam,"[19] each belted with wood more or less thickly, and having on its shore little pebbly creeks rich in agate and cornelian. After a longish drive of 15 miles, made longer of course from absence of all road

18. In her dispatch to the *Tribune* (Sept. 1, 1852) Mrs. Ellet wrote: "About three quarters of a mile westward of Lake Calhoun, we came upon another small, circular lake, equally clear and beautiful, to which the Indians long ago gave a name, signifying 'The Lake of the Isle of Red Cedars.' Some of our party proposed another name, and it was concluded on; but it will undoubtedly retain the first, and should do so." (The last sentence was omitted from *Summer Rambles*.) This lake is still called Cedar Lake; another lake just east of it is called Lake of the Isles—both within the city of Minneapolis.

19. Bright is referring to Lyell, who quotes this line from Thomas Campbell's "Gertrude of Wyoming" (*A Second Visit to the U.S.*, 2:240).

284

whatever after the first few miles, except perhaps in places some Indian trail, near one part of which we saw traces of one encampment, we arrived at the shanty of log where we were to "camp." This was the only place within seven miles; it consisted of one room in which two backwoodsmen lodged, Stephens[20] and Schaeffer (pronounced alas! Shaver), a few blankets in one corner with a mosquito net over them, a stove for cooking, a small looking-glass, a candle stuck into a hunk of wood,—this was the furniture of the house which was most conspicuous, excepting indeed table and chair.[21] They have only lately come here, as this lake, being till within the last 2 or 3 weeks part of the Sioux territory,[22] was known only to Indian traders, and in St. Anthony itself, till last winter, no one knew of its existence, and our friends were the first white ladies who had ever been there.

The Lake itself—Mina-Tanka, "the Great Water," is some little way from the house; perhaps indeed before you fairly get to it you have to go seven miles.[23] A stream which has flowed through a chain of lakes from West to East of perhaps 40 miles in length passed close by, and we all embarked in a skiff under the care of our worthy driver Allan, and our still more worthy host "Shaver"—(the other man was from home). The

20. According to Mrs. Ellet, Simon Stevens, of Saint Anthony, had first explored this region the preceding March, in order to make claims.

21. Mr. Schaeffer, "with ruddy, cheerful countenance . . . welcomed us with much courtesy, apologizing for the homeliness of the accommodation he had to offer, and intimating slightly a wish that we had delayed our visit till 'things had been got a little nicer—a house built, and so forth' " (*Summer Rambles*, pp. 123-24).

22. In 1851 the Sioux sold most of their Minnesota territory to the U.S. government, but the treaty was not ratified until June 23, 1852.

23. "The basket was unpacked, meanwhile, and a hasty lunch taken . . . and leaving our luggage in the wagon, and fastening the horses, we took the footpath to the landing-place, just on the bend of the stream. Some young frogs were taken for bait among the weeds on the margin . . ." (*Summer Rambles*, pp. 125-26).

stream ran through some pretty prairie land, and was "bespankt" with white and yellow water-lilies. At last we entered a small lake, and then a larger, to which we gave the names of "Browning" and of "Bryant,"[24] which will probably adhere to them, as they are as yet nameless, and belong in part at least to Mr. Schaeffer who approved most fully.[25] One word en passant of this backwoodsman, who is by birth however a Pennsylvanian.[26] He is remarkably handsome, with a frank, open face, honest look, and most pleasant manners; he is more than a pleasing—an almost dignified man, he spends his spare time in reading, and was delighted when I gave him a copy of Bryant which I had with me. He is perhaps "one in a thousand;"—were it otherwise, I must confess that no other nation can boast a finer set of fellows—"Nature's noblemen"—than America with her backwoodsmen of the West.[27]

At the junction of these smaller lakes, we dropped Loch and Burder who fished, and had caught on our return three large bass weighing between two and

24. These are the easternmost parts of Lake Minnetonka, now known as Grays Bay and Wayzata Bay.

25. "As we shot over [the lake's] unruffled surface, we asked each other what name should be given to [it] . . . and claiming the right, as the first white women who had ever looked on its beauty, to bestow a name, in compliment to the English portion of our party we called it Lake Browning—after the great poetess. . . . Passing through a narrow strait, we then entered the second lake . . . With due formality, and reverently standing, we gave to the lake the name I had chosen—Lake Bryant— and read aloud a few lines from the poet ["The Prairies"] appropriate to the scene" (*Summer Rambles*, pp. 126-27).

26. Mrs. Ellet says he is from Indiana.

27. According to Mrs. Ellet, Schaeffer was planning to move his family West "if he could buy land that afforded a chance for making a fortune." The stage driver told her that he was worth a hundred thousand dollars already. "With all his rough exterior, he seemed to possess an extensive knowledge of literature; criticized the poetry of Dryden, Pope, and other English classics, and compared with them the poetry of Bryant, Longfellow, and a number of American bards, in a manner that showed he had read and appreciated them" (*Summer Rambles*, p. 90).

three pounds: the rest of us went on to where Lake
Bryant receives the water of Lake Mina-Tanka, a
promontory (on which was found an Indian idol—a
painted stone—by the last gentleman who went
there)[28] stretches out and divides the two Lakes. We
landed on the promontory, and looked over the broad
expanse beyond us, with beautiful wooded islands on
its surface, beautiful wooded slopes along its side.
The red cedar grew luxuriantly on this point of land,
and tossed its wild fantastic branches far over the
waters on either bank; we heard the wild cry of the
loon in the distance, and saw the fish hawk and the
Turkey-buzzard wheel round the low cliffs near us:
the eagle and the pelican are said to haunt this spot!

We returned after once again landing on a spot
where probably no white step has ever trod before, and
after finding an arrowhead of stone (on Cedar Point)
and some few cornelians, one of which Mrs. Ellet
wishes sent to Mrs. Browning.

As we came along, Mrs. Ellet recited cleverly enough
poems of Poe's and Longfellow's, Browning's and Tom
Hood's, and told one or two good stories of absurd
blunders. An American lady whose husband was in
Europe was asked if he had seen the Drachenfels.[29]
"I presume so," she answered, "for he took a great
many letters with him to people." Another gentleman
was desirous of knowing why so many American families prided themselves on their Juggernaut (Hugenot)
blood.

We took up the fishers, and returned to cook and
eat the fish—our dinner. Miss Clark was Soyer of the

---

28. The stone, covered with small yellow spots, was placed upright
between two sticks painted red. "Dr. S. of St. Louis," who found it,
learned from a Sioux chief that it was used for offerings of scalps (*Summer Rambles*, p. 117).

29. A mountain on the Rhine.

Wilds,[30] and excellent, most excelling was the fried bass; hardly so good the tea which was very bitter. Of course we eat out-of-doors, and soon after prepared for bed. The ladies went—rather against their wishes, I think—inside the hut:[31] *we* prepared to "camp" out. A fire was lighted to keep away mosquitoes, and we laid ourselves down under the side of the wooden shanty, on a row of buffalo hides—Allan, Shaver, myself, Loch, Burder—in this order we lay, looking up at the clear, starry skies, and trying to ward off the insidious mosquitoes. How they buzzed round us, and found uncovered corners of flesh, and gloated over them. It was a long time before we could get to sleep; we were quite warm and comfortable, but the mosquitoes and the excitement of our first bivouac, and the wondrous pleasure of lying down and looking up at those glorious heavens with their stars, made us very wakeful. And added to this, the crackling of the fire, and the stamping of the horses which, by the way (as they were tethered close to their heads), kept our poor ladies also awake till late, as we were aware when the hut door opened about midnight and a shower of shawls was thrown upon our beds. At last we got to sleep, and about 4½ got up again rather tired, I must acknowledge, and rather covered with bites. Burder took an axe and commenced an onslaught on some of the trees; Loch helped Miss Clark to "wash up," and I went down to fish with Allan. Burder afterwards turned up and caught a big pike (pickerel they call it); I

30. Alexis Soyer (1809-58), celebrated French chef at London's Reform Club.

31. "Having secured the cabin door, and placed two carriage cushions for pillows, we crept under the netting and lay down on the floor pallet; but no fatigue could bring me repose. The heat, and the fumes of cookery; the gambols of a number of field mice which had got in through the crevices . . . were sufficient to banish slumber" (*Summer Rambles*, p. 133).

288

caught four bass, two small ones, the others from lbs. 2 to 3 each; Allan also caught several, so that we had considerably more than enough for breakfast.[32] "Nature's toilette" was soon performed at the stream, and then we sat down to our repast of fish and water, the luxuries we had brought in shape of pork, beef, &c. being quite despised. "Shaver" tells me he drinks nothing but water, and hardly tastes animal food—he certainly thrives on it!

Soon after breakfast we got again into our carriage and returned after sundry "perils of driving" through this roadless country. Were I to live here I could thank a roadmaker most sincerely, and be in a position to say, like the Scotchman to his friend,

> Had you seen these roads before they were made
> You'd lift up your hands and bless Marshall Wade.[33]

In the fall however, the way to the Lake will be easier, as then the "wild fire" of the Prairies will sweep over these oak openings and leave freer passage to the voyageurs: were it not for this, these young oaks would soon spring to trees, and the country would be dense forest land.

Somehow or other a road *will* and must be made, as a Hotel is to be built near the Shanty (Mr. Stephens'), who expects to have many visitors during the summer months. I'm only glad I've seen it in its wild, really wild state, before civilization has adorned and—spoiled

32. "It seemed but an instant after, when a curious *fizzing* roused me, and the bass they had caught might be seen in the pan, frying under the auspices of Miss C[lark], who showed an admirable knowledge of culinary mysteries on this occasion. In the mean time Mr. S[chaeffer] had arranged the breakfast table on the green, in perfect order, fetched a bucket of cool spring water, and was diligently slicing up a loaf of bread" (*Summer Rambles*, p. 134).

33. The verse ("The Highland Road") refers to General George Wade, who employed 500 soldiers in roadmaking in the Highlands in 1726-29.

it.[34] On our way back to-day we saw a little party of half-breed Indians by a lake-side, with dogs. One was a regular squaw, Madame Brissette, married to a French Canadian; we called at her husband's on Lake Calhoun, and paid $1 for a great number of pebbles picked up about its shore. He's a nice clever person, who speaks 6 Indian dialects and knows of course, much about the various tribes; his wife was a Sioux.[35]

Since dinner we've been sleeping and talking, and are now off to bed.[36]

Steam Boat Dr. Franklin.
Sunday Morning, [August 15].

We left St. Anthony's on Friday, going round by Fort Snelling to St. Paul's.[37] On the way we passed a pretty waterfall—Minnehaha—so called more properly than the great falls of St. Anthony. The water falls in one sheet over a rock of 60 feet in height, and I never saw water more graceful in its leap, or more whitely broken, a *sheet* I have called it—rather, a snowstorm of water, each drop seeming distinct and like a flake of snow falling into and getting lost among the rapids below.

Fort Snelling is beautifully situated, on a rock at the

34. "On the shore of this third lake a location has been chosen, and claims set up for a hundred families who are to remove thither next year. In some remote places we saw them designated by mere slips of board nailed against a tree" (*Summer Rambles*, p. 131).

35. Mrs. Ellet notes that M. Brissette had lived in the vicinity twelve or fourteen years, had a "neat house," and kept boats and fishing tackle to accommodate visitors (*Summer Rambles*, p. 98).

36. Mrs. Ellet concludes her *Tribune* account as follows: "On our return to St. Anthony, we found that the fame of our excursion had spread far and wide, and that many were already emulous of the enterprise." (This sentence was omitted from *Summer Rambles*.)

37. A line of stages ran three times a day between Saint Paul and Saint Anthony, making connections with the steamboats.

From *Appletons' Illustrated Hand-Book of American Travel*, 1857

junction of the St. Peter and the Mississippi rivers; it looks substantial enough, and once, I suppose, was useful, very useless for the future, I imagine.[38] Back to St. Paul's by dinner-time, after which we strolled along, looking at Indian curiosities, and Indians themselves as they prowled into drug stores and grocery stores. At about eleven o'clock we found ourselves going to sleep in the Dr. Franklin which left early next morning, the Excelsior having started a few hours before. Yesterday we saw Lake Pepin better than on our way up; it is very beautiful; and we passed two Indian villages, one, the Kaposia, we had seen before, the other, Red Wing.[39] Dirty, bean-spattered[?] "individdles" again came on board, and again we saw squaw-rowed canoes dart along across us. But now

38. Only a few weeks earlier the House had passed a bill to reduce and define the military reservation at Fort Snelling; in 1854 over 4,500 acres of it were sold (all now included in the city of Saint Paul).

39. Kaposia was a Sioux village (described on p. 277); Red Wing belonged to the Dakota tribe.

we've passed the Indian lands, and shall see no more of this poor ill-fated race; indeed, without going far West or perhaps South in Florida, we should see little more than we have seen already, and an interpreter would be necessary, or a very long residence among them, before one could really *understand* them, their wants and hopes, or judge with certainty what will be their future.

Some in the South must be nearly, if not quite civilized, and many of the Cherokees own *negro slaves*. A propos of this unhappy Red-race, I heard a story which is worth remembering, from Mrs. Ellet.

A missionary tried to convert a very beautiful young girl—of what tribe I forget. He talked to her long and seriously; he told her of the Christ, and how He had lived and worked and died. "Noble, brave," said the Indian girl, "I like that." He told her then how she and all the Indians *must* believe in the Christ, and follow Him and His doctrines, and how the Great Spirit would punish all who did not with punishment to last for ever. She listened, and clapping her hands, woke up the echoes of some near hill—"The Great Spirit laughs," she said, and turning away, left the missionary again for her own loving trusting faith.

14

EASTWARD TO NIAGARA

Chicago, Illinois. Wednesday, August 18.

We are rapidly getting eastward, and have to *put on*
our watches daily. Nor are we sorry to get into civilized
parts again, (especially after the last two days' travel)
or find ourselves in so good a Hotel as is the Tremont
House of Chicago.[1] But now for a history "how short
soever" of our journey from Galena. Mrs. Ellet in a
letter to the Tribune spins her journey between the
same places into two columns of the Tribune newspaper; I shall try to condense it into a couple of pages.

"Forsitan hac olim nobis meminisse juvabit"[2]—true
enough when conscious of a certain heroic or a certain
ludicrous element mixed with one's distresses; very
untrue in any other case; as for example in this trip,
or rather *passage* ("trip" suggests something pleasur-
able) through Illinois. Bad food, a slow coach, jolting
roads, swearing Irishmen, and an all-but-sleepless

1. At the corner of Dearborn and Lake streets.
2. *Forsan et haec olim meminisse juvabit*: "And perhaps sometime it
will be pleasant to recall these things" (*Aeneid* I.203).

night—not much of pleasant memory to be extracted out of these. Leaving Galena (where we landed early in the morning) about eight, we travelled through the flattest country eye ever beheld. A "rolling prairie" was the sublimest thing we saw, and after all, an "un-dulating field" without any trees is much the same in common English. In places too, we saw the flat regular prairie very extensive, and except where wood-belted at the horizon, seemingly boundless; but the grass is hardly more than a foot high, very dusty and brown, and with but few flowers to enliven the dull expanse. As for it waving like a sea, and all that, it's simply nonsense as regards the Prairies of Illinois, farther west I may not answer for.

At Rockford we got into the railway carriages, hop-ing to reach Chicago in good time, that is, by starting at about 5 to be there by a little after ten. " 'Tis not in mortals to command success"[3] or in "cars" either. Through this unenclosed prairie-land of Illinois roam apparently "at their own sweet will," a very con-siderable number of cattle, who are not over particular about trespassing upon the line of rail. This is well known, and before every engine is placed "a cow cradle," to push away any intruding animal. The cow cradle served us in good stead at least twice, I after-wards heard, but unluckily at last while going some-what slowly, some ill-fated calf got before the engine, and from the want of speed at which we went, was not pushed away at once, and remained pressed along by the weight behind it. At last we came to a hollow in the road, into which and under the cow-cradle fell the wretched creature, the wheels went over it, the calf was killed, and the engine ran off the line.

After six hours, and after no small difficulty then,

3. Addison, *Cato*, I.ii.44.

294

Illustrated London News, April 10, 1852

we got away, not quite starved luckily, as a place called Marengo was within a mile and a half of our accident. What a nuisance this was may be easily imagined, and how glad we were at last to find ourselves in Chicago. Not the least part of our pleasure in getting here consists in the fact that here at last we can see the papers, and have a little English news. The N. Y. Herald seems quite an old friend, it is very long since we have seen it. It is laboriously writing down Newport, but inserts an advertisement, the effect of which will doubtless be far greater than Mr. Bennett's editorial. Imagine poor Miss Draper getting into an Inn-keeper's advertisement as a "lion!"[4]

I found a letter from Synge waiting my arrival.

4. In the August 10 issue of James Gordon Bennett's *New York Herald*, an editorial mocks the fact that Newport hotelkeepers, plagued by the Maine Liquor Law, had been forced to attract customers by advertising the names of the ladies staying with them. A column reprinted from the *Newport News*, listing the ladies at the Ocean House, states that "Miss Draper, of New York, is very pretty, sings beautifully, and dances well."

Good-natured fellow! I hope we shall meet in Canada or at Boston!

Chicago is, I think, a stupid town enough, and Lake Michigan a blue sea with low bank, and without (of course) the delicious fresh breeze which a salt sea always bears upon its waters.

The only building, besides the Hotel, which is at all striking is a Church built of some black and white stone, which gives a peculiar half-mourning look to the exterior of it,—rather fantastic than beautiful.[5]

The dinner here to-day was good,—prairie chicken and venison inter alia. To-night we've been to see Julia Bennett in "Lucille," a story taken from Bulwer's "Pilgrims of the Rhine," and we had a good-for-nothing, a droll little farce in which she appeared to much advantage.[6]

Steam Boat Southern Michigan, Lake Erie.
Friday Evening, [August 20].

Seated at a marble table, and sitting on a red velvet-covered chair, I write from the cabin of the "Southern Michigan" of our travels from Chicago.

This is a beautiful boat, and, being low pressure, is safe as well, so that we have a feeling of security never felt on the waters of the Mississippi and Ohio. The accommodations are excellent—on the upper deck, two large saloons, one for "us masculines," the other for the ladies and their gentlemen friends. Below are two

5. The Second Presbyterian Church, a Gothic structure built of a singular pitchy stone, seamed with varicolored streaks.

6. Julia Bennett Barrow (b. 1824) made her American debut in New York in 1851 after establishing a reputation at the Haymarket in London. The adaptation of Bulwer-Lytton's novel was made by William B. Bernard.

other large rooms, a private "tabooed" cabin, for ladies only, and a place for dining—by lamp-light, by the way, as rows of open berths take the place of windows except at the extreme end of the room. Dinner was very good,—turkey and oysters, among other things seen for the first time since we left Washington shores; we are indeed again coming East, and getting into civilized parts—a proposition no one who considers how invariably oysters are a sign of superior civilization, as invariably as other "natives" are of barbarism, would hesitate for a moment to admit.

I have said we feel *safe* to-day—and yet a rumour brought on board by some passenger at Monroe proves, if true, that even with low pressure engines, fine weather, and every favouring circumstance, the carelessness of these people is enough to endanger the finest vessel. The rumour is, that by collision the "Atlantic," bound for Detroit, is lost, and 250 souls gone down in the blue waters of Lake Erie! I trust it may not be true, and I feel sure the loss has been exaggerated, but it's very terrible to think of![7]

We left Chicago yesterday morning at 8½, by the Southern Michigan and Northern Indiana R. R. for Toledo, where we arrived at 10. We chose this line of rail in preference to the other Central one to Detroit, because (other things being about equal) the scenery is said to be better, and the boats from Toledo finer. The scenery was in places extremely pretty—pine woods and little lakes covered with broad-leaved water plants, some good prairie land, greener and fresher than that of Illinois (except where the wild fire had left a blackened tract stretching either side of the line of rail), and small rising towns and villages looking

7. The *Atlantic* collided with another ship off Long Point in dense fog; over one hundred passengers—many of them Norwegian emigrants bound for Wisconsin—were drowned.

more habitable than those of the same size and age in the "Far West."

Jonesville and White Pigeon were the principal towns we past. At the latter place we dined, and (as I said before) it was not till ten or later that we found ourselves supping at Toledo, having been 13 hours or more in doing 250 miles.

This morning we left at seven, and after ten miles of sailing down the river Maumee, we entered Lake Erie, only landing once at Monroe to take up people from the morning train of the West.

Buffalo, N.Y. Saturday, [August 21].

About 7 last night we reached Cleveland, and here we had to wait till one this morning, as the cars from Cincinnati had met with a series of disasters, first running off the line, then running into another train.

This morning we found ourselves out of sight of land, and, quite "at sea," our steamer going at a good pace, and about three o'clock we arrived at Buffalo—again in State of New York. It is a large imposing-looking town, with an admirable Hotel, the American, and some beautiful Churches and other buildings.

Buffalo. Sunday [August 22].

When I next write in my journal, I shall have seen Niagara, and received my letters from home.[8] Niagara

8. HAB received a letter from his father offering to send more money, as his tour was longer than expected. Bright replied on August 23: "I certainly don't intend to let you pay entirely for my Trans-Atlantic tour— £40 or £50 will be ample for presents, books and maps, for, except Indian curiosities and furs, there is very little that our own England will not supply as well and as cheaply."

Gleason's Pictorial Drawing-Room Companion, September 11, 1852

*"The rumour is, that by collision the 'Atlantic,'
bound for Detroit, is lost."*

at last!—really to see Niagara *to-day*—within a few
hours—to have one of my oldest longings satisfied,
and to see in all the grandeur of reality what I have
so often seen mistily and vaguely in day-dreams in
old England![9]

I have this morning been to our Church to hear Mr.
Hosmer.[10] He is very eloquent, but his eloquence is
the least part of the charm and power of his prayers
and sermon. I never heard any one who combined
beauty of style with such *goodness* of matter, by
which I do not mean merely that he preached sensibly
and wisely, but like a true, good Christian, feeling

9. Cf. the ninth stanza of Bright's poem "Noctes Coenaeque Deum,"
written in 1850 (page 447).

10. George Washington Hosmer (1804–81), Unitarian clergyman
noted for his pulpit eloquence, later president of Antioch College and
professor at Meadville Theological School.

every word he spoke, and anxious, as only a good man can be, that we should feel it too. Retribution and Forgiveness of Sin—what each was, and how the two are reconciled—forgiveness for the past sin will not preclude the retribution of ill health, ill fame, lost opportunity which sin brings with it. A very true and awful sermon.[11]

Loch and Burder went to a beautiful Episcopal Church—really beautiful in the Gothic style where the Gothic still has a Norman look of simple beauty unspoiled by ornament![12]

Loch leaves us to-day—one of the nicest and most agreeable fellows I ever met. I don't believe he lost his temper for a moment while he was with us, certainly never when with me. He is a real loss.

Niagara, Canada.
Tuesday Night, [August 24].

Canada!—our own dominions—Niagara!! We arrived here on Sunday night, having driven over, as there was no train and we were too impatient to wait till morning.[13]

11. In the same letter to his father quoted above Bright writes: "This is President Fillmore's Church, and he showed his respect for his pastor by offering to make him Chaplain of the Navy, but Mr. Hosmer . . . is 'too good to live,' and declined it, first because it would countenance war, secondly because it was a sinecure, so Dr. Dewey got the place instead."

12. Saint Paul's Episcopal Church, in brown sandstone with an imposing spire, was designed by Richard Upjohn (1850).

13. "It is with a feeling of positive relief that the English traveller finds himself in Canada. Kindly as he has been treated, perhaps, in the States, and delightful as many of the higher classes there undoubtedly are, he has often been unpleasantly reminded that he is travelling in a 'free and enlightened' republic, where every one he meets (in whatever rank of society, however educated, however clad) is, or considers that he is, on the same level with all the world, and has an indubitable right to fraternize

Two miles from the Falls (with the wind against us) we heard the Niagara roar, and saw the spray rising above the tree tops. We passed the American village with its large Hotel and its <   > Post Office, where we got such a budget of letters! and crossing the suspension bridge, first saw the Falls by the light of the young moon.—On to the Clifton House, where we find ourselves in a beautiful room looking right upon the Falls, which roar us every night to sleep.[14]

The beauty of the river gorge with its green water, its escarped rocks, and its pine woods, struck me very much, as I never heard it mentioned. Without the Falls Niagara would be a lovely spot—with them, it is perhaps the grandest thing in the world.

But how am I to describe Niagara! It is very difficult. A mere outline will give but little idea of it,—a drawing heavy with detail will be finnikin and trifling, unworthy the grandeur of the "regal reality," as Curtis aptly calls it.[15]

I will join in one view Niagara, as seen by me today on the "American," and as I have seen it almost hourly for the last two days, on the Canadian side of the river, and lay down a plan rather than a picture, but a plan not without some of the true colouring of Nature.

Some way above the Falls begin the rapids of the Niagara river. The water, chafed into foam, dashes down little ledges of rock and sweeps along hurriedly and confusedly, except where some green islet with fantastic groups of dark cedar for a moment stops its course.

with anybody and everybody" (anonymous article by HAB entitled "Canada" in *Fraser's Magazine* [February, 1853], p. 184).

14. Niagara's most celebrated hotel on the Canadian side was a huge white structure with three green verandahs and extensive gardens.

15. In the little book of travels called *Lotus-Eating: A Summer Book* (New York, 1852), by George William Curtis.

On again—the islet has been safely passed,—so the water tumbles over another rocky shelf, and away towards the Fall. Again it is checked,—it has now to choose a course, for here is a larger island, and the trees grow down to the very edge of the cataract, and some are wet with the spray from the green depths of the Canadian, and others bend low over the waters of the American Fall. It is a difficult choice, each is so beautiful. On the right is the American fall again broken by a rock, which turns away one stream from the main body of the water,—very small it looks, the stream, like one tress of hair which the wind has carried from its place,—and yet it is as large as any waterfall I ever saw, and is at least 160 feet in height.

But that rock which divides the two? Of that there is a sad story often told, and often yet to tell,—how a lover and his mistress sat upon its turf close to the river side, and how, in sport, he held *her* little sister over the dangerous edge, and how the child fell from his arms into the fatal stream, and he, as he tried again to grasp her, was like her, hurried over by the torrent's power, and perished with her in the whirl below, and his betrothed close by![16]

Yet the spot is very beautiful, and the water glides smoothly and falls gracefully, and splashes up the diamond spray, all unconscious of any wrong; and over the fall leaps a rainbow arch, as if to vie with the leap of the Niagara river, or as if (as I sometimes thought) it would wish to bridge the fall for him who is about to cross in the tossing little ferry-boat beneath—as glorious a bridge the bow would make as the snake in Goethe's "Tale of Tales," but still more frail and dangerous even for naiads of the place.[17]

16. The story is told by Curtis as having happened "two years since."

17. In the "Märchen," which Bright refers to earlier (p. 209), the dragon makes with its body a dazzling bridge across the river.

From *Picturesque America*, ed. W. C. Bryant, Vol. I, 1872

"You can see it best from a little tower—
Terrapin tower they call it."

No less lovely and more sublime is the Horse Shoe Fall of Canada. You can see it best from a little tower—Terrapin tower they call it—which juts out from the end of Goat Island, or rather from the end of some planks communicating with it.

A vast amphitheatre of waters, 158 feet in height, is the Horse Shoe Fall. Part of the water is churned into foam before it reaches the fall, part is still a sheet of clearest green, part you can hardly see for the spray rises high and thick and throws an all but impenetrable veil around it.

But I must give in—I cannot, who can?—describe Niagara! "Words cannot picture a place so fair,"—words cannot give any just impression of the shifting lights and shadows, the motion and the life of this wonderful scene. "Exaggeration, mere verbiage," he who has *not* seen Niagara will say—tame, dull description—the man whose memory is full of it, will think, —and his criticism is but too true.

I shall crowd into one page the mere details of the last two days. Yesterday we went 150 feet or more behind the Horse Shoe Fall, and got well wet for our pains. In the evening we rode to Queenston to inquire after the grave of Burder's uncle,—we were unsuccessful, and he has not been more fortunate to-day, when he went by himself, and I explored Goat Island, &c.

This evening we've called on Mr. Porter, and dine with him to-morrow.[18] He has a nice house on the American side, while we as in duty bound are in Canada, and see more English faces at dinner at the Hotel than I've seen for a long time;—young officers

18. The Porter family had long been established in Niagara: Augustus Porter (d. 1849) was the first judge of Niagara County. This Mr. Porter may have been his eldest son, Augustus S. (1798-1872), formerly U.S. senator from Michigan; or his second son Albert H. (b. 1801), both of whom built houses near their father's old homestead.

in numbers, who are full of brandy and patriotism, and I forgive them the noise they make very heartily, for the pleasure of again hearing "The flag that's braved a thousand years,"[19] and so forth, which they've been bellowing out this evening.

I've just been reading the papers. I see that 12 Unis have been returned to Parliament. Je doute.

Thursday Evening, [August 26].

Here we are moneyless and money-expecting, and here we must remain till Loch and Mr. Irvin remit us the "necessary." Letters have however come from England—from George Melly, and from Temple, and also a short note from Ed[mund] Knight, telling me that we shall probably meet at Montreal or Quebec; I hope with all my heart we shall.

Yesterday Burder and myself spent on Goat Island, and after a bath, dined with Mr. Porter. We had a good English-like dinner, and Porter himself is a capital fellow. Miss Porter is agreeable, and chatty, and told me how a foreigner at Boston was asked to tea to meet a few "minds,"—*minds* in question however, quite appreciating the *bodily* comforts of tea and toast.[20]

A Toronto gentleman told me that Lyon Mackenzie is a "young Canada" man, and worth seeing,[21] but

19. From the song "Ye Mariners of England," set to words by Thomas Campbell.

20. As Bright elsewhere tells the anecdote, the foreigner "preferred meeting a few *soles* at dinner."

21. William Lyon Mackenzie (1795–1861) had led the 1837 rebellion in Upper Canada, after which he escaped to the United States, supporting himself by anti-British journalism. He was permitted to return to Canada in 1849, and in 1851 was elected to the Legislative Assembly for the county

the general feeling in that country is very loyal, and full of attachment to Old England—"home" they often call it, even when for two or three generations the family have lived in Canada.

A Mr. <   > who is now living at Cincinnati (where by the way he met Loch whom he was pleased to believe Attaché to the Court of Vienna) and who was at Cambridge University, Mass:—gave me much information about this very commendable education-factory. The Cantabs go younger than *our* Cantabs generally do; they are not obliged to be in at night, seldom have dinner or supper parties, drink wine and brandy, particularly the latter, and do not affect Debating Societies so much as the students at Southern colleges.

Yale is a *Presbyterian* place.

The best American magazine is the "North American," edited by Mr. Bowen.[22] A Perkins wrote much in it, and well <   > the article on Hildebrand.[23]

After dinner we adjourned to the garden, where we amused ourselves with the "garden engine," as one of the ladies called it, and afterwards received tea from the fair Miss Porter. A concert was going on at one of the Hotels, which all our friends were anxious to patronize,—and we were *pennyless*. We rushed off to the Post Office, but no letter had arrived for us, and finally we slunk back to the Clifton House without giving the Porters any explanation of our (doubtless to them) very eccentric behaviour, and we did not call to-day either, as in duty bound.

---

of Haldimand. At this time he had, as Bright wrote later, "sobered down from a dangerous and most incorrigible demagogue into an amusing and somewhat ridiculous M.P." (*Fraser's Magazine* [February 1853], p. 189).

22. The *North American Review*, founded in Boston in 1815, was edited at this time by the philosopher Francis Bowen (1811–90).

23. Among the contributions of James Handasyd Perkins (1810–49) was a rather colorful essay on Hildebrand, Pope Gregory VII (*North American Review* 61 [1845]: 20–54).

When we had returned, I walked as far as the ci-devant Table Rock to see a lunar rainbow, which is at certain seasons visible, and only at certain seasons. You stand with your back to the moon, and half facing the Clifton House, look into the spray. The bow was perfect, as good as ever solar one in shape—in colour very inferior—a washed-out bow with the merest shading as if to show where the colours would be in the sunshine dazzling you with their violet and orange and purple; or (si vous voulez) we'll call it a phantom bow, the ghost of the one which in daylight leaps down the rocks "streaming among the streams," as the Shelley-sung curls of Arethusa's hair. (I owe Mr. Curtis thanks for reminding me of my favourite poet at Niagara.)[24]

To-day, while Burder bathed, I lay "chewing the cud of sweet and bitter fancies"[25] on one of the islands in the Niagarean Rapids. It is a lovely spot, the water rushing along and hardly stopping to dally with the gnarled and twisted cedar branches which hang into the rivers—the most beautiful cedars with natural seats up among their branches, or down among their roots, —just the place for a lover like George [Melly], or a thinker like Temple, or a dreamer like myself, on a fine, hot, sunny summer day.

Burder however roused me with the news that no letter had come, and after a little natural grumbling, we went to explore the Cave of the Winds, behind the Fall, which I have described as separated by one rock from the main body of the American Fall. A staircase in a wooden tower—yclept Biddle's[26]—leads you under the rocks and brings you to a little house where

24. Curtis opens his chapter on "Niagara, Again" in *Lotus-Eating* with the first stanza of Shelley's "Arethusa."

25. Cf. *As You Like It* IV.iii.102.

26. These stairs were named after Nicholas Biddle of the United States Bank, who had them built.

you take off your "things" and put on a dress they—
a brace of niggers—give you. A half-ladder half-stair-
case affair, slippery with spray is now descended, and
holding hands at the bottom, you edge along some
rocks, while the water splashes over you, and takes
away your breath, and finally, you emerge at the other
side somewhat "done." A small cavity in the rock pro-
tects you for a moment, and to this is given the name
of Cave of the Winds, as in this paper given to certify
to those it may concern, my "pluck."[27]

Sometimes the phenomenon of a perfectly *circular
rainbow* makes the place interesting, otherwise, there
is little to see except a small arch rainbow you can
see better above, and no particular pleasure to experience except that of a shower bath. Still, it is better
worth doing than the feat of going behind the Horse
Shoe Fall, though it is, I think, more difficult; ladies
frequently do it though, and we have seen one emerg-
ing just as we entered to-day, in a dripping costume
in appearance at least, as like that of a Bloomer as
of Undine.[28] Our guide says that gentlemen often
turn back from want of spirit, or enterprize, ladies
far less often.

This afternoon we've spent quietly at home, having
dined rather late and being rather tired with our exertion. I've got through a good deal of letter writing,
—Mr. George, Mr. Irvin, my Father, Aunt Annie,
Nanny, Spencer Perceval[29] and Edmund Knight.

---

27. "This is to certify that —— has passed through the Cave of the Winds
and behind the Central Fall on the American Side, at the foot of Goat
Island."

28. Curtis speaks of "Bloomerized Undines" at Niagara.

29. Spencer Perceval (1828–90), a Cambridge friend.

308

Saturday Night, [August 28].

Our money has arrived to-day, but too late to allow of our going on to Toronto, so here we stay in peace till Monday. Loch was taken ill at Albany, which accounts for the delay in getting the money. Yesterday I wandered over the river, and finding no letters, sent a telegraphic message to Irvin—50 cents or 2/- for 10 words, "We are expecting one hundred dollars, please send them directly," and early this morning we got a telegraphic answer and at half past one, our money.

Burder also crossed a little later and we both met Porter to whom we apologized, offering to call in the evening which we accordingly did, having first driven round by the Whirlpool to see it. It is extremely fine— the river rocks, surpassingly beautiful, have receded and formed a deep bay on the right bank, and here the water is caught and whirls slowly round in foamy circles—round and round, white with struggling for its freedom, and restless in its effort to escape from the wild dance to which it has been forced. The sun had set, and the moon was rising on the opposite side of the river, when we left this sublime scene for our friend's house. We found company there—they always have company there—and spent a pleasant evening chatting with some nice enough ladies, listening to some good music, and promising Mr. Porter to join him (if still at Niagara) in a fishing excursion to-day.

When we came back to Canada—(hasn't it a magnificent sound—Canada spoken of as a *place*—"drive me to *Canada*," one says to a hack man)—well, on our return to Canada, we walked to see the lunar rainbow, which Burder had not seen. We were disappointed—

309

the night was very splendid—the moon holding high court in Heaven, and all the river-gods rising on Niagarean spray to do her homage,—but Iris was not there, and we returned, by no means grateful to that tyrant Aeolus, who kept her out of sight, and deprived his yesterday's guests of a pleasure as great in sooth as a visit to his own wet cave!

To-day we have done the last of the "lions"—the "Maid of the Mist," and the "Devil's Hole." Of the former I shall say nothing, as I do not wish to be upbraided as "Curtis and water,"[30] although the more watery the more truthful my description of the excursion would necessarily be. It was *very* wet work, and supplied the *third* shower bath we've had while lionizing. We were strange unhappy looking creatures during our pleasuring—in great waterproof cloaks and caps, and ranged solemnly on seats, like black rows of Inquisitors, very silent, for the spray blinded us, and the flaps of the weird headdresses deprived us of the sister sense of hearing. The "maid" goes three times a day—at 8, *11*, and 4, and has a daily average of 70; last year altogether she had 11,500 passengers, this year not so many, as "cholera and rumours of cholera" have kept people from Niagara.

About 3½ we arrived at the "Devil's Hole," and left our "buggy" under the charge of "the Proprietor of *this cool retreat*" (as he advertises the place). A path led us down to the water's edge, and when there we found our friends just finishing dinner, which seemed to have been most successful, more so than the fishing, which had resulted in *two* fish. Some Indians in civilized garb were also fishing, and another fish was caught for us by them. Porter fried salt pork, and with

30. Curtis has a rather purple description of the "Maid of the Mist," the little steamer that "dances up to the very foot of the Falls, wrapping herself saucily in the rainbow robe of its own mist."

crackers and the brandy flask we really did very well. Porter talked and caricatured us all; Force and an "Alabama Professor," clerical, severe and dyspeptic, fished very assiduously, Burder ditto; I prowled about at my "own sweet will" and chatted about spearing fish with a German exile—doubtless a Baron Von Somtingtk—and tried it, only failing because there was no fish visible and spearable. A Mr. Kensett, really a distinguished artist, and the man who has illustrated Curtis' "Lotus Eating" was there; I liked his looks and struck up a friendship with him.[31] He admires the Pre-Raphaelites, at least in some degree, and does not approve of Turner's later style;[32] he kindly gave me a card of introduction to a man who has a fine gallery at N[ew] York, and offered to "show me round" if he is there himself when we are. He knew Dr. Furness' *son by name*,[33] and knew Dr. Dewey well,—advises us to go to the White Mountains from the East, &c. &c.

While we were fishing, &c. Mr. Kensett left us and finished a sketch of some of the rocks in the wood above the Devil's Hole; and a strikingly good sketch it was, as we rested to look at it on our way up—a very steep way, by the bye—"facilis descensus *Averni*, sed revocare graduum,"[34] wittily remarked Mr. Porter as we toiled along.

At the top we parted, and *we* crossed the bridge and "cut" the Custom House as we generally do.

As I write, music and dancing are going on in a sit-

31. See p. 92. Kensett was slender and romantic-looking, with a high forehead, straight nose, and long dark wavy hair.

32. Joseph Mallord William Turner (1775-1851), English landscape painter.

33. Dr. Furness's oldest son, William Henry Furness, Jr. (1828-67), was studying to be a portrait painter.

34. "Easy is the descent to hell, but to recall thy steps [*gradum*] . . . " (*Aeneid* VI.126-28).

ting-room close by—they have these gaieties nearly every night, and one night had really a grand "hop." I neither knew nor cared anything about it, and was sitting writing in my room. A negro came up with some water in answer to my bell—"Why not at the ball to-night?" he asked. "I knew nothing of it—besides, I know no ladies here." "Is it possible?" he asked, raising his hands in astonishment, "ladies, fine ladies here from Toronto and Montreal and Quebec—not know any of them?" A propos of balls, I find there has been a large one at Saratoga. My informant is the New York Herald who mentions several of the ladies thinly disguising them with initials.

"Mrs. C. A. D----s of N. Y. was dressed in black and held her bouquet as coquettishly as if one and not two score were her portion of years—her *stylish* daughter was dressed in, &c. &c."[35]

Poor Mrs. Davis! At forty a lady is thought quite old here—antique and to be reverenced. Miss Porter too asserts that she cannot be forty, which is of course the "unkindest cut of all."[36]

Western Hotel, Toronto.
Monday Night, August 30.

Yesterday I went over to the American side, leaving Burder writing. Meeting Porter, Kensett and Force, we strolled along to the "Indian Ladder," the place where, before the days of suspension bridges or pully-propelled cars and ferries, the Red gentlemen descended the rocks when anxious to cross the river.

---

35. " . . . Dressed in white, in an embroidered flounced muslin robe" (*New York Herald*, August 24, 1852).

36. *Julius Caesar* III.ii.187.

Porter was very agreeable, and amused me much by imitating the English way of talking,—"When (are) I see the Honorable gentleman (are) it appears to me that I (are) really never heard," &c. Kensett pressed me to call on him at New York between Broadway and <Fourth St.>; he kindly gave me a card to a Mr. Cozzens who has a fine collection of paintings.[37] In the evening, Burder and myself drove round by Lundy's Lane, to see where we (English) are said to have been beaten; a real curiosity on this account is Lundy's Lane and one which it is not easy to see elsewhere.[38] As matter of fact though, it's doubtful if we were beaten there after all, though for the sake of "political capital" the Whigs make all the use they can of it to get Scott elected,[39] and the English can well afford to give them the benefit of the doubt. The man who shows you the battle-ground, from the top of an observatory by the way, is a character,— very impudent, and amusing, and Buckstone (the actor)-like.[40] He will repeat by the half hour the good answers he's made to absurd questions which "such a dear old lady, good old creature," or "such a delightful little girl," have asked him. According to his own account he bullies the Yankees terribly, asking them "which story they'd like—as they've paid their money, they may have their choice," and so on. "Truth," of course, is what the Yankee wants, and

37. Probably Abraham M. Cozzens (1811-68), amateur painter and patron of the National Academy of Design.

38. On July 25, 1814 a battle was fought here between some 2,600 Americans and 4,500 British. The British were repulsed but later returned and kept possession of the field.

39. For example, speakers at a Lundy's Lane memorial celebration a few weeks before took the occasion of that "early and glorious victory" to extol General Scott as the hero of many battles (*New York Herald*, July 28, 1852).

40. John Baldwin Buckstone (1802-79), genial English comedian.

313

truth, with the old sinner of a showman, consists in swearing that the English won the battle.

We took a long drive, and had to give up going to Porter's as we lost our way, and then thought it too late to intrude upon his "domestic circle." This morning we left the best of Hotels and the best of Landlords (from whom we borrowed $25) and found ourselves at ¼ before eleven on a bus bound for the cars, at eleven, on the cars bound for the boat, and at about half past one on the boat itself bound for Toronto from Queenston.[41]

41. "The 'Chief Justice Robinson' is quite a model of neatness and comfort; the deck is carpeted, furnished with sofas and arm-chairs, the sides hung round with paintings, and ornamented with well occupied stands of gay flowers" (Eliot Warburton, ed., *Hochelaga; or England in the New World* [New York, 1846], 1:126–27).

15

TORONTO TO MONTREAL

[*August 30 Continued.*]

We made some agreeable acquaintance—a lady named,
I don't know what *now*, but in her unmarried days,
Robinson (her father being the "Chief Justice R." after
whom our steamer was named).[1] She was quite a nice
person, and asked if I knew Mr. Heywood[2] who had
dined with them. She seems to have been fascinated
with James and tells me that when with them he said
most fortunately: "You Canadians disagree about
everything except one—everyone speaks well of C[hief]
J[ustice] Robinson,"—ignorant (*she* says) of the near
relationship. A Mr. Clifford, a Mr. Mirehouse (both in
the army) and a Mr. Something with lots of children
(? husband to my lady friend) were also good-natured,
and I am gradually obtaining a good stock of information about Canada of which I'll unburden myself as soon
as my voyage to Toronto is well over. Our steamer gets

1. Sir John Beverley Robinson (1791–1863), chief justice of Upper
Canada, a man of great ability and scrupulous integrity.
2. Bright's cousin James Heywood.

on well through the inky water of this deep—(really very deep) lake. Dinner is over, and a very bad dinner in a dark cellar place, and Mr. ?, whom I've sat next, has been telling me stories of the Mammoth Cave and of the rarity of the fish, asserting very positively that the *Styrian* [i.e., Stygian] fish aren't fish at all, merely eyeless lizards.[3] Here's Toronto at last! Mirehouse has just called us to the upper deck to look at it—a fine harbour, though bad to navigate they tell me; churches, barracks, a lunatic asylum,—these are the striking objects as we near the town. A few minutes more, —we're there! and jumping into a *doorless* hack drive first to a *full* hotel, but making a better shot next time, arrive at the "Western,"—small (as was the other one) and dirty perhaps, but English-looking and snug and comfortable. This seems a fine town; it has some 37,000 inhabitants, good shops, &c., and is building a beautiful Church of England Cathedral.[4] The only Uni Chapel (a hideous conventicle) in Canada or indeed (except in Madras) in our colonies at all, is here,[5] and to-night I've called on our minister to have a little sectarian gossip, but unfortunately he was not at home, and it's doubtful if I *can* call to-morrow.

As for Canada, I agree with James [Heywood]— no two people tell the same story, or leave on you the same impression with regard to the state of the country, or the popularity of the Government.

Divided into Upper and Lower Canada geographically, it is quite as markedly and far more dangerously divided in a social point of view into English Canada and French Canada; two parties of different race, dif-

3. The waters of the river Styx in Mammoth Cave were noted for small blind fish (*Amblyopsis spelaeus*), which were bottled and sold as curiosities.

4. Saint James's Cathedral at King and Church streets.

5. The First Unitarian Church was established in Toronto in 1845 but one was also started in Montreal the same year.

ferent religion, different hopes and wishes, brought into close contact, and mutually hating and mutually fearing each other—it's not an easy matter to have any government which will not excite the jealousy of some one,—happy if it do not gain the hatred of every one.

The nearest approach to the position in which Lord Elgin[6] stands to the two parties, appears to *me* (this is my own, and possibly quite wrong) the position of the Home Government to the Orangemen and Catholics of Ireland. The Government tries to conciliate each in turn, to treat each with fairness, and gradually to do away with the bitterness arising from rival race and religion.

At one time an Orange, at another a Romanish procession has to be prevented; now Smith O'Brien, and now Lord Roden has to be reminded that the preservation of peace is of paramount importance, and that neither at Limerick nor at Dolly's Brae will violation of the law or even impudence, which may lead to violation of the law, be tolerated.[7] "Young Ireland" must be exiled, and the "Nation"[8] silenced, or the head of the Orange Lodge deprived of his magistracy—but Peace must be and is preserved, and the Government is impartial.

So in Canada. The French Canadians rebel—they are "put down," the "Indemnification of Losses Bill" re-

6. James Bruce, 8th earl of Elgin and 12th earl of Kincardine (1811-63), governor-general of Canada, 1847-54. A tactful and wise leader of men, Elgin presided with uncanny insight over the transition in Canada from the old British colonial imperialism to "responsible government" based on local autonomy.

7. William Smith O'Brien (1803-64), Irish nationalist and M.P. for Limerick, was arrested for high treason in 1848 and transported for life. Robert Jocelyn, 3rd earl of Roden (1788-1870), grand master of the Orange Society, was censured for his conduct during riots at Dolly's Brae (July 12, 1849) between Orangemen and Catholics. Several lives were lost, and Roden was deprived of his place on the commission of the peace.

8. The weekly newspaper of the "Young Ireland" movement.

ceives Lord Elgin's assent,[9] and the "rebels" are conciliated, but the "loyalists" are offended, and they in their turn require putting down, by showing them that the Government will have its way, and that if they obstinately go into opposition, the Government must rely still more on, and be linked in closer ties to the French of the Lower Province.

This position of impartiality and conciliation must doubtless in the long run be successful, if honestly maintained, but if the Government ever condescend to the dangerous expedient of playing off the two parties in order to sustain a falling Minister or a tottering Cabinet, the country will of course cease to trust them, and will follow any leaders—however ultra—who may obtain its confidence.

Meanwhile there appear to be four parties.

The Government, headed by Mr. Hincks,[10] and followed by the reasoning liberals of the country, the conciliated French, and the not-estranged-by-the Indemnification-Bill English Canadians—much like Lord Clarendon[11] and the Irish liberals.

The Loyalists—so loyal as to become rebels in the cause,—answering to the Orangemen.

The French rebel party—headed by Papineau[12] and others—resembling the Irish Ribandmen and Catholics.

9. The signing of the Rebellion Losses Bill, on April 25, 1849, was the most dramatic event of Elgin's eight-year Canadian career. The measure was intended to indemnify French Canadians who had suffered property loss during the 1837 rebellion; but it was bitterly contested by conservatives who objected to "rewarding rebels." Elgin's assent to the bill provoked a violent riot by a Tory mob in Montreal who attacked him and then burnt the Parliament Buildings.

10. Francis Hincks (1807–85), Irish-born politician of moderate liberal views, formed in 1851 a reform coalition government with A. N. Morin. This government lasted until September, 1854, when Hincks's involvement in railway scandals forced him to resign.

11. George William Frederick Villiers, 4th earl of Clarendon (1800–1870), lord lieutenant of Ireland, 1847–52.

12. Louis Joseph Papineau (1786–1871) was the leader of the French

And besides these, a fourth or Independent Radical set of light skirmishers (as Lyon Mackenzie—no annexationist) and annexationists.[13]

Of the popularity of the Government I can form as yet no opinion. Almost everyone I meet abuses Mr. Hincks, almost every paper I take up talks of him and Rolph[14] and Cameron[15]—two other miscreants in the Cabinet—as you or I should of a pickpocket or worse, and yet in the very papers that are most virulent in their leading articles, I see "Division" on some motion of Mr. H[incks]'s,—62 for it—5 against it,—and then the Editor talks indignantly about Mr. Hincks *riding roughshod over the minority*, and all the rest of it:—minority of five!

Of the popularity of Mr. Hincks there I can as yet judge nothing, being from the opinion of stray acquaintance in the same pleasing state of uncertainty as was John Bunyan[16] from the advice of his friend:

> Some said John print it—others said no,
> Some thought it might do good—others said not so.

and here for the present I'm fain to leave it.

Canadian *patriotes* who revolted against English rule in 1837. The rebellion was broken within a month, and Papineau fled to the United States with a price on his head. He was now a rather tired lion, no longer a force in the Assembly, and he retired into private life in 1854.

13. Annexationist feeling in Canada, which peaked in 1849, had commercial, not political, roots. Its principal defenders were Montreal merchants of high standing who would gain financially from union with the United States.

14. Dr. John Rolph (1793–1870), English-born physician and a leader of the Reform party, had been implicated in the 1837 rebellion and fled to Rochester, New York, where he practiced medicine until the amnesty allowed him to return to Canada. He was commissioner of crown lands in the Hincks-Morin administration.

15. Malcolm Cameron (1808–76) took no part in the 1837 rebellion but he was, like Rolph, a leader of the so-called "Clear Grits" (Ultra-Reformers). He was now president of the Council.

16. Cf. "The Author's Apology for His Book," *The Pilgrim's Progress.*

The Government of Canada is extremely aristocratic.

Lord Elgin, Governor General, a sort of constitutional Monarch.

Legislative Council, answering to the English House of Lords. All the members chosen for life by the Crown and assuming the title of Honorable.

Legislative Assembly answering to our House of Commons, chosen by household suffrage.

Why don't more emigrants come to Canada? I see in a Toronto paper an advertisement headed—"A few hundred labourers wanted," on some railway or other, it goes on to say.

"The Quebec" from Montreal to Quebec.
Thursday Evening, September 2.

On Tuesday morning at some very ungodly hour before the world was aired or I was awake, the Rev. Mr. Dall honoured me with a call.[17] Of the honour at six o'clock, I was naturally unconscious, at half past eight even I could hardly be said to appreciate a second honour conferred upon me by a second call from the Revd. gentleman, and it was not till about half past ten when I returned his call, that I had the pleasure of seeing him "face to face." Burder had gone after a Shreiber or Schreibber, to whom he had a letter, so that I had an opportunity of being as sectarian as I chose without boring anyone.

Mr. Dall is an intelligent Yankee—*Yankee proper* in State, and equally undeniable in energetic talk and

17. Charles Henry Appleton Dall (1816-86) had been minister-at-large in Saint Louis and Baltimore before coming to Toronto. In 1855 he was sent to Calcutta as the first foreign missionary of the Unitarian church.

accent. Having been for some time Minister to the poor, and having found his health fail him, he "retired into private life" and cut down trees and all the rest of it, like Coverdale (or Hawthorne) in the Blithedale Romance.[18]

When his health returned, he returned with it to the Ministry, and has got on surprizingly at Toronto. His school numbers 70, his congregation 120 each Sunday, and he is about to build a Chapel rather less like a barn than the one he has now. He has barely been there two years, and before him there was only a lay preacher—truly "the harvest is plentiful, but the labourers few." Mr. Hincks does nothing for the faith, except assert in Assembly on the Church Land Preservation Question "I'm independent—I'm a Unitarian," and put down his name for subscriptions, the subscription itself not being forthcoming, nor I hear his money owed to tradesmen! Meanwhile, as I am learning this, we are walking up the avenue which leads to the University of Toronto. It *will be* a splendid building, it *is* in a noble situation, with park-planted trees in clusters on the lawns in front. A splendid building and a noble site, but alas! a "godless" college, and Bishop Strachan has washed his hands of it and is busy about a new college of his own—the College of the "Holy Trinity," very orthodox and requiring the "39, the whole 39 and *nothing but the 39*,"— though the last clause *may be* a libel.[19] Church of

18. Miles Coverdale is a fictional self-portrait in Hawthorne's novel, which was based on his experiences at Brook Farm. The book was only published in July, so Bright must have seen a copy on his travels.

19. John Strachan (1778-1868), militant Anglican bishop of Toronto, was furious when King's College was reorganized in 1850 as the nonsectarian University of Toronto. The charter of his own University of Trinity College provided that the president (himself) be an Anglican clergyman, that the members of the governing council subscribe to the XXXIX Articles, and that degrees in divinity (but not other degrees) be conditioned on the same declaration.

321

Englandism is however, far from rampant, and the last census shows if not a *de*crease, by no means a proportionate *in*crease in the numbers of its followers. Liberalism spreads in Upper Canada, Catholicism is still dominant in the Lower Province. In America however, Mr. Dall tells me, Catholicism is not as it was, or as it was supposed to be, and a Mr. Macumther [?], a Catholic, who endeavoured to ascertain whether there were the 4,000,000 Romanists which it was reported there were in the State, found to his horror and chagrin only 2,000,000.

From the godless college we went to see the Normal Schools,[20] admirably suited for their purpose, and with a fine view from the dome, which (dome) like all other domes and roofs in the Canadian towns are *tinned* over, slates, &c. not standing the winter cold and snow. The new Cathedral as seen from this dome is already a handsome building, and the spire of the Scotch Church "leaps up nobly into the sky," as Mr. Hosmer says, quoth Mr. Dall—let me say, en passant, Mr. Hosmer and Mr. Eliot are the saints, the beaux ideals of Uni-parsons in the opinion of every one I've spoken to.

You may see too, lunatic asylum, and the university grounds, St. Lawrence Hall, and the dark waters of Ontario, forming altogether a striking town view.

Besides the colleges I've mentioned, there are several others, 5 or 6 in all, so that in Toronto, if anywhere, there would seem to be a chance for universal education; but, says my informant, out of 250,000 children in Upper Canada, 100,000 only go to school at all.[21]

20. Founded in 1847 by Egerton Ryerson, superintendent of education in Upper Canada.

21. These statistics were roughly correct for 1852, but thanks largely to the ceaseless efforts of Egerton Ryerson, by 1858 seventy-four percent of Upper Canada's children were in school.

The boat started at one and I left Mr. Dall, leaving $4—a Canadian pound—as a small—small enough—offering towards his new Church.

On the "Princess Royal" we again met Mirehouse, and Captain and Mrs. Clifford, with whom I had a long chat about the Saginaw [Saguenay] (river) and scenery. The evening was spent with Burder talking of home, and it was still early when we turned in to the most comfortable berths I've seen since leaving the "Great Britain." At four in the morning we arrived at Kingston, and here our officer friends left us, and we left our boat for the "St. Lawrence," which was to take us to Montreal. We were sorry to decline all the kind offers of our Kingston friends, especially as the town itself looked tempting, with an extremely handsome City Hall standing well out on the river bank:[22]—but time is short and inexorable, and we must be inexorable too, so, after bidding Mirehouse Godspeed, we stowed away ourselves and our luggage in the Montreal steamer.

Soon after leaving Kingston, the Thousand Islands begin. They are very striking and beautiful; some large enough for a little village, others so small that you wonder where that stunted pine can find nourishment for its roots. They are very different from the Mississippi islands, which too often were sand banks covered with a scrubby brushwood, and running parallel with the river merely narrowed the channel without adding any picturesque feature to the scene: here all or nearly all were rocky, often of fantastic shape, always with weird spruce stretching sharp angular branches over the water. And then the number!— in all 1500! It puzzles you to think how the pilot can steer in so confusing and complicating a course; yet we

22.   Built in 1843, this was a fine example of the late classical style.

go on very smoothly and quietly, and a little after midday find ourselves *"shooting the rapids"*—the water white with foam though so deep, our steamer going near 20 miles an hour. These first rapids are curious, but the "cedars" nearer Montreal are really fine. The sun was setting very large and red as we swept swiftly down them; large islands with cedars thick among the other trees stood blackly out of the white foamy water as we came close along them, and showed blacker yet when we had passed on, and looking back, saw them in relief against the Western sunset sky, while the water itself was chafed into broken waves like the breakers on some rocky shore, and our boat plunged and pitched and heeled as though she fancied herself on the salt Atlantic and not on the beautiful St. Lawrence.

CEDAR RAPIDS OF THE ST. LAWRENCE.

Written between Quebec and Montreal on Steamer Sept. 9th.[23]

Cedar islands of St. Lawrence!
Where the cedar boughs, low bending,
In their dewy fragrance, sweep
Off the white foam from the Rapids,
As they sparkle, as they leap,
As they hurry, night and day,
On their way!

Cedar islands of St. Lawrence!
Where the passing boatman ever
Sings his choicest melodies;
And his voice upon the water
Gently swells, and gently dies,
As his boat is swept along,
With his song!

23. On the return journey a week later.

The evening had closed, and the sun had gone down behind the last of the cedar isles, when we saw a poor raft struggling with the rapids which played with her, and tossed her about as it seemed, like a reed or fallen leaf; the St. Lawrence boatmen though are brave fellows, somehow no doubt they steered her safe, singing as they always do some French barcarolle, some

> Row brothers row, (the stream runs fast
> The Rapids are near and the daylight past)[24]

in their own sweet tongue.

For ourselves, we arrived safely at Lachine, and took the railway—nine miles on to Montreal, where we put up at Donegana's,[25] a first-rate Hotel, with civil people, and an English rather than a Yankee look.

This morning I was up in good time, anxious to see Montreal and get my letters; also to find Edmund Knight.[26] The two first I managed, but Edmund is still, I suppose, at Quebec. I like the looks of Montreal extremely—a respectable French-looking, old-looking town, with fine churches, quaint houses with high roofs, or gable ends, or sculptured entablatures, while in the street our own redcoated soldiers, respectable Indians, bearded Canadians, black-robed priests meet and pass you as you walk along. The Montreal Bank[27] is a fine building, the Catholic Cathedral is also striking, chiefly, I must own, externally, as the inside though of wonderful size (holding they say 15,000 people!) is spoiled by the painted pillars, the tinselled altars, and the bad pictures.[28]

24. Thomas Moore, "A Canadian Boat Song."
25. On Notre-Dame Street.
26. An English friend.
27. A fine example of Corinthian architecture on the Place d'Armes.
28. The huge French Cathedral in the Place d'Armes, with its six towers, was said to be the largest Gothic edifice in the New World.

As we intend returning, we called on no one, but that good-natured Collingwood found us out, and had just left a card for me, when we met him at a hat shop where we were civilizing ourselves. He took us with him to the Wharf to see our boat, and be introduced to the Captain: he took us to "Doley's Chop House" to get some soda water and be introduced to Mr. Doley; and he took us to the News Room that we might feed on English *papers*. (The "Great Britain" is to carry the mails! *they* say!!)

Collingwood reminds me of Mr. Boythorn,[29] he is so truly good-natured and good-hearted, is so anxious to do what he can for us, and is so pressing in his hospitalities, yet listen to him and you think he must be a perfect monster,—hardly any one you mention he does not d--n, blast, broil to all eternity in h--l with the d---l's hottest pepper, &c. &c. (I've expressed this gingerly lest ladies look over my journal!) Poor Hincks suffered much in this way, Mr. Young,[30] Mr. Macken-zie, the Collins' steamers, radicals, and many another. To do Collingwood justice, there are some who escape, and of them he'll tell you "there isn't a better fellow in the world—as good a fellow as ever lived," and so forth. He hears from Bob [Bright][31] but never reads his letters, but *hands them to his family*! He has just returned from a beaver-hunt, this Gordon Cumming of Canada,[32] and has, I believe, been tolerably suc-cessful. Anderdon is soon to join him on a moose expedition—assuredly Mrs. Collingwood has little danger of being bored with her husband.

In the afternoon we drove round "the mountain"

29. In *Bleak House*, then appearing in monthly parts.

30. John Young (1811-78) represented Montreal in the Legislative Assembly as a strong liberal.

31. See p. 51.

32. See p. 207.

where was Lord Elgin's house, now an Hotel,[33] well situated with good view. After dinner we embarked on the "Quebec" and shall be there (D.V.) by six tomorrow.

33. "Monklands" was abandoned because the seat of government had been moved to Toronto and Quebec after the burning of the Montreal Parliament buildings in 1849.

16

QUEBEC

Sunday Morning, [September 5].

Friday morning we reached Quebec, the fortress of which reminds one of Ehrenbreitstein[1] in its beautiful position. It is, without exception, the most picturesque town I ever saw, and whether you see it from the river, or look down upon the river from the walls, you must be equally struck and delighted. You leave the boat and wind up narrow little steep streets, so narrow that two carriages can hardly pass, so steep you wonder any carriage can be drawn up the tortuous ascent. The Hotels are bad—Russell's full, Swords' so far from empty that Burder, myself and a "stranger" (as they'd say in Kentucky) were stowed away in one room.[2] Synge was here, and we were delighted to see him again with his good-natured face and merry laugh. He took us out after breakfast to *do* the people to whom we brought letters. Mr. Hincks we met in the street;

1. A fortress 385 feet above the Rhine.
2. Swords' Hotel was at the corner of Haldimand and Saint Louis streets in the Upper Town.

BOAT-LANDING, QUEBEC

From *Picturesque America*, ed. W. C. Bryant, Vol. II, 1874

*"You leave the boat and wind up
narrow little steep streets."*

he received us with the greatest empressement, and
told me he had expected me long before this. Under
the Prime Minister's guidance we were shown the
Houses of Parliament,—most gentlemanly and elegant
houses, fitted up in the best taste, with royal pictures,
maces of office, a throne and other monarchical in-
signia about them.[3] The library is exquisitely arranged,
and the Chaplain to whom we were introduced showed
us the bibliothetical wonders. Chief ornament is some
British Parliamentary records in 1900 and more
volumes. When the old library was destroyed,[4] it
was supposed to have suffered irreparably by the loss
of a copy of this work, but through the energy of the
Speaker of the English House a fresh copy collected

3. The first session of the new Parliament had opened in Quebec on
August 19.

4. On April 25, 1849, during a riot in connection with the Rebellion
Losses Bill, fire almost totally destroyed the parliamentary library, valued
at £25,000.

329

in single volumes from different quarters, was presented to the Canadian Legislature.

We were likewise introduced to Mr. Langton, Member for Peterborough,[5] who is brother to Mr. L[angton] in Heywood's bank;[6] to the Speaker Mr. M'Donald,[7] to Sir Allan M'Nab leader of the Opposition.[8] Every one was as civil as possible, the Speaker took me to his sanctum, and trotted us about with Hincks—Attaché, Speaker, Premier and Chaplain—a distinguished company indeed! We then went to the Government House where Colonel Antrobus the aide-de-camp introduced us to the Governor General Lord Elgin. He was extremely kind, made us sit down, asked us to dinner for the next day to meet Parliamentary "swells," and gave us a "screed" of doctrine on Canadian politics. He liked to see young Englishmen come and see what Canada was really like; he believed it contrasted well with the United States: the Canadians had now a representative Government just like our own, and a South Carolinian had said to him, "It's madness of Canada to talk of annexation, they've got what South Carolina has been trying for long to get, a *right to govern themselves.*" Then the responsibility of the Government for the acts and words of members of it, is a great advantage they have not in the States, where any Member may support a Motion without inculpating the Government, and where therefore, any Member is liable to corrupt influence actuating him to give votes, and speak in a *private capacity*; hence

5. John Langton (1808–94), a Conservative, born in England and educated at Trinity College, Cambridge.

6. Probably the Liverpool bank of John Pemberton Heywood.

7. John Sandfield Macdonald (1812–72), a veteran Reformer, representing Glengarry in the Legislative Assembly.

8. Sir Allan Napier MacNab (1798–1862), a genial, bluff old soldier, long the accepted leader of the Conservative party.

the individuals of a Government may be and are individually bribed and corrupted without thereby giving political opponents a handle against the Government. It is very dangerous this temptation which the lowness of official salary brings; professing republican simplicity, they pay their public men very little—the style of living in New York, &c. is very sumptuous,—the members of a Government have of course extraordinary expenses, a few hundred dollars for supporting a particular Motion is very tempting, and—. Take Webster himself, "a glorious fellow." He writes a letter to say that he knows only of *one man* fit to be Secretary of State, and he can't afford to accept the office, his income is not sufficient. The Massachusetts Whigs raise a sum of money, Webster of course accepts it, "and although I don't for a moment wish to impute bad motives to Mr. W. I do say that is a bad state of things necessitating such a procedure."[9] But everything in America is more or less venial—the Press for instance.

Synge instanced a riot in Washington, when pistol shots were fired in a Hotel, and the papers took no notice of it, as paper-editors were often treated there. I mentioned how Mrs. Ellet passed free through the States, and how she gave the quid pro quo by calling every innkeeper "most gentlemanly;" each boat she travels on "the best on the river."

"Still," continued Lord E[lgin], "there is this to be said, that the effects of this corruption are not so great as might be supposed, for everybody vetoes everybody else—State L[egislature], Federal L[egislature], President,—all check the other."

9. It is true that before accepting Fillmore's offer to be secretary of state in July, 1850, Webster—who was heavily in debt—made sure of the financial backing of his Boston friends. But he assumed the office with some reluctance.

331

"It has a gentlemanly look," I told Lord E. of the Parliament House. "Exactly, it is what, for the last two years, I've been endeavouring to do—make *gentlemen* of the Representatives."

In Canada itself I hope a good feeling is rising. Canadians are becoming proud of their country in these last two years, and becoming more and more national, and this the Government endeavours by all means to encourage. "Has not this passing of the Fugitive Slave Bill been of use in Canada?" I asked, "as exciting the Abolition feeling against annexation?"[10] Yes, he thought it had, but not to any great extent; there was not the same feeling on behalf of the black in Canada as in England.

The French Canadians are strong against annexation, knowing that in the importation of the Yankee element, their religion and language would be swamped.

Of the loyalty of many of the English Canadians Synge told *me* (not Lord E. in this conversation) an instance. He saw in a shop an up-country farmer with two buxom daughters. The daughters were disputing his taste on some point:—"Don't tell me," he replied, "that you know better than I do. Why! (raising his voice) why, lassies, you've never seen a king, and I've seen *three* and spoken to *one*. Well, why shouldn't I speak out? Yes, and before those officers there too; I'll warrant they've never spoken to a king!"

This is but an outline of the conversation between us four, a conversation which lasted nearly ¾ of an hour, and in which we were put quite at our ease by Lord Elgin's kindness and good-natured, unaffected

10. The Fugitive Slave Law of 1850 authorized the capture of runaway slaves within the northern free states. As increasing numbers of blacks sought safety across the Canadian border, abolitionists came to regard Canada as the Negroes' last refuge.

LORD ELGIN, CA. 1851

Gleason's Pictorial Drawing-Room Companion, November 8, 1851

*"Very pleasant face though not handsome,
with a singularly honest, childlike look."*

manner. He is a man of about 50, I suppose;[11] middle
height, very pleasant face though not handsome, with
a singularly honest, *childlike* look, which makes you
love him at least as much as you respect him, and (as
Burder said) instead of thinking "what a swell!" you
think "what a brick!"

Synge after our audience introduced me to Paget
and Perrin, lieutenants of the 66th regiment, and they
good-naturedly asked us all to dinner in the mess-room
that evening. We lunched there as well, so that we are
getting quite into a military set. Synge was very amusing at dinner (before which we only strolled and
shopped, and talked to Sir W. Gordon, Major of the
66th and our subaltern friends)—a dinner beginning
awkwardly, as they had all sat down and were eating.
I found myself between Perrin and a Mr. Smith of
England. Perrin's a nice gentlemanly fellow, and told
me some military experiences. He had been quartered
in the West Indies, and mentioned one worthy-of-note
fact, that in St. Lucia there are any number of deadly
serpents, in St. Vincent, close by, same climate, soil
and all, there was not a snake of poisonous tendencies to be found. He liked Canada much, but regretted
that from the charms of the ladies many officers found
themselves "victims of locality." But I've forgotten
Synge's stories, they were very good. Imagine a Boston lady saying to him, after he had owned himself
an enthusiast about England, "Not an enthusiast, I
think, Mr. Synge, as much as a *retrospect.*"

Or imagine another lady saying to him of Lord Mark
Kerr—an eccentric half-mad officer at Montreal,—that
Lord Mark is "pas du tout flamboyant, mais tout à
fait agricole."

Of Margaret Fuller *Crampton* told some strange

11. He was 41.

stories, how *he* does not believe in the *marriage*, and that he knows how when in Italy, after looking at some beautiful scenery, she turned to a friend of his who was with her with—"Mon frère, 1--quor."[12]

The dinner was good, the "Badminton" claret-cup excellent, everyone kind and agreeable, people I'd never seen asking us to take wine with them, and the whole thing very pleasant—about 16 I suppose at dinner—after which we sat and talked and strolled to look how the moon played on the waters of the St. Lawrence.

Stupidly enough, I've forgot to say that we went again to the House about 5½ to hear debate; there was nothing to hear except the reading Petitions and the strange effect of French and English going on together.

By the way, I could read French better than the Speaker, indeed he confessed his shortcoming in this respect to Burder.

We were on the floor of the House, and Mr. Young, Mr. Langton, and Sir Allan [MacNab] all came and talked to us; likewise Mr. Hincks at the adjournment, and the Speaker as he solemnly descended from the chair in black robe and cocked hat, and—offered us a cigar![13]

The Speaker is a nice gentlemanly fellow, not unlike Dr. Pope of St. Louis. Mr. Hincks has a little of the attorney cast of feature, speaks deliberately, like

12. Margaret Fuller long kept her marriage to the Marquis Angelo Ossoli a secret, and there was much gossip about her and her child. I can make no sense of the last word: I suppose the two hyphens are the typist's.

13. As Speaker, J. S. Macdonald sat on a dais in a massively carved chair. He was "vain of the post, his sweeping black gown and tricorne hat, and the white kid gloves that he wore with a great carnelian ring over one gloved finger—which made his magisterial gestures all the more impressive" (J. M. S. Careless, *Brown of the Globe*, 1 [Toronto, 1959]: 156).

Beard of Trinity;[14] he seems on good terms with Sir A. M'Nab, and we saw the heads of the Government and the Opposition in friendly, almost affectionate converse.

Yesterday at eleven we started for Lorette, where Mr. Hincks had asked us to a picnic. We had a beautiful drive, and were delighted with the falls of the St. Charles at Lorette. The Indian village is, I think, a take-in, and we didn't care to see it.[15] Mr. and Mrs. Hincks, Major and Mrs. Ready (né Nelly Hincks)[16] Morris and Clay (who turned up just in time),[17] an artist, Captain Hamilton,[18] and a Yankee gentleman with two ladies,—these were the party—and a pleasant party it was, good dinner at the Inn, champagne, &c. &c.

We left them early as we had to dress for Spencer Wood (Lord E[lgin]'s). We arrived there in good time, —the first, or rather, among the first, as Colonel Antrobus and others entered almost with us.

The drive up to the House was pretty, as far as we could judge of it. Torches on the trees partially lit it up, and showed us soldiers pacing along before the house, and at the gates.[19] The house is of wood, and

14. Charles Izard Beard (1827-1916), a physician, who was at Trinity College with Bright.

15. The Indian village at Lorette was built by the government; the Indians had so intermarried with the French that they retained few of their distinctive characteristics.

16. Hincks's older daughter Ellen (1835-1912) married Charles Ready, an officer of the British army.

17. Probably Charles D'Urban Morris (1827-86) and William Dickason Clay (1828-76), both Oxford-educated Englishmen of good family, who were touring America.

18. Augustus Terrick Hamilton of the 71st Regiment, aide-de-camp to Lord Elgin.

19. Two years later Laurence Oliphant described the grounds of Spencer Wood as follows: "From the verandah extends a lawn studded with noble trees to the edge of a steep wooded bank, and among the trees rise the tapering masts of ships, which look as if they were eccentric

though nicely furnished, the rooms look small and rather beneath the dignity of the Queen's Representative. We were received by Colonel Bruce, an excellent specimen of English officer and English gentleman, who after a few words to set us at our ease, turned to receive the others.[20] Luckily, our friends the Speaker and Mr. Langton were there, so that we did very well, and were both busily talking when His Excellency entered. There was at once silence, and he came round shaking hands with us all, and staying some time with the Speaker and Burder; his only decoration was the Star of the Thistle, which glistened on his breast, while the green ribband of the Order crossed from left to right over his waistcoat.

Of course Lady E. did not appear, and we all walked into a dining-room shortly after His Excellency had entered. At a long table Lord Elgin sat in the middle of one side, a Mr. Crawford[21] was placed in a chair opposite to him; on Lord E's right sat Mr. Jackson, an English M.P. and distinguished railway Contractor;[22] on his left, the Speaker, while Colonel Bruce and Colonel Antrobus had possession of the two ends of the table. I sat between Mr. Langton and a Colonel Prince, chiefly noted for having ordered 6 rebels to be shot in cold blood, and who now, I believe—(brute!) avows himself an annexationist.[23] Burder sat nearly opposite to me.

branches" (Margaret O. W. Oliphant, *Memoir of the Life of Laurence Oliphant* [Edinburgh and London, 1891], 1:134.

20. Col. Robert Bruce (1813-62), Elgin's younger brother, had been Elgin's military secretary in Jamaica, and he filled the same role in Canada. Later he was governor to the prince of Wales.

21. Probably George Crawford, an annexationist and moderate Conservative in the Legislative Assembly from Brockville, Canada West.

22. William Jackson, of the English firm Peto, Brassey, Jackson, and Betts, was promoting his company's interest in constructing the Grand Trunk Railway in Canada.

23. The redoubtable Col. John Prince (1796-1870), now representative

337

It was very pleasant, though a good, rather than grand dinner, with not wonderful wine. The plate was beautiful, and for the first time in my life I eat soup, fish, &c. out of silver, dessert out of gold plate! Lord E. talked much and well, getting excited after dinner on the subject of Canada, and having quite a long discussion with Mr. Crawford opposite, while the English M.P. (who disgusted Synge so that he refused to take wine with him) patronized the Canadians and Lord Elgin, and behaved like an impertinent snob as he is. Lord Elgin said, "I wish you all to be *proud* of being Canadians—Canadians in heart and feeling. Of course England can't be expected to understand all of a sudden how you, who have been in a state of chronic rebellion, should, all of a sudden, become peaceable; but it is so, and I know a more loyal people doesn't exist than the Canadians, but the English have to learn this by degrees. England is, I do assure you, proud of and well-disposed to Canada, and so far from Canadians being looked down upon, I can tell you that I have done and can do for Canadians with the Home Government what I, the same person, cannot do for Englishmen. As for Canada itself, if you are discontented with your representation, any mode you yourselves prefer, I will, as far as I can, get carried out. Of course," (he prudently added afterwards) "I don't pledge myself as responsible hereafter for every word I let fall at dinner after a bottle of champagne, but I do wish that your representatives should be as you really judge best."[24]

for Essex in the Legislative Assembly, had commanded a force of Canadian militia in 1838. When a body of invaders crossed from Detroit to Windsor, he ordered the shooting of five of them who had been taken prisoner.

24. Elgin was adept at using champagne as a diplomatic instrument, while pretending to drink a lot himself. Laurence Oliphant, who succeeded Col. Bruce as Elgin's secretary two years later, describes how

This was the sort of conversation which gradually swallowed up the rest, and which became almost a dispute carried on on Lord E's part with a quiet dignity which warded off Mr. Jackson's impertinent bottle-holding, and "Your Excellency is right,—and the feeling in England is, &c.,"as well as Mr. Crawford's contradictions and violently expressed views about Canada being despised and bother of that sort.

There was talk of the Queen coming to Canada, which the annexationist next me [Prince] with a praiseworthy dread of the perils of the ocean and the exposure of her life, becoming cloke for his real fear of the popularity English rule would at once acquire, trusted would never happen.

After a really stormy half hour, there was a pleasant calm in which Lord Elgin talked of Boston, and how at dinners the President must retire at once under plea of convenient stomach ache lest he be asked awkward questions, since he has no fortress in the etiquette which would hedge any other State chief. He also talked of Mr. Bigelow the Mayor of Boston,[25] and his civilities, which opened the way for a good story of Synge's as to how Mr. Bigelow had imagined him acquainted with Lord Elgin and made much of him in consequence, spite of S's disclaimers, "You, Sir, an intimate friend of His Excellency the Earl of Elgin and Kincardine, Knight of the Thistle." Lord E. was much amused and talked of Mr. B. all the rest of dinner as "Knight of the Thistle."

successfully Elgin wined and dined the Democratic senators in Washington, whose votes were needed to pass the Reciprocity Treaty in 1854. It may be noted that Elgin's company on the present occasion included not only two impressionable young Englishmen, but a British diplomat, two avowed annexationists, and a man whose railway interests profoundly affected Canada.

25. John Prescott Bigelow (1797–1872), Whig mayor of Boston, 1849–51.

After dinner we returned to the drawing-room, when to my surprize Lord Elgin came up to me and for ten minutes at least pumped into me his Canadian views. I admire his enthusiasm extremely, and the whole heart he has for the British Empire, his love for the Mother Country, his pride for her Colony of Canada, his own kingdom.

He complained to me how hard a part he had to play, how at last he hoped and believed parties were satisfied, and how, should Mr. Papineau "that incorrigible man" get into power, he'd pin him down to the statements he's made in opposition, and see how he will get on as Minister, with his old opinions. I asked if the state of parties in Canada did not correspond with those in Ireland. "Yes," he answered, "but with this difference,—Ireland can only gain evil and trouble by a rebellion,—for two countries alone, Canada and Belgium, would a rebellion be an apotheosis, they have each something to fall back upon."

We've talked also about the incompetency of American Presidents, and afterwards about a railway near Montreal which he is going to open, and to which Mr. Young has promised me tickets.[26] Lord E. recommends us to see it. He approves also much of Tremenheere's book, which indeed he quoted at dinner as showing how Englishmen do feel towards and write of, Canada.[27]

26. The extension of the infant railway system in Canada was one of the government's most urgent concerns: in this autumn session of 1852, no fewer than 28 railway bills were passed. The line Elgin was to open at Sherbrooke was a section of the Saint Lawrence and Atlantic line between Montreal and Portland, Maine.

27. Hugh Seymour Tremenheere's *Notes on Public Subjects, Made During a Tour in the United States and in Canada* had just been published. It took the line that Canada was insufficiently appreciated in England and provided excellent opportunities for English investment.

He also mentioned at dinner how Lord Wharncliffe[28] had become an "enthusiast about Canada."

But our conversation was coming to an end, the Speaker was waiting to say goodbye, and when he left, we had to leave, Lord Elgin hoping to see more of us before we left. I never enjoyed myself much more.

Among the things I learnt at dinner was that others (Mr. Langton told me) besides myself, have thought that a *consolidation* of the provinces of America with *one Governor-General* would be an advantage: it had struck me for some time.[29] Langton was at Trinity in the days of Praed, Buller, Macaulay.[30]

This morning E. Knight's friend Boswell has called, and [Knight] has gone to Montreal he tells me. Mr. Hincks has also been to ask us to go to Church with him, which I declined, being anxious to write.

Monday Evening, [September 6].

Yesterday, just as I finished my journal, Synge came (at 2 p.m.) to take us to the Protestant Cathedral where the soldiers go to Church—a church full of soldiers is a fine sight—and the music was good. Synge showed me a Spanish prayer-book of the English Liturgy he found in our pew, dated 1707, and praying for Queen Anna and the Princess Sophia. In the preface

28. Cf. p. 246. Elgin made sure that Tremenheere and Lord Wharncliffe absorbed his own views of Canada when they visited there.

29. Confederation was proclaimed on July 1, 1867.

30. Winthrop Mackworth Praed (1802–39), poet; Charles Buller (1806–48), liberal politician; Thomas Babington Macaulay (1800–59), historian—all at Trinity in the 1820s.

it mentions that an edition had been translated in James I. time.

After Service, the soldiers formed and marched orderly away, the chimes rang merrily out, and we, joined by Perrin and Paget "loafed off" to the Citadel. One of their mess was on guard, and under his *full-dress* chaperonage, we looked over the walls, and lounged in the guard room, and made friends with some tame black bears. The view is exquisite—the large vessels at anchor in the river below, the windings of the St. Lawrence with reach after reach, and the hills over the water, and close under the citadel itself the quaint high roofs, and steeples, glittering with the metallic coating always laid on them in this country.

A soldier's funeral was going on—it was the first time I had seen one—it is a sad melancholy sight. The soldiers with their arms reversed, the drums and fifes playing that terrible "Dead March in Saul," and the coffin itself borne by the friends and bearing the arms of the deceased man.

We left our military acquaintance, who pressed us to dine with them, and spent a quiet evening with our books and letters.

This morning B[urder] and myself drove over to the Falls of Montmorency. They are very beautiful and *wilder* than Niagara, and their height is higher; in everything else of course Niagara has the advantage.

The St. Lawrence here has a little opening in its banks, a recess of some little depth, where the slaty rocks rise high, and the pine trees grow black; and, like quartz veins running down the rocks, from a height of 250 feet flow the Falls of the Montmorency river. A beautiful river, which just above the Falls is narrow and wild with dark tawny water and a strange formation of rocks in "Natural steps." <sketch> The "natural steps" are a lion of the place,

342

MONTMORENCY FALLS, LOOKING TOWARD QUEBEC

From *Picturesque America*, ed. W. C. Bryant, Vol. II, 1874

"Wilder than Niagara."

but they are indescribable by *me* at least, either by pen or pencil; imagination or a tour, or ignorance noway blissful are the alternatives.

The villages on your way to Montmorency are French, with crosses and chapels like a Belgian village—the driver of our "calêche" was French, the children who hung about the falls to show them, they were French.

On our return we saw Synge off, and after dinner found our way to the Legislative House. The Speaker ordered us to go to the Legislative Gallery, and we heard part of a debate, or rather series of debates on pottering little questions quite without interest. Hincks gave us for a short time the light of his countenance, and gave me "a bill of fare" which was to have been to-morrow but I believe isn't.

We met Lord E[lgin] to-day on horseback, and he stopped us and made us promise to breakfast with him to-morrow; of his good-natured kindness I cannot speak enough.

This is a horrid Hotel! Imagine Mr. Swords charging £1: 5: 0 for Synge—"for ten baths and extra towels" —when S[ynge] brought his mackintosh bath *with him even!*—in any case, £1: 5: 0 for 10 baths!

Tuesday Afternoon and Evening, [September 7].

We breakfasted this morning at Spencer Wood—ten was the hour and we got there rather before time, I think, and were shown into the pretty drawing-room adorned with pictures of the good lord himself and his children. He soon made his appearance; then Lady Elgin (one of Lord Durham's daughters)[31] came in, a

31. Elgin's second wife was Lady Mary Louisa Lambton, daughter of

344

cousin of hers, young Lambton,[32] and we sat down to breakfast in a pleasant dining-room.

It was delightful!—only we five, and Lord Elgin all to ourselves, with his kind manners and kinder talk, telling us his plans, and views, and wishes as if we were statesmen to be conciliated, not young Englishmen merely, without the slightest claim upon him. I never met anyone though, for whom I felt so soon so great a respect and love. His only fault as far as I can discover seems to be an over-confidence, a want of discretion, which must be as injurious as it is injudicious.

It is of course absurd to suppose that to us alone among English tourists he reveals his confidences; it is the same doubtless to all, and *someday* he may be deceived in the man he has trusted, and great evil may result.

Still his light, chivalrous, open bearing, the love for his country which prompts his every action, his courage and uncompromising conduct—one feels that he is a true nobleman, and that the Canadians would lose incalculably should he be recalled.

At Montreal, he says, he was chiefly hated, and chiefly by the English officers who going home spread every ill report of him, ignorant even of the facts they assert, still more ignorant of the principles of the Government, the politics of the country!

This "Indemnification Bill!"—what are the facts? The Commission to inquire into what property was "wantonly and unnecessarily destroyed, and whether compensation should be granted," was originated by

John George Lambton, 1st earl of Durham (1792-1840). As governor-in-chief of British North America (1838), Durham wrote the famous *Report* that led to the union of Upper and Lower Canada in 1841, and to the introduction of responsible government.

32. Frederick William Lambton was embarking on a military career in the 71st Regiment.

Lord Metcalfe,[33] the Tory beau-ideal, with a pledge that the Government would support the Commission in the views it propounded. Lord Elgin, on coming into power only continued Lord M's Commission with the same men.[34] Their views, condensed into this Bill, passed before Parliament, who carried them by a majority of 80(?) against 18.[35] What could Lord Elgin do? Upset the constitutional government he had laboured to build up, and with a Bill carried by such a majority and supported by the Government? He at once assented to it—and the tumult began. A traveller, he told us, in Canada then, declared that in Quebec, *the* moderate town, he met a man who told him the Governor-General should be *tarred and feathered*, and that this man, spite of this opinion, was *so* moderate that he had to keep loaded pistols in his house—"a moderate man this in *the* moderate city!—judge by rule of three what would be the violent man in the violent city!"

Going to Montreal he was pelted; passing through the streets stones broke through the panels of his carriage, hitting him in several places, while his brother's head was cut open:—"I was in constant danger of being murdered."

It was under these circumstances that he avoided Montreal, and made a tour through the provinces of Upper Canada, where he was well, indeed enthusiastically, received. "Miles of people" followed his carriage through parts where there was not a single

33. Charles Theophilus Metcalfe, 1st baron Metcalfe (1785–1846), governor-general of Canada, 1843–45. Although a Whig in British politics, in Canada his sympathies were entirely with the Tories.

34. Metcalfe's commission had presented a report in April, 1846, listing over 2,000 people in Lower Canada who claimed recompense for losses incurred during the rebellion.

35. Actually 47 to 18.

Frenchman, and this at a time when in England they declared that none but Frenchmen but hated him.

At one place—London (I think)—when some little way from the town, two men came up and warned him not to proceed or there would be a disturbance. "I told them quietly that if my carriage wasn't allowed to pass, I should *walk* through the town." They turned out to be emissaries of the ill-disposed party.

I repeated to Lord E. a remark of Capt. Elliott, that it was not the Indemnification Bill, but the fact of the rebels only being indemnified, that was so offensive.[36] This, he observed, was—must be—pure imagination on the part of my friend, as the lists of those to be indemnified have not yet been made out, and they have (he thought) a strong *royalist* bias, though this should not be repeated.

On the Church Reserve Secularization question, he has not the strong opinions of Mr. Hincks against Church endowment, but undoubtedly there is a strong feeling against such endowment in the country, and a stronger feeling that the country must legislate *for itself* independently of Imperial dictation.[37] It is manifest that the Anglo-Saxon race in America will have freedom, and that any attempt to enforce obnoxious laws on the part of England will only have the effect of causing us to lose Canada; and if on this Church question we peril her loss, we peril at the same time the best interests of the Church itself. What we must

36. This was the common objection, which was voiced in England by Gladstone among others: that the Rebellion Losses Bill rewarded rebels for rebelling.

37. The "Clergy Reserves" question, long a source of bitter controversy, concerned the fate of extensive tracts of public lands that had been reserved for the support of a "Protestant Clergy." Reformers like Hincks believed that the reserves should be secularized—that is, that their endowment should be appropriated to secular uses such as education. A bill to this effect was finally passed in 1854.

347

try to do is to show the Canadians that they have as much freedom as the Americans, but freedom of a better kind from our Monarchical institutions.

"Is not the extreme feeling of *Canadian Independence* to be guarded against?" I asked.

"By no means. They know they can only be independent under British Protection—such a feeling must be encouraged to the utmost, as our safeguard against annexation."

This is but a small part of the conversation we had on Canadian matters. He entered fully into them, but added with a sigh, "No one knows how disheartening it is,—the ignorance of the English on these subjects, and the way in which my best efforts are neutralized by the cool manner in which they talk of giving up Canada. You know the tone everywhere—'Let Canada go, of course she must go sooner or later.' And I—what can I do? It is but picking up one grain of sand here, another there, and trying to build a pyramid of them, so few Englishmen can I affect with the pride they should feel for this country."

We were now walking round the grounds, and had reached a point where we could see the beautiful St. Lawrence just below us, and the large ships riding at anchor at the foot of the fortress-cliffs of Quebec: the scene was altogether *to me* the most splendid I ever saw. "One thing," said Lord Elgin, after a few moments silence, as we stood gazing on the view before us, "one thing the removal of the seat of Government to Toronto and Quebec has done; it has shown the Lower Canadians that there is in the Upper Province as high a cultivation and as fine a country as any in the United States. It has shown the Upper Canadians this glorious rock and made them proud of possessing it."

Of Lord Grey, I may here say he thought well—"the

348

best Colonial Secretary for Canada we ever had,"[38] —of Sir J. Pakington he only knew from favourable hearsay.[39]

At Montreal the rebels hired carriages on which they stood pelting. "I would not let the military in among them, they might pelt me as much as they liked, but I was not going to have a war of races."[40]

"Papineau has behaved shamefully, but we take no steps against him—no persecution, I always say,—we must have none of that. The only thing I do is, that of course I can't doubt any gentleman's word, and that if he asserts himself hostile to the Queen, I won't insult him by disbelieving such assertion, or act as if I disbelieved it by making him Justice of the Peace or other officer, which would necessitate his taking oaths of allegiance: nay, I go one step farther by depriving anyone who speaks of annexation of his magisterial or other office, in order that he may not feel in a false position. So Colonel Prince I deprived of his 'silk gown,' and I believe he now owns I was quite right in so doing, and is coming round."[41] (I told Lord E. I

38. Henry George Grey, 3rd earl Grey (1802-94), secretary for the colonies, 1846-52, decided on the policy of responsible government for Canada that Elgin carried out. The two men worked together in unusual harmony.

39. When Lord John Russell's government fell in February 1852, Sir John Somerset Pakington (1799-1880), an untried administrator, replaced Grey as colonial secretary. Fortunately for Canadian progress, Pakington was in office for less than a year.

40. Cf. the comment of Elgin's secretary, Major Campbell: "He was urged by irresponsible advisers to make use of the military forces at his command, to protect his person in an official visit to the city; but he declined to do so, and thus avoided what these infatuated rioters seemed determined to bring on—the shedding of blood" (Elgin, *Letters and Journals*, p. 85).

41. Elgin removed from office all magistrates, queen's counsels, and militia officers who had signed the annexation manifesto in 1849. During Parliament's 1850 session only six members of the Assembly supported Prince's annexationist views.

heard him muttering praises of the G[overnor] G[eneral]'s talents and cleverness at dinner.)

So far from the Ministry being exclusively French, only 3 out of 10 are.[42] This should not be mentioned (he said) or dwelt on or the French may again get discontented.

The lighter talk was chiefly of Boston. Burder told the "retrospect" I the "Juggernaut" story,[43] Lady E. having led the way by telling us of a Bostonian who showed her a picture by *Chinborayo* for Carlo Boutti (?).[44] She showed us herself some pretty sketches by Mr. Friend of the "natural steps" "Lorette," &c. &c.[45] She is a plain, quiet, kindly, un-Countess-like little woman, with a nice little girl to whom we were introduced as "a young Canadian." Lady E. talked but little besides, but laughed much at our stories.

Lord Elgin was most amusing about Boston; I'll try to describe his visit there as nearly as possible in his own words:—

"They were going to have this fête at Boston which was to last three days.[46] Hincks and all of them wished me to go the first day; this I determined I would not do, but of course kept my reasons to myself. They were these:—I felt that as the President was to be there too, that by arriving the same day before they

42. A. N. Morin, provincial secretary; Jean Chabot, commissioner of public works; P. J. O. Chauveau, solicitor-general for Lower Canada.

43. See pp. 334 and 287.

44. I can make no sense of this and do not know if the question mark is Bright's or the typist's.

45. Washington F. Friend (ca. 1820–ca. 1890) began in 1849 a 5,000-mile tour of Canada during which he painted numerous watercolor sketches for an enormous panorama of Canadian scenery.

46. The occasion was the Jubilee, September 17-19, 1851, celebrating the completion of the railway between Boston and Montreal. So eager were Boston merchants to overcome commercial competition with New York that this event was hailed even in Boston pulpits. Elgin had been especially invited to attend, with a large Canadian delegation that included Hincks, MacNab, and John A. Macdonald.

have got over their reception of him, I should appear in the light of a rival which would be awkward, or of a Provincial Governor and of inferior consequence to him, which would never do. So I kept my own counsel and determined to go there the second day and have my reception all to myself and all my own.[47] When I got there, Crampton and Hincks who had gone before, were delighted that I had *not* got there the previous day, as it appears that Mr. Webster, who is *really*, I believe, well-disposed toward England, had made a disagreeable speech, which it would have been awkward to answer.[48]

"That evening there, after a grand reception, and so on at the railway, I went to six parties and got through the evening that way.

"Next day there was to be a procession and a dinner, but I heard that the President was not going to the dinner, so of course I said I cared nothing about it, but what wasn't good enough for the President wasn't good enough for me, and I shouldn't go.[49] Meanwhile, I was *put into* a procession—the strangest affair—but here the President had the advantage of me, for it was only after I got regularly into it, I found that he was not going too. The only thing I got credit for in the procession was that from some cricket reminiscences I managed to catch the bouquets that were

47. Elgin, arriving at 5 P.M. on September 18, was greeted by representatives of the city government, cadets, and a large crowd of citizens. He "saluted all who approached him by a hearty shake of the hand, and was cheered most enthusiastically" (*New-York Daily Tribune*, Sept. 19, 1851).

48. In his speech Webster not only omitted any mention of Canada but likened the position of the United States to Jove among the gods: "Jove is first, and there is none second."

49. Fillmore was said to be suffering from a stomach ailment. The procession—featuring national lancers, artillery, infantry, representatives of the "mechanical and manufacturing arts," Harvard College students, and schoolchildren—started at 11 A.M. and was two hours and twenty minutes passing the Revere House.

LORD ELGIN IN THE PROCESSION AT THE RAILWAY JUBILEE IN BOSTON, SEPTEMBER 19, 1851

Gleason's Pictorial Drawing-Room Companion, November 15, 1851

thrown me from the windows by the ladies who were so terribly civil that in a hot sun I was obliged to hold my hat in my hand all the time.

"Well, then came this banquet, where, (thanks to the Maine Liquor Law) was nothing to drink but water and coffee.[50] The President did go, it seems, so I went too; the Mayor, our friend 'the Knight of the Thistle' presided and there was a small party of 3500 people. Mr. Bigelow told me that the President was going to leave directly after the cloth was removed, that he must go by some 5 o'clock train, and so forth, and that he was far from well. I said I was very sorry,

50. The dinner, given by the City Corporation, was held under a huge tent on Boston Common. The newspapers noted that although champagne flowed freely the day before, when the visiting dignitaries toured Boston harbor, "the dinner tables on this occasion were furnished with nothing stronger, save coffee, than Adam's ale" (*New-York Daily Tribune*, Sept. 22, 1851).

352

but being the President's guest I should feel bound to leave when he did, unless instead as I was under his orders while in the States he desired me to stay. This was repeated to the President, who after dinner got up and said that he was sorry that he was obliged to go from indisposition, &c., but that he hoped the Governor-General of Canada would stay, and that he was sorry for his own part that he could take no part in their *exercises*. '*Exercises!*'—such an odd word to use! ('dry toasts' was my obvious pun!) This was really what I wanted, so I got up and said that I should have felt bound to go with the President, but that *here* I was *under his orders*. That got me some cheers, of course. Well then, the President went, and the amusing thing was the twofold story the 'Knight of the Thistle' had to tell—he wished at the same time to persuade the people in the room that Fillmore was seriously ill, and the people in the States generally that there was nothing at all the matter with him: so one sentence was meant for the audience, and the next for the telegraph office—'The President was extremely unwell—(nothing at all alarming)—his serious state of health could not allow of his remaining—(he will probably soon be well again).'

"Well, after all this I had to speak, and I never spoke to any audience so much in my power.[51] Extremely excitable, they caught at, and drank down every word I spoke: and I had a difficult task; when

51. Elgin's speech was reported as a thorough success: "In the way of humor, nothing could have been happier than the manner in which he made the acknowledgment of John Bull's 'slowness of speech,' giving utterance as he did to the richest sallies of wit while pretending to stammer out his apology. . . . His lordship showed himself thoroughly up in the various Yankee accomplishments of caucusing, electioneering, pipe-laying and log-rolling; and a gentleman who sat near me remarked that it would require but a few months to transform him into a thorough Yankee" (*New-York Daily Tribune*, Sept. 22, 1851).

Bulwer[52] for instance, had to speak, he had but to praise America;—I had also to praise Canada, and please my own people as much as I did the others.

"I may here tell you, what should not be repeated, that by my visit to Boston, I firmly believe I did more to prevent annexation than by any step I could have taken. Quantities of people were going anyhow, and if I had not gone too, the Canadians would have felt that they were nobody in America, they would have had no spokesman, Canada would have been sneered at, and the Canadians would have gone home ashamed of their country and anxious to join the States. By my going, the tables were turned. They were delighted to find their Governor-General made so much of, and the admiration the Yankees were pleased to express for me had no small effect. I assure you, I was asked several times to remain in America, and they'd make me President 'on the De—mocratic ticket.' (How merrily Lord Elgin laughed as he told us this!)

"I came back with the Mayor and Corporation of Montreal; they wished me to go with them, but they went the first day, so I got out of it in a joking way, —'It will never do to carry my flock to the States, I'll meet them there, and bring them home again.' So I came back with them and they were pleased to make me an address."

He detailed the history of the rebel town's address, and how he offered (having answered it) to shake hands with any one who chose, and how many of the worst disposed made up with him, and how too at Boston the most scurrilous of all the Montreal paper's editors went round the different bars in the town swearing there was no one "like *our Governor-General.*"

52. Sir Henry Bulwer (1801-72), British ambassador at Washington, 1849-51.

"In short, I did much good I feel sure by this trip, and I cannot doubt the country will soon recover altogether the effects of the revolution of '49, as regular a revolution as any experienced by the European States in '48."[53]

Of Lyon Mackenzie Lord E. spoke kindly. He has never called, he says, not because he is ill-disposed, he thinks, but from a motive of delicacy from what has passed in former years.

We arrived at Spencer Wood at 10—left it at 1, having talked all the time, the kind old man walking us round to see the place—and a charming place it is, worthy of its possessor!

On our way back to the town we explored the Plains of Abraham where is a poor monument to Wolfe.[54]

We lunched with the 66th [regiment], and Tupper asked us to dine with them. Burder was unwell and could not go. Paget and Perrin were away at the outposts, and the dinner table not being full, it was rather slow in spite of the band which always plays on Tuesday night.

A Mr. Watson, with whom I made friends, is a nice person. We met him at lunch and also in the *Gardens* in the afternoon, where the band of the 54th was playing, a pretty little garden with monument to Wolfe

53. After his Boston visit, Elgin wrote to his chief: "My little holiday, as you style it, has not been spent altogether in idleness, as I have lately travelled in 8 days nearly 1,500 miles, and met, firstly all the United States, President included, at Boston, and secondly my Montreal friends. I hope that I have broken, or, as I should rather say, thawed a little the ice in the latter place, and as to the former, it is Crampton's opinion, I believe, that I did no harm by my visit there" (Elgin to Grey, Sept. 26, 1851, quoted in J. L. Morison, *The Eighth Earl of Elgin* [London, 1927], p. 151).

54. James Wolfe (1727–59), English general who died victorious at the Battle of Quebec.

and Montcalm,[55] and a nice view of the river, but owing to the number of maids and children and the small proportion of "rank, beauty and fashion," rather too much of a *nursery* garden.

After dinner I went to the House, and found Lyon Mackenzie talking. Langton introduced me to him; he professes the utmost admiration for Mr. Hume "whom he humbly tries to imitate."[56] He is a hideous little man, a plain likeness of Miss French!

I heard Papineau speak a few words, and own myself much pleased with his quiet gentlemanly style and his appearance; he has grey hair, and a nose almost straight from his forehead.

The manner of taking *votes* is peculiar. There are two *Clerks of the House*, one of whom goes round and calls out the names of the Members who stand up one by one, while the other clerk writes down their names on the "aye" list. The "No" Members then rise and are put down in the same way.

Mr. Langton's kindness is very great; directly he saw me he rushed to tell *me* what was going on.

Our landlord comes to me as I write and says:—"Sir, here's a man from *Antigy*[57] with some curiosities—pieces of *putrified wood*, Sir!"

Friday, [September 10].

Wednesday morning we took a drive, hoping to get to a Lake Cabian, and get back for Lady E[lgin]'s

55. Louis Joseph, marquis de Montcalm (1712–59), leader of the French forces in the Battle of Quebec.

56. Mackenzie struck up a friendship with Joseph Hume (1777–1855), the radical politician, in England in 1832.

57. I.e., Antigua?

reception, but Burder was unwell, so we came back at once and haven't called on her ladyship at all.

In the evening was the Speaker's Parliamentary dinner—seven the time, Russell's Hotel the place. We got there in good time and were kindly received by Mr. M'Donald. Clay and Morris were there, Governor Seward of New York,[58] Mr. Jackson M.P., and any number of Canadian Members, &c. The Speaker had forgotten to bespeak a drawing-room for himself, so that we were honoured with the company of some ladies of the States, a fact which caused our host some uneasiness, lest they should be mistaken for his wife and family. Guests came in thickly, poor Mr. Langton was unwell and bolted; but on the other hand, there was Mr. Hincks with his cat-like glide and stoop, there was Mr. Papineau with his white hair brushed back off his forehead, and his quiet, gentlemanly manner; there was Mr. Lyon Mackenzie with turn-down collar and a face all but revolting from its plainness, there was Colonel Bruce the model of a high-bred Englishman, and Colonel Antrobus the beau-ideal of a country gentleman.

We were at our request introduced to Papineau, and Mr. Morris and myself had a good ten minutes' conversation. Papineau speaks English well, but with a strong accent. We talked chiefly of course of Canada, avoiding politics, though I own to some insidious comparisons between the Canadians and the Yankees, not quite to the advantage of the latter or the encouragement of Papineau's favourite annexation. It was strange to meet a *rebel* in such company! Colonel Prince too was there, who bragged at dinner of having had £800 offered for his head.[59]

58. William Henry Seward (1801–72), Whig governor of New York, 1838–42, at this time senator from New York.

59. After Prince's shooting of the five prisoners (see p. 337), placards

Well,—conciliation is doubtless the best policy, unless—it fail to conciliate!

We now moved in to dinner. There was a very long table with a cross *T*-shaped at the top. On going in, a gentleman who had spoken to me before, asked me to sit by him and he would tell me the names of everybody. He sat near the end of the long table, and we were well placed. My friend was a Mr. Forsyth, but that is all I know about him.[60]

The dinner was good, but the waiters were insufficient, and if you *did* set your affections on any particular dish in the carte, the chances were it was finished—one never loved a dear gazelle but it died,[61] —one shouldn't complain therefore at so inferior a loss as that of a dish.

The flags of England hung festooned over the table, and looked hardly well, wanting instead of battles and breezes, the ignoble appliance of the wash-tub before they had appeared in so distinguished an assembly.

After dinner the Speaker proposed the Queen and Lord Elgin—both were drunk with much applause and as loyally—more so indeed—than in England, for here it was no empty form, but an assertion of the loyalty of Canada, and a challenge to any and all of the annexationists.

Then followed "The President of America" in honour of Governor Seward. He spoke in reply and insulted every one. The Canadians, by saying "the country was under the *tutelage* of England," the English, by "expressing a hope that the younger sister

were posted in Detroit offering $1,000 for his capture or $800 for his dead body.

60. Perhaps John Richardson Forsyth, a member of one of Kingston's oldest founding families, who was defeated as a Conservative candidate in 1841.

61. Thomas Moore, *Lalla Rookh*, part 5.

358

would follow the example of the elder in throwing off that tutelage," and the French, by dwelling, as every American does, on the glories of the Anglo-Saxon race, its superiority and its supremacy. Everybody looked disgusted except Colonel Prince who made a speech proposing Seward's health, after Seward's own Toast had been drunk, which was to this effect:— "May the glories of England endure, till her institutions are replaced by freer ones"—may she live till she dies—small thanks, Governor Seward, for so ambiguous a toast as that, as ambiguous as your speech was insulting. People looked sulkily toward the top of the table. Colonel Antrobus longed to kick the Yankee, Colonel Bruce burned to answer him (as each told me), a Mr. M'Donald (not the Speaker) *did* answer him, in a speech redolent of English feeling, proposing Premier Hincks, and throwing slavery in Seward's teeth.[62]

Hincks did his part well, Jackson his better, in reply to his health being drunk, except that (as Col. Bruce said to me) it was bad taste to say to the Canadians, "when you wish to be independent, you shall be independent,—England doesn't wish to oppose you, &c.," and this when their hearts are full of loyalty; they love England, but they feel it hard that their loyalty is not appreciated, and that an English Senator talks coolly of cutting them off and "wishing them God-speed."

I own myself that I entered thoroughly into Colonel Bruce's feelings on this when we bid him good-bye yesterday—"we must keep this splendid country, and with two such wings as Canada and Australia, our

---

62. This was John A. Macdonald (1815-91), who was later to play such a prominent part in Canadian history as chief architect of Confederation and prime minister. At this time he was Conservative member representing Kingston and beginning to emerge as the obvious successor to MacNab as head of the party.

British Empire will be the grandest Empire the world has ever seen."

Soon after Jackson's speech, people began to go, and between twelve and one, I suppose, we found ourselves again at Swords' Hotel; our parting with the kind Speaker being quite affecting!

Yesterday I strolled by myself to see the Seminary Gardens where a wretched flower-show was going on: a few large pumpkins, and some nice cockscombs and honeycombs were the best things there: fuchsias, and all greenhouse plants, devices and all cut flowers were contemptible.

The Chapel of the Seminary I also explored. It has several good pictures, but I had no one to tell me the names. In the courtyard were the boys of the seminary playing in a costume consisting of blue tunic with white braid round it, and a green sash, and the reverend fathers clad like Belgian priests, save their Christian instead of their Trinitarian hats, walked up and down to keep order.

Before we left we paid our respects to Lord Elgin. He was as kind as ever, and hoped to meet us at this railway opening. Colonel Bruce talked to us for some time, as I have already mentioned; at last then, having quarrelled with Mr. Swords for charging two calêches of which we were innocent, we got our luggage on board the "Montreal" for Montreal Steamer.

We were both sorry to leave Quebec, most picturesque of towns,—most strikingly so after the log houses all whitewash we've just seen in the States. The sun was just thinking of setting as we left the quay, and hidden from our view by the lofty rocks of the fortress, we could still see how he shone on certain favoured banks and slopes on the other side of the St. Lawrence, and how the roofs of some houses or chapels gleamed with a silvery lustre in the light. The quay

360

itself is crowded with people,—French, English and Americans, standing to see us off; black-robed fishers of men, and check-shirted fishers of fish mingle together in the throng, while the St. Lawrence is also crowded for its part: Steamboat St. Nicholas and Steamboat Lady Elgin are passing us at nearly the same instant.

Here, guided by a dark-haired French-Canadian, is a raft from the forests of the Ottawa, which has safely weathered the Rapids and is waiting to be split up into planks and carried perhaps to some European market; here is a pleasure boat with its white sails and jaunty air; and here large vessels which have come freighted with goods across the Atlantic, and are lying anchored at their goal. And above all, towers the Rock of Quebec, crowded with its walls and battlements, from the top of which, looking lazily down in pride of possession upon all below it, floats the flag of Old England. As you carry your eye upwards, from the river to the town, from the town to the rock, from the rock to the fortress, and above that again and see there the flag of your country, with nothing between it and God's own Heaven, you feel, or you are no Englishman, such a thrill of national pride as perhaps you never felt before; and then you remember the distance that country is away, and what a tiny ocean speck she is when compared with the nations she has given birth to, and the territories she has won; and as the steamer leaves the quay, and the citadel is now behind you, and the corner being turned, the setting sun shines out full upon the water, you see the Heights which barrier the Plains of Abraham, and you remember the noble Wolfe and how he died there to win new glory for that dear island-country!

An uncomfortable night in a bad steamer, and we find ourselves in the early morning again at Montreal.

361

DALHOUSIE SQUARE, MONTREAL, DURING THE
FIRE OF JULY 8, 1852

Illustrated London News, August 7, 1852

*"The places where the fire has been look
sadly desolate—whole streets in ruin!"*

How tame everything looks after Quebec, and yet
when we first saw Montreal we thought it picturesque
enough. Burder is seedy, so I've been shopping my own
way, reading Mrs. Ellet's account "of three Englishmen of high intelligence and taste,"[63] and calling on
Miss Ingall.[64] I saw Madame sa mère, and rather like
her; of course our conversation was merest gossip, and
by no means worth a farther record. I've also left
cards on Collingwood, and have received a card from
Ed. Knight but no Edmund himself. I go this evening to
the Ingall's for "tea and talk." The places where the

63. "Three of our companions were English gentlemen of high cultivation and taste, who desired to enjoy to the utmost the beauty of the
scenery and novelty of the adventure" (*New-York Daily Tribune*, Sept. 1,
1852).

64. Cf. p. 51.

fire has been look sadly desolate—whole streets in ruin![65]

65. Only two months before, on July 8, fire destroyed some 1,100 houses in Montreal's east end.

17

MONTREAL TO PROVIDENCE

Burlington, on Lake Champlain, Vermont.
Monday Night, [September 13].

Friday evening I spent at the Ingall's, having refused a dinner invitation from Collingwood. Bevies of dames all evidently prepared to make one a "victim of locality," and a droll little Captain Ingall, made up a pleasant evening enough, though I was sorry Burder was not there to do a little "chaffing."

On Saturday morning by time somewhere about seven o'clock I left the Hotel for Longueuil by boat; here the Quebec grandees were to meet us, and with them we were to adventure this new railway. On the boat I met Edmund Knight, and very glad I was to see the old fellow again.

Soon after our arrival at Longueuil, the "John < > " made its appearance, the band struck up "God save the Queen" and Lord Elgin made his appearance, and with uncovered head, but closely surrounded by policemen walked very fast to the "cars" which were to take us to Sherbrooke. I own to a feeling of dis-

appointment and surprize at the precautions the good
lord still thinks it necessary to take when in the vicin-
age of Montreal. A second feeling of regret came over
me at a trivial thing if you like, but still as it appeared
to me, an omen of ill. These carriages meant to tra-
verse that district of Canada where the annexation
feeling is strongest, were all of the *Yankee* build,[1]
and poor Lord Elgin had to sit in a carriage with some
40 others. I was in the same one, but at quite the far
end, so that of course I had no opportunity of speaking
to him. Colonel Bruce however, came up and talked to
me for some little time; I never saw such a "par nobile
fratrum."[2] Mr. Young also told me much of his views
and hopes—how the Provinces are to be connected, and
how as soon as the Canadas contribute to the taxation
of the Empire they will require representation in the
Imperial Parliament. He is anxious that steamers
should run between Liverpool and Quebec with the
mail bags, thereby saving 400 miles over the passage
to Boston.[3]

Lambton was sitting by us all the time, a quiet,
gentlemanly, coxcombical individual.

The country we passed through is very beautiful.
At St. Hyacinthe an address was presented by the
heads of some Catholic Seminary, and we could hear
from our seat part of the Governor's reply, thanking
them for the "paroles éloquents et faciles."[4] At another
place a lady with two little boys spoke to His Excel-

1. Because the Saint Lawrence and Atlantic line to Portland was partly financed by American capital.

2. "A fine pair of brothers" (Horace, *Satires* II.iii.243).

3. The Province of Canada advertised in June, 1852, for bids for just
such a service; but the resulting London, Liverpool, and North American
Screw Steam Ship Company ran into objections from Samuel Cunard, who
had long maintained weekly mail service between Liverpool, Boston, and
New York.

4. Elgin's fluent French was an obvious asset in his position.

lency, one boy waving a flag inscribed "Hurrah for the Bruce," the other handing him—the Bruce—a bouquet chiefly of china asters.

Having left St. Hyacinthe, the road passes through the heart of a pine forest with here and there some settler's hut for the first time laid open to the ken of a "busy curious world," its inhabitants feeling, I imagine, much like ants when you turn over the clod, and let the sun in on their "penetralia." Part of the wood near the line had in places been burnt down, and the charred timber lay as it had fallen, or stood up black and grim among its as yet untouched brethren.

At last we enter the valley of St. Francis, the beautiful stream with pine knolls on its banks was bordered in many places with flourishing farms, and fields in the highest state of cultivation. These "Eastern townships" are worthy all commendation save their Yankee tendencies.[5]

At Sherbrooke there were more addresses in a drizzling rain,—flags and evergreens, some enthusiastic committee men with red ribbons in their button-holes, a band of music, a gun, I believe, and a gaping crowd who looked on, and looked apathetic. This was our reception. Then came a struggle for luncheon, in which we nearly came to "tarnal smash" such was the pressure of a Canadian mob stimulated by a base desire for food, which considering they breakfasted at six, and it wasn't more than two now, was absurd to the last degree. However, they did squeeze, and push and resist all entreaties, "Do take your time, gentlemen," and finally, tumbled rather than walked into the room where the feeding was to go on. Nearly 1000 people at

5. "We know places in both the Canadas perhaps unsurpassed in cultivation by anything in the United States, and to him who tells us of the high farming of Pennsylvania or the valley of the Genessee, we would point out the country round Hamilton and the district which is watered by the St. Francis" (HAB in *Fraser's Magazine* [February, 1853], p. 186.

Illustrated London News, August 14, 1852

*"Flags and evergreens, . . . a band of music,
a gun, I believe, and a gaping crowd."*

divers long tables hard at work on chickens and lobster
salads, and melons and pears—an exhilarating sight
truly, rendered more so by the report of the champagne
corks cracking about you like detonating balls. I was
near Lord Elgin's table, opposite Morris and next Ed.
Knight and Mr. M' Donald of Kingston to whom un-
consciously I praised his own speech at the Speaker's
dinner. The room was hung with evergreens and flags,
among which were the arms of the Bruces with their
grand pathetic motto *"Fuimus"*.[6]

Of the speeches that followed I shall say nothing, as
I expect that there will be a full account of them in
the papers; I will only remark that Lord Elgin's speech
was worthy of him, perfect in elocution and taste, and
sentiment;[7] touching so delicately on the Americans

6. "We have been" (i.e., "We have a history").

7. W. E. Gladstone rated Elgin's natural gift of eloquence as the best
of all their contemporaries at Eton and Oxford.

that he "without sneering taught the rest to sneer,"[8] and speaking so heartily and honestly of Canada that each Canadian's heart must "have burnt within him" at his eloquent words: assuredly if Canada is to be saved, Lord Elgin will save it; if it is not, and if Yankees take away from this fine people "their race and nation," Lord Elgin may at least feel that he has been a "good and faithful servant" to his country, and that the evil he could not avert, was an evil that no English statesman could avert. However, I own I hope and believe no such consummation will happen. In the railway to this place, I talked to a Catholic priest. He believes much in Canada (wheat selling, he says, at 4/6 a bushel) and dislikes the Americans. I talked to an American "raised" in Vermont; he tells me he has been delighted with Canada and has bought a place there, and intends to be a British subject. His place contains, besides a splendid house, 140 acres. One field has 105 acres, and last year produced 240 tons of hay. He gives £3000 for it: he hopes to see the Queen there should she come to Canada, me also, should I revisit Quebec. He gives me his card—his name is "J. R. Benjamin—Brass Spring Trusses!" He seems to have quarrelled with a member of the Canadian legislature, and asked Lord Elgin if his life was in danger in consequence!

However, returning for a moment to annexation, I do not believe there is much feeling for it, malgré Governor Seward's wishes, malgré Captain Ingall's fears.

We got back to Montreal about nine—the last time I saw Lord Elgin being at Sherbrooke when as he stood on a platform, "the cynosure of every eye," he saw me, and beckoning me up, bade me good-bye. "Do we part

8. Cf. Pope, "Epistle to Dr. Arbuthnot."

here, Mr. Bright?" being his first question to which I answered, yes, forgetting that his meaning probably was (in allusion to a question I had asked him at Quebec) "Do you get on to Boston hence instead of returning to Longueuil and Montreal?" I was afterwards very glad I had so bid him goodbye, as at Longueuil the darkness and crush would have prevented it.

Yesterday we called at Collingwood's and got lunch there; saw a memorial in the Papish Cathedral, went to Chapel and heard Mr. Dall (who disgusted Burder with a controversial sermon) and got introduced to "friends," and spent the evening chatting with the Ingalls. Mrs. Collingwood I don't like much; Miss Maxwell is exceedingly pretty. C[ollingwood] talked of his wife's Church as "the dodging shop."

This morning, accompanied by the Ingall girls, we went to buy furs and see nuns. The Convent of the "Grey Sisters" is quite worth seeing.[9] The good women take care of many poor idiots and many little foundling children. The rooms for the former were a sad sight, those devoted to the latter were really most interesting; droll little things of 3 or 4 years old, all so clean and fresh, with the drollest rows of tiny little beds side by side; everything about them neat and cheerful, with rosyfaced nurses and the kind grey sisters themselves to look after them. These poor foundlings are doubtless very happy children, and one feels while looking at them no small admiration for these women devoted to good works, who superintend this glorious institution. We bought some little melon seed bags to commemorate our visit, and after seeing the Chapel and the nuns themselves as they walked two and two to Service there, we returned to Donegana's and bade our fair chaperones a long farewell. Imagine in En-

9. The Grey Nuns, in Foundling Street, was founded in 1692 for the care of lunatics and children.

gland four unmarried ladies and two gentlemen, no relations, walking about a town all alone!

We dined at one, took ticket ($9 for the two) to Troy, and crossing to La Prairie, entered the railway for Burlington, passing St. John's, Rouse's Pt. (where our luggage was examined and we changed cars) and Essex (where we again changed).

The "American" is the hotel here, and it seems a good one. I see here advertisement cards about an Hotel on the White Mts. where you may get "intelligent and *gentlemanly* Guides"—an odd expression which recalls one I saw some time ago in a paper mentioning Mr. Downing who was lost in the "Henry Clay"[10]—"in private character he was intelligent, amiable and *lovely.*"

A very nice Philadelphian is here, and he quite agrees with me about Seward's speech; "he is a firebrand," he says, and he rejoices that he has made himself unpopular in Canada; he often insults people, and as he won't *fight,* "a horsewhipping" is all that remains.

We've just been much amused by the volubility of a New Jersey man of an inquiring turn of mind, who has been pouring forth a 20 minute list of questions to our much-enduring landlord. "What State's this? What county's this? What's the next county to this? What's the best crop in this county? Do you graze at all in this county? Who's your Mayor? How many are there in your Municipality? &c. &c."—a most amusing specimen of a Yankee genuine and undefiled by foreign admixture, his last speech being, "Guess I'm posted now!—a candle, a glass of water, and a waiter to show me my room."[11]

10. A steamer that caught fire on the Hudson on July 27. Hawthorne's sister Louisa was among the passengers drowned.

11. This type is a stock American character as observed by English-

I am heartily sorry to think that we've left Canada. Shall I ever see it again, most noble of our Colonial possessions!

To-morrow we see Lakes Champlain and George!

Caldwell's, Head of Lake George.
Tuesday Night, September 14.

This morning, on looking from our bedroom windows, we saw the beauties of Lake Champlain spread out before us, the view being bounded by a range of high and finely varied hills.

The morning was spent in strolling through Burlington and writing some letters to Mr. Irvin, &c. Burlington is the chief town in Vermont, and is undoubtedly a flourishing little place as far as looks go; its situation is delightful, and as yet I've hardly seen any American town near which a more glorious locality for a country house could be found.

About 10½ our boat arrived, and having got our luggage on board and devoured six greengages which I bought for a halfpenny—(nasty things! they've given me a stomach ache!)—we steamed away down the Lake, near the head of which a stage took us from Ticonderoga to the foot of Lake George, where another steamer conveyed us to this place.

Everyone has heard of the beauty of Lake George, and the praise is well-merited, for it resembles (no satire meant against us travellers in foreign land!)—strongly resembles—a Scotch lake, and in parts our English Ullswater; here, however, instead of heather hills, every mountain side is covered with forest; on

men: cf. Dickens's description of the man he calls "an embodied inquiry" on the canal boat in Pennsylvania (*American Notes*, chap. 10).

371

Gleason's Pictorial Drawing-Room Companion, October 16, 1852

*"The thick oak woods come feathering down
to the water's edge."*

their tops the pine bristles among some bald crags, at their base the thick oak woods come feathering down to the water's edge. The two lakes are much alike except in size, and the hills on the smaller sheet brought closer together rise more imposingly than do those in Lake Champlain; it has also more islands, but they are not so beautiful as those which we used to see from our window at Patterdale.[12] The Hotel here is comfortable, and the day having been intensely cold, we were exceedingly glad to arrive at our journey's end.[13]

In the boat was a man with a glass box containing two rattlesnakes who were in a great excitement, rattling and darting their forked tongues out:—I'm sure I've heard that rattle in Virginia!

12. On Ullswater in the Lake District.

13. "Caldwell is a hamlet at the southern end of the Lake. It is named from an eccentric gentleman . . . who owned the whole region, built a hotel on the wrong spot, determined that no one else should build anywhere" (Curtis, *Lotus-Eating,* p. 128).

372

Troy on the Hudson, N.Y.
Wednesday Night, [September 15].

We have just arrived at this classical city. "Tell no
more the hall of Troy" as the Hellas chorus warns ye,[14]
nor believe again, as Aeneas whispers it in Dido's ear,
that "Troja *fuit*."[15] "Troja est" rather is the truth, and
"many fountained Ida" where Oenone wandered[16]
and where Mrs. Warren to whom Burder has a letter,
still lives. Yes, Ida itself rises within a stone's throw
of our Hotel—and Olympus too! Olympus has become
ungeographical in its hoary age, and when its gods
deserted it, it deserted Greece it would seem, and with
Mt. Ida at its side, and the Troy itself at its feet, it
looks calmly down upon the windings of the Sca-
mander, I mean the Hudson, and views with placid
content the advancing cars not of Greeks but—of railways, as they pass straight through the town and de-
posit their passengers at the Hotel doors.

From Caldwell to Moreau Station is a beautiful
drive of 14 miles by stage or carriage at $1 a head.
On the way we pass Glen's Falls,—pretty Hudson River
falls in a bad situation.[17] From Moreau to Saratoga
the railway takes you in half an hour. Saratoga season is over, the balls have ceased, the belles have returned to New York and town gaiety:—Saratoga is over
—you see at once that it is so; only one omnibus
meets the train at the station, only one Hotel professes to have still a decent show at dinner; the walks
look deserted, there's one boy, and but one, at the
Congress Spring, and no one, except the enterprizing

14. Cf. Shelley, final chorus of *Hellas.*
15. "Troy is no more." Cf. *Aeneid* II.325.
16. Tennyson, "Oenone."
17. "They [the falls] are oppressed by the petty tyranny of a decayed
dynasty of saw-mills" (Curtis, *Lotus-Eating*, pp. 127-28).

373

proprietor at the "Circular Railway," and no one at all at the Observatory. We are quite too late, and a sense of dreariness creeps over you when you think of these large hotels which must now shut up, and like bears or dormice, |<hibernate?> in sleep through the winter months.

Still, in summer Saratoga must be a pleasant place, and is for several reasons to be preferred to the White Sulphur Springs, Va.: it's more accessible to begin with, it's more of a town, it has more foreigners, it has better drives and more of them, and must be far gayer, besides which the water is really delightful, cool and fresh and good to taste as well as to drink.

Per contra, the White Sulphur has infinitely finer scenery round it, though the want of roads or paths up the mountains is a great drawback.

There is in Saratoga one chief street with large and splendid Hotels all along it; the "United States" is thought, I believe, the best, then the "Congress Hall" where we dined close to the Congress Spring, the "Union Hall" with a lovely garden behind it, and seats under trees, and behind trellises and in arbours —nothing could be more tempting for a flirtation or— a cigar: and talking of flirtation, there is a most suggestive advertisement fixed up in the hall of each Hotel,—"Mr. So-and-so will supply De La Rue's Wedding Stationery!"

Leaving Saratoga at 6, we reached Troy at 7½, and are well placed in the Troy House, which we leave for Newport "en bonne heure" to-morrow.

I'm in a moralizing humour, and having seen Saratoga to-day, naturally enough thoughts of fair Americans are uppermost, and one involuntarily compares them with our own countrywomen. "I guess" neither would wish to change their lot: no English *lady* but would feel as much shocked by the accent, the

374

"style" the forwardness of an American girl as she would be delighted with her beauty; no American woman but would shudder at the English restraint, and the English toilette, and chafe inwardly at having any one of higher rank or station than herself. "I would only be an Englishwoman on one condition," said an American to Morris,[18] "that I should be a *Duchess*, otherwise I could not bear it."

Even in England they forget that they have superiors, and Mrs. Abbott Lawrence[19] scarcely exaggerated the complacent self-reverence of her countrywomen when she said, "I entertain for the Queen a feeling, not exactly of friendship, for I am not intimate enough for that, nor of loyalty, for I am not a British subject, but rather a sentiment of attachment and sympathy which one lady in an exalted position always entertains for another." Or to take another instance when she wrote to the Queen begging to present Mrs. Peabody to her, —"I may assure your Majesty in requesting this favour that I am doing what is with me an unusual thing, for at Boston the Lawrences are more in the habit of conferring than of requiring a favour."[20]

Republicanism rarely agrees with a woman except she be a Cornelia[21]—a Madame Roland[22]—it too often excites them to the most disgusting follies by way of showing their independence, as at the Woman's

18. Probably the Morris he saw in Quebec (p. 336).

19. Wife of the wealthy Bostonian manufacturer who was minister to the Court of St. James, 1849-52.

20. Hawthorne records (probably from HAB) the second of these stories as one of the "queer stories . . . the English tell" (*English Notebooks*, p. 281).

21. Roman matron, famous for her virtue and accomplishments, mother of the Gracchi.

22. Madame Roland de la Platière (1754-93), whose salon in Paris was the headquarters of the republicans and Girondists during the Revolution.

Rights Convention held at Syracuse,[23] and an account of which is worth preserving, as the "force of *folly* would no farther go"[24]—an unnatural odious proceeding throughout.

No! Loyalty is the true political feeling for a woman,—the love or affection for what is higher than herself seems a part of her nature, and in woman the purest, truest feelings of loyalty have over and over again been seen—in Joan of Arc when she raised the Cross and drew the sword, blended her love for God with her love for His anointed; in Catherine Douglas when she strove to preserve her monarch's life by that door barred only with her arm;[25] and in Flora M'Donald when she followed the fortunes and shared the perils of the last of the Stuart Princes;[26] in Miss Lane,[27] in the Princess De Lamballe,[28] and in fifty others whose names can never be forgotten so long as heroism commands our admiration and woman possesses our affection and our love.[29]

23. The Woman's Rights Convention, attended by some 2,000 people and featuring such speakers as Lucy Stone, Lucretia Mott, and Samuel J. May, met at Syracuse September 8-10.

24. Cf. Dryden, "Lines on Milton."

25. Catherine Douglass (or "Bar-Lass") tried to save James I of Scotland by barring the door against his assailants (February 20, 1437).

26. Flora Macdonald (1722-90), Scottish Jacobite heroine, who helped the Young Pretender to escape after the battle of Culloden.

27. Jane Lane, afterward Lady Fisher (d. 1689), distinguished for her courage in the service of Charles II.

28. Marie Thérèse Louise de Savoie-Carignan, princess de Lamballe (1749-92), proved her loyalty to Marie Antoinette by refusing to take the oath against the monarchy.

29. It would no doubt be impertinent to note that four out of Bright's five examples of loyal female behaviour resulted in injury, imprisonment, or violent death.

Providence, R.I. Friday Morning, [September 17].

Yesterday after a tiresome twelve hours' journey we arrived here, but only to find that the Newport boat had started and that every hotel was so full that we might think ourselves lucky to get, as we did, beds on the floor. Nor was it much consolation to reflect that our money is getting to an end, and that when we reach Newport we shall probably have a dollarless purse. How I hope the Georges are still there!

Last night after supper, we strolled out seeking "what we might devour"[30] in the sightseeing line. We first made our way to the Musĕum The-ātre, but finding the boxes so full that we could not sit, and the gallery so hot that we could not stand it, we wandered away, and next essayed a lecture-room which we saw brilliantly illuminated from the street; but the lecture was Temperance, a useless topic one would think in a place where the Maine Liquor Law is in full swing, so not being tempted by this, we again went our way. The next amusement we came across was a huge telescope fixed in the street, through which we had the satisfaction of seeing two coloured stars, a nebulous-looking comet at some wonderful distance, and a part of the Milky Way, for which scientific treat we were charged 50 cents a head—villanous "dos" as these Yankees are!

Our journey yesterday was no way remarkable, except for the complication of railways on which we had to travel—one line to Albany, another to Worcester, a third to Providence. We saw Albany well from the opposite river bank, and a very fine town it appears. Springfield, where we dined, is likewise a large place, and the bill of fare is worth preserving to show how a

30. Cf. 1 Peter V.8.

Massachusetts Birmingham treats hungry railway travellers.

The country, soon after entering the old Bay State is very beautiful, and more populous than any American district I have yet seen, and more like the fairer parts of our own England; woody hills, valleys richly cultivated with brawling streams winding through them, white farms and homesteads and sheltered villages:—such is the scenery of Berkshire county where Dr. Dewey has his home,[31] and the authoress of the "Linwoods" also.[32] Dear Massachusetts! where Channing lived and Henry Ware, and so many other great, good men,—country where every one is educated, and where more entirely than in any other State is it true that our people "have kept unstained what there they sought—Freedom to worship God!"[33]— whether in the stern old creed of Calvin, or in the gentle tenets of the martyred servitors; State whence has flowed /so much of good in theology, in science, in poetry, /where the Harvard University exists and flourishes, only surpassed by the old Cambridge and Oxford, surpassing them in her freedom from bond and shackle and conscience-snare,[34] State of the modern Athens where may now be seen such a cluster of great literary men together as perhaps no other country in the world can show;—Prescott and Longfellow, and Emerson, and Parker, and Winthrop, and Sumner, and Everett and Hawthorne,—names held in reverence hardly more in their America than in our own England![35]

31. Orville Dewey was born and died in Sheffield, Mass.

32. Catharine Maria Sedgwick's popular novel *The Linwoods; or, 'Sixty Years Since' in America* was published in 1835.

33. Cf. Felicia Hemans, "The Landing of the Pilgrim Fathers."

34. Because Harvard required no religious tests.

35. Bright met all of these men in Boston except Sumner (whom he had seen in Washington) and Prescott.

18

BOSTON

Monday Night, [September 20].

Veni, vidi, vici! I mean, veni, vidi, and taken tea with Longfellow. However, I'll be coherent and describe the incidents of the last few days though my pen is so bad that writing in *itself* will be very laborious.

On Friday we left Providence for a two hours trip to Newport, where we intended remaining till next day, but when we got there, we found the Georges gone, the Ocean House shut up, and the whole place anything but inviting; we accordingly dined at the Bellevue and came away directly after, full of wonder at people who go to the seaside and live in Hotels where a sea view's an impossibility and not to be had at any price. Two hours to Providence, two more, and we were in Boston: another quarter of an hour and here's the Tremont,[1] and the common with the Frog pond, and the King's Chapel are close at hand; and

---

1. Tremont House, at the corner of Tremont and Beacon streets, built in 1830 as the first "palace hotel" in the world, was described by Dickens as "some trifle smaller than Bedford Square."

streets with fine stores run along in front of our hotel, and as next morning I pass through them to Mr. Reynolds' for our money, I pass the Faneuil Hall and the Quincy Market and Uni. Churches to any number.

However Mr. Reynolds is next day. On Friday we've only time for Signor Blitz the conjuror, who spins plates and ventriloquises Jews Harps, and produces eggs from handkerchiefs, and bullies tame canaries. Next morning I *did* Mr. Reynolds, or rather Mr. Grant his partner,[2] and in the evening we teaed there and were introduced to a club, the Somerset, which seems comfortable and slow, exceedingly the *latter*.[3] Mrs. Grant is a nice ladylike person who had learnt German from M[argaret] Fuller. We also before tea drove out with Dr. Gannett[4] to see the Squires, but alas! they were out and we missed them. Dr. Gannett is a charming old man, who is very lame, but manages to crutch along marvellously, and his kindness in rushing about after us is very great. He is Channing's successor, but is not so popular by any means as my great predecessor, for he is very lachrymose it seems, resembling Dr. Hutton[5] in this; but poor old man, he's had many troubles and does his duty bravely, they all say.

He has taken us to-day to the Athenaeum,[6] where

2. Possibly Moses Grant, philanthropist and deacon of the Brattle Street Church.

3. The Somerset Club had been organized earlier this year, in a granite mansion at the corner of Beacon and Somerset streets.

4. Ezra Stiles Gannett (1801-71) was William Ellery Channing's co-pastor and then his successor at the Federal Street Church. His "many troubles" included the death of his wife and the paralysis of his right leg.

5. Richard Holt Hutton (1826-97), English Unitarian minister and editor of the Unitarian newspaper, the *Inquirer*, 1851-53.

6. An imposing edifice on Beacon Street (opened 1849), housing one of the largest libraries in the nation.

I saw *my* article,[7] and met Mrs. Brooks of New York.[8] She is a charming, fascinating woman and everyone speaks highly of her. The Athenaeum is a beautiful room, well furnished, and well bookcased, and Mr. Folsom the Librarian a pleasant, gentlemanly person.[9] Dr. Gannett likewise took us to see a picture gallery with a Belshazzar's Feast by Allston,[10] and introduced us to Mr. Ticknor, the author of "Spanish Literature;"[11] he has a lovely house with beautiful rooms, and seems an agreeable person; he talked of Uncle Henry, Mr. Kenyon, and William Greg,[12] and introduced us to Lady Lyell,[13] who with her husband is staying at their house.

Yesterday we spent in religious dissipation going to Theodore Parker in the morning, Dr. Peabody[14] in the afternoon, and spending the evening with the Squires.

Theodore Parker preaches in the Melodeon, a place which on week days is used by Mr. Anderson the conjuror; he has a large congregation, as well he may, for such "spiced food" is very tempting and appetiz-

---

7   This was Bright's first appearance in print: a letter in *Fraser's Magazine* (September, 1852) on the presidential election. Viewing the election as "a contest of men, not principles," Bright describes the Democratic convention (see p. 133 n.) and regrets that the Whigs nominated Scott instead of Webster.

8.   Mrs. Sidney Brooks, formerly Miss Fanny Dehon of Boston, a pronounced blonde known for her brilliant conversation.

9.   Charles Folsom (1794-1872), formerly teacher and librarian at Harvard; librarian of the Athenaeum, 1846-56.

10.   "Belshazzar's Feast" was a colossal unfinished painting, commissioned (by Ticknor among others) from Washington Allston (1779-1843), who labored on it for twenty-five years.

11.   George Ticknor (1791-1871), Boston's social autocrat, whose *History of Spanish Literature* appeared in 1849.

12.   William Rathbone Greg (1809-81), essayist and Lancashire mill-owner, whom Ticknor had visited in 1838.

13.   Wife of the great geologist Sir Charles Lyell (1797-1875).

14.   Ephraim Peabody (1807-56), minister of King's Chapel, 1845-56.

ing though perhaps hardly wholesome. After Service I made myself known to him; he was civil, but could offer no hospitality as he is living in the country. His sermon was on atheism, and he took advantage of his subject to inveigh against Louis Napoleon,[15] and praise Kossuth.[16] At times he grew nearly facetious, and a buzz of suppressed laughter sounded through the room, as if the echo of the laughter Mr. Anderson occasioned still haunted it. The King's Chapel is very interesting and contains several nice monuments. They here use the reformed Liturgy.[17] The Squires are in 3rd St., South Boston, and were delighted to see us; *he* told me he went once to an abolition meeting and never heard such *blasphemy* in his life.

This afternoon we started for Cambridge and Longfellow. We've now delivered letters to him, to Theodore Parker, Mr. Ticknor, Mr. Ward,[18] Dr. Gannett and Mr. Grant.

We drove out and got to *his* (L[ongfellow]'s) house about four o'clock. It is a pretty house with nice gardens and verandah; as we drove up a waggon full of his children passed us, all in high glee.

We sent in our letters and waited. Presently we were desired to enter: the house is as pretty inside as out; good pictures and old oak cabinets and bookcases and tables make the drawing-room and study as comfortable and elegant as ever a poet's rooms need be.

15. Napoleon III (1808–73) had executed his coup d'état the preceding December and was to be proclaimed emperor in December, 1852.

16. Louis Kossuth (1802–94), leader of the Hungarian insurrection of 1848, had just concluded a tour of the United States, where he gave six hundred speeches on behalf of his country's independence.

17. Historic King's Chapel, at the corner of Tremont and School streets, was the first Episcopal church in New England (1686) but later became Unitarian. The liturgy was altered in 1785.

18. Probably Thomas Wren Ward (1786–1858), American agent for Baring Brothers, bankers.

LONGFELLOW'S HOUSE IN CAMBRIDGE

Gleason's Pictorial Drawing-Room Companion, June 12, 1852

"It is a pretty house with nice gardens and verandah."

The poet himself! there he stood, holding out his hand to greet us; a short, stout, red-faced man, in personal appearance like Capt. Matthews, is the poet, with grey eyes, and long hair brought over his cheeks with a curl as if to stand for whiskers: a red velvet waistcoat, a blue coat with black velvet collar, and (when he went out) a white hat. Such was the poet's dress. No Grub St. look about *him*, and everybody says he's "a man of the world." He received us very kindly, read our notes from R. Carpenter[19] and Synge .with much apparent interest, and told me that when he saw the former he was a Minister without a charge —"a steekit Minister" as the Scotch say—a phrase trans-

19.   See p. 147.

lated by some French luminary "un ministre apassière [?]."

L. advised us strongly to go and see Miss Sedgwick, and pulled out maps to show us our route, soon after which he drove us to Mt. Auburn, the cemetery near him, which is very pretty and "a lion."

He told us one or two good stories of an old lady who loved nature and hated the Jews. She used to abuse these poor people industriously, and on someone remarking "Our Saviour was a Jew,"—"I can't help it, Sir, I hate the Jews!"

Her love for Nature prompted her to sit transcended on the verandah, and when our canker-worms fell upon her, and raised their heads round the folds of her headdress, she would say, "What matter it, they are our fellow-worms."[20]

He talked of Père-la-Chaise, and how absurd some of the monuments were, and pointed out to us the monuments of Spurzheim[21] and Bowditch[22] in Mt. Auburn.[23]

On our return he introduced us to Mrs. Longfellow, a very nice person, and his children who played and romped, and made a noise in a most exhilarating way, and their father had some trouble to turn them out of the room laughing and screaming, only to return again on all fours like little frogs.[24]

---

20. The old lady was Mrs. Craigie, who once owned the house that was now Longfellow's; as a young Harvard professor he rented a room from her.

21. Kaspar Spurzheim (1776–1832), German phrenologist.

22. Nathaniel Bowditch (1773–1838), navigator and mathematician.

23. Twenty-six years later Bright wrote to Longfellow: "I remember the drive we all took together one Sunday, and how strange it seemed to me to show anyone *ivy* for the first time" (fragmentary letter [1878?] in Harvard College Library).

24. Longfellow's children at this time were Charles (aet. 8), Ernest (7), and Alice (2).

From *National Portrait Gallery of Eminent Americans*, ed. E. A. Duyckinck, Vol. II, 1862

"No Grub St. look about him."

Longfellow told me of the Washington ghost he saw; a figure leading a horse, and standing out in the light flung by a burning barn. He won't acknowledge that he thinks it a ghost, but I suspect he does. He believes the *rappings* are caused by magnetic power, and says that America is so highly electrical that sparks come from you as on a cold night you pull off your stockings, and that some *looms* are full of electricity! He is evidently a *leetle* superstitious,—verily is under scientific slavery!

He collects autographs and showed us his, after tea, promising to send me some good ones in return for some I promised him: this was after tea when two other gents joined us.[25]

He says Prescott is writing "History of Philip II of Spain,"[26] the most difficult subject he has yet undertaken. He admires Mrs. Browning and *swears* by Kingsley and the "Saint's Tragedy."[27] He showed me a collection of things about Faust, and declares that the sermon and the Miracle play in "Golden Legend" are really authentic or nearly so.[28] He says he believes he's been abused for the book; I owned it, but assured him he was much valued in England, and told him how the children loved him. By the way, among his autographs is a letter from Dickens in which he says *his* children have been acting a pantomime which consists of drinking down three glasses of water,

25. Bright sent autographs of Priestley, Kingsley, Elizabeth Gaskell, and Connop Thirlwall; Longfellow returned those of O. W. Holmes, Poe, and Sylvester Judd.

26. William Hickling Prescott (1796–1859) began this history in 1849; two volumes were published in 1855, a third in 1858.

27. Longfellow, reading Charles Kingsley's "The Saint's Tragedy" (1848) for the first time the previous April, wrote in his journal that he wished he had used the theme (of Saint Elizabeth of Hungary) for his own "Golden Legend."

28. See p. 155 and n.

solemnly toasting Longfellow—"Mr. Longfellow, hoorra—!"[29]

He talked about Newport which he likes; it is a curious place, from being so like the Isle of Wight in the names of places and people, and was doubtless settled by some from that place.

We discussed *dialects*, and he told me of a mistake he made when a man spoke to him of a book "of the bards (birds) of England,"—does it not, he asked, include the Irish *Bards* as well?

He spoke highly of Clough's Bothie,[30] and admired the hexameter extremely; the *name* was the obstacle in the way of its success in America when it was reprinted: but Kingsley as an *author* was his great admiration, and he said over the lines at the beginning of the "delicious"—"Go Mary, call the cattle home."[31]

We had altogether a delightful evening and we go to-night to Mr. Appleton's to meet him there.[32]

Wednesday, [September 22].

On the morning of yesterday, Mr. Ticknor called to see us; he's a nice person, and very good-natured, with a good, droll, Socratically-plain face. He offered to

29. The letter (Dec. 29, 1842) is printed in *The Letters of Charles Dickens*, ed. Madeline House, Graham Storey, and Kathleen Tillotson, 3 (Oxford, 1974):407–9. Dickens had entertained the American poet in London in October, 1842, returning Longfellow's hospitality of the preceding January.

30. Arthur Hugh Clough's poem "The Bothie of Tober-na-Vuolich," published in 1848 as "The Bothie of Toper-na-Fuosich," was prompted by a reading of *Evangeline*.

31. From the ballad "The Sands of Dee," published in chap. 26 of *Alton Locke* (1850).

32. Nathan Appleton (1779–1861), wealthy manufacturer and father of Longfellow's wife Fanny.

take us to the Appleton's if we had no other engagement, and advised me about my letters.

Theodore Parker also called. He is not, I think, a very pleasant man when you see him close, or rather I should say he has not the air of *goodness* and piety which even in a Theist Minister one likes to see. He speaks openly and coarsely about such things as Mormon polygamy, and roused up like a war-horse when he spoke of arming the fugitive slaves against the kidnappers; like *his* mother in Clara Vere De Vere "he has the passions of his kind!"[33]

He spoke much about Martineau, was surprized to hear he edited the Westminster, and promises two articles—on Mormonism and on America.[34] I gave him all the information I could on the former subject, not much to be sure, but he seemed glad to get it.

He was much excited about the Fugitive Slave Bill and the harm it has done,—the excitement and the arming—he went round to see that their weapons were in order, "that their powder was dry," and that they "trusted in God." Ellen Craft he has hidden in his own room.[35] He promised to give me some books for James Heywood, and gave us a letter of introduction to Plymouth.

He thinks little of Whewell as a moralist, and says that he praised him in a note to the Discourse on Religion, and has repented it ever since, believing his praise to be false.[36] Whewell however, has always

33. Tennyson, "Lady Clara Vere de Vere." "*His* mother" refers to the mother of the dead suitor in the poem.

34. James Martineau (1805-1900), Unitarian minister at Liverpool (where Parker had met him), did not edit the *Westminster Review* but was a frequent contributor. Nothing came of Parker's promise.

35. Parker not only hid Ellen Craft, fugitive slave from Georgia, in his own house, but married her to William Craft on free soil.

36. Parker praised the "forcible and eloquent remarks" concerning the sacrifices required by religion in Whewell's *Sermons on the Foundation*

sent him his books since. (He sends books to Longfellow also.)[37]

Yesterday too, we made calls as well.

Mr. Everett[38] was icy and courteous as he always
is. Quiet in manner, with suppressed voice, and gliding
step, he freezes you by his reserve, till you get frigid
from very sympathy. He was kind enough, however,
to talk to us for some time about emigration and such
like. He thinks the German a dangerous element in the
population, and tells us that the Irish checked the
Kossuth fever as their priests told them they were not
to be led aside by a hater of Catholics. One-third the
population of Pennsylvania is German, and they always choose a German Governor to keep the people
quiet.

In New York State are still Dutch villages, and also
a Welsh one, &c. &c.

We pilgrimaged to Bunker's Hill, but were too lazy
to get to the top of the mountain.

In the evening, Longfellow's brother-in-law, Tom
Appleton,[39] took us to his father's to a "swarry;" a
nice house, a pretty little supper, and pleasant people
were there, and such elements of course insured success. Longfellow was charming; talked to us of Tennyson whom he dearly loves, and admires the "In
Memoriam" extremely and the art by which such
varied music is played on one thing: "it is the most
English poem, and nowhere can I get a better, clearer

of Morals—"a work well worthy, in its spirit and general tone, of his illustrious predecessors, 'the Latitude men about Cambridge' " (A Discourse
of Matters Pertaining to Religion [1842], book 1, chap. 3).

37. Whewell gave Evangeline a lyrical review in Fraser's Magazine
(March, 1848).

38. Edward Everett (1794–1865), noted American statesman,
formerly minister to England.

39. Thomas Gold Appleton (1812–84) dabbled in literature and art,
but was cherished mainly for his social graces and brilliant talk.

notion of English scenery than from the 'In Memoriam.' " We talked of Virginia forest scenery, and he quoted from Moore's "Dismal Swamp."[40] We talked of Indian dresses, and he reminded us how the Prince de Joinville[41] brought his sister from the Sandwich Isles a bead on a string as the *costume* of the natives. Of Edgar Poe we talked much, and he quoted that "delicious little thing" "Annabel Lee," addressed, he told us, to his poor wife.[42] He told of his death, and also mentioned another sad story of a poor fellow lost in the White Mountains.[43] Longfellow is delightful, and a most kind friend. Mrs. Howe,[44] and a beautiful Miss Allston of S. Carolina I also talked to for some time, also Eliot Norton[45] who delights in John Kenyon, and Mrs. Longfellow.

This morning Tom Appleton has called, offering to take us to Laura Bridgman,[46] Mr. W. Appleton[47] with

40. Probably these lines of Thomas Moore:

> Away to the Dismal Swamp he speeds—
>   His path was rugged and sore,
> Through tangled juniper, beds of reeds,
> Through many a fen, where the serpent feeds,
>   And man never trod before.

("A Ballad, The Lake of the Dismal Swamp"). Longfellow had published his own poem "The Slave in the Dismal Swamp" in 1842.

41. François Ferdinand Philippe Louis Marie d'Orleans, prince de Joinville (1818-1900), French admiral.

42. Poe's child-wife, Virginia, died in 1847; the poem appeared posthumously in the New York *Tribune* (1849).

43. Probably Hawthorne's "The Ambitious Guest," based on a true story of the Samuel Willey family, who were buried by an avalanche in the White Mountains in 1826. Longfellow reviewed his old classmate's *Twice-Told Tales* (1837), where the story appeared.

44. Julia Ward Howe (1819-1910), poet, abolitionist, and wife of Samuel Gridley Howe.

45. Charles Eliot Norton (1827-1908), at this time (like Bright) a merchant who had stronger ties to literature than to commerce. Later he became professor of the history of art at Harvard.

46. Laura Dewey Bridgman (1829-89), blind deaf-mute educated by Dr. Howe at the Perkins Institute. Dickens related her extraordinary story at length in *American Notes*.

invites for the Baring dinner[48] to-night, Mr. Minot[49] with an invitation for Saturday, and Mildmay[50] with a chat about the West and the news that Synge is with his "ladye love" at the Lothrop's,[51] and lastly Synge himself who hurried me off to get a glimpse of "she" and introduce me to old Lothrop himself.

In the afternoon, B[urder] and myself drove over again to Cambridge to see the President Sparks[52] and the college. He received us very kindly, and made me a present of some pamphlets about the University. He's a pleasant-looking person and talks nicely. English books on Political Economy are useless with them in great measure from the large space they devote to Rent (all but unknown in America); they have tried Say and Mill[53] however, but now a book on the subject by an American has come out.

The Library, &c. rather disappointed me.[54] They have a nice Hall for public days[55] with pictures of illustrious Bostonians, any number of Winthrops for instance.

We got back just in time for Everett who had come for us to take us to the dinner. He talked to us about a

47. Perhaps William Appleton, son of Nathan Appleton's brother Joseph.

48. In honor of Thomas Baring (1799–1873), partner of the London banking house.

49. William Minot, Jr. (1817–94), wealthy Boston lawyer, married to a niece of Catharine Maria Sedgwick.

50. One of the brothers mentioned on p. 77.

51. Samuel K. Lothrop (1804–86), minister of the Brattle Street Church (Boston's largest and most fashionable Unitarian church), 1834–76.

52. Jared Sparks (1789–1866), American historian and editor of Washington's manuscripts; president of Harvard, 1849–53.

53. Jean Baptiste Say (1767–1832) and John Stuart Mill (1806–73), authors of numerous works on political economy.

54. The library was housed in Gore Hall (built in 1841), a granite imitation of King's College Chapel; at this time it numbered about 56,000 volumes.

55. University Hall (1815), designed by Charles Bulfinch.

Mr. Downing who had been a person of consequence at Cambridge here, and whose descendant founded Downing College in Cambridge in our country.[56]

The Revere House was full of illustrious people, and Everett introduced us to a considerable number, but I was not particularly fascinated by any one I saw, and was glad to get next Synge at dinner who introduced me to one of the Lawrences[57] on his other hand. Synge was very agreeable, and the whole dinner passed off pleasantly enough, many of the speeches were good, Everett's of course the best, though I think he disappointed me a little; his manner repelled enthusiasm, and indeed how could he be enthusiastic on such a subject,—"Honour to the Rich" being the virtual toast,—and a well buttered one, too,—of the evening. It was humiliating when you thought of it, to hear such praises of Capital and Money and Wealth from one like Everett, and the gloss of saying that they fêted Mr. Baring, not as being rich but as being honourable, made the matter worse. "Would they fête an honourable bankrupt?" muttered Synge indignantly. Only two things struck me in the whole number of speeches, one, a joke of one of the Lawrences, "things must indeed be in a bad way when they are beyong Baring," and a clever antithetical sentence of Everett about the American War,—"There was war upon the land, there was war upon the sea: there was profound peace in that office in Bishopsgate."[58]

After dinner, B[urder], S[ynge] and myself jumped into a carriage and got to Eliot Norton's about ten, I

56. Sir George Downing (?1623–84), second graduate of Harvard College, soldier, and politician; and his grandson, Sir George Downing (?1684–1749), founder of Downing College.

57. There were four Lawrence brothers, all well-to-do Boston merchants: Abbott, Amos, Samuel, and William. Bright says a "James Lawrence" later gives him a letter of introduction when he visits Lowell.

58. I.e., the head office of Baring Brothers.

suppose. He was having a club supper, and I found myself capitally placed between him and Prof. Agassiz.[59] Felton[60] was there, and Tom Appleton, and Davis, and Longfellow and Pringle, an S. C[arolina] man who's written a clever anti-abolitionist book.[61]

Agassiz expressed much admiration of Sedgwick, who is not very prominent, but not the less exceedingly clever.[62] We talked about Unitarianism, and E[liot] Norton told a story of Chas. Sumner in England sitting next a clergyman who offered to introduce him to the Archbishop of Canterbury, but unfortunately let out he should be uncomfortable even at sitting next a Uni. Charles Sumner lost his presence of mind and didn't tell him what he was, but of course did *not* keep his engagement. "Did not tell him?" said Agassiz with foreign accent, "ah! that was bad! I should have said, don't you feel the Devil at your shoulder now?" "That feeling of bigotry wouldn't do here," said Norton, *"we're all Unitarians."*

We talked of Dickens; everyone was loud in his abuse of the "American Notes," and Agassiz remarked that the mere picking out the bad was not worthy of him. I vindicated him, and assured Agassiz that except his anti-slavery violence, his falsely exaggerated language about the Mississippi, and his mistaken facts as regards the Penitentiary system at Philadelphia, I thought the book capital.[63]

59. Jean Louis Rodolphe Agassiz (1807–73), Swiss-born scientist, professor of natural history at Harvard since 1848.

60. Cornelius Conway Felton (1807–62), professor of Greek at Harvard.

61. Edward J. Pringle had published his anonymous pamphlet *Slavery in the Southern States* only a month earlier, in Cambridge. It was an attack on *Uncle Tom's Cabin*, written in answer to a Boston friend who had asked what southerners thought of the book.

62. Catharine Maria Sedgwick's genial brother Charles (1791–1856), clerk of the courts of Berkshire.

63. In *American Notes* Dickens devoted an eloquent chapter to the evils of slavery; he called the Mississippi "an enormous ditch, some-

Tremenheere's book they also abused, but praised Lyell and De Tocqueville.[64]

Agassiz says I should not judge from first impressions; I assured him I thought them most valuable. "I wrote down," he replied, "what I first thought of America when I arrived here, and I read my notes over the other day, and I can't tell you how they amused me; and yet, if I now praise America I'm not prejudiced because I'm not even an American citizen having always refused to be naturalized."

I could only say I was not convinced, for this reason—when you first arrive at a place, you judge it by comparison with the place whence you come: thus, you say the Americans chew, and spit, and the common people are presuming and familiar, and though after you've been in the country some time, and get familiar with these things you don't care about them, and hardly notice them, and think strangers talk in an exaggerated way about them, yet it was your first impression which was the real true one, for *relatively* —when compared with your own nation—they do chew, and spit, and so forth. So a traveller at Niagara can judge better of the waters' roar than he in whose ears it has sounded so long that he never hears it [at] all.

Agassiz called himself "a sad Pagan," and said he had never been to a political meeting in his life, not caring for such things.

He's a fat, good-natured man with a foreign accent and look about him.

times two or three miles wide, running liquid mud"; and he expatiated on the cruel effects of solitary confinement in the Philadelphia penitentiary (see p. 110).

64. Tremenheere's book, though full of praise for Canada, found fault with much in America, particularly the educational system. Lyell published *Travels in North America* in 1845 and *A Second Visit to the United States* in 1849. Alexis de Tocqueville's celebrated *Democracy in America* appeared in 1835-40.

Longfellow talked chiefly to Synge, and (S. told me) thanked him for introducing us.

Tom Appleton discussed various things with Burder, and Norton, Pringle and myself talked <Christian> Socialism among the rest.

We got home between one and two, after a delightful evening.[65]

Saturday Morning, [September 25].[66]

On Thursday at twelve we three started for Concord to see Emerson and Hawthorne.[67] We got there in about an hour. It was a beautiful day, and I felt in particular good spirits and health. It was a bright early Autumn day, a light fresh wind played among the trees and blew away a leaf here and there, and reddened the tints on the maples and the oaks, as we walked along the broad lanes of Concord. Like an English village is the Concord of Massachusetts and of Emerson. Huge trees stand singly out between the footpath and the road, and most of all the drooping

65. Bright reminisced about this supper in a letter to Norton nine years later: "I remember . . . a supper at your house and Longfellow the life of the party,—so kind and genial. . . . I remember a friend of yours, a South Carolinian (Mr. Pringle, was he not?) was present,—and I remember the kindly way in which *then* the South was spoken of" (letter of Sept. 7, 1861, in Harvard College Library).

66. In a letter to his friend Robert Temple, Bright described his visit to Concord, repeating many of the details given here. See William Sherman, "Henry Bright in New England: His First Meeting with Hawthorne," *New England Quarterly* 46 (March, 1973): 124-26.

67. Longfellow supplied a letter of introduction to Hawthorne: "I write you this 'Scarlet Letter,' [the stationer's device was red] in order to present two readers and admirers of your books, Mr. Bright and Mr. Burder, of Liverpool and London, who go to Concord expressly to see you and Emerson. . . . I am sure my young friends from England will find a door and a welcome" (*The Letters of Henry Wadsworth Longfellow*, ed. Andrew Hilen, 3 [Cambridge, Mass., 1972]: 355-56).

elms bend over us as we pass. White houses with gardens before them are on each side of the way. A little girl with straw hat and clever face, and school book under her arm is standing on our track, and we ask her where Emerson is living. "Watch," she replied, "keep down the road and past the meeting house, and when you've turned to the right you'll see his house amidst a grove of pines."

There it is! the door is standing wide open, and the girl who answers our bell shows us into his study. The study is surrounded with well-filled and badly arranged book-cases, the table is covered with well read and badly bound books. Over the chimney-piece is a picture of the Three Fates, in an open drawer is a collection of ripening pears.

But here is Emerson;—a tall, thin, angular figure, with quiet gentlemanly manner, unaffected look and pleasant voice. He's by no means awful or incomprehensible. He talked to Synge about International Copyright,[68] he talked to me of Martineau, and the Westminster, and attributed the articles on American Literature to Dr. Griswold.[69] We walked in his garden with him; he is interested in pear-trees and pumpkins, and told us of one of the early settlers who asserted that "in America God Almighty feeds His people with pumpkins."

He took us to see Hawthorne, and as we went along, talked pleasantly all the way. Hawthorne's house is an

68. At Synge's request, Emerson had drawn up a petition, signed by prominent local writers, urging protection for British authors, who received no payment for their works published in America. Dickens, among others, lobbied vehemently for International Copyright, but Congress did not reach an agreement until 1891.

69. The *Westminster Review* (under the new editorship of John Chapman) initiated in January, 1852, a series of articles on "Contemporary Literature of America," parts of which were indeed written by Rufus Wilmot Griswold (1815–57), whose anthologies of American literature were widely valued.

old one—100 years old—and a hill rises pleasantly behind it. Hawthorne leads an almost hermit life; he's a
strange man, so shy and retiring that he is rarely seen,
and hardly speaks when he is seen. He is so gentle
and mild that you feel as if speaking to a girl, said
Emerson, when speaking to him. "Yet there is a pang
of bitterness which is most plainly visible in everything
he writes. Sometimes too, he comes out with truths
which show so great a worldly knowledge, that involuntarily you say, where did the man learn all this."

Here however is Hawthorne—a man with an eye so
black and piercing you shrink away as he fixes it
steadily upon you, with a brow so grand and massive,
that had you not seen Webster you'd say it was the
most wonderful you ever saw; yet with awkward gait
and manner, and a shyness which oppresses you as
much as himself, yet he asks us in, and talks slightly
in answer to questions and so forth. Emerson does
most of the conversation, and we go deeply into the
mysteries of the heathen and Christian Socialism.[70]
When we rise to go, Hawthorne promises Emerson to
join us at dinner at four, and we bid him goodbye.
E[merson] and B[urder] had already left the garden
when the hermit novelist asked us to come and see his
view from the hill, and an old summer-house built by
a man called Alcott, a man Longfellow told me of, as
Emerson's "Skimpole Plato,"[71] and the man whom
Carlyle abused to Tom Appleton, (he (Alcott) is a vege-
tarian it seems.) "The man came here with his potatoe
gospel, and at last I said to him, 'Sir, I'd rather talk

70. Bright promised to send Emerson copies of the *Christian Socialist*
on his return to England; but the journal expired while he was in America,
and he could only send some back numbers.

71. Amos Bronson Alcott (1799–1888), Transcendentalist and educational theorist. The sobriquet was Fanny Longfellow's—a glance at Harold
Skimpole in *Bleak House* (just then being published), who disguises his
selfishness under an assumption of childish irresponsibility.

to any old woman, or child, or lunatic, or donkey than to you, let us never meet again,' and he replied, 'Mr. Carlyle, you've exactly expressed my sentiments with regard to you.' And so we parted."[72]

Back to the arbour in Hawthorne's garden. It is now tumbling to decay, but he seems very fond of it, and told us he would not have it touched. It commands a good view, and from the hill top is a better view still. Hawthorne tells me he likes it better than his view at Lenox—"that mountain scenery was stereotyped in my mind, this never wearies me." He spoke of England, and how he longed to see it, and how deeply he and all New Englanders felt towards it. The asters were growing all over the hill top, and reminded me of my favourite lines in Emerson.[73]

When we got back we found a scientific gent, a Mr. Hunt from Montreal[74] waiting to see Emerson—they got very deep as we perambulated the garden and lin-

---

72. Carlyle wrote to Emerson, August 29, 1842: "The good Alcott and I have prospered, I am afraid, almost as ill as it was possible for two honest men kindly affected towards one another to do. . . . When we two came to part, [he] answered my, 'When shall I see you again?' by a solemn 'Never, I guess!' It was really too ridiculous. . . . I wish you would tell this good man that my whole heart is kindly affected to him; that I do esteem his Potatoe-gospel a mere imbecillity which *cannot* be discussed in this busy world at this time of day;—but that he ought really to come back to me!" (*The Correspondence of Emerson and Carlyle*, pp. 329–30).

73. From "The Apology":

> Chide me not, laborious band,
>   For the idle flowers I brought;
> Every aster in my hand
>   Goes home loaded with a thought.

Cf. a letter from Bright to Hawthorne, Sept. 8, 1860: " . . . Possibly all England looks by this time nothing but mistland, and you believe only in Concord and its white houses, and the asters on the hill behind your house, and the pumpkins in the valley below" (Lathrop, *Memories of Hawthorne*, p. 464).

74. Possibly Thomas Sterry Hunt (1826–92), geologist and chemist, on the staff of the Geological Survey of Canada.

From *Homes of American Authors*, 1853

gered in *Emerson's* arbour, the prettiest I ever saw, and invented by Mr. Alcott who "starting one morning in aspiration worthy of Michael Angelo went into the woods and cut down trees and built it." Hunt and Emerson certainly did get deep, and we heard for the first time in our lives that "a gas is a vacuum for every other gas," as intelligible, T. Appleton said when we told him, as if "a vacuum were a gas to every other vacuum."

Hawthorne arrived, and seemed in decent spirits and all right. Unluckily, a moment or two before dinner Emerson maliciously said "I hear Hawthorne that Miss Bremer makes honourable mention of you." "Where?" asked Hawthorne; Emerson appealed to Burder who had mentioned to Emerson the story I had told him about Miss Bremer: Burder threw the onus of it all on me, and I had to blurt out that I didn't know that anything was printed, Miss B. had mentioned Mr. H. in private conversation. "My interview with Miss Bremer was not a very successful one," said Hawthorne,[75] and, dinner being announced, he said he

75. Frederika Bremer had spent an evening (Sept., 1850) trying unsuccessfully to engage Hawthorne in conversation; her accent (so Hawthorne wrote later) prevented him from understanding what she was

could not stay, and vanished, to my annoyance and Emerson's amusement.

Before dismissing Hawthorne, I must mention his children,—a long-haired red-haired Una, and a beautiful glorious boy called Julian.[76] Hawthorne is a democrat and will be promoted by his friend Pierce, perhaps (as T. Appleton says) "as Minister to some aesthetic Court."[77]

At dinner we were introduced to Mrs. Emerson, "a < > -acting woman," Synge calls her; a woman always nagging at her husband is Burder's expression. She believes in Rapping, though the spirits told her all wrong, a point on which Emerson is sceptical, and justly so. By the way, the scientific credulous ones say it's done by electricity, but I've been thinking this over, and proved last night to my own and Mrs. Squire's satisfaction that this is absurd. These raps, &c. may doubtless be produced by electricity, but it's not the mere rapping, but the way these rappings answer questions and so forth which is the curious point.

Now the believer is reduced to this dilemma by the sceptic:—granted that raps come by electricity, since questions are answered and revelations made by the raps, these questions and revelations are due to electricity. But if so, electricity must have a mind, and sense to make these answers, &c., i.e. electricity must be an intelligence; or if they say electricity is only the agent of an intelligence, I say then *that* intelligence must necessarily exist either in the spirit or in the flesh. If in the spirit, you allow of spiritual agency,

saying. Her account of the interview did not appear in print until 1853, but Bright probably picked up some gossip, perhaps from Longfellow.

76. Una was 8 at this time, Julian 6, Rose a baby of 16 months.

77. Hawthorne's campaign biography of Franklin Pierce had just appeared; his appointment as consul to Liverpool was confirmed the following March.

and then there is no occasion for your scientific theory of electricity, you gain nothing by it, and are as
credulous as the silliest of them. Or, if you believe
that the mind of the *medium* directs the electricity,
then he, who all the while pretends a spirit to be at
work, and to have no hand himself in these rappings,
then he is a charlatan and a knave, and the revelations
are the work of his own brain.

Believe in this flimsy science notion, and you believe
either that electricity has a mind, or that spirits are
at work, or that the medium is deceiving you. Which
will you have? At the same time, T. Appleton, the
Longfellows, and the Squires have all witnessed what
is incomprehensible and uncanny. But I have still
much to say of Emerson. He spoke of "that wicked
Carlyle with his musket worship,"[78] of Rogers, on
whom all the good jokes are fathered as once on Sydney Smith, &c.[79]

He spoke of the Blithedale Romance, and the truths
contained in it, and how in the real Brook Farm, Labour, Capital, and Intellect received the same wages,
"the ploughman and he who sketched him from the
window being treated alike."[80] A girl was really
drowned, but a commonplace person unlike Zeno-
bia.[81]

78. Emerson might have been thinking of a recent letter (June 25,
1852) from Carlyle, who was then reading (not yet writing) about Frederick
the Great: "I confess also to a real love for F[rederick]'s dumb followers:
the Prussian *soldiery*—I often say to myself, 'Were not *here* the real
priests and virtuous martyrs of that loud-babbling rotten generation!'"
(*The Correspondence of Emerson and Carlyle*, p. 484).

79. Samuel Rogers (1763-1855), celebrated for his table-talk, as was
the witty Sydney Smith.

80. George Ripley, inviting Emerson to join the cooperative community
near West Roxbury, wrote that his aim was "to insure a more natural
union between intellectual and manual labor than now exists." Hawthorne was a member of Brook Farm from April to November, 1841.

81. This was Martha Hunt, a schoolmistress and daughter of a poor
Concord farmer. Hawthorne was roused in the middle of the night (July

Emerson told us a story of Everett and his daughter (Mrs. Wise) calling to see Miss Bremer. She had somehow taken a prejudice against him, and as he talked, she went on knitting and silent. Subject after subject was tried, row after row was finished, and at last poor Everett gave up the task, baulked entirely by the Swedish lady. Emerson says Clough is going to stay with him and find some work to do at Harvard; he, Emerson, was with him at Paris,[82] but he never suspected that he was a poet, his "Bothie" was the fusion of thought caused by reading "Evangeline" and Homer.

We left Emerson's by train at about seven.

We went for an hour on our return to see Julia Bennett as Rosalind in "As You Like It."

Yesterday the Squires spent with us, we went to Faneuil Hall and Mt. Auburn, where we saw Channing's and Tuckerman's graves.[83] Also to Mr. Waterston's Church, which is beautiful Gothic,[84] with a chapel within the building for prayer-meetings, &c. Mr. Squire tells me that the Unitarians are divided into Conservative and Evangelical Unis, the latter being Huntington and Coolidge chiefly.[85] I made S[quire] take $10 for South Boston congregation.[86]

9, 1845) to help find her drowned body—an event he recollected in the novel.

82. Emerson had urged Clough (1819-61) to come to America with the promise of "unlimited opportunities of employment"; in the event, Clough tutored only a handful of students during his stay in Cambridge (November, 1852, to June, 1853).

83. William Ellery Channing's tomb was designed by Washington Allston, the inscription written by George Ticknor. Joseph Tuckerman (1778-1840) was another influential Unitarian minister and philanthropist.

84. Robert C. Waterston's church was the Church of the Saviour, a handsome stone building on Bedford Street.

85. Huntington's preaching had impressed Bright in New York (see p. 73). James I. T. Coolidge was minister of the Thirteenth Congregational Church, 1842-58.

86. A year later Burder wrote to Bright about Mr. Squire: "I shall never forget that excellent man, wrapped in a plaid, serenely sick, and ever evangelical" (letter of May 23, [1853] at Trinity College, Cambridge).

After a capital dinner we gave them at our Hotel, we drove off to Lothrop's. He is a fat merry fellow, Mrs. L. a good-natured agreeable woman, whose "crutch makes music at every step," as Emerson told Synge. The daughter is piquante and pretty. Some sons of Mr. Peabody's were there and sang nigger songs, &c. very cleverly; Synge gave the "Shan Van Vogh"[87] with much enthusiasm, and the evening was very pleasant and successful, and I only refrain from saying more about it, because my arm aches with writing.

Sunday Morning, [September 26].

Yesterday in the morning we received visits from our dearest Boston friends, Dr. Gannett and Longfellow. Longfellow was much amused about Hawthorne, and made us promise to come and spend an evening with him at Cambridge. Dr. Gannett told us that Emerson's party is very small, that the Dial[88] died prematurely away, that Emerson himself sits at the feet of Alcott, thereby at least evincing his humility, as no one else thinks much of this friend of his. Alcott wrote in the Dial himself; he has theories about the angelic nature of children, and leads a queer dreaming life; the building a summer-house being the most practical thing the good Dr. ever heard of him doing.

At two o'clock Mr. Minot called to take us to his country place, some six miles off on the Providence

87. "Shan van Vocht" ("the little old woman"), an Irish revolutionary song of 1798.

88. The organ of the Transcendentalist movement. Edited by Margaret Fuller and then by Emerson, it lasted from July, 1840, to April, 1844.

railway.[89] It is prettily situated in a fir plantation of 16 acres, and here live a colony—Mr. Minot, his brother and his father. Mrs. Minot is a particularly nice person, a Sedgwick of Lenox, niece of *the* Catharine. Here I saw a portrait of a bag-wigged ancestor Minot, a thing I've not seen in America.

The brother and a Mr. Parker were there, and we had a very pleasant party, but do not think I gained any great amount of information worth noting down. The Sedgwicks are great Mrs. Butlerites, and Mrs. M. told me that Mr. B[utler] was a horrid man, but that she (the wife) bore with his infidelity and everything else till he took her children from her.[90] Mr. Parker told me that Charles Sumner is intensely vain, and that he is quite out of Boston society, Longfellow being his only friend *now*. The chief Boston families I learn from Parker are the Eliots (Mrs. Ticknor was one), the Appletons, and the Lawrences. Dr. Putnam[91] is the most eloquent Uni. Minister in Boston, Dr. Walker[92] is very good, Mr. Huntington is a rising fellow.

We left the Minots rather early as we wished to go to a concert given by a Mr. Dempster,[93] but it was atrociously bad, and we came away again very soon, giving me a good quiet evening for letter-writing and

89. The Minots lived at Woodbourne, a large country house in West Roxbury.

90. After the divorce, Butler retained custody of Fanny Kemble's two daughters. Kate Sedgwick Minot was one of Fanny's dearest friends.

91. George Putnam, minister of the First Church in Roxbury, 1830–76.

92. James Walker (1794–1874), at this time professor of religion at Harvard, later its president (1853–60).

93. William R. Dempster earned his reputation as a ballad singer in New York City.

so forth, besides a half hour at the Athenaeum where I saw the Chronicle Review of Fane's poems.[94]

Monday night, [September 27].

Yesterday Burder went to Theodore Parker, and I, after wandering about found myself at 1st Church, only, I'm ashamed to say, a short time before the sermon began. The Minister was some stranger and his sermon was not striking, but the Church is trebly interesting, as the oldest Church in Boston, as the Church Mr. Prescott attends, and as the Church in which and on which Sprague wrote his beautiful "Winged Worshippers."[95] In the afternoon we went to hear Father Taylor.[96] Charles Norton took us, and I certainly never heard a more splendid discourse than the old man delivered. A sailor who "received a call," he turned preacher in this Methodist Church, and the good he does is incalculable. Much that he said was very fine indeed; his description (a cut at *us*) of the man who says "he's free will" and that "God is good," trusting to this and leading a wicked life. "He's been going down the stream so long that even if he now tries to make head against it, his arm is feeble, and he still drifts down, and he hears a scream of terror from

94. Julian Henry Charles Fane (1827-70), whose *Poems* had just been published, had been at Trinity College with Bright.

95. "The Winged Worshippers. Addressed to two swallows that flew into Chauncey Place Church during divine service" by Charles Sprague (1791–1875), Boston poet.

96. Edward Thompson Taylor (1793–1871), minister of the Seamen's Bethel, whose extraordinary pulpit manner was described by Dickens in *American Notes* (probably the incentive for HAB's account) and reproduced by Melville in Father Mapple's sermon (*Moby-Dick*, chap. 9).

405

FATHER TAYLOR, CA. 1870

Harper's Weekly, May 6, 1871

the shore—'the rapids!' Yes, he's in the rapids now. How much for his free-agency? He has it still—free-agency in the Rapids it is now! O yes, the will is very powerful, and there's something of omnipotence in that arm of his, but somehow it seems useless now—he's in the Rapids—and he's driving down them, lulling himself with the thought that God is good even in the Rapids. Yes, God is good, but the time is past when he who repeats this cry could experience that goodness; he must go now the way he has chosen, he's borne away, and now only Hell remains for him, and there he must go and there he will be kept, never to come back even for the spirit rappers!"

He spoke of the Apostles, "with only 12 feeble pairs of hands, yet lifting up the world with them, and giving it an offering to God." He spoke of the best periods for conversion as being between 12 and 15, and 20 and 25 years of age, and said that after 45 a conversion was very rare,—"the winter is too near." "You can't sow the seed of religion on a snow bed." He uses much gesticulation, now as of a rower, now a fiddler, and so forth. Over his head is a picture of ships at sea. He's an extraordinary fellow. Mr. Lothrop once preached for him, and used a *book*; this didn't do for his audience, so he threw it aside, and Father Taylor congratulated him:—"Now you'll preach." When he had finished, he said, "Well, you didn't preach,"—Mr. Lothrop looked uncomfortable, "no, you didn't preach, it was your Master who preached."

Norton told me this, and also told me some curious things of Dr. Channing; how he lost his influence by his anti-slavery line, and by his toleration of Parker's infidelity.[97] He was very egotistical in his sermon,

---

97. Norton's account is colored by his own conservative views: his father, Andrews Norton, the "Unitarian Pope," was the most outspoken

and having sent one to be printed, and complaining of delay, the printer explained that he had used all his large *I* types in the first half sermon, and was waiting to get more cast.

At 5½ we dined with Mr. Ticknor, his wife, two daughters and Norton: we had a good dinner and pleasant evening. Mr. T. has a beautiful library and some capital autographs of Luther, Ferdinand and Isabella, &c., and a whole play of Lope de Vega, a whole poem of Robert Southey.[98] He gave me several nice ones. He has known everybody, Buonapartes without end, Byron, Wordsworth, &c. &c., in short, everyone.

We stayed late, talking and looking at pictures and autographs. Mr. Parker, whom we met at the Minots, came in. A nice person, anxious to do anything for us.

To-day I saw Mr. Bishop, and had a long—chiefly slavery—conversation with him. I called on Mr. Winthrop[99] who was equally agreeable and courteous. T. Appleton tells me he exactly resembles his ancestor in face.

I've spent a little fortune in books and pictures; have spent one hour with Mrs. Longfellow, half an hour with Mrs. Grant (while Burder solaced to his heart's content). In short, I've spent a day of busy idleness, and it's tired me quite enough for a good night's sleep.

At Longfellow's (who was himself out) I saw an autograph letter of Laura Bridgman's to Mr. Longfellow, which Mrs. L. allowed me to copy.

opponent of Parker and the Transcendentalists. Channing's active anti-slavery stand began with his pamphlet *Slavery* (1835).

98. Ticknor gave his fabulous Spanish collection to the Boston Public Library, which he helped establish. The Lope de Vega play was probably *El castigo sin venganza*; the Southey manuscript, promised to Ticknor by the poet himself, was the unfinished "Oliver Newman."

99. Robert Charles Winthrop, descended from the first governor of Massachusetts Bay, was former representative and senator from Massachusetts (see p. 157).

From Justin Winsor, *The Memorial History of Boston*, Vol. III. 1881

My dear Sir,

I will address you. A very dear friend of mine, Mrs. Goodwin, was very kind, who gave me a book from which she read to me. I prize it so highly. I will always think of you when I touch the book which is copied by you. I am so much interested in thinking of Evangeline who devoted all her time in doing so very much good to the sick and afflicted during her life. I sympathize with her so far in her afflictions. I love her very dearly. She is so lovely and sweet. She is one of Christ's very dear sisters. I enjoyed myself very much in reading about Evangeline and her most benevolent duties.

I should love to meet her with my soul in Heaven, when I die on the earth.

From

Laura Bridgman.

Feb. 8th, 1852.

Longfellow sent her a *copy* of his book; she confounds the meaning of the <copy?> with that of the <manuscript?>

Tuesday Night, [September 28].

At twelve this morning Burder and myself started for Lowell, an hour's drive, and after a poor man's dinner started under the direction and guidance of the Hon. Linus Child "to see what we *should* see." We had a letter to him from James Lawrence through Mr. Parker.

He is agent to the Boott Mills, and gave us more useful information than I could easily write down or remember. In his mill he employs 1,000 girls and 2 or 3,000 men; the girls receive per week $2.25 when they begin, which is raised to $3 or 4.25, of this $1.25 goes to the mistress of the boarding-house where they are obliged to live, and where they experience a species of college discipline, dining together and having to be in by 10 every evening under threat of expulsion, and a girl expelled from one mill is never taken in by another. The girls generally come for 3 years and then marry or go back to their parents' houses; they would consider it a great degradation to go out as servants.

They are generally most moral, and out of 10,000 girls employed in Lowell, hardly 3 children will be born in the year. They work 12 hours a day, not including dinner-time.

Enough of statistics:—assaye[100] Sathanas!

There are some eight *rows* of brick boarding-houses belonging to the Boott Mills, and into two of these

100. Probably the typist's misreading of the Greek $(\upsilon\pi\alpha\gamma\epsilon)$ for "Begone" (Matthew IV.10).

410

The Boott Cotton Mills at Lowell, Massachusetts

Gleason's Pictorial Drawing-Room Companion, May 29, 1852

"Remarkable only for its size, cleanliness, and the clean, pleasant, well-to-do look of the girls at work there."

houses Mr. Child took us. One was entirely for women; on the ground floor was a common parlour, above were rooms with double beds: a room for two was called par excellence "a bed room," one for four, having two beds, our informant said was "a square room." In the next house, there was a part set aside for men, and these were explored. I asked "Did the men and women dine together?" "No," replied the landlady, "the ladies dine in one room, the gentlemen in another." In the men's rooms we saw a harp, and a fiddle, a Dombey & Son, an Uncle Tom, and many other books, generally religious, such as Barnes on the Acts.[101]

They are generally orthodox Methodists or Congregationalists, perhaps not more than 20 Unis among them, and our two congregations at Lowell are entirely supported by the professional men and merchants who have come from Boston. This I learnt from a Mr.

101. Albert Barnes, *Notes, Explanatory and Practical, on the Acts* (1841).

411

Miles, our Minister,[102] and an excellent person to whom Dr. Gannett gave us a letter and whom we saw after *doing* the Mill—a cotton mill, remarkable only for its size, cleanliness, and the clean, pleasant, well-to-do-look of the girls at work there. There are 10,000 out of 35,000 Irish at Lowell, and the Irish often apply for work there, but the supply is barely equal to the demand.

The Lowell Offering[103] originated in a sort of L[ondon?] D[ebating?] S[ociety?] among the girls and some Minister; their I <articles?> then appeared in the papers, thence in a separate form. It died out though a year ago, non-contributing Lowellers grew jealous, encouraging Bostonians grew tired of it, and so it died.

We took tea at the Ticknors and went with them to see Anderson's conjuring tricks:[104] after feather beds had been pulled out of Mr. Ticknor's hat, and all the rest of it, we went back to a fruit supper and talk.

Miss Ticknor told me of a lady who was a medium and *rapped* sounds from a wood and marble table, moving it moreover to the edification of beholders, not to the opening of the eyes or benefit of the shins however of two sceptics, who having twirled their legs round table aforesaid, received several violent kicks—from the spirit, *of course!*

Mr. T. said that a negro had come to him for money to help him to free his wife; he told Mr. T. he did so for he had before helped him, and he might see from the list of names he brought that the case was a gen-

---

102. Henry Adolphus Miles (1809–95), Unitarian minister, author of a history of Lowell and several theological works.

103. In *American Notes* Dickens drew attention to this periodical, which contained original articles written exclusively by women employed in the mills.

104. Professor Anderson, "the Wizard of the North," was a Scotsman whose London debut in 1840 heralded an enormously successful career.

Gleason's Pictorial Drawing-Room Companion, September 25, 1852

uine one. "Why don't you apply to *these* men for money?" asked Mr. Ticknor, seeing Charles Sumner, Dr. Palfrey[105] and others on the list. "Ah, Sir," was the reply, "it isn't them that says Lord, Lord, that does the thing."

Lenox, Mass. Saturday Night, October 2.

On Wednesday morning we breakfasted with Dr. Howe.[106] He has a nice house in South Boston, and is

105. John Gorham Palfrey (1796–1881), Unitarian clergyman and former editor of the *North American Review*.

106. Samuel Gridley Howe (1801–76) organized the Massachusetts

413

a nice person, and peculiar as being the only man I've yet met who believes in Kossuth and T. Parker. Of Kossuth he says: "He is a noble, honest man, and unselfishly devoted to Hungary." Mrs. Howe is an agreeable person, fond of quoting French, and so *susceptible* that when Tom Appleton once tried to electrify (spirit rap) a table, the "virtue" went into *her* by mistake, and she jumped up and followed him round the room.

She is quite capable of talking transcendentalism, and assured me in answer to my story of Mrs. Hudson's dressing for a Duchess or a commoner, "I'd no notion the female element was so expansive," to which I answered, "Yes, very much so indeed."

Dr. Howe may literally sit under his own vine, as fruit-laden it hangs round the porch of his pretty house; his pears, &c. look delicious. He told me the meaning of speaking for Bunkum, i.e. speaking to your village and constituency in the Senate instead of to the Senate.[107] Bunkum was a Carolinian place.

He took us after breakfast to see the Idiot School, where some 40 children are trained to habits of order, and at least to some intelligence. It was a melancholy sight, these poor, poor children, and yet a touching one to see his kindness to them, and how they rush to meet him so gladly, they all know him, and "Howe," "Dr. Howe" came lisping out from their scarcely-articulating tongue.

The Blind Asylum is beautifully situated, and still more gloriously arranged. In one room we heard them sing, in another we heard them asked questions in geography, in a third, in arithmetic.

School for the Blind in 1831 and the Massachusetts School for Idiotic and Feeble-Minded Youth in 1848.

107. The phrase originated during the debate on the Missouri question in 1820, when a congressman insisted on making a speech for his county of Buncombe, North Carolina.

Gleason's Pictorial Drawing-Room Companion, July 24, 1852

"Beautifully situated, and still more gloriously arranged."

Girls of 14 or 15 were sitting on benches and answering questions in algebra on their slates with moveable types of an oblong cube shape, the ends of which fit into little cells in the honeycombed surface of the slate. There were only two types, one (as represented) forming or representing according to the position of the raised stamps in each end, eight differing digits; the other, denotes the remaining two. These girls did their sums with surprizing speed, and they were sums quite as hard as we accomplish for a Cambridge Degree.

(What is Square Root of 1444?)

(Two Nos: as 5 : 4 have the difference of their 2nd powers 9. Find Nos.)

(Find two Nos: whose sum is to the less as 15 : 4, and whose sum x by the less = 135?)

Laura Bridgman we also saw, and the wonderful way in which she talks upon her fingers. She is disappoint-

415

ing looking, but was unwell when we saw her, complaining of cold and fearful of consumption. She wrote for me, and shook hands with me, saying "my hand was like a lady's, so delicate!" She is now 23 years of age!

Dr. Howe tells us that smallness in head is no sign of idiocy, *they* generally have large heads; a small head of fine texture of hair is often the best in every way. He told us how ignorant the blind are of what seem to us ordinary things;—a girl believing a hen to have four legs, for example.

At half past two we left for Milton Hill, the Lothrops; dined there, teaed there, and came away after a very pleasant evening. Miss L. is very agreeable, Mrs. lively, the gentleman amusing and with much information, though I don't approve of a Minister going to and talking of Baron Nicholson's at London.[108] He was at Cambridge with the Freshfields whom they picked up abroad.

Unitarianism, he tells me, received a great blow from Theo. Parker, and from the secular feeling which the absence of a clergyman at the head of Harvard since Dr. Kirkland, has given birth to.[109] Webster is still a Uni; that is, he sends for Lothrop on important occasions; he has much religious feeling, and when his son died 4 years since, he sent for his pastor.[110] "I now feel,

108. Renton Nicholson (1809-61), known as "Lord Chief Baron," edited a society journal and a sporting paper, and presided over mock trials at the "Garrick's Head."

109. John T. Kirkland (1770-1840) was a much-beloved president, whose era at Harvard (1810–28) was nostalgically dubbed the "Augustan Age." He was succeeded by the more business-like Josiah Quincy (1829–45), the first layman in that office in over a hundred years. Edward Everett (1846–49) and Jared Sparks (1849–53) were both Unitarian clergymen; but Everett's interests were mainly political, Sparks's historical.

110. Dr. Lothrop conducted the religious service for Major Edward Webster, who died in the Mexican-American war, January 23, 1848.

Dr. Lothrop, how worthless are power and glory, and pomp, and everything, except the religion of Jesus. When I am gone, I would wish, if it did not seem to my friends to savour of vanity and presumptuous pride, I wish them to be on my tomb—only these words —'a believer in the religion of Jesus.' "

Dr. Lothrop told me that the passing of slaves from State to State was *the* great evil, and that it may be doubted whether it is even legal. A slave is a slave in his own State, he is not necessarily so in another!

The Lothrops made us promise to write, &c.[111]

On Friday morning we went round the High Schools with Lothrop and heard the boys catechized in algebra, geography, and French, they certainly get a glorious education and—gratis.

We dined with Longfellow. His sister Mrs. M'Intosh, a daughter-in-law to Sir James, was there, and seemed a very nice person.[112] Longfellow himself charming as ever, hearty and affectionate, and sorry to part with us.[113]

We talked of Cambridge, and Mrs. L. and I looked over a book of plates of the old place together. Longfellow quoted curious old poems, one of which talks of Death's "envious casque" hitting a man. He had a capital little dinner, good hock, and Spanish wine from Spain's eastern coasts. He wants some English milk

111. Bright wrote to Hawthorne, Sept. 8, 1859: "Dr. Lothrop was over here [Liverpool] the other day.—I didn't like him quite so well as I fancied I remembered liking him.—He is,—well, never mind what he is;—I don't like being censorious on paper,—and he was certainly very kind to me, and his daughter is certainly very beautiful" (letter in Berg Collection, New York Public Library, printed (with minor variants) in *Nathaniel Hawthorne and His Wife*, 2:229–30.

112. Mary Appleton (Mrs. Longfellow's sister) married Robert James Mackintosh, whose father, Sir James Mackintosh (1765–1832) was a celebrated philosopher.

113. Longfellow wrote in his journal: "At dinner we have Mr. Bright and Mr. Burder, who makes themselves very agreeable. They are off tomorrow, homeward bound" (MS journal in Harvard College Library).

punch sent him.[114] He spoke of Richard Rathbone's "ardent letters" to Charles Sumner.[115] He told us of frightening a lady by invoking the statue on Cologne Bridge, as did Don Giovanni, to supper. He told us how in going into Mr. Fox's[116] chapel at Finsbury he heard them singing his own "Psalm of life." He composes music for his pieces, he tells me, walking by himself on the sea shore, but never writes it down.

He admires the Portuguese Sonnets, and the "Lady Geraldine" most of Mrs. Browning's poems. Mrs. L. told me the latter was written at the last moment to fill up the volume.[117] He told us of a black preacher who after various efforts to excite his audience, stood on his head and clapped his feet together.

We passed the evening with the Grants, the Winthrops, and the Ticknors. Taking the Winthrops first; he is a perfect gentleman, and his wife is quite a pleasing person. We discussed great living men, young Stanley (now Lord Derby), who, it seems, stammers, &c. &c.[118] He gave us some fine grapes,—"should the Liquor Law continue, we must soon ask our friends to take a grape with us." The Ticknors were most civil.

114. Bright obliged. Clough, newly arrived in Boston, writes on Nov. 27, 1852, of a feast at Longfellow's: "We had quite an English dinner— he had just received a present of grouse, pheasants, and milk punch (!) from some one whom he had been civil to, and issued immediately his invitations: Norton, Felton, Lowell, and me" (*The Correspondence of Arthur Hugh Clough* 2:338).

115. Richard Rathbone was so impressed by Sumner's oration "The True Grandeur of Nations" (1845) that he arranged for the Peace Society of Liverpool to publish and circulate an abridgment of it.

116. William Johnson Fox (1786-1864) was disowned by the Unitarians because of his marital difficulties and independent views, but continued much in vogue as a preacher.

117. True. Mrs. Browning wrote 140 lines of "Lady Geraldine's Courtship" in one day to fill up the first volume of *Poems* (1844).

118. Edward Henry Stanley, 15th earl of Derby (1826-93), later a distinguished politician, was at this time undersecretary for foreign affairs. His stammer did not keep him from becoming an impressive speaker.

"Can we do anything for you?" I asked. "Only come soon back again," was the old man's answer.[119] Everett had introduced Clay and Morris[120] to him.

At Winthrop's, by the way, we saw a beautiful picture of Webster taken in his up-gazing attitude on the Bunker's Hill festival.

Yesterday Charles Norton called three times to bid us goodbye; he is a capital fellow, and is really most kind.[121]

We dined at Dr. Gannett to meet the Squires and Mr. Bishop, and directly after dinner (at three) we left for the cars to Pittsfield, taking one glimpse at a beautiful picture of Channing which hangs in the old man's study.

We reached Pittsfield at 10½ and started this morning for Lenox where we sleep; our pleasant adventures I shall, and must, postpone.

NOTES ON BOSTON

The *tone* of Boston generally is a tone of calm respectability, a horror of "isms," cant or extremes of any sort; a dislike of transcendentalism, but a respect for intellect—chiefly of the practical kind. Talent is held in high esteem, genius, as savouring of eccentricity, in very little. Prescott and Ticknor are good

119. Nearly a quarter of a century later, reviewing Ticknor's biography, HAB reminisced about "one of the pleasantest of houses, one of the kindliest of hosts. . . . the street that faced the green elms on the Boston Common, the well-known door, the hospitable greeting" (*Athenaeum*, April 22, 1876, p. 562).

120. The Clay and Morris whom Bright saw in Canada (see p. 336).

121. Some months before his death, Bright wrote to Norton: "Only yesterday I was looking over old letters, and came across one,—such a kind one,—you wrote to me 31 years ago!—as I was leaving America" (letter of Sept. 5, 1883, in Harvard College Library).

specimens of Bostonians, certainly the latter, I speak it from knowledge, and Miss Sedgwick confirmed it. To have written a successful book, one which shows knowledge and reading, is a great feather in your cap in Boston, and this Ticknor has done. To have travelled in Europe and to correspond with illustrious Englishmen, this is another feather; to be benevolent and liberal, and to be rather moral than religious; to profess a Unitarianism which is only apparent by attendance at the fashionable church, and which entails no sacrifice and demands no asceticisms or long prayers, or difficult duties,—all this is requisite for a model Bostonian, and all this our friend Ticknor fulfils to the letter. Mr. Grant and maybe Mr. Minot are likewise true children of the modern Athens. The most conservative of men, staunch Whigs, orthodox Unitarians, courteous, well-educated and agreeable, they are only bitter at mention of abolitionists or Theodore Parker, or Emerson. The existence of the latter indeed, they affect to ignore "I met Emerson to-day," says Burder. "Which Emerson?" innocently asks the author of "Spanish Literature."

Their liberality about religion is truly edifying. *I* call it *liberality*, others might say (an they dared) indifference. They subscribe only to the *Unitarian* Association on condition that some of the funds go to Methodists and the like.[122] While in Washington, in England, it's often convenient to do as the Romans do, and Mr. Fillmore, and Mr. Lawrence[123] attend the Episcopal or the Scotch Church.

122. Cf. the observation of James Freeman Clarke, after some years' experience as secretary of the American Unitarian Association: "The Unitarian churches in Boston see no reason for diffusing their faith. They treat it as a luxury to be kept for themselves, as they keep Boston Common" (quoted in Cooke, *Unitarianism in America*, p. 160).

123. Abbott Lawrence (1792–1855), recently returned from three years as minister to the Court of St. James.

Still, I do admire much about the Bostonians extremely, and their real philanthropy is beyond all praise, while their love of literature and their respect for intellect raises them infinitely above the wealth-worshippers and Mammonites of New York.

There is also in Boston another set, or rather another class, for the best men in Boston form one set, and all know each other,—Dr. Howe, Longfellow, Tom Appleton and others are more liberal, more credulous, and more interesting than the stiff and orthodox: all these have abolition tendencies which are very *shocking*, and likewise make much of mesmerism, and talk of spirit-rapping scientifically, which is very extraordinary. Dr. Howe admires Parker and Kossuth, and is therefore only on the verge of respectability. Longfellow is intimate with Charles Sumner, and Mrs. L. calls him "a noble fellow," but everyone else in Boston has cut him, and Longfellow must be careful what he does. Tom Appleton mesmerises himself, but his family, and his wit, and his goodnature preserve him from losing caste in Boston, besides, he's travelled, and is well off, and a host of et ceteras which all count for something.

C. Eliot Norton evidently leans to the highly respectable, and talks pityingly of Dr. Channing's anti-slavery course; his connexion with Longfellow as club-mate may save him from this fate: Time will show. Parker of course no one knows but Dr. Howe. "Have you never heard him?" I ask Miss Ticknor. "Oh no, but you might; gentlemen can go where ladies can not." The depths of unfathomed respectability! The heights of Olympus high exalted "gigmanity" (to use Carlyle's word) which Mr. Everett possesses is really marvellous to contemplate.

Abolitionists in Boston are few, and not generally in the best set.

421

Transcendentalists fewer yearly. The Dial died an early death, and Emerson has never been able to establish a club in the City chiefly because folk fear being bored by Alcott.

Boston girls are well educated, read Latin and so forth, but are agreeable and not *blue*.

Longfellow has married twice; he proposed to his present wife (Miss Appleton) 6 months after his first wife's death, and she refused him for 7 years.[124]

124. Longfellow's first wife, Mary Storer Potter, died in 1835; he met Fanny Appleton the following summer and courted her until their marriage in 1843.

19

THE BERKSHIRES AND THE HUDSON RIVER VALLEY

Lebanon Springs.
Sunday Evening, October 3.

It was a beautiful morning when we left Pittsfield for Lenox, 6 miles distant, after yesterday's breakfast. The scenery of Berkshire,—the Switzerland of America they love to call it—the Lake District of America I should rather say—every view whenever the woods allow of one—is rich and varied, and lovely:—in every season this is a glorious country,—how much more so when the first autumn has taken nothing from the summer, but has touched the woods with its own bright scarlet, and yellow, and crimson, and brown,—and hill side and valley are clad in a garment "of many colours."

The oak and the maple are most gorgeous and you see freshest green, and richest red, both upon the branches of the same trees, while the dark pine, and many another tree mingle their boughs with them, and form the most exquisite studies of forest scenery that ever gladdened traveller's heart, or drove poor artist to despair. It was a perfect blending of summer and of autumn.

There was autumn in the tint which lay upon the woods. There was autumn in the sheaves of ripe Indian corn, and the orange pumpkins lying in the sun,—and there was autumn in the orchards bent with the weight of apples. But on the other hand there was summer in the warm clear sunshine,—there was summer in the roses which hung round the Sedgwicks' house, the loveliest of which Miss S. plucked for me, and most of all was there summer in the merry smile with which the kind old lady herself greeted us, already heralded by Mrs. Minot as Mr. Kenyon's friend. The house in which she lives is wooden, it commands a beautiful view and is curious as having been *moved* literally from the place where it stood before and which had no view at all:—literally in four months the house was moved, furniture and all, nearly a quarter of a mile.[1]

There is a large Sedgwick family, and complicated.[2] Miss Sedgwick and her brother Charles live at Lenox, others of the family live at New York, and Mrs. Sedgwick and three daughters from there were staying at Lenox at the time.—Others again are at Stockbridge. No wonder the puzzled Katydids repeat the name "Sedgwick, Sedgwick."[3]

Our interview with Miss Sedgwick was shortened by her having to drive with her sister[-in-law], but she made us promise to come to tea with them, and promised also that her brother should take us a drive. We agreed to stay and meanwhile went back to Pittsfield

1. It was in May, 1850, that Charles Sedgwick's house was moved from its cramped position in the village of Lenox to this hilltop. Miss Sedgwick occupied a wing of the house.

2. Catharine Maria and Charles were at this time the only survivors of a family of ten children; they had innumerable nephews and nieces.

3. Bright probably heard this from Longfellow, who recorded the remark in his journal (August 8, 1848).

for our "things," which we left at the little Inn at Lenox,—and then strolled out, being taken up before long by Mr. Sedgwick in his carriage with Miss Sedgwick herself, and Miss Lizzie,[4] a great friend of Mr. Kenyon, an intelligent, pleasant girl. We had a delightful drive past a house, the "Walker House" where Mrs. Kemble wished to live, near a house where she is going to live, by Hawthorne's house, and to a beautiful lake "Mountain Mirror," a sentimental name for which Miss S. half apologised telling me at the same time the Indian one (meaning "the Bowl,") which is certainly so hard to pronounce, that the romance-sounding appellative is quite excusable.[5] We were drawn by two good white horses one of which I was told had somewhat the spirit of his mistress, Mrs. Kemble, a little fiery, though the Sedgwicks' love of her is so intense that they can hardly bear to insinuate anything like a fault in one so perfect. Mr. Butler was, they say, in every way unsuited to her. Depraved, a slaveholder, cold, uneducated, he could never really agree with one so very opposite.

As we went along I was told a characteristic story of a Western man, who when Judge [Charles Sedgwick?] of Mass. was on the Mississippi was placed in the same cabin with him,—in the morning he got up and taking the Judge's watch-chain in his hand said admiringly, "Well now, I reckon this watch-chain is exactly like that of Jim Smith's, Judge, on my word it is." The Judge answered somewhat coldly, when the Western man, seeing it, said, "I say, Judge, reckon you'll like that ere cabin to yourself,—well, I don't mind it, I'll not mind sleeping outside the door," and he was as good as his word. On our return we had tea, and after

4. Elizabeth Ellery Sedgwick (1824–98), eldest daughter of Robert Sedgwick, later Mrs. Francis James Child.

5. The Indian name was Quecheeochook.

425

tea (with "food for angels" as Mrs. Jameson[6] called it, other folk, "tomato sweet-meats,") talk to any amount.

Here are a few notes of our conversation hastily put down.

Miss S. is a strong Unitarian and told me how, when in her European tour, while in a Channel steamer she shocked an Evangelical Lady, who asked her if the Unitarians had managed to creep into New York, by at once avowing herself.

Mr. Martineau's and Mr. *Fox's* writings she particularly admires. Dr. Dewey she thinks has been misunderstood, Dr. Channing was with her just before his death and read her [an?] unpublished sermon, when she (her eyes were weak) sat *shelling peas.*[7]

Of modern authors she talked much,—admires Bryant more than Longfellow, and thinks his pieces unimprovable, "a mirror of nature." Tupper she doesn't like at all, neither the man nor the "Proverbial Philosophy" (in this Longfellow agrees with her). When Tupper was at New York he met Mr. Bellows[8] at a supper party and rushing up to him startled our poor Minister by "Is this the distinguished Bellows?" He then said, "now Mr. Bellows what are your ideas on the Trinity?" a query Mr. Bellows of course declined to answer *then.*

At another time at Church just as he was kneeling down he said to a lady by his side, "Do you know I lecture to-morrow?" Margaret Fuller, Miss S. never

6. Anna Brownell Murphy Jameson (1794–1860), British author who visited America in 1837, a great friend of Miss Sedgwick.

7. Channing died in 1842 after spending the summer in Lenox. Miss Sedgwick wrote: "I should never have known the affectionateness, the divine *simplicity*, the gentle playfulness of his character but for the intimate intercourse of this summer" (*Life and Letters of Catharine M. Sedgwick*, ed. Mary E. Dewey [New York, 1871], pp. 282–83).

8. See p. 73. He was a close friend of Miss Sedgwick, as was Orville Dewey.

426

knew beyond the repelling point, she laughed very heartily at Temple's name for her life. She talked of the "Mutual Admiration Society"[9] and told me how Chas. Sumner, Felton, and Longfellow are said to have entered a bookseller's shop one after another, just after "In Memoriam" came out, and made the elegantly turned remark each of them, "Now Tennyson has done for friendship, what Petrarch has done for Love."

I spoke of Rappers with Mrs. S., and Miss Lizzie told me that one enlightened table raised itself on its hind legs and rocked a cradle with its fore legs!

Miss S. liked Lord Carlisle[10] extremely,—it was at Mr. Lowndes' house that she arrived so late for dinner.[11] She thinks Mrs. Browning's Portuguese sonnets the best of her works. She doesn't like Helps' works, and when I offered to send as the best of them "Essays in intervals of business,"[12] "No," she said, "I would rather have none but works of authors I esteem from those I like." She is the kindest soul, and when we left them after breakfast this morning she gave me the tomatoes I liked to take home, and some shaker baskets, begging I would write to her when I got home. I asked if I could send her nothing from England. "Nothing but to hear you are safe again at home, where I feel very sure they will be indeed glad to see you." Compliments, or kind sayings from so kind, good a person as Miss Sedgwick are indeed precious,

9. A group of friends in Cambridge (also calling themselves "The Five of Clubs"): Longfellow, Sumner, Felton, George S. Hillard, and Henry R. Cleveland.

10. I.e., Lord Morpeth (see p. 77) who became 7th earl of Carlisle in 1848.

11. In her *Letters from Abroad to Kindred at Home* (1841), Miss Sedgwick described her embarrassment at arriving nearly two hours late at a London dinner party. Mr. Lowndes was perhaps William Thomas Lowndes (d. 1843), the bibliographer.

12. Published by Sir Arthur Helps in 1841.

and good wishes from her are not without a value. "Dear Aunt Kitty!" I am going to send a picture of Mr. Martineau's Church,[13] and "Libbie Marsh"[14] and any[thing] else I can think of to her.[15]

She has given us a letter to her brother to [sic] New York through whom we may see Washington Irving,[16] and she has promised to send her traveller friends to me. We had a pleasant breakfast, and the baked apples, and "rye drops" were excellent. There was too a lordly tea-cup which the good lady insisted on my using as "a visitor." Miss Sedgwick looks about fifty, is energetic and active, interested in flowers, head of committee on them in an approaching flower-show, "zealous in good works."[17]

We reached Lebanon[18] in about an hour from Lenox and having passed through the neat village and left horse and buggy under care of a "darkie" we entered the Church. There were about 100 women and as many men and boys.

13. James Martineau's church for many years was the Paradise Street Chapel in Liverpool; in October, 1849, a new church building was opened in Hope Street.

14. Elizabeth Gaskell published *Libbie Marsh's Three Eras. A Lancashire Tale* in 1850.

15. Just before he sailed from New York, HAB wrote to Longfellow: "Our expedition to Lenox was most successful, and we feel that we are much indebted to you for having persuaded us to undertake it:—there are few people I have met in America whom I should have lost more by not calling on, than Miss Sedgwick" (letter of [October 12? 1852] in Harvard College Library).

16. Washington Irving (1783–1859) was living at "Sunnyside," near Tarrytown, New York.

17. Twenty years later Bright drew on his diary account of Miss Sedgwick in a review of her *Life and Letters* (*Athenaeum*, July 20, 1872, p. 73). He quotes from letters she wrote to him, in one of which (ca. 1856), speaking of her delight in Mrs. Gaskell's *Cranford*, she adds: "We have a female community, an out-of-doors nunnery at Stockbridge. The women are of a high order, not intellectually at all related to the Cranford set; but we have the ludicrous incidents common to feminine communities."

18. Mount Lebanon, New York, was the site of the first complete Shaker community in the United States (1787). Miss Sedgwick used it in her novel *Redwood* (1824).

There were many visitors sitting near the door while the devotees were arranged in rows, men, one side, women the other side of the Church, at an acute angle, at the apex of which stood the Minister. They were singing as we entered and seemed orderly enough. The men in brown coats and chocolate breeches with long back hair, the women in chocolate dresses with white tippets of linen fastened in a point and queer looking caps, and nothing over their arms. After this hymn two Ministers in turn addressed the congregation. Then the men went and hung up their coats and with shirt sleeves nobly displayed began to dance, forming in rows facing us, and dancing sometimes towards us, sometimes towards the singers, moving to and receding from them like the dancers in "L'Eté."

Occasionally too they clapped their hands in time to the music, and admirable time legs and hands kept, not a hitch or mistake anywhere—admirably drilled they were to be sure. The tunes are very gay—"Drops of Brandy" and other popular airs—and their dancing grows more and more lively, especially when they form again differently and shaking their hands before them, like the paws of so many dancing bears, follow one another in rows of three deep in some what of this sort <sketch> but rather more perplexed and convoluted, yet the two sexes never came in contact in the least. It was almost too sad, and humiliating to human nature for laughter and yet its absurdity seemed too great for serious feeling. Imagine God worshipped in this wise! After an hour's dancing the men recoated themselves, sang a hymn like Christians, standing, and then listened to a bad sermon from a Minister, after which they broke up, and as we drove away we saw some of them, I think from a neighbouring village, walking off in grim unmixed procession.

The "Springs" are two miles from the village, we've

good quarters and have taken a most pleasant drive
this afternoon our own way.

Albany. Monday Night, [October 4].

This morning after breakfast we drove over to the
Shaker village to buy specimens of celibe [i.e., Ce-
lebes?] basket-work. It was pouring with rain, but
the leathern apron of the "buggy" came up to our
noses, and the reins passed through a slit in front so
that not even our hands got wet.

The Shakers were all busy as we entered the village,
some driving an oxen team in a wagon, some carpenter-
ing, and a very tidy woman at a store ready to sell
us what we wanted. There are, she told us, 600 in
this village, and from others in our way I learnt they
are most charitable people, putting by all their old
twice-mended clothes into a common store for the poor,
to whom they also give food and often a night's lodg-
ing. They are recruited[?] by children sent to them by
poor people in the neighbourhood, who can't afford
to bring them up themselves. Sometime—some two
years ago,—we heard, their religious worship was most
extraordinary, having pas seuls, like the Eastern Der-
vishes (see Dickens).[19] About then too they used to
meet upon the hills round "to chase the Devil" who
passed through their Church and escaped them. They
now have afternoon services to which strangers are
not admitted; we saw the only public one.

19. "These people are called Shakers from their peculiar form of ado-
ration, which consists of a dance, performed by the men and women of all
ages, who arrange themselves for that purpose in opposite parties. . . .
They accompany themselves with a droning, humming noise, and dance
until they are quite exhausted, alternately advancing and retiring in a
preposterous sort of trot" (*American Notes*, chap. 15).

430

From the Shaker Village we went to Pittsfield some seven miles from the Springs where we only stayed to pick up our luggage, and reached Pittsfield just in time for the train which gets to Albany in about 1¾ hours. This is a beautiful city on the Hudson, we've strolled about it, and peeped into two theatres; an "inadequate female" was acting "Mrs. Haller" in one, Mrs. Cora Mowatt[20] was performing "Rosalind" in the other. She acts well, but the whole thing was very inferior to the Julia Bennett performance in Boston.

At tea to-night we saw a sight only equalled by that mentioned by M'Kinton[21]—a little girl of about seven, *sitting next* her mother (there was no parental ignorance in the case) "went in for" tea and tongue, five slices of which disappeared, jam followed, and then, turning composedly round, she asked the waiter for a *beef-steak*. That also disappeared, and as she now took some cake I imagined her tea was coming to an end at last, innocent as I still was of the gastronomic powers, the ostrichian stomach of an American child. "A glass of milk and some more tongue," and this finished, roll and cake followed; and tea at length over, the repletionized child rolled away from the table, followed by her sister, an infant of about four who had meanwhile been alternately gnawing a slice of tongue, and sucking a jam bedabbled spoon—and then they talk about the climate making them dyspeptic.

We found our way this evening into a confectioner's eating house, as good if not better than Taylor's in New

20. Anna Cora Ogden Mowatt (1819-70), American actress and playwright.

21. Captain Lauchlan B. Mackinnon in *Atlantic and Transatlantic: Sketches Afloat and Ashore* (1852) describes a nine-year-old boy (with "no appetite" according to his mother) gorging himself in her absence on molasses, butter, and pickles.

York, and had there some good fried oysters and peach-
es, a moderate supper, and light,—oh, the horrors of that
dyspeptic child with her heavy tea.

Mountain House of the Catskills, 2,500 ft.
Above the Sea. Tuesday Night, [October 5].

We left Albany this morning at eleven, and crossing
the Hudson got "on board" the "cars" for Oakhill,
where we "disembarked" (they always use nautical
terms here) and once more crossing to the right bank
found ourselves in about an hour and a half after leaving Albany in the little village of Catskill. The river
is not broad and the banks are not high, but within
a mile or two of Catskill Village rise, covered with
wood, the Catskill Mountains, the most romantic spot—
as far at least as tradition may make a spot romantic,
—of which the States may boast. For was it not here
that on a memorable evening long, long ago Rip Van
Winkle fell in with those old ghostly Dutchmen?
And were not these grey rocks the only things un-
changed in all this changing wood, and reddening leaf,
were not these old rocks round which the fern is
growing and over which the oak and ash are bending,
weren't these the very rocks which then rang with the
echo of merry laugh and dashing bowl, and which
doubtless would, if they could, tell strange weird stories
of the old lords of the land, and where they are rest-
ing and how they pass the time, stories which would
rival those which haunt the hill at Salzburg and im-
mortalize with dubious renown the name of Frederick
Barbarossa?[22] And if you chose to be sceptical, why

22. Salzburg was the scene of various struggles with Frederick Ba
barossa (?1123-90), Holy Roman Emperor.

432

is it not confirmation of the legend "strong as Holy writ" to find obscure little tavern half-way up the mountain with picture of the famous Dutchman as he awakes and muttering imprecations on the flagon asks "What excuse shall I make to Dame Van Winkle?"

A hasty dinner at the village and we prepare to ascend the mountain, a distance of 12 miles in all and requiring well nigh four hours for two stout horses to pull us up.

The road at first is along the valley below the mountain, but we are gradually ascending; at last we reach the foot of the mountain itself, and then come 3 miles of steepest hill, all through the woods. It was, I need hardly say, very glorious: fading leaves, like setting sun or dying dolphin showing fairest at the last,[23] and every now and then some opening through the foliage giving glimpses of fields, and woods and villages, and Hudson far below all bathed in the light of the evening sun. We are now at the top, the air is bitterly cold, but the kitchen fire at the Hotel is bright and glowing and the old negress, who, now the season is over, lives alone in her glory taking care of the house, is as fat and resplendent and jolly as ever negress need be, and welcomes us with a hearty chuckle. But the view! we must see that, so we leave the glowing fire and the jolly negress, and stand at the brink of a rock close to the house, and look down upon the world. There marked out like map or model the miles of rich fair country, and the Hudson, like a girdle, flowing in a straight unbending course between pasture land and wood-land and fields of sheaves, Indian corn, while here and there like some fair gem, gleams the white sail of tiny pleasure boat or fishing smack upon that beautiful river belt.

23. Cf. *Childe Harold's Pilgrimage*, IV.29.

The Mountain House, the Catskills

"We . . . stand at the brink of a rock close to the house, and look down upon the world."

It is very still! not a sound! we and the negress and a carpenter or so are the only human creatures near the place; there is no grasshopper among the grass, no katydid or song bird upon the trees, and the sounds of life from the world below never curl up on high, as do the morning mists, it is quite still! The only thing with motion, (for the air is still too, and the branches are all at rest) the only thing that moves is the shadow of the mountain, which, for the sun is setting behind, glides solemnly along the plain and chases away the sunlight as it goes. It has now reached the Hudson, and the air is very chilly, and we turn in, and in a little room, by a tiny open stove, with tea and fried beef and preserved prunes upon the table, and with "Up country letters"[24] and other pleasant books in our hands, we sit together, and the evening like the mountain shadow passes slowly and tranquilly along, but does not chase away a ray of brightness from fire or book or heart.[25]

Philadelphia. Saturday Evening, [*October 9*].

On Wednesday morning we descended from our eyrie and at noon recross the Hudson, entered the cars and in a couple of hours found ourselves at Cold Spring opposite West Point. A ferry boat took us across and landed us in a spot which will only take a second place in our memory to Quebec, so far at least as natural scenery goes. I remember now one view on the

24. Published anonymously by Lewis William Mansfield in 1852. A year or so later Hawthorne sent Bright a copy of this book, urging him to talk or write about it in England.

25. This passage seems to be an effort at studied prose before the diary's hasty concluding pages.

Rhine comparable with this at West Point, the two miles (on either side the river) covered with autumnal wood flowing with <   >. [A] craggy rock rises up nobly and boldly from the water, and the river here, unlike the Hudson at the Catskills, winds gracefully round each promontory and jutting point of land, till the miles shut it from our sight.

We called on Mr. Dwight, a cadet at the military college, and had a conversation with Col. Lee[26] to whom Mrs. Wainwright gave me a letter. In the morning he put us under the charge of Lieut. Williams with whom as guide we saw the model rooms, library, Koskiusko's[27] garden and all the rest of it. Also an artillery drill, and some cavalry practise for the young gentlemen cadets. They have extremely hard work. They remain here four years during which they have eight examinations, and what the examinations are, may be inferred from the fact that the *whole* of algebra is required for the first at the end of six months. They have no recreation during the day except for 1½ hours, nor any furlough during their residence except for two months at the end of the second year. The cadets are appointed by the representatives to congress who each select one. Many leave, however, not being able to stand the work, or not being competent to perform it. The Library is extremely pretty, and some of the models, etc., interesting. Mr. Williams told us much about fortification. Any citadel can, he said, be taken by regular approaches. The perfect understanding of fortification is the hardest thing that the cadet has to do.

26. Robert E. Lee (1807-70) had just been appointed superintendent of the U.S. Military Academy, against his wishes.

27. Thaddeus Kosciusko (1746-1817), Polish military hero, directed the construction of fortifications at West Point.

436

WEST POINT, LOOKING NORTH FROM THE ARTILLERY-GROUNDS

From *Our Native Land*, ed. George T. Ferris, 1886

"A spot *which will only take a second place*
in our memory to Quebec."

The whole of Thursday we wasted at West Point looking for a boat, which, however, came not, so we got into the evening cars and at nine o' the clock found ourselves at New York, where driven from pillar to post, from New York House to Waverley House, we at last got rooms and rushed to call on Irvin. Unfortunately New Yorkers go to bed early and our cab-man's ring at the bell was answered by a night-gowned Mrs. Irvin.

Nothing remained for us but a theatre and we honoured Burton's and saw the farce "Frightened to Death," Burton acting "his own ghost."[28] Yesterday we saw Irvin and Loch, and started at 5½ for Philadelphia which we reached in 4½ hours. A tiresome journey in dark cars, too dark to read in; Lola Montez was a fellow passenger.

To-day we've spent talking to the Furnesses and Peters. Miss Furness sang for us Montrose's "Love song" and the "Three students." She is a charming girl, and the Doctor delightful; we tea with them to-morrow though Dr. Furness thinks it hard that we must go to Church with them in the evening when he never likes people to go, as he can't get the steam up twice and he likes his own congregation to be "well fed in the morning." Miss F. promises us sacred music at the Lothrops; she would sing anything she says!

Mrs. Peter seems intelligent and agreeable. She talked to Burder while I held converse with the old man. He told me one or two noticeable things. When Lord Carlisle left America his last words to Peter were "As good a Whig as ever, but certainly no Republican." The Governor of the Philadelphia Prison says that it is extraordinary the difference intellectually

28. William Evans Burton (1804–60), English actor-manager, was a celebrated comedian.

438

between the blacks whose families have been for some time free, and those only just <liberated?>.[29]

He describes the places in Charleston where slaves are flogged as horrible, the operator receiving a slip of paper with the number of lashes marked on it, and having to administer punishment for a crime of which he knows absolutely nothing.

Dr. Furness has been to Niagara this summer, his congregation paying his expenses; he talked enthusiastically (as did Mr. Peter) of "Uncle Tom." He admires Garrison and May[30] and the very "extremes." Miss F. told me that Emerson always says he keeps his friends at arm's length, therefore, he's without a heart.

This evening we've shopped and been to hear the Bateman Children in "Her Royal Highness" and "The Young Couple." They are really wonderful, and there is nothing unpleasant about the performance *except* the *thought* of it. The younger Ellen acts gloriously as male.[31]

A message from [S.K.] George says he'll come on Monday night.

Friday, [October 15].

Last Sunday morning we spent in going to church, and in the evening we went to the Furnesses to tea and when Dr. F. and his wife went to evening church we staid talking to Miss Furness on our way. Monday Dr. F. took us to see the statue of Hero and Leander

---

29. Cf. p. 116 and n.

30. William Lloyd Garrison (1805–79) and Samuel Joseph May (1797–1871), leading abolitionists.

31. At the Walnut Street Theatre Ellen (aged 7, as Charles de Blenville) and Kate (aged 9, as Henrietta de Vigny) were repeating the success they had had in New York.

at the Academy of arts,[32] and also introduced us to Mrs. Rush's husband who showed us over his "convenient" house, and told us how he contrived to prevent peeping into the supper room.[33] In the evening the Georges came, and we went to the Furnesses for the *last time*, and heard "Young Romily" and other glorious old ballads.[34] We called on Allibone next morning, after an abortive attempt to see Independence Hall, we fell in with Mrs. Wharton, and an hour or two later went on to New York with the Georges by the Amboy Line.

We got to the Clarendon,[35] and spent the evening (Tuesday) seeing "School for Scandal."[36] On our way home we fell in with Loch, and on Wednesday he and Jay called on us, took us to a plant shop and to the library to see magazines. We dined at our Hotel to meet Mr. Draper and Judge Forsyth, and afterwards called on the Davises, who were as usual. Supped at Taylor's[37] with Loch and to bed.

32. In fact a group of statuary (1848), by Carl Johann Steinhauser (1813–79).

33. Cf. p. 122. Dr. James Rush (1786–1869), who could accommodate 800 guests in his "convenient house," did not share his wife's enthusiasm for social gatherings.

34. See Bright's poem "On a Lady Singing English Ballads at Philadelphia" (page 456).

35. The Clarendon Hotel on Fourth Avenue and 18th Street, an Elizabethan edifice favored by English families.

36. Sheridan's favorite was performed this night (October 12) at two theaters—Burton's and Wallack's.

37. A gilded palace of mirrors and marble at 365 Broadway. In his pamphlet *Free Blacks and Slaves* HAB relates the following incident: "The traveller in New York will remember a pastrycook's shop—Taylor's, I believe, is the name—about half-way up Broadway. At the back of this shop is a room, fitted up like our own Regent Street Verry's, with little dinner-tables, which are well supplied with 'all the luxuries of the season,' and well attended by the fashionable loungers of 'the Empire City.' One day in last year, to the natural horror of the patrons of Taylor's, a small party of swarthy individuals were observed to enter, and place themselves at one of the tables. 'Coloured people!' was the immediate exclamation, 'and sitting down and eating dinner in the same room!

Yesterday we saw the N. Y. fair, bright "buffalos," and called on Bryant at his office. He is uninteresting and stiff. How unlike Longfellow! In the evening we dined at Jays' ourselves, a Mrs. Gerhand and Miss Jay were the party. Jay showed us a fine Claret jug (silver) given him by Mr. Gardner, who wrote some fine accounts of the "Model Republic" in Blackwood.[38] Jay says that Canada is wanted to extend the arm of freedom in the States. The Southerners look to Cuba and the Sandwich Islands, South California and Mexico for the opposite reason. The internal slave trade must be abolished. He admires Sumner. Wishes to see any of my friends and will send me his.

To-day I've been busy packing, for England, and dined with the Irvins for the last as for the first time some five months ago. David Kennedy was there, and Robert Bunch our V[ice] Consul, who was "civi lest" or most civil. A Mr. Haddon and other uninteresting people made up the party besides Georges and us there. Madiera excellent, a white Ariadne not too warmly clad sat in vanille ice on a pink ice panther.

Was any thing so shocking!' Louder grew the murmurs, and, on pain of losing his fair-skinned customers, the proprietor of the shop must dismiss the obnoxious intruders. He expostulates, he desires them to go; they, however, still retain their seats, for they assure the worthy pastrycook, that it is Indian and not negro blood which darkens their faces: all are at once satisfied, and the most squeamish and sensitive New Yorker eats his ice, and peels his banana, in comfort and contentment" (p. 10).

38.   Two articles entitled "How they manage matters in 'the Model Republic,'" which criticized everything in the United States from slavery to children's manners, appeared in *Blackwood's Magazine* 59 (April, 1846) and 61 (April, 1847). The author, a representative of an English commercial firm, is identified in the Wellesley Index only as "Mr. Gardner."

20

THE VOYAGE HOME

Jay, George and Irvin came to see us off, kindest and best of friends. Loch too, dear old fellow, was there too, and Mr. Williams. Miss W[illiams] and Mrs. Pell are pleasant fellow passengers, the rest, brutes. Time spent in semi-sea-sickness.

A Mr. Pell of New York was a nice gentlemanly fellow and we saw him again in Liverpool as he dined with us.

On Sunday the Catholic Bishop of New York gave us an harangue all dressed in his robes of state, violet and white, ring and rosary and all. He prayed for Pius.

Longfellow told us of a black preacher who, despairing of rousing his congregation otherwise, stood on his head and clapped his feet together.

Dr. Furness told us how Mr. Norton was once asked at college by a scoffing reprobate, "I hear, Norton, you were drunk yesterday,—is it true?" He answered with characteristic gravity, "And I hear you were sober, which is the more extraordinary?"[1]

1. This would be Andrews Norton (1786–1853), Charles Eliot Norton's

On being told there was no better college than Harvard he cuttingly replied, "Nor any worse."

Synge told us how General Scott corrected Mr. Pine at Washington for saying "St. John." "Sinjohn, Sir, Sinjohn—the distinguished family of that name in England always pronounce it so."

The dinners on board were good and the attendance decent.

A murky morning entering Liverpool, and the Custom House arrangement was as bad as bad could be.

Reached Liverpool Wednesday [October 27] at 10, having been eleven days and $<$ $>$ hours.[2]

father, who ruled the Harvard Divinity School when Furness was a student there.

2. On returning home, Bright wrote to Longfellow: "Our voyage across the Atlantic was so far successful that we arrived safe at last, but not without experiencing a storm on our last two nights;—in the middle of which a wave burst in the little window of my cabin and set books and boots floating, and completely swamped me as I lay dozing in my berth: —you will be amused when I tell you how much one line of your poems [from "The Building of the Ship"] haunted and consoled me as I lay in a state of semi-consciousness, repeating over the words 'Wrecks in the great *September* gales' and finding my consolation in the reflection that as this was *October*, the dangerous storms were probably over for a time at least, and we had nothing to fear" (letter of [November, 1852] in Harvard College Library).

THE POEMS

Poems by Henry Arthur Bright

The poems printed here have some bearing on Bright's American tour; several of them, in fact, were written during the journey. He never published them and would have been the last person to claim for them any particular poetic merit. "The writing of poetry," he said in one of his reviews, "always blesses him who gives, even when it has no such power for him who takes" (*Athenaeum*, July 24, 1875, p. 114). The texts, with one exception, are taken from a pamphlet prepared after HAB's death: *Poems by Henry Arthur Bright* (London: privately printed at the Chiswick Press, 1885). I am again indebted to Mrs. Elizabeth Lloyd for knowledge of this pamphlet.

"Nights and feasts of the Gods": a tribute to university life at Cambridge. The initials below the title stand for Robert Temple and Henry Bright. The tag is from Horace, *Satires* II.vi.65.

NOCTES COENAEQUE DEÛM

R. T. AND H. B.

(1850)

Evenings spent as evenings never
  Will be spent by us again;
Time, a very flowing river,
  Flows but once along a plain;
Kisses once its flowered garland,
  Whispers once a murmuring sigh,
Hurries on to seek some far land,
  In a wild inconstancy.

Yet, as one who plucks pale sedges,
  And the Iris' golden gleam,
And, from off the river edges,
  Sends them whirling down the stream,
So would I send, recollections
  Of what has been, floating on;
Time shall bear their bright reflections,
  When all fresher flowers are gone.

Evenings spent—we two together;
  How those evenings sped away!
Had time's wing another feather,
  From the quills that round us lay,
You would tell me of the mountains
  Of your Celtic land of leeks,
Of its health-bestowing fountains,
  Of its maidens' ruddy cheeks:

Of each strange and wild tradition,
    Haunted well, and fairy crew—
Of the grave, where superstition
    Says the green grass never grew;
Of each ancient hero's prowess,
    Stately hall and lofty tower
Of the doughty Prince of Powis,
    Of Sir Watkin's regal power.

Checking soon your merry stories,
    With a smile and half a sigh,
Talk no more of bygone glories
    While for bread the people cry.
Rather think we how to aid them
    As they toil their life away,
For a year's work may be paid them
    What the rich spend in a day.

How we loved the lines of Shelley,
    And his "mind of human kind,"
Listened to his "lark's reveillé,"
    Heard the sough of his West Wind.
Cursed with him the ermined Eldon,
    Breathed with Proserpine the prayer,
Saw where Arethusa welled on,
    From her mountain bleak and bare.

How we both laughed at the folly
    Of the Bowdlers of the day;
Drowning all our melancholy
    With deep draughts of Rabelais.
Ofttimes we were Unionic,
    Settling matters of the state;
Now and then we waxed Byronic—
    Women's fans, and woman's fate.

Hand in hand we two would wander
   In a metaphysic maze,
Turning at each step to ponder
   Which to take of many ways.
One was far too broad and trodden,
   One too wild and brambled round;
One with blackest slime was sodden,
   Nettles cropped another's ground.

Evenings in a lonely College!
   In an oaken panelled room,
Where the very walls breathed knowledge,
   Knowledge somewhat mixed with gloom.
Often have we sat, and rambled
   By St. Lawrence' woody shore,
To Niag'ra brows have scrambled,
   Heard, dear friend, its thunders roar.

Dreamed we oft of law's high honours,
   Or the Senate of the land,
With men's waiting gaze upon us,
   While we speak with outstretched hand.
We would talk of spirit's warning,
   By the fire's dying light;
You were bravest in the morning,
   I was bravest in the night.

Or we chased mesmeric fancies
   In the mystic stream of life,
And half feared the spectral dances
   Of Alonzo and his wife.
While the room seemed growing fuller,
   Full of darkness and of dread,
While the embers burnt still duller,
   And shades flickered overhead.

While your dog that lay beside you,
  Leaping up upon your knee,
Seemed as if he sought to hide you
  From a *shade* you could not see.
Evenings past and gone for ever,
  River banks left far behind;
Time flows on, but never, never
  Fairer blossoms shall we find.

The "golden, golden day" was Friday, June 4, when Bright drove to Harrisburg, Pennsylvania, from Baltimore. (See page 136).

THE SUSQUEHANNA RIVER

(Song)

'Twas a golden, golden day,
As there we stood together,
In the hot and summer weather,
Where the Susquehanna River
Rolls swiftly on its way.

'Twas a bright and balmy day,
And the white acacia blossom
Shed its tribute on the bosom
Of the Susquehanna River,
Rolling swiftly on its way.

Long past and far away
Seem those bright and golden hours,
And the white acacia flowers,
And the Susquehanna River
Rolling swiftly on its way.

Bright was much struck with the beauty of the flowering kalmia around the Virginia springs. (See pages 175 and 181)

TWO VIEWS OF ONE OBJECT; OR,
THE KALMIA BRAKE

(Written at Lewisburg, June 28th, 1852.)

The noonday glows in the valley,—
    The shadows are buried in light,—
And the burning air has a lurid glare,
    And the sun a furnace might.
Then up to the mountain stream,
    Your eager thirst to slake;
Then up to the mountain, and lay you down,
    In the cool of the Kalmia brake.

The night is thick in the heaven,—
    The stars are lost in the dark,—
And the dark winds sigh as they hurry by,
    And quenched is the fire-fly's spark.
Then down, from the mountain down,
    From your careless sleep awake;
Down from the mountain,—the dew falls fast,
    On the sickly Kalmia brake.

The morning glows in the valley,—
    But the woods are cool to-day,
And sings the wild bee in the tulip-tree,
    The wild bird on a locust spray.
Then up when the mountain winds
    A gentle murmur make;
Then up where the mountains are crimsoned o'er,
    With the beautiful Kalmia brake.

452

The night is thick in the heavens,
   The dew is thick on the trees,
And all is still, save the Whip-poor-Will,
   As he wails to the wailing breeze.
Then down, from the mountain down,
   Hark! the noise of the warning snake!
Down from the mountain, and hurry away
   From the deadly Kalmia brake.

This poem and the next one were written during the two weary weeks Bright had to spend at Blue Sulphur while waiting for money. (See page 214.)

SOUL'S MEMORIES

(Written at the Blue Sulphur Springs,
Virginia, U.S., July 9th, 1852.)

Sweet sad tune!
But what is its meaning,
   Floating like bird on the wing?
Where does its power dwell,
   Which, as a magic spell,
Round me a mystical coil doth fling?

Sweet, strange thought!
But where is its fountain?
   Wanderer through my brain,
Stream of a hidden source,—
   Bright'ning along its course
Buds that I ne'er thought would bloom again.

Sweet fair face!
But why does it move me,
   Face never gazed on before?
While, as it passes by,
   Feelings, half memory,
Rise up and haunt me for evermore.

Memories all!
Of a time unremembered,—
   Time never told by the sun:
Flowers of a spirit wreath,
   Fanned by some living breath
Into new freshness ere life is done.

To HAB's favorite poet.

A DEBT OF GRATITUDE TO SHELLEY

*(Written at the Blue Sulphur Springs,
Virginia, U.S., July 11th, 1852.)*

Thy Spirit, Shelley, haunts me like a dream,—
By day, thy skylark sings above the hill;
By night, thy west wind sighs, all else being still,
All else being dark, thy orbed maiden's beam
On loving hearts doth pour a memory stream,
As light and fair as silvery mountain rill,
Or hoary castle. Wander where I will,
Each thing memorial of its bard will seem.

In commerce-marts upon the Mersey shore;
In college-room 'mid ancient Hero lore;
In forests of the New World's virgin soil;
In Flemish cities, quaint as towns of yore,—
Thy spirit still was with me;—evermore
May it abide, rich sweetener of life's toil.

The lady was Annis Lee Furniss. (See pages 114, 123, 438 and 440.)

ON A LADY SINGING ENGLISH BALLADS
AT PHILADELPHIA

Sing on, sing on,—the air is filled
  With the billowy waves of song.
Sing on, fair lady—our hearts are thrilled
  As thy rich voice floats along;
And heart and air are tremulous each,—
But not with *our* passion, and not with *our* speech.

Sweet sounds "that hurt not" are round us still,
  As in Prospero's haunted isle,
  But Miranda has stol'n from Ariel's skill:
  'Tis she who is singing!—the while
Unnumbered Ferdinands linger near,
And *thine* the command of their smile or their tear.

Sing on from thy far-off home in the West
  Old songs of the Motherland;
And let kind thoughts spring within thy breast
  By old ballad memories fanned—
Thoughts of that England Isle so fair,
And some thought of a friend who awaits thee there.

Julian Hawthorne tells how Christmas day at Mrs. Blodgett's household in Liverpool was celebrated with mistletoe and kissing games. Bright, in a piece of fun written (1855) in the metre of *The Song of Hiawatha* (which he reviewed in the *Examiner*) teases Hawthorne about this. The text is taken from Julian Hawthorne's *Nathaniel Hawthorne and His Wife*, 2:78–80.

SONG OF CONSUL HAWTHORNE

Should you ask me, "Who is Hawthorne?
Who this Hawthorne that you mention?"
I should answer, I should tell you,
"He's a Yankee, who has written
Many books you must have heard of;
For he wrote 'The Scarlet Letter'
And 'The House of Seven Gables,'
Wrote, too, 'Rappacini's Daughter,'
And a lot of other stories;—
Some are long, and some are shorter;
Some are good, and some are better.
And this Hawthorne is a Consul,
Sitting in a dismal office,—
Dark and dirty, dingy office,
Full of mates, and full of captains,
Full of sailors and of niggers,—
And he lords it over Yankees."

But you ask me, "Where the dwelling,
Where the mansion, of this Hawthorne?"
And I answer, and I tell you,
" 'T is a house in upper Duke Street,—
'T is a red brick house in Duke Street."
Should you ask me further, saying,
"Where this house in upper Duke Street?"
I should answer, I should tell you,
" 'T is the house of Missis Todgers,—
House of good old widow Todgers,
Where the noble Yankee captains

457

Meet, and throng, and spend their evening,
Hairy all, and all dyspeptic,
All of them with nasal voices,
Speaking all through nasal organs,
All of them with pig tobacco,
All of them with Colt's revolvers."

Should you ask me what they do there,—
What the manners and the customs
Of this house of widow Todgers,—
I should tell you that at Christmas
Mistletoe hangs in the parlors,
Mistletoe on hall and staircase,
Mistletoe in every chamber;
And the maids at widow Todgers',
Slyly laughing, softly stealing,
Whisper, "Kiss me, Yankee Captain,—
Kiss or shilling, Yankee Captain!"
Slyly laughing, softly saying,
"Kiss from you too, Consul Hawthorne!
Kiss or shilling, Consul Hawthorne!"[1]—
I should tell you how, at midnight
Of the last day in December,
Yankee Captain, Consul Hawthorne,
Open wide the mansion's front door,—
Door that opens into Duke Street,—
Wait to see the hoary Old Year
Pass into the frosty starlight,—
Wait to see the jocund New Year
Come with all its hopes and pleasures,
Come into the gas and firelight.

Do you ask me, "Tell me further
Of this Consul, of this Hawthorne"?
I would say, he is a sinner,—
Reprobate and churchless sinner,—
Never goes inside a chapel,

1. A fib!—N. H.

458

Only sees outsides of chapels,
Says his prayers without a chapel!
I would say that he is lazy,
Very lazy, good-for-nothing;
Hardly ever goes to dinners,
Never goes to balls or soirées;
Thinks one friend worth twenty friendly;
Cares for love, but not for liking;
Hardly knows a dozen people,—
Knows old Baucis[1] and Philemon,[2]
Knows a Beak,[3] and knows a Parson,[4]
Knows a sucking, scribbling merchant,[5]—
Hardly knows a soul worth knowing,—
Lazy, good-for-nothing fellow!

1. A. M. Heywood [Mrs. J. P. Heywood of Norris Green].
2. J. P. Heywood [John Pemberton Heywood, Liverpool banker].
3. J. S. Mansfield [Liverpool magistrate].
4. W. H. Channing [William Henry Channing, minister of the Renshaw Street Chapel].
5. H. A. Bright.

HAB sent Longfellow the following sonnet in 1868 after Charles Eliot Norton reassured him that Longfellow would be pleased. A manuscript in HAB's hand is among the Longfellow papers at Harvard. The poem was printed (with the variant reading "Glows forth afresh" instead of "Has glowed afresh" in the last line) in Samuel Longfellow's *Life of Henry Wadsworth Longfellow* (Boston and New York, 1896), 3:345.

SONNET TO LONGFELLOW

In England

(July, 1868.)

An English greeting to the Bard, who bears
  His chaplet of sweet song from that far West
  Where pine woods, with their branches low depressed,
Cease not lamenting to the scented airs,—
For Hiawatha, as he disappears,
  Swift sailing to the Island of the Blest,—
  And for Evangeline, who, now at rest,
With our own Gertrude's self the amaranth shares.—

Glad greeting! for, in many an English home,
  The poet's voice has pierced the silent night
With chants of high Resolve, and Joys that come
  At Duty's summons;—then Hope's answering light,—
Clear as the red star watching o'er the earth,—
Has glowed afresh on life's rekindled hearth.

Swinburne's Memorial Sonnet

Bright met Swinburne in 1865 at Lord Houghton's house. "He is the strangest little fellow, this new poet,—an odd nervous, vain, twitchy boy,—looking, some one says 'like a red spider,'—or (as some one else says) 'like a Duke of Argyll, possessed with the devil.'" (HAB to C. E. Norton, August 4, 1865, in Harvard College Library.) Years later Bright corresponded with Swinburne and visited him a number of times in London, before and after the poet's removal to "The Pines" in Putney. In the following sonnet (from *A Midsummer Holiday*, 1884), Swinburne refers to *A Year in a Lancashire Garden*, a book that delighted him.

IN MEMORY OF HENRY A. BRIGHT

Yet again another, ere his crowning year,
   Gone from friends that here may look for him no more.
   Never now for him shall hope set wide the door,
Hope that hailed him hither, fain to greet him here.
All the gracious garden-flowers he held so dear,
   Oldworld English blossoms, all his homestead store,
   Oldworld grief had strewn them round his bier of yore,
Bidding each drop leaf by leaf as tear by tear;
Rarer lutes than mine had borne more tuneful token,
   Touched by subtler hands than echoing time can wrong,
   Sweet as flowers had strewn his graveward path along.
Now may no such old sweet dirges more be spoken,
Now the flowers whose breath was very song are broken,
   Nor may sorrow find again so sweet a song.

INDEX

464

467

468

469

470

471

Hobson, John Cannon, 162 and n, 164, 174

Hobson ("Junior," son of above) 164-65, 167

Hollywood Cemetery, Richmond, 162 and n

Holmes, Oliver Wendell, 386 n

Home, John: *Douglas*, 60 n

Hood, Thomas, 287

Hope, Mr. (HAB's teacher), 267 n

Hope, Thomas, 274 and n

Horace: HAB quotes, 67, 206, 365, 447

Hosmer, George Washington, 26, 299 and n, 300 and n, 322

Hospitality. *See* American people

Hotels: Bath Alum Springs, 181-82; Blue Sulphur Springs, 195; Buffalo, 298; Burlington, 370; Charlottesville, 169 and n; Cincinnati, 229 and n; Lexington, Va., 182; Louisville, 233; Montreal, 325; Newport, 295 n, 379; New York City, 67, 72, 438, 440; Niagara Falls, 301 and n; Philadelphia, 98-99, 104 and n; Quebec, 328, 344; Richmond, 161 and n; Rockbridge Alum Springs, 175 and n, 182; St. Louis, 248 and n; St. Paul, 278 and n; Saratoga, 373-74; Staunton, Va., 172; Toronto, 316; Warm Springs, 181-82; Washington, 141 and n; White Sulphur Springs, 183-84

Houdon, Jean Antoine, 153 and n, 168 and n

Houghton, Lord, 10, 14, 18, 149 n, 156 and n, 461; article on HAB, 8, 20-21

House of Representatives, 144, 147

Houses: Baltimore, 125; New York City, 71, 74; outside New York City, 95; Philadelphia, 105-6; St. Louis, 254; Washington, 154

Howard, George William Frederick, viscount Morpeth, 7th earl of Carlisle. *See* Carlisle, Lord

Howe, Julia Ward, 29, 390 and n, 414

Howe, Dr. Samuel Gridley, 390 and n, 413 and n, 414-16, 421

Howells, William Dean, 29

Hudson, Mrs., 414

Hudson River, 373, 431-36

Hughes, Thomas, 16; *Tom Brown's Schooldays*, 7

Hume, Joseph, 356 and n

Hunt, Miss (HAB's teacher), 267 n

Hunt, Mr., 255

Hunt, Martha, 401 and n

Hunt, Mr. (Thomas Sterry?), 398 and n, 399

Hunt, Washington, 82-85

Hunter, Dr. John A., 189 and n, 197-98, 200, 204, 207-8, 214, 217

Huntington, Frederic Dan, 73 and n, 402 and n, 404

Hutton, Richard Holt, 380 and n

Hydesville, New York, 28, 220

Icarians, 263 and n, 265 and n

Icebergs, 58

Illinois, 293-98

Indemnification of Losses Bill. *See* Rebellion Losses Bill

Independence Hall, Philadelphia, 440

Indians, 172, 270-72, 277, 291-92

Ingall, Captain, 364, 368

Ingall, Miss, 51, 54, 60, 63, 71, 73, 362, 369

Ingersoll, Charles Jared, 120 and n

Ingersoll, Joseph Reed, 120 and n

Inglis, Miss, 256

Innes, Miss, 63, 74

Inquirer (Unitarian newspaper), 27, 380 n

Inquisitiveness. *See* American people

Insects, 190, 224, 244-45, 288

473

477

478

479

480

481

City, 73, 92 and n; Philadelphia, 102–4; St. Louis, 256–57

Unitarianism: in America, 21–28, 115, 178, 208; in Boston, 393, 402, 416–17, 420; and A. J. Davis, 210, 213; HAB's, 7–8, 21–28, 102; in Liverpool, 22; in Massachusetts, 205–6, 378; in Parliament, 305; in St. Louis, 257

Unitarian ministers, 322, 381, 402. *See also* Bellows, H. W.; Burnap, G. W.; Dall, C. H. A.; Dewey, O.; Eliot, W. G.; Furness, W. H.; Gannett, E. S.; Heywood, J. H.; Hosmer, G. W.; Huntington, F. D.; Livermore, A. A.; Lothrop, S. K.; Miles, H. A.; Parker, T.; Squire, E.

United States Bank of Pennsylvania, 122 n

United States Hotel: Philadelphia, 98–99; Saratoga, 374

Universities. *See* Education

Upjohn, Richard, 79 n, 300 n

Upper Canada (Canada West), 316–18, 322 and n, 337 n, 344 n, 346, 348

Utah Territory, 280

Vega, José de la, 154 and n

Vega, Lope de, 408

Vermont, 364, 368, 370–71

Villiers, George William Frederick, 4th earl of Clarendon. *See* Clarendon, Lord

Violence. *See* American people

Virgil: *Aeneid*, HAB quotes, 55, 293, 311, 373

Virginia Military Institute, 174 and n

Virginia Springs, 174–88, 194–218

Virginia, University of, 170, 172 and n, 203

Wainwright, Mrs., 436

Walker, James, 404 and n

Wallack's Theater, New York City, 440 n

Walnut Street Theatre, Philadelphia, 439 n

Ward, Thomas Wren, 382 and n

Ware, Miss, 114–15

Ware, Henry, 378

Ware, Henry, Jr., 114 and n

Warm Springs, Virginia, 181–82

Warr, Major, 93

Warren, Mrs., 373

Washington, George, 152–53

Washington, John Augustine, 152 and n, 153–54

Washington, D.C., 141–60; Dickens on, 249, 250 n; HAB describes, 148

Washington Monument, Baltimore, 132 and n

Watchman, Mr., 134 and n

Waterston, Robert C., 402 and n

Watson, Mr., 355

Waverley House, New York City, 438

Webster, Daniel, 121 and n, 146 and n, 151, 154 n, 191, 206, 231, 257, 419; death, 12, 151 n; HAB meets, 13, 38–39, 146, 149–50, 158–60; Lord Elgin on, 331, 351; religion, 416–17; speeches, 206, 351 and n

Webster, Mrs. Daniel, 149, 157–58

Webster, Major Edward, 416 and n

West, Benjamin, 113 and n

Western Hotel, Toronto, 316

Westminster Review, 209 n, 388 and n, 396 and n. *For HAB's reviews in, see* Bright, H. A.: Reviews

West Point, New York, 435–37

Wharncliffe, Lord, 246 and n, 341 and n

Wharton, Thomas Isaac, 32, 106 and n, 107–8, 112

Wharton, Mrs. (Thomas Isaac?), 440